The Civil Rights Reader

THE CIVIL

RIGHTS READER

American Literature from Jim Crow to Reconciliation

Julie Buckner Armstrong | Editor

Amy Schmidt | Associate Editor

The University of Georgia Press | Athens and London

About the front cover illustration: Monitoring devices
similar to the one shown were sometimes attached to
the heads of slaves who were considered flight risks.

Published by the University of Georgia Press
Athens, Georgia 30602
www.ugapress.org

Designed by April Leidig-Higgins
Set in Minion, Pikelet, and The Serif by
Copperline Book Services, Inc.

Printed and bound by Sheridan Books

The paper in this book meets the guidelines for
permanence and durability of the Committee on
Production Guidelines for Book Longevity of the
Council on Library Resources.

Printed in the United States of America
12 11 10 09 08 C 5 4 3 2 1
12 11 10 09 08 P 5 4 3 2 1

Library of Congress Cataloging-in-Publication Data
The civil rights reader : American literature from Jim
Crow to reconciliation / Julie Buckner Armstrong, editor ;
Amy Schmidt, associate editor.
     p. cm.
Includes bibliographical references and index.
ISBN-13: 978-0-8203-3181-2 (alk. paper)
ISBN-10: 0-8203-3181-3 (alk. paper)
ISBN-13: 978-0-8203-3225-3 (pbk. : alk. paper)
ISBN-10: 0-8203-3225-9 (pbk. : alk. paper)
1. Civil rights — United States — Literary collections.
2. Civil rights movements — United States — Literary
collections.   3. African Americans — Literary collections.
4. American literature — African American authors.
5. American literature — 19th century.   6. American
literature — 20th century.   I. Armstrong, Julie
Buckner.   II. Schmidt, Amy, 1983–
PS508.N3C58   2009
810.8'0896073 — dc22   2008020385

British Library Cataloging-in-Publication Data available

Prepared through support of the
William Winter Institute for
Racial Reconciliation at the
University of Mississippi

Contents

Section Two. The Fall of Jim Crow 105

Section Three. Reflections and Continuing Struggles 253

Contents by Genre

Contents by Theme

Integration, Segregation, Separatism, and Nationalism

Oppression and Violence

Race, Class, and Economics

Reconciliation and Healing

Significant Issues

CRIME AND PUNISHMENT

EDUCATION

Significant People, Places, and Events (only those with two or more texts are listed in this category)

Preface

This book began with a conversation between two civil rights educators who regularly use literary works in their classes and discussion groups, and who just as regularly complain about the process of gathering materials. Those who focus on civil rights history face their yearly dilemmas as well, having to choose just one of the many, excellent textbooks that continue to appear with increasing regularity. Those who want to use creative writing face a different problem, however. A wealth of civil rights literature does exist (too much for one book, the editors of this one now realize) but not in any central print or online source. Instead, finding literature means scouring through Web sites, individual author collections, and anthologies organized around other themes, *and then* double-checking the history books to make sure nothing obvious was overlooked. The conversation ended with one of those educators, Julie Buckner Armstrong, promising to edit an anthology, and the other, Susan Glisson, offering resources from the University of Mississippi's William Winter Institute for Racial Reconciliation to make Julie's editorial promise a reality. Winter Institute graduate assistant Amy Schmidt soon joined the project, and the idea for *The Civil Rights Reader: American Literature from Jim Crow to Reconciliation* was born.

The idea part was easy. The hard part was what to do next. All we had were questions, a lot of them. What did we mean by "civil rights movement"? What did we mean by "literature"? What, and who, would we include in this book? What, and who, would we leave out? How could we coherently present a broad range of political ideas and artistic styles? How might we organize this diverse material — by chronology, genre, theme? Who was our target audience — college students, high school students, general readers? How much was this book going to cost anyway? And who was going to pay for it? Like most English majors, Julie and Amy saved the financial issues for the end and tackled the conceptual ones first. For help, we consulted other civil rights educators across the country — high school teachers, college professors, and community discussion leaders — about the kind of anthology they would want to use. This initial feedback led us to a preliminary table of contents that we refined, along with our questions, over the next year while we presented our work at professional conferences and used material from this book in courses taught at the University of Mississippi and the University of South Florida St. Petersburg. Although we still find ourselves debating these larger questions, even English majors must one day stop theorizing and actually do something. We submitted a proposal to the University of Georgia Press, which agreed with us that a literature anthology would complement its already strong civil rights line. When an editor there suggested that our readers may have some of the questions that we started with, we decided to include this preface to address those questions.

Thus, here we are, at another kind of beginning. What do the editors of this book mean by "the civil rights movement"? As our subtitle, *From Jim Crow to Reconciliation*, indicates, we take a broader view than some readers might expect. For many Americans, the civil rights movement occupies a specific historical moment and geographical location, with a clearly defined philosophy, aims, and goals. According to that simple yet compelling story, the Supreme Court's 1954 *Brown v. Board of Education* decision to outlaw segregation in public schools provided the first step toward ending racism in America, a problem that endured primarily in the South. After *Brown*, extraordinary individuals like Rosa Parks and Martin Luther King Jr. began challenging other forms of segregation. These individuals met violent, sometimes deadly opposition, but their protests, based in the philosophy of nonviolent direct action, prevailed with the help of the federal government, which first brought in troops and then enacted laws to protect them. The era came to a tragic close with King's 1968 assassination, but by the time of his death, his followers had achieved in a legal, if not yet a practical, sense equal access to voting, housing, jobs, public facilities, and all the rights entitled to them as Americans.

Over the past decade, civil rights scholars and activists have challenged this narrative for leaving out too much. In terms of leadership, focusing on a handful of high-profile, nationally recognized figures fails to recognize the hard work of everyday people who made change happen in ways small and large. Limiting the geographical scope to the South does not acknowledge the persistence of racism across the country, and limiting the philosophical scope to nonviolent direct action does not acknowledge more radical methods of protest and resistance. In terms of chronology, focusing on the 1954 to 1968 years leaves out everything that came before or happened after. At a minimum, one must recognize the decades-long legal road-building that led to the Supreme Court's 1954 decision and the community organizing efforts of civil rights groups that had been working since the turn of the twentieth century. One might even raise a question about whether the movement began with the first protests against segregation, or with those against slavery, a defining question of civil rights in America. Equally vexing is the question of when, or if, the movement ended. Many of the solutions that midcentury legislation was supposed to provide have either been undermined or become controversies themselves. Racism has proven to be a subtle force, intrinsic to our institutions, rather than an identifiable obstacle that federal law or Supreme Court decisions can weed out. And the struggle against it, inevitably, continues.

The Civil Rights Reader: American Literature from Jim Crow to Reconciliation draws from this expanded historical vision in making its literary selections. We begin our survey with the post-Reconstruction period, where the system of racial segregation known familiarly as "Jim Crow" became fully entrenched in law and custom. The civil rights movement as we characterize it involves a struggle between those who would extend constitutional guarantees to all U.S. citizens, no matter who they are or where they come from, and those who would limit those rights to protect their own economic and political power. African Americans have resided at the heart of that struggle since the Constitution forged its definitions of freedom from the crucible of slavery. While we acknowledge that the black freedom struggle has roots that go deeper and spread wider than the late nineteenth-century United States, we have chosen to begin our book with literature that focuses on a place and time when the terms of debate shifted dramatically. Slavery's end forced the nation to negotiate new meanings for words such as "freedom," "equality," "justice," and "democracy," and Jim Crow marked the striking gap between American ideals and realities. The 1954–68 years that many associate with the civil rights movement proper put an end to Jim Crow, but as many would argue, the gap between the idea and the reality still seems impossible to close. The struggle and its legacies, moreover, continue to inform attitudes and behaviors in ways that many of us in the present day do not always recognize. As W. E. B. Du Bois predicted in 1903, "The problem of the Twentieth Century is the problem of the color-line." And, as some of our contemporary selections demonstrate, that line still trips up even the most careful and well intentioned. For this reason, we bring the book's chronological focus into the present day. "Reconciliation," the term of hope with which we end our title, refers to ongoing, widespread efforts to solve the color-line problem. A primary guiding principle behind this volume is that "movement," with respect to civil rights, happened long before and continues well after the 1950s and 1960s.

Another guiding principle is that the response to the civil rights movement is multifaceted in form and content, which brings us to another set of questions: what do we mean by "literature," and what have been our criteria for selecting this anthology's texts? With the first part of that equation, we might again surprise some readers. When "literature" and "civil rights" come together in one sentence, most people think of the familiar speeches, political writings, and memoirs that document the twentieth century's sweeping changes with regard to race. This book provides examples of those texts, but it features more prominently the poetry, fiction, and drama that often receive less attention in histories of the period. Creative writers (and artists more generally) have always been an integral part of the fight for civil rights: raising awareness about particular issues, claiming and celebrating an identity that some would try to invalidate, honoring those who risked or gave their lives to the struggle, and helping individuals to make sense out of a complicated, shifting world. Just as focusing on one fourteen-year period obscures a bigger civil rights picture, focusing on documentary literature alone leaves out an important part of the story. America's civil rights movement was, and continues to be, about more than changing laws. The movement is about changing a nation — in mind, heart, and soul — for the better, for all of its people. Creative writing can reveal those changes in ways that documentary literature cannot, although both are important for the broad view of the American civil rights movement that this book presents.

Just as this volume offers a variety of literary forms, it also presents a range of subject positions and ideological views. Talking about civil rights change in terms of "movement" has never meant that everyone moving agreed on the direction to take. One popular misconception is that civil rights has been literally and metaphorically a black and white issue. The powerful visual images of the 1954–68 years especially can give the impression that battle lines were clearly drawn between races, between right and wrong, between nonviolent protest and angry, violent opposition. Another misconception, more either-or than black and white, is that debates within the movement can be neatly bracketed into oppositional ideologies represented by key leaders such as Booker T. Washington and W. E. B. Du Bois, or Martin Luther King Jr. and Malcolm X. From this perspective, our own times seem much more complicated. With so many gray areas, so many perspectives and possibilities from which to choose, how can we ever know which direction to take, which solutions to contemporary problems are right? But choices are easy only from a distance or in hindsight. The documentary literature and the creative writing, and the historical and the contemporary selections, represented in this volume help provide a more nuanced view: from conservative, liberal, and radical thinkers; from those whose acts of protest are public and those whose acts are private; from those who practice nonviolence, those who advocate self-defense, and those who are not sure what to believe; and from those not caught up in big decisions at all, just everyday people doing everyday things, going to school or work, spending time with friends and family, trying to treat others and to be treated with basic human dignity and claim basic human rights.

The problem raised by creating a more nuanced view of civil rights literature is that we wanted only a one-volume anthology. At the beginning stages of this project we jokingly referred to *The Civil Rights Reader* as our thirty-thousand-page book. Along the way we had to decide what texts to leave out. Most of these decisions were very difficult. In the initial feedback we received from civil rights educators, several suggested that we include political cartoons, journalism, and song lyrics — all excellent ideas. But space limitations would not allow us to provide the historical coverage we wanted, draw attention to the creative writing that has yet to receive its due in civil rights anthologies, *and* diversify our genres even further. Other documentary writings, conversely, seemed mandatory for this anthology. We could not imagine a volume without some of the essays, speeches, and memoirs included here. Another difficult decision was limiting our focus to African American civil rights. We initially thought that this book might also include readings from the black freedom movement worldwide and related struggles of other groups within the United States. Such a project quickly became overwhelming, especially (once again) given the historical and literary scope that we wanted. The wealth of literature in these areas would have given us far more than a thirty-thousand-page book; we would have had a multivolume set.

Some of our choices were easier, however. Many decisions were made for us, although we cannot say that their ease made them preferable. We sometimes could not obtain permission to reprint a selection, or something simply cost too much. For readers who wonder why an essential text of civil rights literature is not included here, copyright permission or price is the most likely reason. We have also chosen to include a few selections that feature violence and adult language or situations, even though we imagine that this volume will be read in high school and college classrooms, or in church and community discussion groups. While most scenes are quite tame when compared to today's television, radio, and movie content, we want readers to know up front that we have not toned down any situations. In some cases, a work's shock value is an intrinsic part of the message itself. Finally, we have not included overtly racist writings, although some reviewers have rightly suggested that those texts provide a useful historical context. We believe that the writers represented here do a more than adequate job of demonstrating what civil rights activists have been fighting against. And, once again, given budget and space restraints, we want to spend our dollars and word counts on those who have written in support of civil rights, or on those who have at least struggled in good faith with the sometimes overwhelming changes that the struggle has wrought.

As a closing note on organization, we have set up this book to accommodate multiple uses by a range of audiences. We have divided it into three roughly chronological sections, "The Rise of Jim Crow," "The Fall of Jim Crow," and "Reflections and Continuing Struggles." Each section begins with an introduction that surveys historical and literary developments. Within each section, we have organized material by author birth date, finding this arrangement to be the best way to maintain coherence and flexibility at the same time. Head notes preceding the literary texts provide biographic and bibliographic information on each writer and relevant context for understanding specific selections. Our intention with this loose chronological structure is not to arrange selections so that they tell a specific civil rights story, but to provide a user-friendly anthology. To further achieve that goal, we also include two alternative tables of contents that group material by genre (drama, essay/memoir/speech, fiction, and poetry) and by theme (agency and resistance; coalition building and related struggles; immigration and migration; integration, segregation, separatism,

and nationalism; oppression and violence; race, class, and economics; reconciliation and healing; and significant issues). Closing the book are a chronology
of publication dates and historical events, and a list of selected readings in civil
rights studies. Our bibliography, like this anthology, is by no means the final
word on the subject. There is always more to read, always more to talk about in
terms of civil rights in America. Just as this book began with a conversation, we
hope that it will continue to facilitate dialogue that goes well beyond its pages.

Acknowledgments

The editors would like to thank, first and foremost, Susan Glisson, director of the William Winter Institute for Racial Reconciliation at the University of Mississippi. Without the Winter Institute's generosity of resources and Susan's generosity of spirit, this book never would have gone from idea to reality. Anyone who knows Susan can attest that she both talks the talk and walks the walk. Under her guidance, the Winter Institute has become a model of positive racial discourse and progressive social change. Working there during the first stages of preparing this manuscript, during the 2005–6 academic year, was a joy that we will always remember. We would like to thank as well our colleagues from that year: Judith Barlow-Roberts, Richard Glisson, April Grayson, Annette Hollowell, Ron McDaniel, and Kirk Sims.

This project's success has also depended upon those who have given feedback on various stages of the manuscript: Deborah Menkart and Jenice L. View, Teaching for Change; Craig Gill, the University Press of Mississippi; Derrick Alridge, University of Georgia; Sterling L. Bland, Rutgers University–Newark; Sharon Lynette Jones, Wayne State University; Anne P. Rice, Lehman College, City University of New York; Charles Wilson, University of Mississippi; an anonymous reviewer for the University of Georgia Press; and especially Christopher Metress from Samford University, whose suggestions have been thorough and gracious from beginning to end. We also would like to extend our thanks to John Young of Marshall University, whose panel on Race and Textual Scholarship at the 2006 Modern Language Association conference in Philadelphia, Pennsylvania, allowed us to hone some of the volume's controlling questions. Finally, anyone who has ever worked with Nancy Grayson at the University of Georgia Press knows that she is one of the best editors in the business. We cannot sing enough praises for her.

Assembling an anthology can be prohibitively expensive, and the process of obtaining permissions laborious at best. We must therefore single out for special gratitude those writers or their representatives who allowed us to use material free of charge, at affordable rates, or reduced their fees upon request, and those who were especially helpful with copyright permissions: Wanda Coleman, Anthony Grooms, Michael Harper, Haki Madhubuti, the family of Howard Sackler, the estate of Martin Luther King Jr., and literary representatives for Amiri Baraka, Cyrus Cassells, Lucille Clifton, Honorée Fanonne Jeffers, June Jordan, and Dudley Randall.

Amy: I am particularly grateful to my family, especially my parents, Angie and Fred Schmidt, not only for their support and encouragement, but also for teaching me that all people deserve to be treated with dignity, respect, and compassion. I also owe a great debt to several professors for profoundly and positively influencing my conceptions of race and social justice; these include, but are not limited to, Julie Armstrong, Susan Glisson, Jeff Jackson, and Nancy Bercaw.

Julie: I have multitudes to thank, beginning with my partner Thomas Hallock, whose work at the University of Mississippi initially brought me into the conversation with Susan Glisson where the idea for this book was born. Now that we are both at the University of South Florida St. Petersburg, Tom was kind enough to take on an extra course one semester so that I could fulfill administrative duties and have time to work on this anthology. He has also given this book more than one thorough proofread. I have to admit as well that I am thoroughly dependent upon him for titles, first lines, and knowing when to stop working and have fun. Most important, however, is the way he helps me stay true to my best self.

This volume has a long history that goes back to a 1998 National Endowment for the Humanities Institute, Teaching the History of the Civil Rights Movement, directed by Waldo Martin, Patricia Sullivan, and Henry Louis Gates Jr. While there, I was part of a working group on the arts and civil rights, and drafted a syllabus for using poetry in the classroom. That syllabus eventually formed the core of this book, although I had no thoughts at the time of assembling an anthology. I did, however, coedit another volume with three Institute participants, Susan Hult Edwards, Houston Roberson, and Rhonda Williams. The experience, the book, and the colleagues were all invaluable resources for preparing this manuscript. I used Houston's excellent chronology as the starting point for the one here; I also drew upon the bibliography, in which we all had a hand, to prepare this one. Rhonda provided feedback on the preliminary table of contents for this manuscript as well.

Working with Amy Schmidt has been a real pleasure. She started off as the project's graduate assistant, quickly proved capable of taking on more responsibility, and finished out her time at UM as my colleague and friend. Additional editorial assistance on the volume was provided by Amanda Coffey and Kyle Draper at the University of South Florida St. Petersburg, who scanned, converted, and proofread several manuscripts expertly and efficiently.

Last — but in some ways first — I want to thank the students who have tested different versions of this anthology. Those enrolled in LIBA 102 at UM in the spring of 2006 and AML 3604 at USFSP in the fall of 2006 and the fall of 2007 deserve much credit for being victims of a two-year-long experiment. On the serious side, I want to acknowledge the difficulty of talking about civil rights movement literature. We live in a society that discourages reading and critical thinking, where students come into the classroom with very little knowledge of history, and where few people know how to have an open, honest dialogue about race. USFSP students Juan Diaz, Jimmy Martell, Sarah Edwards, Jamie Simpson, and Erin Jensen deserve special notice for carrying the classroom conversation forward through Students for Social Justice. However, I celebrate all three UM and USFSP classes for their faith in what this book ultimately represents: that art can make the world a better place.

THE RISE OF JIM CROW

uring the 1830s a character named "Jim Crow" became popular in American minstrel shows, where white performers donned blackface makeup to caricature African American vernacular forms of dancing and singing. Thomas Dartmouth "Daddy" Rice, a struggling New York actor, modeled Jim Crow on either an old slave who had trouble walking or a stable boy dressed in rags. The character's jerky moves, tattered clothes, and trademark lyrics were a hit with white audiences across the country:

> Weel about and turn about and do jis so,
> Eb'ry time I weel about I jump Jim Crow.

By the end of the decade the term "Jim Crow," like the names of other minstrel figures "Sambo" and "Coon," was being used as a racial epithet. By the end of the nineteenth century, the term had come to embody the interlocking systems of segregation, disfranchisement, socioeconomic controls, and racist violence that prevailed across the South and reached into other parts of the nation. Although Jim Crow's movements originated as caricature, they offered an ironic prophecy. Many African Americans trying to negotiate the ever-shifting racial codes that prevailed through the middle of the twentieth century — where penalties for trespass could be as extreme as death — found themselves performing a strange social dance. Sometimes everyday life meant jumping Jim Crow.

Although Jim Crow has been a figure associated with black oppression since the days of slavery, he met a tough opponent in the "New Negro," a figure associated with uplift and resistance that emerged around 1900. Many people believe that the term originated with Alain Locke, who edited a March 1925 special issue of the journal *Survey Graphic* and later that same year an anthology called *The New Negro*. The collections heralded a burgeoning artistic explosion that came to be known as the "Harlem" or "New Negro" Renaissance. In his introductory essay, Locke states that a "younger generation is vibrant with a new psychology" and a "new spirit is awake in the masses," which mark "a spiritual Coming of Age" among African Americans. Although Locke claims that spirit for a younger generation, the term and the attitude had actually been around for several decades at least. The words "New Negro" first appeared in print in 1895, when a *Cleveland Gazette* editorial praised a "new class of people, the 'New Negro' [that] has arisen since the War, with education, refinement and money." The piece suggested that this new class would demand the rights and privileges that came with the increased access to these benefits. Well before Locke celebrated the New Negro in an essay, this class had begun to flex its political awareness and muscle through the work of organizations such as the National Association for the Advancement of Colored People (NAACP; formed in 1909) and the National Association for Colored Women (NACW; formed in 1896), and through the efforts of outspoken individuals such as Ida B. Wells, who initiated a one-woman antilynching campaign in 1892. The spirit of the New Negro was also apparent in acts of everyday resistance performed by people from all classes. Sometimes it was possible not only to jump Jim Crow but also to trip him.

"The Rise of Jim Crow," the first section of *The Civil Rights Reader: American Literature from Jim Crow to Reconciliation*, surveys literary expression from the early 1890s through the early 1950s, a period when it seemed as if Jim Crow might actually defeat the New Negro. A more accurate depiction of the era is one of significant gains and losses, where political, social, and cultural assertions of the New Negro spirit met on all fronts a Jim Crow backlash, which in turn met renewed civil rights efforts. The transitional period between the post-Reconstruction years and those of modern civil rights was hardly an easy one for most Americans. It was a time of great change throughout the United States in general, as the country became an international player on the battlefield and in the marketplace and as technological developments like assembly-line production, home electricity, radios, movies, television, telephones, automobiles, airplanes, and, near the period's end, the threat of nuclear annihilation forever changed the way people lived. Even modes of creative expression changed dramatically, as writers, visual artists, and others sought new ways to represent a new, modern world. What came to be called "modernism" forced individuals to rethink their relationships to artistic media and traditions, as well as the relationship between the arts and society. Perhaps the battle between Jim Crow and the New Negro indicated a parallel shift in thinking. As the United States entered the modern world, the nation clearly needed to renegotiate the gap between its constitutional ideals and its brutal realities. Some of the period's best writers memorably demonstrate, however, that no great change happens without great struggle.

History and Literature from the Nadir to Red Summer

At least the struggle was forward, although it did not always seem that way for those involved. The turn-of-the-century years offered cause for much hope and despair, leading African American intellectual W. E. B. Du Bois to surmise, in 1903, that "the problem of the Twentieth Century is the problem of the color-line." The 1890s were especially difficult. By then, most of the Reconstruction-era promises were clearly broken. African Americans elected to state and federal offices had been voted out, lynching violence had reached record levels, and Supreme Court rulings had effectively nullified most legislation that would have protected black rights. In 1896 the *Plessy v. Ferguson* decision gave legal precedent to Jim Crow, institutionalizing racial segregation in public facilities and accommodations. In the decades after *Plessy*, blacks and whites across the country, but especially in the South, ate, worked, worshiped, played, and traveled in different spheres. In theory, separate meant equal, but in reality, this was rarely the case. Public accommodations for blacks, even for those of higher classes, did not measure up to those for whites. The color line was also very closely policed. Racially mixed individuals counted as "black" unless they could pass as "white." Interracial interaction was acceptable as long as strict social hierarchies, such as employer and employee, were maintained. Crossing the color line for romantic relationships, especially for black men, was punishable by death. Under the rule of Jim Crow, even the word "interracial" itself became taboo.

Historians commonly refer to the 1890s as the "nadir" of American race relations; this decade and the ones to follow, however, signal the New Negro's growing strength. In 1892, the same year that Homer Plessy lost a Supreme Court battle to ride a "whites only" Louisiana train car, the National Association of Colored Women formed, a significant force in civil rights activism during the coming decades. Several NACW members also became part of the National Association for the Advancement of Colored People, influential in civil rights work throughout the twentieth century. The NAACP was in one sense breaking the ultimate Jim Crow rule by being an *interracial* organization. Resistance to segregation took many colors and forms. Perhaps most creatively, people fought back with their feet. By the 1910s, what would later be called the "Great Migration" was well under way, as thousands of African Americans left the southern states for areas north and west. That people had to leave, resist, and organize to fight for what the U.S. Constitution mandated by law but many states did not grant in practice was an irony that New Negroes and progressive whites did not miss. When the United States entered into World War I, in order to "make the world safe for democracy," as President Woodrow Wilson explained, that irony gained a new focal point. Black soldiers served their country heroically, but on their return found oppression and violence nearing 1890s levels. The summer of 1919 saw so much white-led rioting and bloodshed that it was dubbed "Red Summer." A subtle shift had occurred between the nadir and Red Summer, however. Jim Crow was still in power, but civil rights efforts were gaining momentum.

The period's literature documents this shift as well as its corresponding moments of hope and despair. Turn-of-the-century selections reveal a national concern, or more accurately an obsession, with the color line. Fiction by Frances E. W. Harper and Charles W. Chesnutt, Booker T. Washington's "Atlanta Exposition Address," and W. E. B. Du Bois's essay "Of Our Spiritual Strivings" offer multiple points of view about the role that African Americans should play in society and also show just how heated debates over this issue could grow. In Harper's novel, excerpted here, a racially mixed character must choose whether to identify as "black" or "white," a choice with serious implications that she does not take lightly. The penalties for transgressing Jim Crow's ever-shifting boundaries are made brutally clear in works by Chesnutt, Paul Laurence Dunbar, and Mary Burrill. Also evident throughout the literature, conversely, is the New Negro presence in a variety of guises. Harper's character Iola Leroy devotes her life to the cause of racial uplift. Dunbar and Du Bois honor the persistence of spirit in a culture that tries to deny the existence of humanity. Chesnutt's character Josh and Burrill's John both go out fighting, just like the speaker of Claude McKay's Red Summer classic, "If We Must Die."

In some ways, the literature's presence itself is the best testimony to the existence of the New Negro. Women like Harper and men like Du Bois believed that the fight against Jim Crow demanded all the weapons at their disposal — political, social, and artistic. The selections represented here therefore employ the various literary and rhetorical styles available to late nineteenth- and early twentieth-century authors. The poetry in the earlier part of this section (such as Dunbar's) is more traditional in form than that published later (such as Langston Hughes's), when modernist experimentation began to take hold. Burrill, however, was already experimenting with a new genre, the anti-lynching play, that had been around for only a few years. With fiction, excerpts from novels by Harper and Chesnutt begin by setting up debates that expose the "un-Reconstructed" southern viewpoint, but from there each takes a different tack, depending upon the audience in mind. Harper focuses on the sentimental for her primarily female readers, while Chesnutt, for a racially mixed readership, exposes stereotypes and makes a powerful statement about black self-defense. Audience plays a key role in nonfiction selections as well. As much as one might focus on the historical antagonism between Washington and Du Bois, one might also note how the rhetorical circumstances of the selections reprinted here demand entirely different approaches. Washington was speaking in the Deep South, on behalf of Tuskegee Institute; Du Bois was writing a cultural autobiography and call to arms. For the authors represented here, literature served different purposes at different times. It was a method of social protest, a means of rallying forces, a way to make sense of the world, and above all a necessary outlet for creative expression when the soul needed it most.

History and Literature from the Harlem Renaissance to the Cold War

The Red Summer of 1919, like Freedom Summer forty-five years later, signaled a key battle between the forces of oppression and resistance. Multiple white-led riots and a peak in the number of lynchings gave the year its name, but texts like McKay's "If We Must Die" and Burrill's *Aftermath* memorialize a resulting fighting spirit. Some scholars date the beginnings of a new literary era to 1919, others to 1925 with Locke's anthology. Either way, the New Negro or Harlem Renaissance had arrived, named for the concentration of writers, musicians, visual artists, and other talented individuals in the area of New York City above 125th Street—but the cultural explosion was by no means confined to those blocks. Renaissance actually marked the confluence of two important artistic developments: the advent of modernism and increased attention to black vernacular modes of expression. The modernist movement had been percolating in Europe and the Americas for several years when it erupted around World War I. Painters such as Marcel Duchamp and Pablo Picasso and writers such as James Joyce and Ezra Pound changed the very notion of what art could and should do. Stylistic innovation, rather than adherence to traditions and strict forms, was the new rule for what many saw as the new, "modern" twentieth century, where the old rules no longer seemed to work or apply. Many modern artists were drawn to African and African American modes—visual art, music, dance, and linguistic expression in particular—because they appeared so original and fresh when compared to the European and neoclassical styles that had previously dominated Western art. Negroes were now "new" in another sense as well; they were fashionable, in vogue.

The elevation of blues, jazz, folk stories, dialect, and other vernacular forms to high art became a mixed blessing. Writers found a plethora of publication outlets, from black-sponsored journals like the *Crisis* and *Opportunity* to white patrons and magazines. But a white patronage system was not exactly what Du Bois had in mind when he wrote in *The Souls of Black Folk* that African Americans should claim their rightful place as "coworker[s] in the kingdom of culture." Nor did increased visibility for African Americans as artists and entertainers translate into increased political and economic opportunity. The NAACP tried and failed in 1922 to get Congress to pass antilynching legislation. Sharecropping and peonage labor had become new forms of slavery in the former Confederate states. The Great Migration offered something better than Jim Crow, but that was hardly saying much. When the Great Depression arrived in 1929, hard times hit people of all races. The boom times for the Harlem Renaissance also began drawing to a close, although marking the period's end is just as difficult as marking its beginning. Literature from the period captures the feeling of boom and bust. Poems like Langston Hughes's "I, Too" look forward to a new day of racial equality, but his "Song for a Dark Girl" remains skeptical about justice in this world or the hereafter. In poems such as "America," McKay seems as determined to have faith and to persevere, despite his outsider status, as he is to fighting back in his other well-known work. Angelina Weld Grimké, in "The Black Finger" and "Tenebris," watches the signs and appears optimistic. On some days the black hand of fate points upward; on others, it slowly picks away at the foundations of white society.

As modern art became increasingly experimental, abstract, and occasionally surreal, some artists began to debate the relationship between politics and creative expression. Did artists really have an ability to change the world? Did they have an obligation? These questions were especially important to African American artists and activists; the Harlem Renaissance flowered while the battle between Jim Crow and the New Negro raged. For Du Bois, art and activism went hand in hand. As editor of the NAACP's magazine the *Crisis*, he published poetry alongside exposé. Conversely, Zora Neale Hurston, author of the 1937 novel *Their Eyes Were Watching God*, did not see herself as part of what she called the "sobbing school of Negrohood" that used its writing in service of social causes. Unfortunately for Hurston, she expressed such sentiments during the heyday of politicized art in the United States. Civil rights literature during the 1930s and 1940s did exactly what Grimké predicted: strive to undermine the foundations of white economic and political privilege. Many artists and activists during this time were drawn to Marxist and other forms of leftist critique for modern solutions to old problems of injustice and inequality. Communism promised a utopian, nonhierarchical world where labor's burdens could be shared and resources could be distributed fairly. The benefits were clear to anyone who had witnessed Jim Crow and similar forms of oppression in action. Although Communism still had a bad reputation in the United States at the time — its major target, after all, was Capitalism — it found a fairly broad audience during the Great Depression, when the capitalist economy seemed to have failed the bulk of America's citizens. Some of the federal government's solutions to the Depression's economic woes even drew from the political left, through large-scale public works projects, including those devoted to art. In a Marxist world, of course, all art should be political art, a notion under which writers like Hurston chafed. For Erskine Caldwell, Lillian Smith, and Richard Wright, however, the opportunity to expose Jim Crow's ugly underbelly was more than liberating. Although Wright was the only one of these three authors to identify specifically with the Communist Party, each participated in the times' general tendency toward writing as political critique.

The backlash against Communism in the decades surrounding World War II led to a decrease in politicized art. An upsurge in patriotism during the war years, combined with fears about Communism's spread during the Cold War that followed, led to a series of investigations of U.S. citizens in the late 1940s and early 1950s. This period, known as the "McCarthy Era" after Senator Joseph McCarthy (a rabid anti-Communist), understandably prevented many artists from making overt political statements in their work and kept many people from making political statements at all. Still, civil rights literature and activism continued throughout World War II and the Cold War. As in World War I, African Americans could hardly miss the irony of sending soldiers to fight for democracy and justice overseas, when democracy and justice were severely lacking at home.

Outside the war effort, individuals and groups were laying the foundation for enormous social transformations that would take place in the coming decades. During the 1940s, much was going on. The NAACP was building a series of legal precedents that would ultimately overthrow the Supreme Court's 1896 *Plessy* decision and, thus, Jim Crow. A. Phillip Randolph was conceiving the idea for a March on Washington. The Congress of Racial Equality was founded and initiated the first version of the Freedom Rides. President Harry Truman appointed a committee to investigate civil rights and desegregated the military. And, in 1947, a high-profile turning point took place: Jackie Robinson became the first African American to play Major League Baseball. Unfortunately, literature from the period makes these events seem optimistic only from the perspective of hindsight. In 1951, Hughes was still asking in his poem "Harlem," "What happens to a dream deferred?" One year later, Ralph Ellison published his landmark of literary modernism, *Invisible Man*, which follows its protagonist from the South to the North while the New Negro battles Jim Crow. As the novel's first chapter (reprinted here) indicates, Ellison's protagonist has a long road ahead of him. It would be another few years before Jim Crow would fall.

Frances E. W. Harper (1825–1911)

arper was born Frances Ellen Watkins on September 24, 1825, in Baltimore, Maryland, to free parents, both of whom died while she was still a child. She then moved in with an aunt and uncle and went to William Wilson's Academy for Negro Youth. After the Fugitive Slave Act passed in 1850, she moved to Columbus, Ohio, and began teaching at Union Seminary (later Wilberforce University), becoming the first female professor at the school. Not long after that, Harper would leave Ohio for Philadelphia, where she would join the abolitionist movement, participating in the Underground Railroad, writing poetry to convey her passion for the cause, and speaking on its behalf throughout New England, the Midwest, and Canada. In 1860 she married Fenton Harper and returned to Ohio, but after Fenton's death in 1864 she began touring the South, speaking on social issues that were affecting recently freed men and women. She died on February 20, 1911, after a long period of health problems.

Harper is often known for her poetry, but she successfully wrote prose and nonfiction as well. Much of her writing deals with issues of gender and racial equality in ways unprecedented during her era, and she occasionally focuses on issues of temperance and class. Her best-known novel is *Iola Leroy: Or, Shadows Uplifted* (1892), which, when published, was praised for its treatment of racial equality during Reconstruction. No copies survive of her first published collection of poetry, *Fallen Leaves* (1845). However, *Poems on Miscellaneous Subjects* (1854), with an introduction by William Lloyd Garrison, sold so many copies that twenty editions of it were published in less than twenty years. Harper also wrote essays on abolition for a number of journals, and her short story "The Two Offers," published in 1859, may be the first short story published by an African American author. Her recently republished works include *Minnie's Sacrifice, Sowing and Reaping, Trial and Triumph: Three Rediscovered Novels* (1994).

In addition to her writing Harper was well known for her social-justice work. In the 1860s she joined the American Equal Rights Association, and in 1896 she helped found and later served as vice president for the National Association of Colored Women. For a time she directed the American Association of Colored Youth, and she was often a featured speaker at conferences and meetings on suffrage for African Americans and women, and on the general rights of those two groups.

Two sections of Harper's *Iola Leroy* appear below. In "Open Questions," characters argue over the place of African Americans in post-Reconstruction society, with their viewpoints closely mirroring real debates of the time. In "Diverging Paths," one of those characters, a white man named Dr. Gresham, proposes to the novel's protagonist, Iola Leroy, who served as his nurse during the Civil War. The racially mixed Iola must now choose one side of the color line.

Selections from *Iola Leroy*

Chapter 26, Open Questions

In the evening Robert and Rev. Carmicle called on Dr. Gresham, and found Dr. Latrobe, the Southerner, and a young doctor by the name of Latimer, already there. Dr. Gresham introduced Dr. Latrobe, but it was a new experience to receive colored men socially. His wits, however, did not forsake him, and he received the introduction and survived it.

"Permit me, now," said Dr. Gresham, "to introduce you to my friend, Dr. Latimer, who is attending our convention. He expects to go South and labor among the colored people. Don't you think that there is a large field of usefulness before him?"

"Yes," replied Dr. Latrobe, "if he will let politics alone."

"And why let politics alone?" asked Dr. Gresham.

"Because," replied Dr. Latrobe, "we Southerners will never submit to negro supremacy. We will never abandon our Caucasian civilization to an inferior race."

"Have you any reason," inquired Rev. Carmicle, "to dread that a race which has behind it the heathenism of Africa and the slavery of America, with its inheritance of ignorance and poverty, will be able, in less than one generation, to domineer over a race which has behind it ages of dominion, freedom, education, and Christianity?"

A slight shade of vexation and astonishment passed over the face of Dr. Latrobe. He hesitated a moment, then replied: —

"I am not afraid of the negro as he stands alone, but what I dread is that in some closely-contested election ambitious men will use him to hold the balance of power and make him an element of danger. He is ignorant, poor, and clannish, and they may impact him as their policy would direct."

"Any more," asked Robert, "than the leaders of the Rebellion did the ignorant, poor whites during our late conflict?"

"Ignorance, poverty, and clannishness," said Dr. Gresham, "are more social than racial conditions, which may be outgrown."

"And I think," said Rev. Carmicle, "that we are outgrowing them as fast as any other people would have done under the same conditions."

"The negro," replied Dr. Latrobe, "always has been and always will be an element of discord in our country."

"What, then, is your remedy?" asked Dr. Gresham.

"I would eliminate him from the politics of the country."

"As disfranchisement is a punishment for crime, is it just to punish a man before he transgresses the law?" asked Dr. Gresham.

"If," said Dr. Latimer, "the negro is ignorant, poor, and clannish, let us remember that in part of our land it was once a crime to teach him to read. If he is poor, for ages he was forced to bend to unrequited toil. If he is clannish, society has segregated him to himself."

"And even," said Robert, "has given him a negro pew in your churches and a negro seat at your communion table."

"Wisely, or unwisely," said Dr. Gresham, "the Government has put the ballot in his hands. It is better to teach him to use that ballot aright than to intimidate him by violence or vitiate his vote by fraud."

"To-day," said Dr. Latimer, "the negro is not plotting in beer-saloons against the peace and order of society. His fingers are not dripping with dynamite, neither is he spitting upon your flag, nor flaunting the red banner of anarchy in your face."

"Power," said Dr. Gresham, "naturally gravitates into the strongest hands. The class who have the best brain and most wealth can strike with the heaviest hand. I have too much faith in the inherent power of the white race to dread the competition of any other people under heaven."

"I think you Northerners fail to do us justice," said Dr. Latrobe. "The men into whose hands you put the ballot were our slaves, and we would rather die than submit to them. Look at the carpet-bag governments the wicked policy of the Government inflicted upon us. It was only done to humiliate us."

"Oh, no!" said Dr. Gresham, flushing, and rising to his feet. "We had no other alternative than putting the ballot in their hands."

"I will not deny," said Rev. Carmicle, "that we have made woeful mistakes, but with our antecedents it would have been miraculous if we had never committed any mistakes or made any blunders."

"They were allies in war," continued Dr. Gresham, "and I am sorry that we have not done more to protect them in peace."

"Protect them in peace!" said Robert, bitterly. "What protection does the colored man receive from the hands of the Government? I know of no civilized country outside of America where men are still burned for real or supposed crimes."

"Johnson," said Dr. Gresham, compassionately, "it is impossible to have a policeman at the back of each colored man's chair, and a squad of soldiers at each cross-road, to detect with certainty, and punish with certainty, each invasion of his rights. We tried provisional governments and found them a failure. It seemed like leaving our former allies to be mocked with the name of freedom and tortured with the essence of slavery. The ballot is our weapon of defense, and we gave it to them for theirs."

"And there," said Dr. Latrobe, emphatically, "is where you signally failed. We are numerically stronger in Congress to-day than when we went out. You made the law, but the administration of it is in our hands, and we are a unit."

"But, Doctor," said Rev. Carmicle, "you cannot willfully deprive the negro of a single right as a citizen without sending demoralization through your own ranks."

"I think," said Dr. Latrobe, "that we are right in suppressing the negro's vote. This is a white man's government, and a white man's country. We own nineteen-twentieths of the land, and have about the same ratio of intelligence. I am a white man, and, right or wrong, I go with my race."

"But, Doctor," said Rev. Carmicle, "there are rights more sacred than the rights of property and superior intelligence."

"What are they?" asked Dr. Latrobe.

"The rights of life and liberty," replied Rev. Carmicle.

"That is true," said Dr. Gresham; "and your Southern civilization will be inferior until you shall have placed protection to those rights at its base, not in theory but in fact."

"But, Dr. Gresham, we have to live with these people, and the North is constantly irritating us by its criticisms."

"The world," said Dr. Gresham, "is fast becoming a vast whispering gallery, and lips once sealed can now state their own grievances and appeal to the conscience of the nation, and, as long as a sense of justice and mercy retains a hold upon the heart of our nation, you cannot practice violence and injustice without rousing a spirit of remonstrance. And if it were not so I would be ashamed of my country and of my race."

"You speak," said Dr. Latrobe, "as if we had wronged the negro by enslaving him and being unwilling to share citizenship with him. I think that slavery has been of incalculable value to the negro. It has lifted him out of barbarism and fetich worship, given him a language of civilization, and introduced him to the world's best religion. Think what he was in Africa and what he is in America!"

"The negro," said Dr. Gresham, thoughtfully, "is not the only branch of the human race which has been low down in the scale of civilization and freedom, and which has outgrown the measure of his chains. Slavery, polygamy, and human sacrifices have been practiced among Europeans in bygone days; and when Tyndall tells us that out of savages unable to count to the number of their fingers and speaking only a language of nouns and verbs, arise at length our Newtons and Shakspeares [sic], I do not see that the negro could not have learned our language and received our religion without the intervention of ages of slavery."

"If," said Rev. Carmicle, "Mohammedanism, with its imperfect creed, is successful in gathering large numbers of negroes beneath the Crescent, could not a legitimate commerce and the teachings of a pure Christianity have done as much to plant the standard of the Cross over the ramparts of sin and idolatry in Africa? Surely we cannot concede that the light of the Crescent is greater than the glory of the Cross, that there is less constraining power in the Christ of Calvary than in the Prophet of Arabia? I do not think that I underrate the difficulties in your way when I say that you young men are holding in your hands golden opportunities which it would be madness and folly to throw away. It is your grand opportunity to help build up a new South, not on the shifting sands of policy and expediency, but on the broad basis of equal justice and universal freedom. Do this and you will be blessed, and will make your life a blessing."

After Robert and Rev. Carmicle had left the hotel, Drs. Latimer, Gresham, and Latrobe sat silent and thoughtful awhile, when Dr. Gresham broke the silence by asking Dr. Latrobe how he had enjoyed the evening.

"Very pleasantly," he replied. "I was quite interested in that parson. Where was he educated?"

"In Oxford, I believe. I was pleased to hear him say that he had no white blood in his veins."

"I should think not," replied Dr. Latrobe, "from his looks. But one swallow does not make a summer. It is the exceptions which prove the rule."

"Don't you think," asked Dr. Gresham, "that we have been too hasty in our judgment of the negro? He has come handicapped into life, and is now on trial before the world. But it is not fair to subject him to the same tests that you would a white man. I believe that there are possibilities of growth in the race which we have never comprehended."

"The negro," said Dr. Latrobe, "is perfectly comprehensible to me. The only way to get along with him is to let him know his place, and make him keep it."

"I think," replied Dr. Gresham, "every man's place is the one he is best fitted for."

"Why," asked Dr. Latimer, "should any place be assigned to the negro more than to the French, Irish, or German?"

"Oh," replied Dr. Latrobe, "they are all Caucasians."

"Well," said Dr. Gresham, "is all excellence summed up in that branch of the human race?"

"I think," said Dr. Latrobe, proudly, "that we belong to the highest race on earth and the negro to the lowest."

"And yet," said Dr. Latimer, "you have consorted with them till you have bleached their faces to the whiteness of your own. Your children nestle in their bosoms; they are around you as body servants, and yet if one of them should attempt to associate with you your bitterest scorn and indignation would be visited upon them."

"I think," said Dr. Latrobe, "that feeling grows out of our Anglo-Saxon regard for the marriage relation. These white negroes are of illegitimate origin, and we would scorn to share our social life with them. Their blood is tainted."

"Who tainted it?" asked Dr. Latimer, bitterly. "You give absolution to the fathers, and visit the misfortunes of the mothers upon the children."

"But, Doctor, what kind of society would we have if we put down the bars and admitted everybody to social equality?"

"This idea of social equality," said Dr. Latimer, "is only a bugbear which frightens well-meaning people from dealing justly with the negro. I know of no place on earth where there is perfect social equality, and I doubt if there is such a thing in heaven. The sinner who repents on his death-bed cannot be the equal of St. Paul or the Beloved Disciple."

"Doctor," said Dr. Gresham, "I sometimes think that the final solution of this question will be the absorption of the negro into our race."

"Never! Never!" exclaimed Dr. Latrobe, vehemently. "It would be a death blow to American civilization."

"Why, Doctor," said Dr. Latimer, "you Southerners began this absorption before the war. I understand that in one decade the mixed bloods rose from one-ninth to one-eighth of the population, and that as early as 1663 a law was passed in Maryland to prevent English women from intermarrying with slaves; and, even now, your laws against miscegenation presuppose that you apprehend danger from that source."

"Doctor, it is no use talking," replied Dr. Latrobe, wearily. "There are niggers who are as white as I am, but the taint of blood is there and we always exclude it."

"How do you know it is there?" asked Dr. Gresham.

"Oh, there are tricks of blood which always betray them. My eyes are more practiced than yours. I can always tell them. Now, that Johnson is as white as any man; but I knew he was a nigger the moment I saw him. I saw it in his eye."

Dr. Latimer smiled at Dr. Latrobe's assertion, but did not attempt to refute it; and bade him good-night.

"I think," said Dr. Latrobe, "that our war was the great mistake of the nineteenth century. It has left us very serious complications. We cannot amalgamate with the negroes. We cannot expatriate them. Now, what are we to do with them?"

"Deal justly with them," said Dr. Gresham, "and let them alone. Try to create a moral sentiment in the nation, which will consider a wrong done to the weakest of them as a wrong done to the whole community. Whenever you find ministers too righteous to be faithless, cowardly, and time serving; women too Christly to be scornful; and public men too noble to be tricky and too honest to pander to the prejudices of the people, stand by them and give them your moral support."

"Doctor," said Latrobe, "with your views you ought to be a preacher striving to usher in the millennium."

"It can't come too soon," replied Dr. Gresham.

Chapter 27, Diverging Paths

On the eve of his departure from the city of P —, Dr. Gresham called on Iola, and found her alone. They talked awhile of reminiscences of the war and hospital life, when Dr. Gresham, approaching Iola, said: —

"Miss Leroy, I am glad the great object of your life is accomplished, and that you have found all your relatives. Years have passed since we parted, years in which I have vainly tried to get a trace of you and have been baffled, but I have found you at last!" Clasping her hand in his, he continued, "I would it were so that I should never lose you again! Iola, will you not grant me the privilege of holding this hand as mine all through the future of our lives? Your search for your mother is ended. She is well cared for. Are you not free at last to share with me my Northern home, free to be mine as nothing else on earth is mine." Dr. Gresham looked eagerly on Iola's face, and tried to read its varying expression. "Iola, I learned to love you in the hospital. I have tried to forget you, but it has been all in vain. Your image is just as deeply engraven on my heart as it was the day we parted."

"Doctor," she replied, sadly, but firmly, as she withdrew her hand from his, "I feel now as I felt then, that there is an insurmountable barrier between us."

"What is it, Iola?" asked Dr. Gresham, anxiously.

"It is the public opinion which assigns me a place with the colored people."

"But what right has public opinion to interfere with our marriage relations? Why should we yield to its behests?"

"Because it is stronger than we are, and we cannot run counter to it without suffering its penalties."

"And what are they, Iola? Shadows that you merely dread?"

"No! no! the penalties of social ostracism North and South, except here and there some grand and noble exceptions. I do not think that you fully realize how much prejudice against colored people permeates society, lowers the tone of our religion, and reacts upon the life of the nation. After freedom came, mamma was living in the city of A —, and wanted to unite with a Christian church there. She made application for membership. She passed her examination as a candidate, and was received as a church member. When she was about to make her first communion, she unintentionally took her seat at the head of the column. The elder who was administering the communion gave her the bread in the order in which she sat, but before he gave her the wine some one touched him on the shoulder and whispered a word in his ear. He then passed mamma by, gave the cup to others, and then returned to her. From that rite connected with the holiest memories of earth, my poor mother returned humiliated and depressed."

"What a shame!" exclaimed Dr. Gresham, indignantly.

"I have seen," continued Iola, "the same spirit manifested in the North. Mamma once attempted to do missionary work in this city. One day she found an outcast colored girl, whom she wished to rescue. She took her to an asylum for fallen women and made an application for her, but was refused. Colored girls were not received there. Soon after mamma found among the colored people an outcast white girl. Mamma's sympathies, unfettered by class distinction, were aroused in her behalf, and, in company with two white ladies, she went with the girl to that same refuge. For her the door was freely opened and admittance readily granted. It was as if two women were sinking in the quicksands, and on the solid land stood other women with life-lines in their hands, seeing the deadly sands slowly creeping up around the hapless victims. To one they readily threw the lines of deliverance, but for the other there was not one strand of salvation. Sometime since, to the same asylum, came a poor fallen girl who had escaped from the clutches of a wicked woman. For her the door would have been opened, had not the vile woman from whom she was escaping followed her to that place of refuge and revealed the fact that she belonged to the colored race. That fact was enough to close the door upon her, and to send her back to sin and to suffer, and perhaps to die as a wretched outcast. And yet in this city where a number of charities are advertised, I do not think there is one of them which, in appealing to the public, talks more religion than the managers of this asylum. This prejudice against the colored race environs our lives and mocks our aspirations."

"Iola, I see no use in your persisting that you are colored when your eyes are as blue and complexion as white as mine."

"Doctor, were I your wife, are there not people who would caress me as a white woman who would shrink from me in scorn if they knew I had one drop of negro blood in my veins? When mistaken for a white woman, I should hear things alleged against the race at which my blood would boil. No, Doctor, I am not willing to live under a shadow of concealment which I thoroughly hate as if the blood in my veins were an undetected crime of my soul."

"Iola, dear, surely you paint the picture too darkly."

"Doctor, I have painted it with my heart's blood. It is easier to outgrow the dishonor of crime than the disabilities of color. You have created in this country an aristocracy of color wide enough to include the South with its treason and Utah with its abominations, but too narrow to include the best and bravest colored man who bared his breast to the bullets of the enemy during your fratricidal strife. Is not the most arrant Rebel to-day more acceptable to you than the most faithful colored man?"

"No! no!" exclaimed Dr. Gresham, vehemently. "You are wrong. I belong to the Grand Army of the Republic. We have no separate State Posts for the colored people, and, were such a thing proposed, the majority of our members, I believe, would be against it. In Congress colored men have the same seats as white men, and the color line is slowly fading out in our public institutions."

"But how is it in the Church?" asked Iola.

"The Church is naturally conservative. It preserves old truths, even if it is somewhat slow in embracing new ideas. It has its social as well as its spiritual side. Society is woman's realm. The majority of church members are women, who are said to be the aristocratic element of our country. I fear that one of the last strong-holds of this racial prejudice will be found beneath the shadow of some of our churches. I think, on account of this social question, that large bodies of Christian temperance women and other reformers, in trying to reach the colored people even for their own good, will be quicker to form separate associations than our National Grand Army, whose ranks are open to black and white, liberals and conservatives, saints and agnostics. But, Iola, we have drifted far away from the question. No one has a right to interfere with our marriage if we do not infringe on the rights of others."

"Doctor," she replied, gently, "I feel that our paths must diverge. My life-work is planned. I intend spending my future among the colored people of the South."

"My dear friend," he replied, anxiously, "I am afraid that you are destined to sad disappointment. When the novelty wears off you will be disillusioned, and, I fear, when the time comes that you can no longer serve them they will forget your services and remember only your failings."

"But, Doctor, they need me; and I am sure when I taught among them they were very grateful for my services."

"I think," he replied, "these people are more thankful than grateful."

"I do not think so; and if I did it would not hinder me from doing all in my power to help them. I do not expect all the finest traits of character to spring from the hot-beds of slavery and caste. What matters it if they do forget the singer, so they don't forget the song? No, Doctor, I don't think that I could best serve my race by forsaking them and marrying you."

"Iola," he exclaimed, passionately, "if you love your race, as you call it, work for it, live for it, suffer for it, and, if need be, die for it; but don't marry for it. Your education has unfitted you for social life among them."

"It was," replied Iola, "through their unrequited toil that I was educated, while they were compelled to live in ignorance. I am indebted to them for the power I have to serve them. I wish other Southern women felt as I do. I think they could do so much to help the colored people at their doors if they would look at their opportunities in the light of the face of Jesus Christ. Nor am I wholly unselfish in allying myself with the colored people. All the rest of my family have done so. My dear grandmother is one of the excellent of the earth, and we all love her too much to ignore our relationship with her. I did not choose my lot in life, and the simplest thing I can do is to accept the situation and do the best I can."

"And is this your settled purpose?" he asked, sadly.

"It is, Doctor," she replied, tenderly but firmly. "I see no other. I must serve the race which needs me most."

"Perhaps you are right," he replied; "but I cannot help feeling sad that our paths, which met so pleasantly, should diverge so painfully. And yet, not only the freedmen, but the whole country, need such helpful, self-sacrificing teachers as you will prove; and if earnest prayers and holy wishes can brighten your path, your lines will fall in the pleasantest places."

As he rose to go, sympathy, love, and admiration were blended in the parting look he gave her; but he felt it was useless to attempt to divert her from her purpose. He knew that for the true reconstruction of the country something more was needed than bayonets and bullets, or the schemes of selfish politicians or plotting demagogues. He knew that the South needed the surrender of the best brain and heart of the country to build, above the wastes of war, more stately temples of thought and action.

(1892)

Booker T. Washington   (c. 1856–1915)

Booker Taliaferro Washington was born into slavery in 1856 on a plantation in Hale's Ford, Virginia. Owned by James Burroughs, Washington's mother worked as a cook on the plantation, and his father may have been a member of the Burroughs family. After the Civil War the recently emancipated Washington and his mother moved to Malden, West Virginia, with his mother's husband, Washington Ferguson, with whom Booker worked in a salt-packing plant. While working in the plant and in coal mines Washington taught himself to read, assisted by a teacher from the local African American school. In 1872 Washington began his studies at the Hampton Institute, where he worked as a janitor to pay his tuition and board.

After graduating from the institute in 1875 he returned to West Virginia and taught school until an administrator from the Hampton Institute asked him to create a school for African Americans in Tuskegee, Alabama. In 1881 Washington received a two-thousand-dollar grant from the federal government to build the Tuskegee Normal and Industrial Institute (now Tuskegee University). He borrowed money to purchase a plantation for the school's permanent site and served as the institute's president from 1881 to 1915, during which time he traveled widely, speaking in order to raise funds.

The school's focus was economic independence for racial progress. What W. E. B. Du Bois called Washington's accommodationist approach won white support for the institute on the national and local levels. Washington emphasized cooperation, industrial education, and economic independence at a time when racial violence was common, but because he refrained from pushing for legal and political changes, many southern whites supported him and the institute. Although Washington's approach was effective and innovative, his emphasis on cooperation was eventually replaced by what many early-twentieth-century activists believed was a more aggressive political stance.

In 1895 Washington attended the Cotton States and International Convention in Atlanta and gave an address, reprinted below, about economic cooperation between blacks and whites. Called "The Atlanta Exposition Address" in his autobiography, it was also known as "The Atlanta Compromise Speech" for its advocacy of "separate but equal" racial spheres. Throughout his career Washington published over twenty books, including a biography of Frederick Douglass, several textbooks, and the autobiography, *Up from Slavery* (1901), which received international critical acclaim because of its impact on racial attitudes in the South.

Washington died at his home in Tuskegee on November 14, 1915. He left behind one of the best-supported black educational institutions in the country.

The Atlanta Exposition Address

Selection from *Up from Slavery*, Chapter 14

Mr. President [of the Exposition] and Gentlemen of the Board of Directors and Citizens:

One-third of the population of the South is of the Negro race. No enterprise seeking the material, civil, or moral welfare of this section can disregard this element of our population and reach the highest success. I but convey to you, Mr. President and Directors, the sentiment of the masses of my race when I say that in no way have the value and manhood of the American Negro been more fittingly and generously recognized than by the managers of this magnificent Exposition at every stage of its progress. It is a recognition that will do more to cement the friendship of the two races than any occurrence since the dawn of our freedom.

Not only this, but the opportunity here afforded will awaken among us a new era of industrial progress. Ignorant and inexperienced, it is not strange that in the first years of our new life we began at the top instead of at the bottom; that a seat in Congress or the state legislature was more sought than real estate or industrial skill; that the political convention of stump speaking had more attraction than starting a dairy farm or truck garden.

A ship lost at sea for many days suddenly sighted a friendly vessel. From the mast of the unfortunate vessel was seen a signal, "Water, water; we die of thirst!" The answer from the friendly vessel at once came back, "Cast down your bucket where you are." A second time the signal, "Water, water; send us water!" ran up from the distressed vessel, and was answered, "Cast down your bucket where you are." And a third and fourth signal for water was answered, "Cast down your bucket where you are." The captain of the distressed vessel, at last heeding the injunction, cast down his bucket, and it came up full of fresh, sparkling water from the mouth of the Amazon River. To those of my race who depend on bettering their condition in a foreign land or who underestimate the importance of cultivating friendly relations with the Southern white man, who is their next-door neighbour, I would say: "Cast down your bucket where you are" — cast it down in making friends in every manly way of the people of all races by whom we are surrounded.

Cast it down in agriculture, mechanics, in commerce, in domestic service, and in the professions. And in this connection it is well to bear in mind that whatever other sins the South may be called to bear, when it comes to business, pure and simple, it is in the South that the Negro is given a man's chance in the commercial world, and in nothing is this Exposition more eloquent than in emphasizing this chance. Our greatest danger is that in the great leap from slavery to freedom we may overlook the fact that the masses of us are to live by the productions of our hands, and fail to keep in mind that we shall prosper in proportion as we learn to dignify and glorify common labour and put brains and skill into the common occupations of life; shall prosper in proportion as we learn to draw the line between the superficial and the substantial, the ornamental gewgaws of life and the useful. No race can prosper till it learns that there is as much dignity in tilling a field as in writing a poem. It is at the bottom of life we must begin, and not at the top. Nor should we permit our grievances to overshadow our opportunities.

To those of the white race who look to the incoming of those of foreign birth and strange tongue and habits for the prosperity of the South, were I permitted I would repeat what I say to my own race, "Cast down your bucket where you are." Cast it down among the eight millions of Negroes whose habits you know, whose fidelity and love you have tested in days when to have proved treacherous meant the ruin of your firesides. Cast down your bucket among these people who have, without strikes and labour wars, tilled your fields, cleared your forests, built your railroads and cities, and brought forth treasures from the bowels of the earth, and helped make possible this magnificent representation of the progress of the South. Casting down your bucket among my people, helping and encouraging them as you are doing on these grounds, and to education of head, hand, and heart, you will find that they will buy your surplus land, make blossom the waste places in your fields, and run your factories. While doing this, you can be sure in the future, as in the past, that you and your families will be surrounded by the most patient, faithful, law-abiding, and unresentful people that the world has seen. As we have proved our loyalty to you in the past, in nursing your children, watching by the sick-bed of your mothers and fathers, and often following them with tear-dimmed eyes to their graves, so in the future, in our humble way, we shall stand by you with a devotion that no foreigner can approach, ready to lay down our lives, if need be, in defence of yours, interlacing our industrial, commercial, civil, and religious life with yours in a way that shall make the interests of both races one. In all things that are purely social we can be as separate as the fingers, yet one as the hand in all things essential to mutual progress.

There is no defence or security for any of us except in the highest intelligence and development of all. If anywhere there are efforts tending to curtail the fullest growth of the Negro, let these efforts be turned into stimulating, encouraging, and making him the most useful and intelligent citizen. Effort or means so invested will pay a thousand per cent interest. These efforts will be twice blessed—"blessing him that gives and him that takes."

There is no escape through law of man or God from the inevitable:

> The laws of changeless justice bind
>   Oppressor with oppressed;
> And close as sin and suffering joined
>   We march to fate abreast.

Nearly sixteen millions of hands will aid you in pulling the load upward, or they will pull against you the load downward. We shall constitute one-third and more of the ignorance and crime of the South, or one-third its intelligence and progress; we shall contribute one-third to the business and industrial prosperity of the South, or we shall prove a veritable body of death, stagnating, depressing, retarding every effort to advance the body politic.

Gentlemen of the Exposition, as we present to you our humble effort at an exhibition of our progress, you must not expect overmuch. Starting thirty years ago with ownership here and there in a few quilts and pumpkins and chickens (gathered from miscellaneous sources), remember the path that has led from these to the inventions and production of agricultural implements, buggies, steam-engines, newspapers, books, statuary, carving, paintings, the management of drug-stores and banks, has not been trodden without contact with thorns and thistles. While we take pride in what we exhibit as a result of our independent efforts, we do not for a moment forget that our part in this exhibition would fall far short of your expectations but for the constant help that has come to our educational life, not only from the Southern states, but especially from Northern philanthropists, who have made their gifts a constant stream of blessing and encouragement.

The wisest among my race understand that the agitation of questions of social equality is the extremest folly, and that progress in the enjoyment of all the privileges that will come to us must be the result of severe and constant struggle rather than of artificial forcing. No race that has anything to contribute to the markets of the world is long in any degree ostracized. It is important and right that all privileges of the law be ours, but it is vastly more important that we be prepared for the exercises of these privileges. The opportunity to earn a dollar in a factory just now is worth infinitely more than the opportunity to spend a dollar in an opera-house.

In conclusion, may I repeat that nothing in thirty years has given us more hope and encouragement, and drawn us so near to you of the white race, as this opportunity offered by the Exposition; and here bending, as it were, over the altar that represents the results of the struggles of your race and mine, both starting practically empty-handed three decades ago, I pledge that in your effort to work out the great and intricate problem which God has laid at the doors of the South, you shall have at all times the patient, sympathetic help of my race; only let this be constantly in mind, that, while from representations in these buildings of the product of field, of forest, of mine, of factory, letters, and art, much good will come, yet far above and beyond material benefits will be that higher good, that, let us pray God, will come, in a blotting out of sectional differences and racial animosities and suspicions, in a determination to administer absolute justice, in a willing obedience among all classes to the mandates of law. This, this, coupled with our material prosperity, will bring into our beloved South a new heaven and a new earth.

(1895)

Charles W. Chesnutt   (1858–1932)

harles W. Chesnutt was one of the best-known African American writers at the turn of the twentieth century. He was born Charles Waddell Chesnutt on June 20, 1858, in Cleveland, Ohio, to free parents, Andrew and Ann Marie Chesnutt, who moved to Ohio to escape the racially hostile environment of North Carolina. At the close of the Civil War, however, Chesnutt's family moved back to Fayetteville, North Carolina, where Chesnutt attended the Howard School, established for African Americans by the Freedmen's Bureau in 1865. To help support his family, Chesnutt began teaching at age fourteen, when he also published his first short story in a local weekly newspaper. Chesnutt moved to Charlotte, North Carolina, to teach full-time before returning to Fayetteville in 1877 to serve as the Howard School's assistant principal and later as its principal.

In 1878 Chesnutt married fellow teacher Susan Utley Perry, and in 1883 he left the Howard School when the couple moved to New York City. In New York, Chesnutt held a series of jobs, including those of stenographer and journalist, before moving to Cleveland, Ohio, where his wife and four children joined him in 1884, to work as a clerk for the Nickel Plate Railway Company. While working as a stenographer for the railway's lawyer, Chesnutt studied law and passed the Ohio bar. In 1890 he established a stenography business but abandoned it with the onset of his literary success. Chesnutt, however, later reopened his stenography business in order to support his family when his work was not selling well. Chesnutt died in Cleveland on November 15, 1932.

During the 1880s Chesnutt began publishing a series of popular and critically acclaimed short stories in *McClure's* newspaper and the *Atlantic Monthly* about a character named Julius MacAdoo, a tall-tale-telling former slave. These and other stories were published in two collections, *The Conjure Woman* (1899) and *The Wife and His Youth and Other Stories of the Color Line* (1900). In addition to his short stories, Chesnutt produced a biography of Frederick Douglass (1899) and three novels: *The House behind the Cedars* (1900), *The Marrow of Tradition* (1901), and *The Colonel's Dream* (1905). Chesnutt's first and second novels received favorable reviews from critics but sold poorly. His final work, the autobiographical essay "Post-Bellum, Pre-Harlem," was published in 1931, but several of Chesnutt's novels were published posthumously, including *Mandy Oxendine* (1997), *Paul Marchland, F.R.C.* (1999), and *The Quarry* (1999). Excerpts from *The Marrow of Tradition*, based on the 1898 race riots in Wilmington, North Carolina, appear below. "The Editor at Work" is set in the office of Major Carteret, a wealthy white newspaper editor, and focuses on the ways that powerful southerners conspired to maintain white supremacy. "Mine Enemy, O Mine Enemy!" looks at the violent results (detrimental to both blacks and whites) of decisions made in the first selection's conversation.

Many of Chesnutt's works examine racial attitudes in the postbellum South through the themes of miscegenation and the intraracial prejudices against light-skinned African Americans. Although his writing often depicts the physical and psychological consequences of oppression, Chesnutt emphasizes the strength and ability to persevere and overcome oppression, challenging racist assumptions while celebrating African American folk traditions and dialect. Because of his contributions to African American literature, Chesnutt received the National Association for the Advancement of Colored People's Spingarn Medal in 1928, and he is often credited with being one of the first writers to establish the short-story tradition in African American literature.

Selections from *The Marrow of Tradition*

Chapter 3, The Editor at Work

To go back a little, for several days after his child's birth Major Carteret's chief interest in life had been confined to the four walls of the chamber where his pale wife lay upon her bed of pain, and those of the adjoining room where an old black woman crooned lovingly over a little white infant. A new element had been added to the major's consciousness, broadening the scope and deepening the strength of his affections. He did not love Olivia the less, for maternity had crowned her wifehood with an added glory; but side by side with this old and tried attachment was a new passion, stirring up dormant hopes and kindling new desires. His regret had been more than personal at the thought that with himself an old name should be lost to the State; and now all the old pride of race, class, and family welled up anew, and swelled and quickened the current of his life.

Upon the major's first appearance at the office, which took place the second day after the child's birth, he opened a box of cigars in honor of the event. The word had been passed around by Ellis, and the whole office force, including reporters, compositors, and pressmen, came in to congratulate the major and smoke at his expense. Even Jerry, the colored porter,— Mammy Jane's grandson and therefore a protégé of the family,— presented himself among the rest, or rather, after the rest. The major shook hands with them all except Jerry, though he acknowledged the porter's congratulations with a kind nod and put a good cigar into his outstretched palm, for which Jerry thanked him without manifesting any consciousness of the omission. He was quite aware that under ordinary circumstances the major would not have shaken hands with white workingmen, to say nothing of negroes; and he had merely hoped that in the pleasurable distraction of the moment the major might also overlook the distinction of color. Jerry's hope had been shattered, though not rudely; for the major had spoken pleasantly and the cigar was a good one. Mr. Ellis had once shaken hands with Jerry,— but Mr. Ellis was a young man, whose Quaker father had never owned any slaves, and he could not be expected to have as much pride as one of the best "quality," whose families had possessed land and negroes for time out of mind. On the whole, Jerry preferred the careless nod of the editor-in-chief to the more familiar greeting of the subaltern. Having finished this pleasant ceremony, which left him with a comfortable sense of his new dignity, the major turned to his desk. It had been much neglected during the week, and more than one matter claimed his attention; but as typical of the new trend of his thoughts, the first subject he took up was one bearing upon the future of his son. Quite obviously the career of a Carteret must not be left to chance,— it must be planned and worked out with a due sense of the value of good blood.

There lay upon his desk a letter from a well-known promoter, offering the major an investment which promised large returns, though several years must elapse before the enterprise could be put upon a paying basis. The element of time, however, was not immediately important. The Morning Chronicle provided him an ample income. The money available for this investment was part of his wife's patrimony. It was invested in a local cotton mill, which was paying ten per cent, but this was a beggarly return compared with the immense profits promised by the offered investment,— profits which would enable his son, upon reaching manhood, to take a place in the world commensurate with the dignity of his ancestors, one of whom, only a few generations removed, had owned an estate of ninety thousand acres of land and six thousand slaves.

This letter having been disposed of by an answer accepting the offer, the major took up his pen to write an editorial. Public affairs in the state were not going to his satisfaction. At the last state election his own party, after an almost unbroken rule of twenty years, had been defeated by the so-called "Fusion" ticket, a combination of Republicans and Populists. A clean sweep had been made of the offices in the state, which were now filled by new men. Many of the smaller places had gone to colored men, their people having voted almost solidly for the Fusion ticket. In spite of the fact that the population of Wellington was two thirds colored, this state of things was gall and wormwood to the defeated party, of which the Morning Chronicle was the acknowledged organ. Major Carteret shared this feeling. Only this very morning, while passing the city hall, on his way to the office, he had seen the steps of that noble building disfigured by a fringe of job-hunting negroes, for all the world — to use a local simile — like a string of buzzards sitting on a rail, awaiting their opportunity to batten upon the helpless corpse of a moribund city.

Taking for his theme the unfitness of the negro to participate in government, — an unfitness due to his limited education, his lack of experience, his criminal tendencies, and more especially to his hopeless mental and physical inferiority to the white race,— the major had demonstrated, it seemed to him clearly enough, that the ballot in the hands of the negro was a menace to the commonwealth. He had argued, with entire conviction, that the white and black races could never attain social and political harmony by commingling their blood; he had proved by several historical parallels that no two unassimilable races could ever live together except in the relation of superior and inferior; and he was just dipping his gold pen into the ink to indite his conclusions from the premises thus established, when Jerry, the porter, announced two visitors.

"Gin'l Belmont an' Cap'n McBane would like ter see you, suh."

"Show them in, Jerry."

The man who entered first upon this invitation was a dapper little gentleman with light-blue eyes and a Vandyke beard. He wore a frock coat, patent leather shoes, and a Panama hat. There were crow's-feet about his eyes, which twinkled with a hard and, at times, humorous shrewdness. He had sloping shoulders, small hands and feet, and walked with the leisurely step characteristic of those who have been reared under hot suns. Carteret gave his hand cordially to the gentleman thus described.

"How do you do, Captain McBane," he said, turning to the second visitor.

The individual thus addressed was strikingly different in appearance from his companion. His broad shoulders, burly form, square jaw, and heavy chin betokened strength, energy, and unscrupulousness. With the exception of a small, bristling mustache, his face was clean shaven, with here and there a speck of dried blood due to a carelessly or unskillfully handled razor. A single deep-set gray eye was shadowed by a beetling brow, over which a crop of coarse black hair, slightly streaked with gray, fell almost low enough to mingle with his black, bushy eyebrows. His coat had not been brushed for several days, if one might judge from the accumulation of dandruff upon the collar, and his shirt-front, in the middle of which blazed a showy diamond, was plentifully stained with tobacco juice. He wore a large slouch hat, which, upon entering the office, he removed and held in his hand.

Having greeted this person with an unconscious but quite perceptible diminution of the warmth with which he had welcomed the other, the major looked around the room for seats for his visitors, and perceiving only one chair, piled with exchanges, and a broken stool propped against the wall, pushed a button, which rang a bell in the hall, summoning the colored porter to his presence.

"Jerry," said the editor when his servant appeared, "bring a couple of chairs for these gentlemen."

While they stood waiting, the visitors congratulated the major on the birth of his child, which had been announced in the Morning Chronicle, and which the prominence of the family made in some degree a matter of public interest.

"And now that you have a son, major," remarked the gentleman first described, as he lit one of the major's cigars, "you'll be all the more interested in doing something to make this town fit to live in, which is what we came up to talk about. Things are in an awful condition! A negro justice of the peace has opened an office on Market Street, and only yesterday summoned a white man to appear before him. Negro lawyers get most of the business in the criminal court. Last evening a group of young white ladies, going quietly along the street arm-in-arm, were forced off the sidewalk by a crowd of negro girls. Coming down the street just now, I saw a spectacle of social equality and negro domination that made my blood boil with indignation,— a white and a black convict, chained together, crossing the city in charge of a negro officer! We cannot stand that sort of thing, Carteret,— it is the last straw! Something must be done, and that quickly!"

The major thrilled with responsive emotion. There was something prophetic in this opportune visit. The matter was not only in his own thoughts, but in the air; it was the spontaneous revulsion of white men against the rule of an inferior race. These were the very men, above all others in the town, to join him in a movement to change these degrading conditions.

General Belmont, the smaller of the two, was a man of good family, a lawyer by profession, and took an active part in state and local politics. Aristocratic by birth and instinct, and a former owner of slaves, his conception of the obligations and rights of his caste was nevertheless somewhat lower than that of the narrower but more sincere Carteret. In serious affairs Carteret desired the approval of his conscience, even if he had to trick that docile organ into acquiescence. This was not difficult to do in politics, for he believed in the divine right of white men and gentlemen, as his ancestors had believed in and died for the divine right of kings. General Belmont was not without a gentleman's distaste for meanness, but he permitted no fine scruples to stand in the way of success. He had once been minister, under a Democratic administration, to a small Central American state.

Political rivals had characterized him as a tricky demagogue, which may of course have been a libel. He had an amiable disposition, possessed the gift of eloquence, and was a prime social favorite.

Captain George McBane had sprung from the poor-white class, to which, even more than to the slaves, the abolition of slavery had opened the door of opportunity. No longer overshadowed by a slaveholding caste, some of this class had rapidly pushed themselves forward. Some had made honorable records. Others, foremost in negro-baiting and election frauds, had done the dirty work of politics, as their fathers had done that of slavery, seeking their reward at first in minor offices,— for which men of gentler breeding did not care,— until their ambition began to reach out for higher honors.

Of this class McBane — whose captaincy, by the way, was merely a polite fiction — had been one of the most successful. He had held, until recently, as the reward of questionable political services, a contract with the State for its convict labor, from which in a few years he had realized a fortune. But the methods which made his contract profitable had not commended themselves to humane people, and charges of cruelty and worse had been preferred against him. He was rich enough to escape serious consequences from the investigation which followed, but when the Fusion ticket carried the state he lost his contract, and the system of convict labor was abolished. Since then McBane had devoted himself to politics: he was ambitious for greater wealth, for office, and for social recognition. A man of few words and self-engrossed, he seldom spoke of his aspirations except where speech might favor them, preferring to seek his ends by secret "deals" and combinations rather than to challenge criticism and provoke rivalry by more open methods.

At sight, therefore, of these two men, with whose careers and characters he was entirely familiar, Carteret felt sweep over his mind the conviction that now was the time and these the instruments with which to undertake the redemption of the state from the evil fate which had befallen it.

Jerry, the porter, who had gone downstairs to the counting-room to find two whole chairs, now entered with one in each hand. He set a chair for the general, who gave him an amiable nod, to which Jerry responded with a bow and a scrape. Captain McBane made no acknowledgment, but fixed Jerry so fiercely with his single eye that upon placing the chair Jerry made his escape from the room as rapidly as possible.

"I don' like dat Cap'n McBane," he muttered, upon reaching the hall. "Dey says he got dat eye knock' out tryin' ter whip a cullud 'oman, when he wuz a boy, an' dat he ain' never had no use fer niggers sence,— 'cep'n' fer what he could make outen 'em wid his convic' labor contrac's. His daddy wuz a' overseer befo' 'im, an' it come nachul fer him ter be a nigger-driver. I don' want dat one eye er his'n restin' on me no longer 'n I kin he'p, an' I don' know how I'm gwine ter like dis job ef he's gwine ter be comin' roun' here. He ain' nothin' but po' w'ite trash nohow; but Lawd! Lawd! look at de money he's got,— livin' at de hotel, wearin' di'mon's, an' colloguin' wid de bes' quality er dis town! 'Pears ter me de bottom rail is gittin' mighty close ter de top. Well, I s'pose it all comes f'm bein' w'ite. I wush ter Gawd I wuz w'ite!"

After this fervent aspiration, having nothing else to do for the time being, except to remain within call, and having caught a few words of the conversation as he went in with the chairs, Jerry, who possessed a certain amount of curiosity, placed close to the wall the broken stool upon which he sat while waiting in the hall, and applied his ear to a hole in the plastering of the hallway. There was a similar defect in the inner wall, between the same two pieces of studding, and while this inner opening was not exactly opposite the outer, Jerry was enabled, through the two, to catch in a more or less fragmentary way what was going on within.

He could hear the major, now and then, use the word "negro," and McBane's deep voice was quite audible when he referred, it seemed to Jerry with alarming frequency, to "the damned niggers," while the general's suave tones now and then pronounced the word "niggro," — a sort of compromise between ethnology and the vernacular. That the gentlemen were talking politics seemed quite likely, for gentlemen generally talked politics when they met at the Chronicle office. Jerry could hear the words "vote," "franchise," "eliminate," "constitution," and other expressions which marked the general tenor of the talk, though he could not follow it all,— partly because he could not hear everything distinctly, and partly because of certain limitations which nature had placed in the way of Jerry's understanding anything very difficult or abstruse.

He had gathered enough, however, to realize, in a vague way, that something serious was on foot, involving his own race, when a bell sounded over his head, at which he sprang up hastily and entered the room where the gentlemen were talking.

"Jerry," said the major, "wait on Captain McBane."

"Yas, suh," responded Jerry, turning toward the captain, whose eye he carefully avoided meeting directly.

"Take that half a dollar, boy," ordered McBane, "an' go 'cross the street to Mr. Sykes's, and tell him to send me three whiskies. Bring back the change, and make has'e."

The captain tossed the half dollar at Jerry, who, looking to one side, of course missed it. He picked the money up, however, and backed out of the room. Jerry did not like Captain McBane, to begin with, and it was clear that the captain was no gentleman, or he would not have thrown the money at him. Considering the source, Jerry might have overlooked this discourtesy had it not been coupled with the remark about the change, which seemed to him in very poor taste.

Returning in a few minutes with three glasses on a tray, he passed them round, handed Captain McBane his change, and retired to the hall.

"Gentlemen," exclaimed the captain, lifting his glass, "I propose a toast: 'No nigger domination.'"

"Amen!" said the others, and three glasses were solemnly drained.

"Major," observed the general, smacking his lips, "I should like to use Jerry for a moment, if you will permit me."

Jerry appeared promptly at the sound of the bell. He had remained conveniently near,— calls of this sort were apt to come in sequence.

"Jerry," said the general, handing Jerry half a dollar, "go over to Mr. Brown's,— I get my liquor there,— and tell them to send me three glasses of my special mixture. And, Jerry,— you may keep the change!"

"Thank y', gin'l, thank y', marster," replied Jerry, with unctuous gratitude, bending almost double as he backed out of the room.

"Dat's a gent'eman, a rale ole-time gent'eman," he said to himself when he had closed the door. "But dere's somethin' gwine on in dere,— dere sho' is! 'No nigger damnation!' Dat soun's all right,— I'm sho' dere ain' no nigger I knows w'at wants damnation, do' dere's lots of 'em w'at deserves it; but ef dat one-eyed Cap'n McBane got anything ter do wid it, w'atever it is, it don' mean no good fer de niggers,— damnation'd be better fer 'em dan dat Cap'n McBane! He looks at a nigger lack he could jes' eat 'im alive."

"This mixture, gentlemen," observed the general when Jerry had returned with the glasses, "was originally compounded by no less a person than the great John C. Calhoun himself, who confided the recipe to my father over the convivial board. In this nectar of the gods, gentlemen, I drink with you to 'White Supremacy!'"

"White Supremacy everywhere!" added McBane with fervor.

"Now and forever!" concluded Carteret solemnly.

When the visitors, half an hour later, had taken their departure, Carteret, inspired by the theme, and in less degree by the famous mixture of the immortal Calhoun, turned to his desk and finished, at a white heat, his famous editorial in which he sounded the tocsin of a new crusade.

At noon, when the editor, having laid down his pen, was leaving the office, he passed Jerry in the hall without a word or a nod. The major wore a rapt look, which Jerry observed with a vague uneasiness.

"He looks jes' lack he wuz walkin' in his sleep," muttered Jerry uneasily. "Dere's somethin' up, sho's you bawn! 'No nigger damnation!' Anybody'd 'low dey wuz all gwine ter heaven; but I knows better! W'en a passel er w'ite folks gits ter talkin' 'bout de niggers lack dem in yander, it's mo' lackly dey're gwine ter ketch somethin' e'se dan heaven! I got ter keep my eyes open an' keep up wid w'at's happenin'. Ef dere's gwine ter be anudder flood 'roun' here, I wants ter git in de ark wid de w'ite folks,— I may haf ter be anudder Ham, an' sta't de cullud race all over ag'in."

Chapter 35, Mine Enemy, O Mine Enemy!

The proceedings of the day—planned originally as a "demonstration," dignified subsequently as a "revolution," under any name the culmination of the conspiracy formed by Carteret and his colleagues—had by seven o'clock in the afternoon developed into a murderous riot. Crowds of white men and half-grown boys, drunk with whiskey or with license, raged through the streets, beating, chasing, or killing any negro so unfortunate as to fall into their hands. Why any particular negro was assailed, no one stopped to inquire; it was merely a white mob thirsting for black blood, with no more conscience or discrimination than would be exercised by a wolf in a sheepfold. It was race against race, the whites against the negroes; and it was a one-sided affair, for until Josh Green got together his body of armed men, no effective resistance had been made by any colored person, and the individuals who had been killed had so far left no marks upon the enemy by which they might be remembered.

"Kill the niggers!" rang out now and then through the dusk, and far down the street and along the intersecting thoroughfares distant voices took up the ominous refrain, —"Kill the niggers! Kill the damned niggers!"

Now, not a dark face had been seen on the street for half an hour, until the group of men headed by Josh made their appearance in the negro quarter. Armed with guns and axes, they presented quite a formidable appearance as they made their way toward the new hospital, near which stood a schoolhouse and a large church, both used by the colored people. They did not reach their destination without having met a number of white men, singly or in twos or threes; and the rumor spread with incredible swiftness that the negroes in turn were up in arms, determined to massacre all the whites and burn the town.

Some of the whites became alarmed, and recognizing the power of the negroes, if armed and conscious of their strength, were impressed by the immediate necessity of overpowering and overawing them. Others, with appetites already whetted by slaughter, saw a chance, welcome rather than not, of shedding more black blood. Spontaneously the white mob flocked toward the hospital, where rumor had it that a large body of desperate negroes, breathing threats of blood and fire, had taken a determined stand.

It had been Josh's plan merely to remain quietly and peaceably in the neighborhood of the little group of public institutions, molesting no one, unless first attacked, and merely letting the white people see that they meant to protect their own; but so rapidly did the rumor spread, and so promptly did the white people act, that by the time Josh and his supporters had reached the top of the rising ground where the hospital stood, a crowd of white men much more numerous than their own party were following them at a short distance.

Josh, with the eye of a general, perceived that some of his party were becoming a little nervous, and decided that they would feel safer behind shelter.

"I reckon we better go inside de hospittle, boys," he exclaimed. "Den we'll be behind brick walls, an' dem other fellows'll be outside, an' ef dere's any fightin', we'll have de bes' show. We ain' gwine ter do no shootin' till we're pestered, an' dey'll be less likely ter pester us ef dey can't git at us widout runnin' some resk. Come along in! Be men! De gov'ner er de President is gwine ter sen' soldiers ter stop dese gwines-on, an' meantime we kin keep dem white devils f'm bu'nin' down our hospittles an' chu'ch-houses. Wen dey comes an' fin's out dat we jes' means ter pertect ou' prope'ty, dey'll go 'long 'bout deir own business. Er, ef dey wants a scrap, dey kin have it! Come erlong, boys!"

Jerry Letlow, who had kept out of sight during the day, had started out, after night had set in, to find Major Carteret. Jerry was very much afraid. The events of the day had filled him with terror. Whatever the limitations of Jerry's mind or character may have been, Jerry had a keen appreciation of the danger to the negroes when they came in conflict with the whites, and he had no desire to imperil his own skin. He valued his life for his own sake, and not for any altruistic theory that it might be of service to others. In other words, Jerry was something of a coward. He had kept in hiding all day, but finding, toward evening, that the riot did not abate, and fearing, from the rumors which came to his ears, that all the negroes would be exterminated, he had set out, somewhat desperately, to try to find his white patron and protector. He had been cautious to avoid meeting any white men, and, anticipating no danger from those of his own race, went toward the party which he saw approaching, whose path would cross his own. When they were only a few yards apart, Josh took a step forward and caught Jerry by the arm.

"Come along, Jerry, we need you! Here's another man, boys. Come on now, and fight fer yo' race!"

In vain Jerry protested. "I don' wan' ter fight," he howled. "De w'ite folks ain' gwine ter pester me; dey're my frien's. Tu'n me loose,— tu'n me loose, er we all gwine ter git killed!"

The party paid no attention to Jerry's protestations. Indeed, with the crowd of whites following behind, they were simply considering the question of a position from which they could most effectively defend themselves and the building which they imagined to be threatened. If Josh had released his grip of Jerry, that worthy could easily have escaped from the crowd; but Josh maintained his hold almost mechanically, and, in the confusion, Jerry found himself swept with the rest into the hospital, the doors of which were promptly barricaded with the heavier pieces of furniture, and the windows manned by several men each, Josh, with the instinct of a born commander, posting his forces so that they could cover with their guns all the approaches to the building. Jerry still continuing to make himself troublesome, Josh, in a moment of impatience, gave him a terrific box on the ear, which stretched him out upon the floor unconscious.

"Shet up," he said; "ef you can't stan' up like a man, keep still, and don't interfere wid men w'at will fight!" The hospital, when Josh and his men took possession, had been found deserted. Fortunately there were no patients for that day, except one or two convalescents, and these, with the attendants, had joined the exodus of the colored people from the town.

A white man advanced from the crowd without toward the main entrance to the hospital. Big Josh, looking out from a window, grasped his gun more firmly, as his eyes fell upon the man who had murdered his father and darkened his mother's life. Mechanically he raised his rifle, but lowered it as the white man lifted up his hand as a sign that he wished to speak.

"You niggers," called Captain McBane loudly,— it was that worthy, —"you niggers are courtin' death, an' you won't have to court her but a minute er two mo' befo' she'll have you. If you surrender and give up your arms, you'll be dealt with leniently,— you may get off with the chain-gang or the penitentiary. If you resist, you'll be shot like dogs."

"Dat's no news, Mr. White Man," replied Josh, appearing boldly at the window. "We're use' ter bein' treated like dogs by men like you. If you w'ite people will go 'long an' ten' ter yo' own business an' let us alone, we'll ten' ter ou'n. You've got guns, an' we've got jest as much right ter carry 'em as you have. Lay down yo'n, an' we'll lay down ou'n,— we didn' take 'em up fust; but we ain' gwine ter let you bu'n down ou' chu'ches an' school'ouses, er dis hospittle, an' we ain' comin' out er dis house, where we ain' disturbin' nobody, fer you ter shoot us down er sen' us ter jail. You hear me!"

"All right," responded McBane. "You've had fair warning. Your blood be on your" — His speech was interrupted by a shot from the crowd, which splintered the window-casing close to Josh's head. This was followed by half a dozen other shots, which were replied to, almost simultaneously, by a volley from within, by which one of the attacking party was killed and another wounded. This roused the mob to frenzy.

"Vengeance! vengeance!" they yelled. "Kill the niggers!"

A negro had killed a white man,— the unpardonable sin, admitting neither excuse, justification, nor extenuation. From time immemorial it had been bred in the Southern white consciousness, and in the negro consciousness also, for that matter, that the person of a white man was sacred from the touch of a negro, no matter what the provocation. A dozen colored men lay dead in the streets of Wellington, inoffensive people, slain in cold blood because they had been bold enough to question the authority of those who had assailed them, or frightened enough to flee when they had been ordered to stand still; but their lives counted nothing against that of a riotous white man, who had courted death by attacking a body of armed men.

The crowd, too, surrounding the hospital, had changed somewhat in character. The men who had acted as leaders in the early afternoon, having accomplished their purpose of overturning the local administration and establishing a provisional government of their own, had withdrawn from active participation in the rioting, deeming the negroes already sufficiently overawed to render unlikely any further trouble from that source. Several of the ringleaders had indeed begun to exert themselves to prevent further disorder, or any loss of property, the possibility of which had become apparent; but those who set in motion the forces of evil cannot always control them afterwards. The baser element of the white population, recruited from the wharves and the saloons, was now predominant.

Captain McBane was the only one of the revolutionary committee who had remained with the mob, not with any purpose to restore or preserve order, but because he found the company and the occasion entirely congenial. He had had no opportunity, at least no tenable excuse, to kill or maim a negro since the termination of his contract with the state for convicts, and this occasion had awakened a dormant appetite for these diversions. We are all puppets in the hands of Fate, and seldom see the strings that move us. McBane had lived a life of violence and cruelty. As a man sows, so shall he reap. In works of fiction, such men are sometimes converted. More often, in real life, they do not change their natures until they are converted into dust. One does well to distrust a tamed tiger.

On the outskirts of the crowd a few of the better class, or at least of the better clad, were looking on. The double volley described had already been fired, when the number of these was augmented by the arrival of Major Carteret and Mr. Ellis, who had just come from the Chronicle office, where the next day's paper had been in hasty preparation. They pushed their way towards the front of the crowd.

"This must be stopped, Ellis," said Carteret. "They are burning houses and killing women and children. Old Jane, good old Mammy Jane, who nursed my wife at her bosom, and has waited on her and my child within a few weeks, was killed only a few rods from my house, to which she was evidently fleeing for protection. It must have been by accident,— I cannot believe that any white man in town would be dastard enough to commit such a deed intentionally! I would have defended her with my own life! We must try to stop this thing!"

"Easier said than done," returned Ellis. "It is in the fever stage, and must burn itself out. We shall be lucky if it does not burn the town out. Suppose the negroes should also take a hand at the burning? We have advised the people to put the negroes down, and they are doing the job thoroughly."

"My God!" replied the other, with a gesture of impatience, as he continued to elbow his way through the crowd; "I meant to keep them in their places,— I did not intend wholesale murder and arson."

Carteret, having reached the front of the mob, made an effort to gain their attention.

"Gentlemen!" he cried in his loudest tones. His voice, unfortunately, was neither loud nor piercing.

"Kill the niggers!" clamored the mob.

"Gentlemen, I implore you" —

The crash of a dozen windows, broken by stones and pistol shots, drowned his voice.

"Gentlemen!" he shouted; "this is murder, it is madness; it is a disgrace to our city, to our state, to our civilization!"

"That's right!" replied several voices. The mob had recognized the speaker. "It is a disgrace, and we'll not put up with it a moment longer. Burn 'em out! Hurrah for Major Carteret, the champion of 'white supremacy'! Three cheers for the Morning Chronicle and 'no nigger domination'!"

"Hurrah, hurrah, hurrah!" yelled the crowd.

In vain the baffled orator gesticulated and shrieked in the effort to correct the misapprehension. Their oracle had spoken; not hearing what he said, they assumed it to mean encouragement and cooperation. Their present course was but the logical outcome of the crusade which the Morning Chronicle had preached, in season and out of season, for many months. When Carteret had spoken, and the crowd had cheered him, they felt that they had done all that courtesy required, and he was good-naturedly elbowed aside while they proceeded with the work in hand, which was now to drive out the negroes from the hospital and avenge the killing of their comrade.

Some brought hay, some kerosene, and others wood from a pile which had been thrown into a vacant lot near by. Several safe ways of approach to the building were discovered, and the combustibles placed and fired. The flames, soon gaining a foothold, leaped upward, catching here and there at the exposed woodwork, and licking the walls hungrily with long tongues of flame.

Meanwhile a desultory firing was kept up from the outside, which was replied to scatteringly from within the hospital. Those inside were either not good marksmen, or excitement had spoiled their aim. If a face appeared at a window, a dozen pistol shots from the crowd sought the spot immediately.

Higher and higher leaped the flames. Suddenly from one of the windows sprang a black figure, waving a white handkerchief. It was Jerry Letlow. Regaining consciousness after the effect of Josh's blow had subsided, Jerry had kept quiet and watched his opportunity. From a safe vantage-ground he had scanned the crowd without, in search of some white friend. When he saw Major Carteret moving disconsolately away after his futile effort to stem the torrent, Jerry made a dash for the window. He sprang forth, and, waving his handkerchief as a flag of truce, ran toward Major Carteret, shouting frantically: —

"Majah Carteret — O majah! It's me, suh, Jerry, suh! I didn' go in dere myse'f, suh — I wuz drag' in dere! I wouldn' do nothin' 'g'inst de w'ite folks, suh, — no, 'ndeed, I wouldn', suh!"

Jerry's cries were drowned in a roar of rage and a volley of shots from the mob. Carteret, who had turned away with Ellis, did not even hear his servant's voice. Jerry's poor flag of truce, his explanations, his reliance upon his white friends, all failed him in the moment of supreme need. In that hour, as in any hour when the depths of race hatred are stirred, a negro was no more than a brute beast, set upon by other brute beasts whose only instinct was to kill and destroy.

"Let us leave this inferno, Ellis," said Carteret, sick with anger and disgust. He had just become aware that a negro was being killed, though he did not know whom. "We can do nothing. The negroes have themselves to blame, — they tempted us beyond endurance. I counseled firmness, and firm measures were taken, and our purpose was accomplished. I am not responsible for these subsequent horrors, — I wash my hands of them. Let us go!"

The flames gained headway and gradually enveloped the burning building, until it became evident to those within as well as those without that the position of the defenders was no longer tenable. Would they die in the flames, or would they be driven out? The uncertainty soon came to an end.

The besieged had been willing to fight, so long as there seemed a hope of successfully defending themselves and their property; for their purpose was purely one of defense. When they saw the case was hopeless, inspired by Josh Green's reckless courage, they were still willing to sell their lives dearly. One or two of them had already been killed, and as many more disabled. The fate of Jerry Letlow had struck terror to the hearts of several others, who could scarcely hide their fear. After the building had been fired, Josh's exhortations were no longer able to keep them in the hospital. They preferred to fight and be killed in the open, rather than to be smothered like rats in a hole.

"Boys!" exclaimed Josh, — "men! — fer nobody but men would do w'at you have done,— the day has gone 'g'inst us. We kin see ou' finish; but fer my part, I ain' gwine ter leave dis worl' widout takin' a w'ite man 'long wid me, an' I sees my man right out yonder waitin',— I be'n waitin' fer him twenty years, but he won' have ter wait fer me mo' 'n 'bout twenty seconds. Eve'y one er you pick yo' man! We'll open de do', an' we'll give some w'ite men a chance ter be sorry dey ever started dis fuss!"

The door was thrown open suddenly, and through it rushed a dozen or more black figures, armed with knives, pistols, or clubbed muskets. Taken by sudden surprise, the white people stood motionless for a moment, but the approaching negroes had scarcely covered half the distance to which the heat of the flames had driven back the mob, before they were greeted with a volley that laid them all low but two. One of these, dazed by the fate of his companions, turned instinctively to flee, but had scarcely faced around before he fell, pierced in the back by a dozen bullets.

Josh Green, the tallest and biggest of them all, had not apparently been touched. Some of the crowd paused in involuntary admiration of this black giant, famed on the wharves for his strength, sweeping down upon them, a smile upon his face, his eyes lit up with a rapt expression which seemed to take him out of mortal ken. This impression was heightened by his apparent immunity from the shower of lead which less susceptible persons had continued to pour at him.

Armed with a huge bowie-knife, a relic of the civil war, which he had carried on his person for many years for a definite purpose, and which he had kept sharpened to a razor edge, he reached the line of the crowd. All but the bravest shrank back. Like a wedge he dashed through the mob, which parted instinctively before him, and all oblivious of the rain of lead which fell around him, reached the point where Captain McBane, the bravest man in the party, stood waiting to meet him. A pistol-flame flashed in his face, but he went on, and raising his powerful right arm, buried his knife to the hilt in the heart of his enemy. When the crowd dashed forward to wreak vengeance on his dead body, they found him with a smile still upon his face.

One of the two died as the fool dieth. Which was it, or was it both?

"Vengeance is mine," saith the Lord, and it had not been left to Him.

But they that do violence must expect to suffer violence. McBane's death was merciful, compared with the nameless horrors he had heaped upon the hundreds of helpless mortals who had fallen into his hands during his career as a contractor of convict labor.

Sobered by this culminating tragedy, the mob shortly afterwards dispersed. The flames soon completed their work, and this handsome structure, the fruit of old Adam Miller's industry, the monument of his son's philanthropy, a promise of good things for the future of the city, lay smouldering in ruins, a melancholy witness to the fact that our boasted civilization is but a thin veneer, which cracks and scales off at the first impact of primal passions.

(1901)

W. E. B. Du Bois   (1868–1963)

O ne of the most important political and literary figures of the era, William Edward Burghardt Du Bois was born on February 23, 1868, in Great Barrington, Massachusetts, to Alfred and Mary Sylvania Du Bois. While attending Great Barrington High School, Du Bois worked odd jobs to help support his family, also editing his school's newspaper and contributing articles to the *Springfield Republican* and the *New York Age* (now the *New York Globe*). After graduating high school in 1885 Du Bois attended Fisk University in Nashville, Tennessee, where he edited the school's literary magazine, until 1888, when he graduated and received a scholarship to Harvard. Classified as a junior upon his entrance, Du Bois earned his bachelor's degree in 1890 and a master's in 1891. After studying at the University of Berlin for two years, Du Bois returned to Harvard and in 1895 became the first African American to earn a doctor of philosophy in history. His dissertation, *The Suppression of the African Slave-Trade to the United States of America* (1896), was published as the first volume of the Harvard Historical Series.

After graduating from Harvard, Du Bois taught Greek and Latin at Wilberforce University in Ohio. In 1896 he married Nina Gomer, and in 1897 he was awarded a research fellowship position at the University of Pennsylvania to study the city's poverty-stricken Seventh Ward. The findings of his research were published as *The Philadelphia Negro* (1899), the first sociological study of a black community published in the United States. Du Bois then moved to Atlanta University, where he later served as chair of the sociology department, to teach economics and history.

In 1905 he cofounded the Niagara Movement — an organization demanding racial social equality — which was restructured in 1909 as the National Association for the Advancement of Colored People (NAACP). Afterward, Du Bois began serving on the NAACP's executive board as the director of publications and research. As such, he founded and edited the organization's literary and political journal, the *Crisis*, for twenty-four years, during which time he promoted the work of many Harlem Renaissance writers. His later years with the NAACP, however, were embroiled in controversy over the direction that the organization should take.

As Du Bois moved away from the national organization that he helped establish, he began taking an increasingly international view of the black freedom struggle. He helped organize and attended all five of the Pan-African conferences held between 1919 and 1945, and in 1945 he served as a consultant at the founding conference of the United Nations. Several years later, after the death of his first wife, Du Bois married Shirley Graham, and the two traveled widely in Europe, the Soviet Union, and China. In 1960, after an invitation from the newly independent country's first president, he moved to Ghana, where he died on August 27, 1963.

Du Bois's most critically acclaimed work, *The Souls of Black Folk* (1903), is a collection of essays on the history and challenges of African Americans in the United States, and it profoundly influenced racial attitudes throughout the twentieth century. His other published books include *Dark Water: Voices within the Veil* (1920), *Africa: Its Place in Modern History* (1930), *Black Reconstruction* (1935), *Worlds of Color* (1961), and several novels, including *The Quest of the Silver Fleece* (1911) and *Dark Princess: A Romance* (1928). In addition to essays in *Dial* and *Atlantic Monthly*, Du Bois published numerous sociological studies dealing with economic, spiritual, and educational issues, including *The Negro in Business* (1899), *The Negro Common School* (1901), *The Negro Artisan* (1902), and *The Negro Church* (1903). Du Bois's fiction and nonfiction emphasize education, political and social empowerment, and economic justice, providing a philosophical foundation for writers of the Harlem Renaissance and beyond.

Selection from *The Souls of Black Folk*

Chapter 1, Of Our Spiritual Strivings

O water, voice of my heart, crying in the sand,
All night long crying with a mournful cry,
As I lie and listen, and cannot understand
The voice of my heart in my side or the voice of the sea,
O water, crying for rest, is it I, is it I?
All night long the water is crying to me.

Unresting water, there shall never be rest
Till the last moon droop and the last tide fail,
And the fire of the end begin to burn in the west;
And the heart shall be weary and wonder and cry like the sea,
All life long crying without avail,
As the water all night long is crying to me.
— Arthur Symons

Between me and the other world there is ever an unasked question: unasked by some through feelings of delicacy; by others through the difficulty of rightly framing it. All, nevertheless, flutter round it. They approach me in a half-hesitant sort of way, eye me curiously or compassionately, and then, instead of saying directly, How does it feel to be a problem? they say, I know an excellent colored man in my town; or, I fought at Mechanicsville; or, Do not these Southern outrages make your blood boil? At these I smile, or am interested, or reduce the boiling to a simmer, as the occasion may require. To the real question, How does it feel to be a problem? I answer seldom a word.

And yet, being a problem is a strange experience,— peculiar even for one who has never been anything else, save perhaps in babyhood and in Europe. It is in the early days of rollicking boyhood that the revelation first bursts upon one, all in a day, as it were. I remember well when the shadow swept across me. I was a little thing, away up in the hills of New England, where the dark Housatonic winds between Hoosac and Taghkanic to the sea. In a wee wooden schoolhouse, something put it into the boys' and girls' heads to buy gorgeous visiting-cards — ten cents a package — and exchange. The exchange was merry, till one girl, a tall newcomer, refused my card,— refused it peremptorily, with a glance. Then it dawned upon me with a certain suddenness that I was different from the others; or like, mayhap, in heart and life and longing, but shut out from their world by a vast veil. I had thereafter no desire to tear down that veil, to creep through; I held all beyond it in common contempt, and lived above it in a region of blue sky and great wandering shadows. That sky was bluest when I could beat my mates at examination-time, or beat them at a foot-race, or even beat their stringy heads. Alas, with the years all this fine contempt began to fade; for the words I longed for, and all their dazzling opportunities, were theirs, not mine. But they should not keep these prizes, I said; some, all, I would wrest from them. Just how I would do it I could never decide: by reading law, by healing the sick, by telling the wonderful tales that swam in my head,— some way. With other black boys the strife was not so fiercely sunny: their youth shrunk into tasteless sycophancy, or into silent hatred of the pale world about them and mocking distrust of everything white; or wasted itself in a bitter cry, Why did God make me an outcast and a stranger in mine own house? The shades of the prison-house closed round about us all: walls strait and stubborn to the whitest, but relentlessly narrow, tall, and unscalable to sons of night who must plod darkly on in resignation, or beat unavailing palms against the stone, or steadily, half hopelessly, watch the streak of blue above.

After the Egyptian and Indian, the Greek and Roman, the Teuton and Mongolian, the Negro is a sort of seventh son, born with a veil, and gifted with second-sight in this American world,— a world which yields him no true self-consciousness, but only lets him see himself through the revelation of the other world. It is a peculiar sensation, this double-consciousness, this sense of always looking at one's self through the eyes of others, of measuring one's soul by the tape of a world that looks on in amused contempt and pity. One ever feels his twoness,— an American, a Negro; two souls, two thoughts, two unreconciled strivings; two warring ideals in one dark body, whose dogged strength alone keeps it from being torn asunder.

The history of the American Negro is the history of this strife,— this longing to attain self-conscious manhood, to merge his double self into a better and truer self. In this merging he wishes neither of the older selves to be lost. He would not Africanize America, for America has too much to teach the world and Africa. He would not bleach his Negro soul in a flood of white Americanism, for he knows that Negro blood has a message for the world. He simply wishes to make it possible for a man to be both a Negro and an American, without being cursed and spit upon by his fellows, without having the doors of Opportunity closed roughly in his face.

This, then, is the end of his striving: to be a co-worker in the kingdom of culture, to escape both death and isolation, to husband and use his best powers and his latent genius. These powers of body and mind have in the past been strangely wasted, dispersed, or forgotten. The shadow of a mighty Negro past flits through the tale of Ethiopia the Shadowy and of Egypt the Sphinx. Through history, the powers of single black men flash here and there like falling stars, and die sometimes before the world has rightly gauged their brightness. Here in America, in the few days since Emancipation, the black man's turning hither and thither in hesitant and doubtful striving has often made his very strength to lose effectiveness, to seem like absence of power, like weakness. And yet it is not weakness,— it is the contradiction of double aims. The double-aimed struggle of the black artisan — on the one hand to escape white contempt for a nation of mere hewers of wood and drawers of water, and on the other hand to plough and nail and dig for a poverty-stricken horde — could only result in making him a poor craftsman, for he had but half a heart in either cause. By the poverty and ignorance of his people, the Negro minister or doctor was tempted toward quackery and demagogy; and by the criticism of the other world, toward ideals that made him ashamed of his lowly tasks. The would-be black *savant* was confronted by the paradox that the knowledge his people needed was a twice-told tale to his white neighbors, while the knowledge which would teach the white world was Greek to his own flesh and blood. The innate love of harmony and beauty that set the ruder souls of his people a-dancing and a-singing raised but confusion and doubt in the soul of the black artist; for the beauty revealed to him was the soul-beauty of a race which his larger audience despised, and he could not articulate the message of another people. This waste of double aims, this seeking to satisfy two unreconciled ideals, has wrought sad havoc with the courage and faith and deeds of ten thousand thousand people,— has sent them often wooing false gods and invoking false means of salvation, and at times has even seemed about to make them ashamed of themselves.

Away back in the days of bondage they thought to see in one divine event the end of all doubt and disappointment; few men ever worshipped Freedom with half such unquestioning faith as did the American Negro for two centuries. To him, so far as he thought and dreamed, slavery was indeed the sum of all villainies, the cause of all sorrow, the root of all prejudice; Emancipation was the key to a promised land of sweeter beauty than ever stretched before the eyes of wearied Israelites. In song and exhortation swelled one refrain — Liberty; in his tears and curses the God he implored had Freedom in his right hand. At last it came,— suddenly, fearfully, like a dream. With one wild carnival of blood and passion came the message in his own plaintive cadences: —

> "Shout, O children!
> Shout, you're free!
> For God has bought your liberty!"

Years have passed away since then,— ten, twenty, forty; forty years of national life, forty years of renewal and development, and yet the swarthy spectre sits in its accustomed seat at the Nation's feast. In vain do we cry to this our vastest social problem: —

> "Take any shape but that, and my firm nerves
> Shall never tremble!"

The Nation has not yet found peace from its sins; the freedman has not yet found in freedom his promised land. Whatever of good may have come in these years of change, the shadow of a deep disappointment rests upon the Negro people,— a disappointment all the more bitter because the unattained ideal was unbounded save by the simple ignorance of a lowly people.

The first decade was merely a prolongation of the vain search for freedom, the boon that seemed ever barely to elude their grasp,— like a tantalizing will-o'-the-wisp, maddening and misleading the headless host. The holocaust of war, the terrors of the Ku-Klux Klan, the lies of carpet-baggers, the disorganization of industry, and the contradictory advice of friends and foes, left the bewildered serf with no new watchword beyond the old cry for freedom. As the time flew, however, he began to grasp a new idea. The ideal of liberty demanded for its attainment powerful means, and these the Fifteenth Amendment gave him. The ballot, which before he had looked upon as a visible sign of freedom, he now regarded as the chief means of gaining and perfecting the liberty with which war had partially endowed him. And why not? Had not votes made war and emancipated millions? Had not votes enfranchised the freedmen? Was anything impossible to a power that had done all this? A million black men started with renewed zeal to vote themselves into the kingdom. So the decade flew away, the revolution of 1876 came, and left the half-free serf weary, wondering, but still inspired. Slowly but steadily, in the following years, a new vision began gradually to replace the dream of political power,— a powerful movement, the rise of another ideal to guide the unguided, another pillar of fire by night after a clouded day. It was the ideal of "book-learning"; the curiosity, born of compulsory ignorance, to know and test the power of the cabalistic letters of the white man, the longing to know. Here at last seemed to have been discovered the mountain path to Canaan; longer than the highway of Emancipation and law, steep and rugged, but straight, leading to heights high enough to overlook life.

Up the new path the advance guard toiled, slowly, heavily, doggedly; only those who have watched and guided the faltering feet, the misty minds, the dull understandings, of the dark pupils of these schools know how faithfully, how piteously, this people strove to learn. It was weary work. The cold statistician wrote down the inches of progress here and there, noted also where here and there a foot had slipped or some one had fallen. To the tired climbers, the horizon was ever dark, the mists were often cold, the Canaan was always dim and far away. If, however, the vistas disclosed as yet no goal, no resting-place, little but flattery and criticism, the journey at least gave leisure for reflection and self-examination; it changed the child of Emancipation to the youth with dawning self-consciousness, self-realization, self-respect. In those sombre forests of his striving his own soul rose before him, and he saw himself,— darkly as through a veil; and yet he saw in himself some faint revelation of his power, of his mission. He began to have a dim feeling that, to attain his place in the world, he must be himself, and not another. For the first time he sought to analyze the burden he bore upon his back, that dead-weight of social degradation partially masked behind a half-named Negro problem. He felt his poverty; without a cent, without a home, without land, tools, or savings, he had entered into competition with rich, landed, skilled neighbors. To be a poor man is hard, but to be a poor race in a land of dollars is the very bottom of hardships. He felt the weight of his ignorance,— not simply of letters, but of life, of business, of the humanities; the accumulated sloth and shirking and awkwardness of decades and centuries shackled his hands and feet. Nor was his burden all poverty and ignorance. The red stain of bastardy, which two centuries of systematic legal defilement of Negro women had stamped upon his race, meant not only the loss of ancient African chastity, but also the hereditary weight of a mass of corruption from white adulterers, threatening almost the obliteration of the Negro home.

A people thus handicapped ought not to be asked to race with the world, but rather allowed to give all its time and thought to its own social problems. But alas! while sociologists gleefully count his bastards and his prostitutes, the very soul of the toiling, sweating black man is darkened by the shadow of a vast despair. Men call the shadow prejudice, and learnedly explain it as the natural defence of culture against barbarism, learning against ignorance, purity against crime, the "higher" against the "lower" races. To which the Negro cries Amen!

and swears that to so much of this strange prejudice as is founded on just homage to civilization, culture, righteousness, and progress, he humbly bows and meekly does obeisance. But before that nameless prejudice that leaps beyond all this he stands helpless, dismayed, and well-nigh speechless; before that personal disrespect and mockery, the ridicule and systematic humiliation, the distortion of fact and wanton license of fancy, the cynical ignoring of the better and the boisterous welcoming of the worse, the all-pervading desire to inculcate disdain for everything black, from Toussaint to the devil,—before this there rises a sickening despair that would disarm and discourage any nation save that black host to whom "discouragement" is an unwritten word.

But the facing of so vast a prejudice could not but bring the inevitable self-questioning, self-disparagement, and lowering of ideals which ever accompany repression and breed in an atmosphere of contempt and hate. Whisperings and portents came home upon the four winds: Lo! we are diseased and dying, cried the dark hosts; we cannot write, our voting is vain; what need of education, since we must always cook and serve? And the Nation echoed and enforced this self-criticism, saying: Be content to be servants, and nothing more; what need of higher culture for half-men? Away with the black man's ballot, by force or fraud,—and behold the suicide of a race! Nevertheless, out of the evil came something of good,—the more careful adjustment of education to real life, the clearer perception of the Negroes' social responsibilities, and the sobering realization of the meaning of progress.

So dawned the time of *Sturm und Drang*: storm and stress to-day rocks our little boat on the mad waters of the world-sea; there is within and without the sound of conflict, the burning of body and rending of soul; inspiration strives with doubt, and faith with vain questionings. The bright ideals of the past, —physical freedom, political power, the training of brains and the training of hands,—all these in turn have waxed and waned, until even the last grows dim and overcast. Are they all wrong,—all false? No, not that, but each alone was over-simple and incomplete,—the dreams of a credulous race-childhood, or the fond imaginings of the other world which does not know and does not want to know our power. To be really true, all these ideals must be melted and welded into one. The training of the schools we need to-day more than ever,—the training of deft hands, quick eyes and ears, and above all the broader, deeper, higher culture of gifted minds and pure hearts. The power of the ballot we need in sheer self-defence,—else what shall save us from a second slavery? Freedom, too, the long-sought, we still seek,—the freedom of life and limb, the freedom to work and think, the freedom to love and aspire. Work, culture, liberty,—all these we need, not singly but together, not successively but together, each growing and aiding each, and all striving toward that vaster ideal that swims before the Negro people, the ideal of human brotherhood, gained through the unifying ideal of Race; the ideal of fostering and developing the traits and talents of the Negro, not in opposition to or contempt for other races, but rather in large conformity to the greater ideals of the American Republic, in order that some day on American soil two world-races may give each to each those characteristics both so sadly lack. We the darker ones come even now not altogether empty-handed: there are to-day no truer exponents of the pure human spirit of the Declaration of Independence than the American Negroes; there is no true American music but the wild sweet melodies of the Negro slave; the American fairy tales and folklore are Indian and African; and, all in all, we black men seem the sole oasis of simple faith and reverence in a dusty desert of dollars and smartness. Will America be poorer if she replace her brutal dyspeptic blundering with light-hearted but determined Negro humility? or her coarse and cruel wit with loving jovial good-humor? or her vulgar music with the soul of the Sorrow Songs?

Merely a concrete test of the underlying principles of the great republic is the Negro Problem, and the spiritual striving of the freedmen's sons is the travail of souls whose burden is almost beyond the measure of their strength, but who bear it in the name of an historic race, in the name of this the land of their fathers' fathers, and in the name of human opportunity.

And now what I have briefly sketched in large outline let me on coming pages tell again in many ways, with loving emphasis and deeper detail, that men may listen to the striving in the souls of black folk.

(1903)

Paul Laurence Dunbar   (1872–1906)

During the late nineteenth and early twentieth centuries Paul Laurence Dunbar was the best-known black poet in the United States. He was born on June 27, 1872, in Dayton, Ohio, to Matilda Murphy and Joshua Dunbar, a former Kentucky slave who escaped to Canada but returned during the Civil War to enlist in one of the first all-black regiments for the Union. As a child the author attended public schools in Dayton, and in 1891 he graduated from Central High School, where he was editor of the school newspaper, president of a literary club, and the senior class poet. While in high school he also edited the *Dayton Tattler*, an African American newspaper, and published his first poem, "Our Martyred Soldiers." After high school Dunbar began working as an elevator attendant to support himself and his mother. In 1891 the Kellogg Newspaper Company in Chicago published Dunbar's first short story, "The Tenderfoot," and Dunbar received national attention when his poems were published in a syndicated column.

Dunbar's first collection of poems, *Oak and Ivy*, which contains both conventional poems and those written in dialect, was published in 1893 to the acclaim of critics, both black and white. In 1893 he recited his poetry at the World's Columbian Exhibition in Chicago, and several years later his second collection of poems, *Majors and Minors* (1895), became a critical and commercial success, particularly due to Dunbar's use of dialect. After a volume of poems collected from his first two, *Lyrics of Lowly Life* (1896), appeared, Dunbar went on a six-month reading tour in England, where he collaborated with Samuel Coleridge-Taylor on an opera, *Dream Lover: An Operatic Romance*, which was produced in 1898. Upon his return to the states, Dunbar married Alice Ruth Moore, a schoolteacher and writer, and the couple moved to Washington, D.C., where Dunbar worked as a clerk for the Library of Congress. In 1898 his first collection of short stories, *Folks from Dixie*, and his first novel, *The Uncalled*, were published.

After struggling with tuberculosis-related health problems, Dunbar resigned from his clerk position, but he kept writing, and his fourth volume of poetry, *Lyrics of the Hearthside* (which contains the poem "Sympathy"), was published in 1899, and another volume of short stories, *The Strength of Gideon and Other Stories*, appeared in 1900. Dunbar also published three more novels: *A Love of Landry* (1900), *The Fanatics* (1901), and *The Sport of the Gods* (1902), which received critical acclaim as a social protest novel. Dunbar's other volumes of poetry include *Lyrics of Love and Laughter* (1903), where the poem "The Haunted Oak" appears; *Poetry: Lyrics of Sunshine and Shadow* (1905); and *Howdy, Howdy, Howdy* (1905) — a collection of previously published poems. His collections of short stories also include *In Old Plantation Days* (1903) and *The Heart of the Happy Hollow* (1904). Dunbar was one of the first African American writers to receive international recognition for his poetry, and as such he profoundly influenced the writers who followed him. Paul Laurence Dunbar died on February 9, 1906.

Sympathy

I know what the caged bird feels, alas!
When the sun is bright on the upland slopes;
When the wind stirs soft through the springing grass,
And the river flows like a stream of glass;
When the first bird sings and the first bud opes,
And the faint perfume from its chalice steals —
I know what the caged bird feels!

I know why the caged bird beats his wing
Till its blood is red on the cruel bars;
For he must fly back to his perch and cling

When he fain would be on the bough a-swing;
And a pain still throbs in the old, old scars
And they pulse again with a keener sting —
I know why he beats his wing!

I know why the caged bird sings, ah me,
When his wing is bruised and his bosom sore, —
When he beats his bars and he would be free;
It is not a carol of joy or glee,
But a prayer that he sends from his heart's deep core,
But a plea, that upward to Heaven he flings —
I know why the caged bird sings!

(1899)

The Haunted Oak

Pray why are you so bare, so bare,
    Oh, bough of the old oak-tree;
And why, when I go through the shade you throw,
    Runs a shudder over me?

My leaves were green as the best, I trow,
    And sap ran free in my veins,
But I saw in the moonlight dim and weird
    A guiltless victim's pains.

I bent me down to hear his sigh;
    I shook with his gurgling moan,
And I trembled sore when they rode away,
    And left him here alone.

They'd charged him with the old, old crime,
    And set him fast in jail:
Oh, why does the dog howl all night long,
    And why does the night wind wail?

He prayed his prayer and he swore his oath,
    And he raised his hand to the sky;
But the beat of hoofs smote on his ear,
    And the steady tread drew nigh.

Who is it rides by night, by night,
    Over the moonlit road?
And what is the spur that keeps the pace,
    What is the galling goad?

And now they beat at the prison door,
    "Ho, keeper, do not stay!
We are friends of him whom you hold within,
    And we fain would take him away

"From those who ride fast on our heels
    With mind to do him wrong;
They have no care for his innocence,
    And the rope they bear is long."

They have fooled the jailer with lying words,
    They have fooled the man with lies;
The bolts unbar, the locks are drawn,
    And the great door open flies.

Now they have taken him from the jail,
    And hard and fast they ride,
And the leader laughs low down in his throat,
    As they halt my trunk beside.

Oh, the judge, he wore a mask of black,
    And the doctor one of white,
And the minister, with his oldest son,
    Was curiously bedight.

Oh, foolish man, why weep you now?
    'T is but a little space,
And the time will come when these shall dread
    The mem'ry of your face.

I feel the rope against my bark,
    And the weight of him in my grain,
I feel in the throe of his final woe
    The touch of my own last pain.

And never more shall leaves come forth
    On the bough that bears the ban;
I am burned with dread, I am dried and dead,
    From the curse of a guiltless man.

And ever the judge rides by, rides by,
    And goes to hunt the deer,
And ever another rides his soul
    In the guise of a mortal fear.

And ever the man he rides me hard,
   And never a night stays he;
For I feel his curse as a haunted bough,
   On the trunk of a haunted tree.

(1903)

Mary Burrill   (1879–1946)

ary Powell Burrill was born in Washington, D.C., to John H. and Clara E. Burrill. She spent most of her early life in the city, graduating from M Street School (later Dunbar High School) in 1901, and then moved to Boston to attend Emerson College (later University), graduating in 1904. Burrill later returned to Emerson for another degree, a bachelor's of literary interpretation, in 1929. Still, she spent most of her adult life in Washington, where she taught English, speech, and drama at Dunbar High School, and where she was a colleague and close friend to Angelina Weld Grimké. From 1907 to 1911 Burrill also served as director of the Washington Conservatory of Music's School of Expression, where she taught public speaking and drama. During the 1920s Burrill was active in Washington's community theater, directing several classical plays. She retired from Dunbar High in 1944 and moved to New England, where she died on March 13, 1946. Her partner of twenty-five years was Lucy Diggs Stowe, dean of women at Howard University.

Burrill is best remembered for her efforts to use her playwriting talents as a means of raising awareness about race and gender issues. Both of her published works came out in 1919. *They That Sit in Darkness*, possibly the first feminist play written by a black woman, focuses on a poor woman who dies from having too many children and emphasizes the necessity of education for getting out of poverty. The play appeared in a special issue of *Birth Control Review*, a journal edited by Margaret Sanger and devoted to female reproductive choice. The issue, "The Negroes' Need for Birth Control, As Seen by Themselves," also included pieces by Grimké and W. E. B. Du Bois. Burrill's *Aftermath* (included below) appeared in the *Liberator*, in the same edition as Claude McKay's poem, "If We Must Die." The play was later produced in New York City on May 8, 1928, as a joint effort of the Krigwa Players Little Negro Theatre and the Workers' Drama League. The play dramatizes the reactions of a black soldier who returns from World War I to find that his father has been lynched. The antilynching drama was a relatively new genre in 1919, pioneered mostly by women like Burrill, Grimké, and another Washington writer, Georgia Douglas Johnson.

These plays often drew attention to the effects of lynching on black families and communities, and their authors hoped to gain support for federal antilynching legislation. Like her female peers Burrill offers a sympathetic portrait of a family paralyzed by fear and mourning, but like McKay she also portrays the spirit of resistance common to returning soldiers at the time.

Aftermath

CHARACTERS
Millie (A young woman)
Mam Sue (An old woman)
Rev. Luke Moseby (A clergyman)
Lonnie (A young man)
Mrs. Hawkins (A friend)
John (A soldier)

TIME: The present [1919]
PLACE: The Thornton cabin in South Carolina

It is late afternoon of a cool day in early spring. A soft afterglow pours in at the little window of the Thornton cabin. The light falls on MILLIE, *a slender brown girl of sixteen, who stands near the window ironing. She wears a black dress and a big gingham apron. A clothes-horse weighted down with freshly ironed garments is nearby. In the rear there is a door leading out to the road. To the left, another door leads into the other room of the cabin. To the right there is a great stone hearth blackened by age. A Bible rests on the mantel over the hearth. An old armchair and a small table on which is a kerosene lamp are near the hearth. In the center of the room sits a well-scrubbed kitchen table and a substantial wooden chair. In front of the hearth, the smouldering woodfire, sits* MAM SUE *busily sewing. The many colors in the old patchwork quilt that she is mending, together with the faded red of the bandana on her head, contrast strangely with her black dress.* MAM SUE *is very old. Her ebony face is seamed with wrinkles; and in her bleared, watery eyes there is a world-old sorrow. A service flag containing one star hangs in the little window of the cabin.*

Mam Sue: *(Crooning the old melody)*
> O, yes, yonder comes mah Lawd,
> He is comin' dis way
> Wid his sword in his han'
> O, yes, yonder comes —

(A burning log falls apart, and MAM SUE *suddenly stops singing and gazes intently at the fire. She speaks in deep mysterious tones to* MILLIE, *who has finished her task and has come to the hearth to put up her irons.)*

See dat log dah, Millie? De one fallin' tuh de side dah wid de big flame lap-pin' 'round hit? Dat means big doin's 'round heah tonight!

Millie: *(With a start)* Oh Mam Sue, don' you go proph'sying no mo'! You seen big doing's in dat fire de night befo' them w'ite devuls come in heah an' tuk'n po' dad out and bu'nt him!

Mam Sue: *(Calmly)* No Millie, Ah didn' see no big doin's dat night — Ah see'd evul doin's an' Ah tole yo' po' daddy to keep erway f'om town de nex' day wid his cotton. Ah jes knowed dat he wuz gwine to git in a row wid dem w'ite debbils — but he wou'd'n lis'n tuh his ole mammy — De good Lawd sen' me deses warnin's in dis fiah, jes lak He sen' His messiges in de fiah to Moses. Yo' chillun bettah lis'n to —

Millie: *(Nervously)* Oh, Mam Sue, you skeers me when you talks erbout seein' all them things in de fire —

Mam Sue: Yuh gits skeered cause yuh don' put yo' trus' in de good Lawd! He kin tek keer o' yuh no mattuh whut com'!

Millie: *(Bitterly)* Sometimes I thinks that Gawd's done fu'got us po' cullud people. Gawd didn' tek no keer o' po' dad and he put his trus' in Him! He useter set evah night by dis fire at dis here table and read his Bible an' pray — but jes' look whut happen' to dad! That don' look like Gawd wuz tekin' keer —

Mam Sue: *(Sharply)* Heish yo' mouf, Millie! Ah ain't a-gwine to 'ave dat sinner-talk 'roun' hyeah! *(Derisively)* Gawd don't tek no keer o' yuh? Ain't yuh bin prayin' night an' mawnin' fo' Gawd to sen' yo' brudder back f'om de war 'live an' whole? An' ain't yuh git dat lettah no longer'n yistiddy sayin' dat de fightin's all done stopp't an' dat de blessid Lawd's done brung yo' brud-der thoo all dem battuls live an' whole? Don' dat look lak de Lawd's done 'membered yuh?

Millie: *(Thoughtfully)* I reckon youse right, Mam Sue. But ef anything had a-happen' to John I wuz' nevah going to pray no mo'!

(MILLIE *goes to the clothes-horse and folds the garments and lays them carefully into a large basket.* MAM SUE *falls again to her crooning.)*

Mam Sue:

O, yes, yonder comes mah Lawd,
He's comin' dis way-a.

Millie: Lonnie's so late gittin' home tonight; I guess I'd bettah tek Mis' Hart's wash home tonight myse'f.

Mam Sue: Yas, Lonnie's mighty late. Ah reckons you'd bettah slip erlon' wid hit. (MILLIE *gets her hat from the adjoining room and is about to leave with the basket when* MAM SUE *calls significantly)* Millie?

Millie: Yas, Mam Sue.

Mam Sue: *(Firmly)* Don' yo' fu'git to drap dat lettah fu' John in de Pos' Awfus ez yuh goes by. Whah's de lettah?

Millie: *(Reluctantly)* But, Mam Sue, please don' let's —

(A knock is heard. MILLIE *opens the door and* REV LUKE MOSEBY *enters.* MOSEBY *is a wily little old man with a black, kindly face, and bright, searching eyes; his woolly hair and beard are snow-white. He is dressed in a rusty black suit with a coat of clerical cut that comes to his knees. In one hand he carries a large Bible, and in the other, a stout walking stick.)*

Millie: Good evenin', Brother Moseby, come right in.

Moseby: Good eben', Millie. Good eben', Mam Sue. Ah jes drap't in to see ef you-all is still trus'in de good Lawd an' —

Mam Sue: Lor', Brudder Moseby, ain't Ah bin trus'n de good Lawd nigh onter dese eighty yeah! Whut fu' yuh think Ah's agwine to quit w'en Ah'm in sight o' de Promis' Lan'? Millie, fetch Brudder Moseby dat cheer.

Moseby: *(Drawing his chair to the fire)* Dat's right, Mam Sue, you jes a-keep on trus'n prayin' an evahthing's gwine to come aw-right. *(Observing* MILLIE *is about to leave)* Don lemme 'tain yuh, Millie, but whut's all dis good news wese bin heahin' bout yo' brudder John? Dey say he's done won some kind o' medal ober dah in France?

Millie: *(Brightening up)* Oh, yes, we got a lettah day befo' yestiddy f'om John tellin us all erbout it. He's won de War Cross! He fought off twenty Germuns all erlone an' saved his whole comp'ny an the gret French Gen'rul come an' pinned de medal on him, hisse'f.

Moseby: De Lawd bles' his soul! Ah know'd dat boy wud mek good!

Millie: *(Excited by the glory of it all)* An' he's been to Paris, an' the fines' people stopp't him when they seen his medal, an' shook his han' an' smiled at him — an' he kin go evahwhere, an' dey ain't nobody all the time a-lookin' down on him, an' a-sneerin' at him 'cause he's black; but evahwhere they's jes gran' to him! An' he sez it's the firs' time evah in his life he's felt lak a real, sho-nuf man!

Moseby: Well, honey don't de Holy Book say, "De fust shill be las' and the las' shill be fust"?

Mam Sue: *(Fervently)* Dat hit do! An' de Holy Book ain't nebber tole no lie!

Moseby: Folks ober in Char'ston is sayin' dat some sojers is gwine to lan' dah today or tomorrer. Ah reckons day'll all be comin' 'long soon now dat de war's done stopp't.

Millie: I jes hates the thought of John comin' home an' hearin' 'bout Dad!

Moseby: *(In astonishment)* Whut! Yuh mean to say yuh ain't 'rite him 'bout yo' daddy, yit?

Mam Sue: Dat she ain't! Millie mus' 'ave huh way! She 'lowed huh brudder ough'n be tole, an' dat huh could keep on writin' to him jes lak huh dad wuz livin' — Millie allus done de writin' — An' Ah lets huh 'ave huh way —

Moseby: *(Shaking his head in disapproval)* Yuh mean tuh say —

Millie: *(Pleading)* But, Brother Moseby, I couldn't write John no bad news w'ilst he wuz way over there by hisse'f. He had nuf to worry him with death a-starin' him in the face evah day!

Mam Sue: Yas, Brudder Moseby, Millie's bin carryin' on dem lies in huh let-tahs fu' de las' six months; but today Ah jes sez to huh — Dis war done stopp't now, an' John, he gwine to be comin' home soon, an' he ain't agwine to come hyeah an' fin' me wid no lie on mah soul! An' Ah med huh set down an' tell him de whole truf. She's gwine out to pos' dat lettah dis minute.

Moseby: *(Still disapproving)* No good nebber come —

(The door is pushed violently open, and LONNIE, *a sturdy black boy of eighteen, rushes in breathlessly.)*

Lonnie: Mam Sue! Millie! Whut'da yuh think? John's come home!

Millie: *(Speechless with astonishment)* John? Home? Where's he at?

Mam Sue: *(Incredulously)* Whut yuh sayin'? John done come home? Bles' de Lawd! Bles' de Lawd! Millie, didn' Ah tell yuh sumpin wuz gwine tuh happen?

Lonnie: *(Excitedly)* I wuz sweepin' up de sto' jes befo' leavin' an' de phone rung — it wuz John — he wuz at Char'ston — jes landid! His comp'ny's waitin' to git de ten o'clock train fu' Camp Reed, whah dey's goin' to be mustered out.

Moseby: But how's he gwine to get erway?

Lonnie: Oh, good evenin', Brother Moseby, Ise jes so 'cited I didn' see yuh — Why his Cap'n done give him leave to run over heah 'tell de train's ready. He ought tuh be heah now 'cause it's mos' two hours sence he wuz talkin' —

Mam Sue: Whuffo yuh so long comin' home an' tellin' us?

Lonnie: *(Hesitatingly)* I did start right out but when I git to Sherley's corner I seen a whole lot of them w'ite hoodlums hangin' 'round de feed sto' — I jes felt like dey wuz jes waitin' dah to start sumpin, so I dodged 'em by tekin' de long way home.

Millie: Po' Lonnie! He's allus dodgin' po' w'ite trash!

Lonnie: *(Sullenly)* Well, yuh see whut Dad got by not dodgin' 'em.

Moseby: *(Rising to go)* Ah mus' be steppin' long now. Ah got to stop in to see ole man Hawkins; he's mighty sick. Ah'll drap in on mah way back fu' a word o' prayer wid John.

Mam Sue: Lonnie, yu'd bettah run erlon' as Brudder Moseby go an tote dat wash tuh Mis' Ha't. An drap in Mis' Hawkins' sto' an git some soap an' starch; an' Ah reckons yu'd bettah bring me a bottle o' linimint — dis ole pain done come back in mah knee. *(To* MOSEBY) Good eben, Brudder Moseby.

Moseby: Good eben, Mam Sue; Good eben, Millie, an' Gawd bles' yuh.

Lonnie: *(As he is leaving)* Tell John I'll git back fo' he leaves.

(LONNIE *and* MOSEBY *leave.* MILLIE *closes the door behind them and then goes to the window and looks out anxiously.*)

Millie: *(Musingly)* Po' John! Po' John! *(Turning to* MAM SUE*)* Mam Sue?
Mam Sue: Yas, Millie.
Millie: *(Hesitatingly)* Who's goin' to tell John 'bout Dad?
Mam Sue: *(Realizing for the first time that the task must fall to someone.)* Dunno. Ah reckons yu'd bettah.
Millie: *(Going to* MAM SUE *and kneeling softly at her side)* Mam Sue, don' let's tell him now! He's got only a li'l hour to spen' with us — an' it's the firs' time fu' so long! John loved Daddy so! Let 'im be happy jes a li'l longer — we kin tell 'im the truth when he comes back fu' good. Please, Mam Sue!
Mam Sue: *(Softened by* MILLIE*'s pleading)* Honey chile, John gwine to be askin' for his daddy fust thing — dey ain't no way —
Millie: *(Gaining courage)* Oh, yes, 'tis! We kin tell 'im Dad's gone to town — anything, jes so's he kin spen' these few li'l minutes in peace! I'll fix the Bible jes like Dad's been in an' been a-readin' in it! He won't know no bettah!

(MILLIE *takes the Bible from the mantel and opening it at random lays it on the table; she draws the old armchair close to the table as her father had been wont to do every evening when he read his Bible.*)

Mam Sue: *(Shaking her head doubtfully)* Ah ain't much on actin' dis lie, Millie.

(*The soft afterglow fades and the little cabin is filled with shadows.* MILLIE *goes again to the window and peers out.* MAM SUE *falls again to her crooning.*)

Mam Sue: *(Crooning)*:
    O, yes, yonder comes mah Lawd,
    He's comin' dis way
    Wid his sword in his han' —
(To MILLIE*)* Millie, bettah light de lamp, it's gittin' dark.
    He's gwine ter hew dem sinners down
    Right lebbal to de groun'
    O, yes, yonder comes mah Lawd —

(*As* MILLIE *is lighting the lamp, whistling is heard in the distance.* MILLIE *listens intently, then rushes to the window. The whistling comes nearer; it rings out clear and familiar —"Though the boys are far away, they dream of home."*)

Millie: *(Excitedly)* That's him! That's John, Mam Sue!

(MILLIE *rushes out of doors. The voices of* JOHN *and* MILLIE *are heard from without in greetings. Presently,* JOHN *and* MILLIE *enter the cabin.* JOHN *is tall and straight — a good soldier and a strong man. He wears the uniform of a private in the American Army. One hand is clasped in both of* MILLIE's. *In the other, he carries an old-fashioned valise. The War Cross is pinned on his breast. On his sleeve three chevrons tell mutely of wounds suffered in the cause of freedom. His brown face is aglow with life and the joy of homecoming.)*

John: *(Eagerly)* Where's Dad? Where's Mam Sue?

Mam Sue: *(Hobbling painfully to meet him)* Heah's ole Mam Sue! (JOHN *takes her tenderly in his arms)* Bles' yo' heart, chile, bles' yo' heart! Tuh think dat de good Lawd's done lemme live to see dis day!

John: Dear old Mam Sue! Gee, but I'm glad to see you an' Millie again!

Mam Sue: Didn' Ah say dat yuh wuz comin' back hyeah?

John: *(Smiling)* Same old Mam Sue with huh faith an' huh prayers. But where's Dad? *(He glances toward the open Bible)* He's been in from de field, ain't he?

Millie: *(Without lifting her eyes)* Yes, he's come in but he had to go out ag'in — to Sherley's feed sto'.

John: *(Reaching for his cap that he has tossed upon the table)* That ain't far. I've jes a few minutes so I'd bettah run down there an' hunt him up. Won't he be surprised!

Millie: *(Confused)* No — no. John — I fu'got; he ain't gone to Sherley's, he's gone to town.

John: *(Disappointed)* To town? I hope he'll git in befo' I'm leavin'. There's no tellin' how long they'll keep me at Camp Reed. Where's Lonnie?

Mam Sue: Lonnie's done gone to Mis' Ha't's wid de wash. He'll be back toreckly.

Millie: *(Admiring the medal on his breast)* An' this is the medal? Tell us all erbout it, John.

John: Oh, Sis, it's an awful story — wait 'til I git back fu' good. Let's see whut I've got in dis bag fu' you. *(He places the worn valise on the table and opens it. He takes out a bright-colored dress pattern)* That's fu' you, Millie, and quit wearin' them black clothes.

(MILLIE takes the silk and hugs it eagerly to her breast; suddenly there sweeps into her mind the realization that she cannot wear it, and the silk falls to the floor)

Millie: *(Trying to be brave)* Oh, John, it's jes lovely! *(As she shows it to Mam Sue)* Look, Mam Sue!

John: *(Flourishing a bright shawl)* An this is fu' Mam Sue. Mam Sue'll be so gay!

Mam Sue: *(Admiring the gift)* Who'd evah b'lieved dat yo' ole Mam Sue would live to be wearin' clo'es whut huh gran'chile done brung huh f'om Eu'ope!

John: Never you mind, Mam Sue, one of these days I'm goin to tek you an' Millie over there, so's you kin breathe free jes once befo' yuh die.

Mam Sue: It's got tuh be soon, 'cause dis ole body's mos' wo'e out; an de good Lawd's gwine to be callin' me to pay mah debt 'fo' long.

John: *(Showing some handkerchiefs, with gay borders)* These are fu' Lonnie. *(He next takes out a tiny box that might contain a bit of jewelry.)* An this is fu' dad. Sum'pin he's been wantin' fu' years. I ain't goin' to open it 'till he comes.

*(*MILLIE *walks into the shadows and furtively wipes a tear from her eyes.)*

John: *(Taking two army pistols from his bag and placing them on the table)* An' these las' are fu' youahs truly.

Millie: *(Looking at them, fearfully)* Oh, John, are them youahs?

John: One of' 'em's mine; the other's my Lieutenant's. I've been cleanin' it fu' him. Don' tech 'em — 'cause mine's loaded.

Millie: *(Still looking at them in fearful wonder)* Did they learn yuh how to shoot 'em?

John: Yep, an' I kin evah mo' pick 'em off!

Millie: *(Reproachfully)* Oh, John!

John: Nevah you worry, li'l Sis, John's nevah goin' to use 'em less it's right fu' him to. *(He places the pistols on the mantel — on the very spot where the Bible has lain.)* My! but it's good to be home! I've been erway only two years but it seems like two cent'ries. All that life ovah there seems like some awful dream!

Mam Sue: *(Fervently)* Ah know it do! Many's de day yo' ole Mam Sue set in dis cheer an' prayed fu' yuh.

John: Lots of times, too, in the trenches when I wuz dog-tired, an' sick, an' achin' wid the cold I uster say: well, if we're sufferin' all this for the op-pressed, like they tell us, then Mam Sue, an' Dad, an Millie come in on that — they'll git some good ou'n it if I don't! An' I'd shet my eyes an' fu'git the cold, an' the pain, an' them old guns spittin' death all 'round us; an' see you folks settin' here by this fire — Mam Sue, noddin', an' singin'; Dad a spellin' out his Bible — *(He glances toward the open book.)* Let's see whut he's been readin' — *(*JOHN *takes up the Bible and reads the first passage upon which his eye falls.)* "But I say unto you, love your enemies, bless them that curse you, an' do good to them that hate you" — *(He lets the Bible fall to the table.)* That ain't the dope they been feedin' us soljers on! "Love your en-emies?" It's been — git a good aim at 'em, an' let huh go!

Mam Sue: *(Surprised)* Honey, Ah hates to hyeah yuh talkin' lak dat! It sound lak yuh done fu'git yuh Gawd!

John: No, Mam Sue, I ain't fu'got God, but I've quit thinkin' that prayers kin do ever'thing. I've seen a whole lot sence I've been erway from here. I've seen some men go into battle with a curse on their lips, and I've seen them same men come back with never a scratch; an' I've seen men whut read their Bibles befo' battle, an' prayed to live, left dead on the field. Yes, Mam Sue, I've seen a heap an' I've done a tall lot o' thinkin' sence I've been erway from here. An' I b'lieve it's jes like this — beyon' a certain point prayers ain't no good! The Lawd does jes so much for you, then it's up to you to do the res' fu' yourse'f. The Lawd's done His part when He's done give me strength an' courage; I got tuh do the res' fu' myse'f!

Mam Sue: *(Shaking her head)* Ah don' lak dat kin' o' talk — it don' bode no good.

(The door opens and Lonnie enters with packages. He slips the bolt across the door.)

John: *(Rushing to* LONNIE *and seizing his hand)* Hello, Lonnie, ole man!

Lonnie: Hello, John, gee, but Ah'm glad tuh see yuh!

John: Boy, you should 'ave been with me! It would 'ave taken some of the skeeriness out o' yuh, an' done yuh a worl' o' good.

Lonnie: *(Ignoring* JOHN's *remark)* Here's the soap an' starch, Millie.

Mam Sue: Has yuh brung mah linimint?

Lonnie: Yassum, it's in de packige.

Millie: *(Unwrapping the package)* No, it ain't, Lonnie.

Lonnie: Mis' Hawkins give it tuh me. Ah mus' a lef' it on de counter. Ah'll git it w'en Ah goes to de train wid John.

Millie: *(Showing him the handkerchief)* See whut John done brought you! An' look on de mantel! *(Pointing to the pistols)*

Lonnie: *(Drawing back in fear as he glances at the pistols)* You'd bettah hide them things! No cullud man bettah be seen wid dem things down heah!

John: That's all right, Lonnie, nevah you fear. I'm goin' to keep 'em an' I ain't a-goin' to hide 'em either. See them. *(Pointing to the wound chevrons on his arm.)* Well, when I got them wounds, I let out all the rabbit-blood 'at wuz in me! *(Defiantly)* Ef I kin be trusted with a gun in France, I kin be trusted with one in South Car'lina.

Mam Sue: *(Sensing trouble)* Millie, yu'd bettah fix some suppah fu' John.

John: *(Looking at his watch)* I don' want a thing. I've got to be leavin' in a little while. I'm 'fraid I'm goin' to miss Dad after all.

(The knob of the door is turned as though someone is trying to enter. Then there is a loud knock on the door.)

John: *(Excitedly)* That's Dad! Don't tell him I'm here!

*(*JOHN *tips hurriedly into the adjoining room. Lonnie unbolts the door and* MRS. SELENA HAWKINS *enters.)*

Mrs. Hawkins: Lonnie fu'got de liniment so I thought I' bettah run ovah wid hit, 'cause when Mam Sue sen' fu' dis stuff she sho' needs hit. Brudder Moseby's been tellin' me dat John's done come home.

John: *(Coming from his hiding place and trying to conceal his disappointment)* Yes, I'm here. Good evenin' Mis' Hawkins. Glad to see you.

Mrs. Hawkins: *(Shaking hands with* JOHN*)* Well, Lan' sakes alive! Ef it ain't John sho' nuf! An' ain't he lookin' gran'! Jes look at dat medal a-shinin' on his coat! Put on yuh cap, boy, an' lemme see how yuh look!

John: Sure! *(*JOHN *puts on his overseas cap and, smiling, stands at attention a few paces off while* MAM SUE, LONNIE, *and* MILLIE *form an admiring circle around him.)*

Mrs. Hawkins: Now don' he sholy look gran'! I knows yo' sistah an' gran' mammy's proud o' yuh! *(A note of sadness creeps into her voice.)* Ef only yuh po' Daddy had a-lived to see dis day!

*(*JOHN *looks at her in amazement.* MILLIE *and* MAM SUE *stand transfixed with terror over the sudden betrayal.)*

John: *(Looking from one to the other and repeating her words as though he can scarcely realize their meaning)* "Ef your po' Daddy had lived —" *(To* MIL-LIE*)* Whut does this mean?

*(*MILLIE *sinks sobbing into the chair at the table and buries her face in her hands.)*

Mrs. Hawkins: Lor' Millie, I thought you'd tole him!

(Bewildered by the catastrophe that she has precipitated, MRS. HAWKINS *slips out of the cabin.)*

John: *(Shaking* MILLIE *almost roughly)* Come, Millie, have you been lyin' to me? Is Dad gone?

Millie: *(Through her sobs)* I jes hated to tell you — you wuz so far erway —

John: *(Nervously)* Come, Millie, for God's sake don' keep me in this su'pense! I'm a brave soldier — I kin stan' it — did he suffer much? Wuz he sick long?

Millie: He wuzn't sick no time — them w'ite devuls come in heah an' dragged him —

John: *(Desperately)* My God! You mean they lynched Dad?

Millie: *(Sobbing piteously)* They burnt him down by the big gum tree!

John: *(Desperately)* Whut fu', Millie? Whut fu'?

Millie: He got in a row wid ole Mister Withrow 'bout the price of cotton — an' he called Dad a liar an' struck him — an' Dad he up an' struck him back —

John: *(Brokenly)* Didn' they try him? Didn' they give him a chance? Whut'd the Sheriff do? An' the Gov'nur?

Millie: *(Through her sobs)* They didn't do nothin'!

John: Oh, God! Oh, God! *(Then recovering [from his] first bitter anguish and speaking)* So they've come into ouah home, have they! *(He strides over to Lonnie and seizes him by the collar.)* An' whut wuz you doin' when them hounds come in here after Dad?

Lonnie: *(Hopelessly)* They wuz so many of 'em come an' git 'im — whut could Ah do?

John: Do? You could 'ave fought 'em like a man!

Mam Sue: *(Pleadingly)* Don't be too hard on 'im, John, we'se ain't got no gun 'round heah!

John: Then he should 'ave burnt their damn kennels ovah their heads! Who was it leadin' 'em?

Millie: Old man Withrow and the Sherley boys, they started it all.

(Gradually assuming the look of a man who has determined to do some terrible work that must be done, John walks deliberately toward the mantel where the revolvers are lying.)

John: *(Bitterly)* I've been helpin' the w'ite man git his freedom, I reckon I'd bettah try now to get my own!

Mam Sue: *(Terrified)* Whut yuh gwine ter do?

John: *(With bitterness growing in his voice)* I'm sick o' these w'ite folks doin's — we're "fine, trus'worthy feller citizuns" when they're handin' us out guns, an' Liberty Bonds, an' chuckin' us off to die; but we ain't a damn thing when it comes to handin' us the rights we done fought an' bled fu'! I'm sick o' this sort o' life — an' I'm goin' to put an end to it!

Millie: *(Rushing to the mantel, and covering the revolvers with her hands)* Oh, no, no, John! Mam Sue, John's gwine to kill hisse'f!

Mam Sue: *(Piteously)* Oh, mah honey, don' yuh go do nothin' to bring sin on yo' soul! Pray to de good Lawd to tek all dis fiery feelin' out'n yo' heart! Wait 'tel Brudder Moseby come back — he's gwine ter pray —

John: *(His speech growing more impassioned and bitter)* This ain't no time fu' preachers or prayers! You mean to tell me I mus' let them w'ite devuls send me miles erway to suffer an' be shot up fu' the freedom of people I ain't nevah seen, while they're burnin' an' killin' my folks here at home! To Hell with 'em! *(He pushes* MILLIE *aside, and, seizing the revolvers, thrusts the loaded one into his pocket and begins deliberately to load the other.)*

Millie: *(Throwing her arms about his neck)* Oh, John, they'll kill yuh!

John: *(Defiantly)* Whut ef they do! I ain't skeered o' none of 'em! I've faced worse guns than any sneakin' hounds kin show me! To Hell with 'em! *(He thrusts the revolver that he has just loaded into Lonnie's hands.)* Take this, an' come on here, boy, an' we'll see what Withrow an' his gang have got to say!

(Followed by LONNIE, *who is bewildered and speechless,* JOHN *rushes out of the cabin and disappears in the gathering darkness.)*

Curtain

(1919)

Angelina Weld Grimké (1880–1958)

ngelina Weld Grimké hailed from a long line of race and gender activists. Her great-aunts, Sarah and Angelina Grimké (she was named for the latter), were famous abolitionist and feminist sisters. Her great-uncle Theodore Weld was a noted educator; her aunt Charlotte Forten Grimké was also a writer; and her uncle Francis Grimké pastored a Unitarian church. Angelina was born on February 27, 1880, in Boston, Massachusetts, to Sarah Stanley Grimké, the daughter of a prominent white clergyman, and Archibald Grimké, who held several NAACP offices. In 1883 Grimké's mother left her father, taking the young girl with her. Four years later Angelina moved back in with Archibald and never saw her mother again. She attended some of the best schools in Massachusetts, including the Cushing and the Carleton academies, and after high school she attended the Boston Normal School of Gymnastics, graduating in 1902 with a degree in physical education. Grimké taught gym for five years before moving to Washington, D.C., where she taught at the Armstrong Manual Training School until 1916, when she moved to M Street High School (later known as Dunbar High School) to teach English. She worked there (along with colleague Mary Burrill) until she retired in 1926 to take care of her father, whose health was failing.

Grimké published essays and poems in numerous periodicals, including the *Colored American Magazine, Boston Transcript, Opportunity,* and *Pilot.* Of her short stories, "The Closing Door," published in 1919 in *The Birth Control Review,* garnered the most acclaim. Her poems also appeared in the anthologies *The New Negro* (1925) and *Caroling Dusk: An Anthology of Verse by Black Poets* (1927). Two of Grimké's most famous poems, reprinted here, are "The Black Finger" (1925), which compares a cypress tree to a black finger pointing upward, and "Tenebris" (1927), which compares a nighttime shadow to a black hand. Both poems express a desire for social justice and hint at the barriers to such a goal. In addition to poetry, Grimké wrote plays, including the antilynching drama *Rachel,* which was produced in Washington, D.C., in 1916 and published in book form in 1920. Written in response to W. E. B. Du Bois's call for black theater, the play received mixed reviews, but critics hailed it as the first drama written by an African American for an African American audience and a pioneering effort at using the theater for political activism.

Grimké's writing often addresses racial oppression, and her imagery portrays a need for social equality and despair over the lack of it. Her work also depicts the negative psychological and physical effects of racial oppression and violence. Some of Grimké's writings allude to erotic relationships with women, and poems and letters published posthumously reference her homosexuality, although she never explicitly addresses sexual orientation in works that were published before her death. Becoming frustrated with the social restrictions of race, gender, and sexuality, Grimké stopped publishing in the 1930s. She died on June 10, 1958.

The Black Finger

I just saw a beautiful thing
    Slim and still,
Against a gold, gold sky,
    A straight cypress,
    Sensitive
    Exquisite,
A black finger
Pointing upwards.
Why, beautiful, still finger are you black?
And why are you pointing upwards?

(1925)

Tenebris

There is a tree, by day,
That, at night,
Has a shadow,
A hand huge and black,
With fingers long and black.
    All through the dark,
Against the white man's house,
    In the little wind,
The black hand plucks and plucks
    At the bricks.
The bricks are the color of blood and very small.
    Is it a black hand,
    Or is it a shadow?

(1927)

Claude McKay

Born Festus Claudius McKay in Clarendon Parish, Jamaica, Claude McKay was the son of farmers, Thomas and Anne McKay, whose families were enslaved and brought to Jamaica from West Africa. McKay lived with his brother, Uriah, who taught school and who also taught Claude literature and philosophy. McKay left school to work as a police constable in Kingston but returned to Clarendon Parish, where he lived until 1912, when he immigrated to the United States to study agriculture at Tuskegee Institute (now Tuskegee University) and Kansas State College. Over the next decade McKay published his poetry widely. He put out two volumes in 1912, *Songs of Jamaica* and *Constab Ballads*. In 1917 he began publishing under a pseudonym, Eli Edwards, but after he was discovered he began circulating his work under his real name to multiple literary magazines, including Marcus Garvey's *Negro World* and the activist journal *The Liberator*. His third volume, *Spring in New Hampshire*, appeared in 1920, and in 1922 McKay published his most successful collection, *Harlem Shadows*.

That same year, McKay traveled to Russia, where he addressed the Fourth Congress of Communist International, and then visited Spain and northern Africa before settling in Paris. In France, he wrote his first novel, *Home to Harlem* (1928), the first book by an African American to become a best seller, which went through five editions in two months. McKay's second novel, *Banjo: A Story without a Plot*, appeared in 1929, and his third, *Banana Bottom*, in 1933. After publishing *Gingertown* (1932), a collection of short stories, McKay returned to the United States in 1934.

McKay then became involved in the Friendship House, a Catholic community center in Harlem, and converted to Catholicism in 1944. Afterward, he moved to Chicago and taught for the Catholic Youth Organization before dying of heart failure on May 22, 1948. Two of his volumes were published posthumously: his second autobiography, *My Green Hills of Jamaica* (1979), and a collection of poetry, *Selected Poems of Claude McKay* (1953). Other works include his autobiography, *A Long Way from Home* (1937), and a collection of essays, *Harlem: Negro Metropolis* (1940). In 1977 the Jamaican government named McKay the national poet and awarded him the Order of Jamaica.

McKay's writing, much of which uses dialect, encourages blacks to fight racism and violence, and his work often depicts the poverty of urban life. The selections reprinted here reveal a spirit determined to triumph over the vicissitudes of racial oppression. One of the poems, "If We Must Die," was inspired by the racial violence of 1919 in Chicago. Both poems first appeared in *The Liberator* and were reprinted in *Harlem Shadows*.

If We Must Die

If we must die, let it not be like hogs
Hunted and penned in an inglorious spot,
While round us bark the mad and hungry dogs,
Making their mock at our accursed lot.
If we must die, O let us nobly die,
So that our precious blood may not be shed
In vain; then even the monsters we defy
Shall be constrained to honor us though dead!
O kinsmen we must meet the common foe!
Though far outnumbered let us show us brave,
And for their thousand blows deal one deathblow!
What though before us lies the open grave?
Like men we'll face the murderous, cowardly pack,
Pressed to the wall, dying, but fighting back!

(1919)

America

Although she feeds me bread of bitterness,
And sinks into my throat her tiger's tooth,
Stealing my breath of life, I will confess
I love this cultured hell that tests my youth!
Her vigor flows like tides into my blood,
Giving me strength erect against her hate.
Her bigness sweeps my being like a flood.
Yet as a rebel fronts a king in state,
I stand within her walls with not a shred
Of terror, malice, not a word of jeer.
Darkly I gaze into the days ahead,
And see her might and granite wonders there,
Beneath the touch of Time's unerring hand,
Like priceless treasures sinking in the sand.

(1921)

Lillian Smith

(1897–1966)

illian Smith was born in Jasper, Florida, in 1897 and moved to Rabun County, Georgia, in 1915. She attended Piedmont College before moving to Baltimore to study music at the Peabody Conservatory. In 1922 she moved to Huchow, China, where she taught at a Methodist girls' school until 1925 — an experience that provided her with a new cultural perspective on the effects of segregation. Smith left China to return to Georgia and serve as the director of her father's summer camp for girls, Laurel Falls, where she worked until its close in 1948. While directing the camp, she met Paula Snelling, who became her lifelong partner.

In 1936 Smith began coediting and publishing a magazine, *Pseudopodia* (later renamed *North Georgia Review* and then *South Today*), which contained literary reviews written by white and black authors, and which catered to southern liberal intellectuals. Her first novel, *Strange Fruit*, appeared in 1944 and faced censorship for its portrayals of racial violence and an interracial love affair. The following year, a stage adaptation of the novel ran on Broadway. In 1949 her autobiography, *Killers of the Dream* was published (the first chapter from that book is excerpted below). Smith, who was white, explores the relationships between religion, race, sexuality, class, and gender, exposing white fears over miscegenation and providing a social commentary on racism and the childhood lessons that perpetuate it. Smith's second autobiographical work, *The Journey*, appeared in 1954, followed by *Now Is the Time*, which attempted to persuade southern white readers to accept the Supreme Court's *Brown v. Board of Education* decision. Many stores refused to sell the book, and Smith's home was burned. Her other works include a second novel, *One Hour* (1959), which responds to anti-Communist sentiment during the McCarthy era; *Memory of a Large Christmas* (1962), a childhood memoir; and *Our Faces, Our Words* (1964), a collection of fictional monologues by civil rights activists working for the Southern Conference for Human Welfare and the Congress of Racial Equality (CORE).

Smith died of breast cancer in 1966. Although she never spoke out about her sexual orientation, her writing often deals with gender norms and sexuality, making her one of the few white southern authors of her generation to draw connections between gender stereotyping and racism. Smith viewed all sorts of discrimination as part of the same, larger problem.

Selection from *Killers of the Dream*

Chapter 1, When I Was a Child

Even its children know that the South is in trouble. No one has to tell them; no words said aloud. To them, it is a vague thing weaving in and out of their play, like a ghost haunting an old graveyard or whispers after the household sleeps — fleeting mystery, vague menace, to which each responds in his own way. Some learn to screen out all except the soft and the soothing; others deny even as they see plainly, and hear. But all know that under quiet words and warmth and laughter, under the slow ease and tender concern about small matters, there is a heavy burden on all of us and as heavy a refusal to confess it. The children know this "trouble" is bigger than they, bigger than their family, bigger than their church, so big that people turn away from its size. They have seen it flash out like lightning and shatter a town's peace, have felt it tear up all they believe in. They have measured its giant strength and they feel weak when they remember.

This haunted childhood belongs to every southerner. Many of us run away from it but we come back like a hurt animal to its wound, or a murderer to the scene of his sin. The human heart dares not stay away too long from that which hurt it most. There is a return journey to anguish that few of us are released from making.

We who were born in the South call this mesh of feeling and memory "loyalty." We think of it sometimes as "love." We identify with the South's trouble as if we, individually, were responsible for all of it. We defend the sins and sorrows of three hundred years as if each sin had been committed by us alone and each sorrow had cut across our heart. We are as hurt at criticism of our region as if our own name were called aloud by the critic. We have known guilt without understanding it, and there is no tie that binds men closer to the past and each other than that.

It is a strange thing, this umbilical cord uncut. In times of ease, we do not feel its pull, but when we are threatened with change, suddenly it draws the whole white South together in a collective fear and fury that wipe our minds clear of reason and we are blocked off from sensible contact with the world we live in.

To keep this resistance strong, wall after wall has been thrown up in the southern mind against criticism from without and within. Imaginations close tight against the hurt of others; a regional armoring takes place to keep out the "enemies" who would make our trouble different — or maybe rid us of it completely. For it is a trouble that we do not want to give up. We are as involved with it as a child who cannot be happy at home and cannot bear to tear himself away, or as a grown-up who has fallen in love with his own disease. We southerners have identified with the long sorrowful past on such deep levels of love and hate and guilt that we do not know how to break old bonds without pulling our lives down. *Change* is the evil word, a shrill clanking that makes us know too well our servitude. *Change* means leaving one's memories, one's sins, one's ancient prison, the room where one was born. How can we do this when we are tied fast!

The white man's burden is his own childhood. Every southerner knows this.

Though he may deny it even to himself, yet he drags through life with him the heavy weight of a past that never eases and is rarely understood, of desire never appeased, of dreams that died in his heart.

IN THIS SOUTH I was born and now live. Here it was that I began to grow, seeking my way, as do all children, through the honeycomb cells of our life to the bright reality outside. Sometimes it was as if all doors opened inward.... Sometimes we children lost even the desire to get outside and tried only to make a comfortable home of the trap of swinging doors that history and religion and a war, man's greed and his guilt had placed us in at birth.

It is not easy to pick out of such a life those strands that have to do only with color, only with Negro-white relationships, only with religion or sex, for they are knit of the same fibers that have gone into the making of the whole fabric, woven into its basic patterns and designs. Religion ... sex ... race ... money ... avoidance rites ... malnutrition ... dreams — no part of these can be looked at and clearly seen without looking at the whole of them. For, as a painter mixes colors and makes of them new colors, so religion is turned into something different by race, and segregation is colored as much by sex as by skin pigment, and money is no longer a coin but a lost wish wandering through a man's whole life.

A child's lessons are blended of these strands however dissonant a design they make. The mother who taught me what I know of tenderness and love and compassion taught me also the bleak rituals of keeping Negroes in their place. The father who rebuked me for an air of superiority toward schoolmates from the mill and rounded out his rebuke by gravely reminding me that "all men are brothers," trained me in the steel-rigid decorums I must demand of every colored male. They who so gravely taught me to split my body from my feelings and both from my "soul," taught me also to split my conscience from my acts and Christianity from southern tradition.

Neither the Negro nor sex was often discussed at length in our home. We were given no formal instruction in these difficult matters but we learned our lessons well. We learned the intricate system of taboos, of renunciations and compensations, of manners, voice modulations, words, feelings, along with our prayers, our toilet habits, and our games. I do not remember how or when, but by the time I had learned that God is love, that Jesus is His Son and came to give us more abundant life, that all men are brothers with a common Father, I also knew that I was better than a Negro, that all black folks have their place and must be kept in it, that sex has its place and must be kept in it, that a terrifying disaster would befall the South if ever I treated a Negro as my social equal and as terrifying a disaster would befall my family if ever I were to have a baby outside of marriage. I had learned that God so loved the world that He gave His only begotten Son so that we might have segregated churches in which it was my duty to worship each Sunday and on Wednesday at evening prayers.

I had learned that white southerners are a hospitable, courteous, tactful people who treat those of their own group with consideration and who as carefully segregate from all the richness of life "for their own good and welfare" thirteen million people whose skin is colored a little differently from my own.

I knew by the time I was twelve that a member of my family would always shake hands with old Negro friends, would speak gently and graciously to members of the Negro race unless they forgot their place, in which event icy peremptory tones would draw lines beyond which only the desperate would dare take one step. I knew that to use the word "nigger" was unpardonable and no well-bred southerner was quite so crude as to do so; nor would a well-bred southerner call a Negro "mister" or invite him into the living room or eat with him or sit by him in public places. I knew that my old nurse who had patiently cared for me through long months of illness, who had given me refuge when a little sister took my place as the baby of the family, who comforted me, soothed, fed me, delighted me with her stories and games, let me fall asleep on her deep warm breast, was not worthy of the passionate love I felt for her but must be given instead a half-smiled-at affection similar to that which one feels for one's dog. I knew but I never believed it, that the deep respect I felt for her, the tenderness, the love, was a childish thing which every normal child outgrows, that such love begins with one's toys and is discarded with them, and that somehow — though it seemed impossible to my agonized heart — I too, must outgrow these feelings. I learned to give presents to this woman I loved, instead of esteem and honor. I learned to use a soft voice to oil my words of superiority. I learned to cheapen with tears and sentimental talk of "my old mammy" one of the profound relationships of my life. I learned the bitterest thing a child can learn: that the human relations I valued most were held cheap by the world I lived in.

From the day I was born, I began to learn my lessons. I was put in a rigid frame too intricate, too complex, too twisting to describe here so briefly, but I learned to conform to its slide-rule measurements. I learned that it is possible to be a Christian and a white southerner simultaneously; to be a gentlewoman and an arrogant callous creature in the same moment; to pray at night and ride a Jim Crow car the next morning and to feel comfortable in doing both. I learned to believe in freedom, to glow when the word democracy is used, and to practice slavery from morning to night. I learned it the way all of my southern people learn it: by closing door after door until one's mind and heart and conscience are blocked off from each other and from reality.

I closed the doors. Or perhaps they were closed for me. Then one day they began to open again. Why I had the desire or the strength to open them or what strange accident or circumstance opened them for me would require in the answering an account too long, too particular, too stark to make here. And perhaps I should not have the insight or wisdom that such an analysis would demand of me, nor the will to make it. I know only that the doors opened, a little; that somewhere along that iron corridor we travel from babyhood to maturity, doors swinging inward began to swing outward, showing glimpses of the world beyond, of that clear bright thing we call "reality."

I BELIEVE THERE IS one experience in my childhood which pushed these doors open, a little. And I am going to tell it here, although I know well that to excerpt from a life and family background one incident and name it as a "cause" of a change in one's life direction is a distortion and often an irrelevance. The profound hungers of a child and how they are filled have too much to do with the way in which experiences are assimilated to tear an incident out of a life and look at it in isolation. Yet, with these reservations, I shall tell it, not because it was in itself so severe a trauma, but because it became for me a symbol of buried experiences that I did not have access to. It is an incident that has rarely happened to other southern children. In a sense, it is unique. But it was an acting-out, a special private production of a little script that is written on the lives of most southern children before they know words. Though they may not have seen it staged this way, each southerner has had his own dramatization of the theme.

I should like to preface the account by giving a brief glimpse of my family and background, hoping that the reader, entering my home with me, will be able to blend the ragged edges of this isolated experience into a more full life picture and in doing so will see that it is, in a sense, everybody's story.

I was born and reared in a small Deep South town whose population was about equally Negro and white. There were nine of us who grew up freely in a rambling house of many rooms, surrounded by big lawn, back yard, gardens, fields, and barn. It was the kind of home that gathers memories like dust, a place filled with laughter and play and pain and hurt and ghosts and games. We were given such advantages of schooling, music, and art as were available in the South, and our world was not limited to the South, for travel to far places seemed a simple, natural thing to us, and usually there was one of the family in a remote part of the earth.

We knew we were a respected and important family of this small town but beyond this knowledge we gave little thought to status. Our father made money in lumber and naval stores for the excitement of making and losing it—not for what money can buy nor the security which it sometimes gives. I do not remember at any time wanting "to be rich" nor do I remember that thrift and saving were ideals which our parents considered important enough to urge upon us. Always in the family there was an acceptance of risk, a mild delight even in burning bridges, an expectant "what will happen now!" We were not irresponsible; living according to the pleasure principle was by no means our way of life. On the contrary we were trained to think that each of us should do something that would be of genuine usefulness to the world, and the family thought it right to make sacrifices if necessary, to give each child adequate preparation for this life's work. We were also trained to think learning important, and books, but "bad" books our mother burned. We valued music and art and craftsmanship but it was people and their welfare and religion that were the foci around which our lives seemed naturally to move. Above all else, the important thing was what we "planned to do with our lives." That each of us must do something was as inevitable as breathing for we owed a "debt to society which must be paid." This was a family commandment.

While many of our neighbors spent their energies in counting limbs on the family tree and grafting some on now and then to give symmetry to it, or in reliving the old bitter days of Reconstruction licking scars to cure their vague malaise, or in fighting each battle and turn of battle of that Civil War which has haunted the southern conscience so long, my father was pushing his nine children straight into the future. "You have your heritage," he used to say, "some of it good, some not so good; and as far as I know you had the usual number of grandmothers and grandfathers. Yes, there were slaves, far too many of them in the family, but that was your grandfather's mistake, not yours. The past has been lived. It is gone. The future is yours. What are you going to do with it?" Always he asked this question of his children and sometimes one knew it was but an echo of the old question he had spent his life trying to answer for himself. For always the future held my father's dreams; always there, not in the past, did he expect to find what he had spent his life searching for.

We lived the same segregated life as did other southerners but our parents talked in excessively Christian and democratic terms. We were told ten thousand times that status and money are unimportant (though we were well supplied with both); we were told that "all men are brothers," that we are a part of a democracy and must act like democrats. We were told that the teachings of Jesus are real and important and could be practiced if we tried. We were told also that to be "radical" is bad, silly too; and that one must always conform to the "best behavior" of one's community and make it better if one can. We were taught that we were superior not to people but to hate and resentment, and that no member of the Smith family could stoop so low as to have an enemy. No matter what injury was done us, we must not injure ourselves further by retaliating. That was a family commandment too.

We had family prayers once each day. All of us as children read the Bible in its entirety each year. We memorized hundreds of Bible verses and repeated them at breakfast, and said "sentence prayers" around the family table. God was not someone we met on Sunday but a permanent member of our household. It never occurred to me until I was fourteen or fifteen years old that He did not see every act and thought and chalk up the daily score on eternity's tablets.

Despite the strain of living so intimately with God, the nine of us were strong, healthy, energetic youngsters who filled our days with play and sports and music and books and managed to live much of our lives on the careless level at which young lives should be lived. We had our times of profound anxiety of course, for there were hard lessons to be learned about the body and "bad things" to be learned about sex. Sometimes I have wondered how we ever learned them with a mother so shy with words.

She was a wistful creature who loved beautiful things like lace and sunsets and flowers in a vague inarticulate way, and took good care of her children. We always knew this was not her world but one she accepted under duress. Her private world we rarely entered, though the shadow of it lay at times heavily on our hearts.

Our father owned large business interests, employed hundreds of colored and white laborers, paid them the prevailing low wages, worked them the prevailing long hours, built for them mill towns (Negro and white), built for each group a church, saw to it that religion was supplied free, saw to it that a commissary supplied commodities at a high price, and in general managed his affairs much as ten thousand other southern businessmen manage theirs.

Even now, I can hear him chuckling as he told my mother how he won his fight for Prohibition. The high point of the campaign was election afternoon, when he lined up the entire mill force of several hundred (white and black), passed out a shining silver dollar to each one of them, marched them in and voted liquor out of our county. It was a great day in his life. He had won the Big Game, a game he was always playing with himself against all kinds of evil. It did not occur to him to scrutinize the methods he used. Evil was a word written in capitals; the devil was smart; if you wanted to win you outsmarted him. It was as simple as that. He was a practical, hardheaded, warmhearted, high-spirited man born during the Civil War, earning his living at twelve, struggling through bitter decades of Reconstruction and post-Reconstruction, through populist movement, through the panic of 1893, the panic of 1907, on into the twentieth century accepting his region as he found it, accepting its morals and its mores as he accepted its climate, with only scorn for those who held grudges against the North or pitied themselves or the South; scheming, dreaming, expanding his business, making and losing money, making friends whom he did not lose, with never a doubt that God was always by his side whispering hunches as to how to pull off successful deals. When he lost, it was his own fault. When he won, God had helped him.

Once while we were kneeling at family prayers the fire siren at the mill sounded the alarm that the mill was on fire. My father did not falter from his prayer. The alarm sounded again and again — which signified that the fire was big. With quiet dignity he continued his talk with God while his children sweated and wriggled and hearts beat out of their chests in excitement. He was talking to God — how could he hurry out of the presence of the Most High to save his mills! When he finished his prayer, he quietly stood up, laid the Bible carefully on the table. Then, and only then, did he show an interest in what was happening in Mill Town.

When the telegram was placed in his hands telling of the death of his beloved favorite son, he gathered his children together, knelt down, and in a steady voice which contained no hint of his shattered heart, loyally repeated, "God is our refuge and strength, a very present help in trouble. Therefore will we not fear, though the earth be removed, and though the mountains be carried into the midst of the sea." On his deathbed, he whispered to his old Business Partner in Heaven: "I have fought the fight; I have kept the faith."

AGAINST THIS BACKDROP the drama of the South was played out one day in my life:

A little white girl was found in the colored section of our town, living with a Negro family in a broken-down shack. This family had moved in only a few weeks before and little was known of them. One of the ladies in my mother's club, while driving over to her washerwoman's, saw the child swinging on a gate. The shack, as she said, was hardly more than a pigsty and this white child was living with ignorant and dirty and sick-looking colored folks. "They must have kidnapped her," she told her friends. Genuinely shocked, the clubwomen busied themselves in an attempt to do something, for the child was very white indeed. The strange Negroes were subjected to a grueling questioning and finally grew frightened and evasive and refused to talk at all. This only increased the suspicion of the white group, and the next day the clubwomen, escorted by the town marshal, took the child from her adopted family despite their tears.

She was brought to our home. I do not know why my mother consented to this plan. Perhaps because she loved children and always showed tenderness and concern for them. It was easy for one more to fit into our ample household and Janie was soon at home there. She roomed with me, sat next to me at the table; I found Bible verses for her to say at breakfast; she wore my clothes, played with my dolls and followed me around from morning to night. She was dazed by her new comforts and by the interesting activities of this big lively family; and I was as happily dazed, for her adoration was a new thing to me; and as time passed a quick, childish, and deeply felt bond grew up between us. But a day came when a telephone message was received from a colored orphanage. There was a meeting at our home, whispers, shocked exclamations. All afternoon the ladies went in and out of our house talking to Mother in tones too low for children to hear. And as they passed us at play, most of them looked quickly at Janie and quickly looked away again, though a few stopped and stared at her as if they could not tear their eyes from her face. When my father came home in the evening Mother closed her door against our young ears and talked a long time with him. I heard him laugh, heard Mother say, "But Papa, this is no laughing matter!" And then they were back in the living room with us and my mother was pale and my father was saying, "Well, work it out, honey, as best you can. After all, now that you know, it is pretty simple."

In a little while my mother called my sister and me into her bedroom and told us that in the morning Janie would return to Colored Town. She said Janie was to have the dresses the ladies had given her and a few of my own, and the toys we had shared with her. She asked me if I would like to give Janie one of my dolls. She seemed hurried, though Janie was not to leave until next day. She said, "Why not select it now?" And in dreamlike stiffness I brought in my dolls and chose one for Janie. And then I found it possible to say, "Why? Why is she leaving? She likes us, she hardly knows them. She told me she had been with them only a month."

"Because," Mother said gently, "Janie is a little colored girl."

"But she can't be. She's white!"

"We were mistaken. She is colored."

"But she looks — ."

"She is colored. Please don't argue!"

"What does it mean?" I whispered.

"It means," Mother said slowly, "that she has to live in Colored Town with colored people."

"But why? She lived here three weeks and she doesn't belong to them, she told me she didn't."

"She is a little colored girl."

"But you said yourself that she has nice manners. You said that," I persisted.

"Yes, she is a nice child. But a colored child cannot live in our home."

"Why?"

"You know, dear! You have always known that white and colored people do not live together."

"Can she come over to play?"

"I don't understand."

"I don't either," my young sister quavered.

"You're too young to understand. And don't ask me again, ever again, about this!" Mother's voice was sharp but her face was sad and there was no certainty left there. She hurried out and busied herself in the kitchen and I wandered through that room where I had been born, touching the old familiar things in it, looking at them, trying to find the answer to a question that moaned in my mind like a hurt thing.

And then I went out to Janie, who was waiting, knowing things were happening that concerned her but waiting until they were spoken aloud.

I do not know quite how the words were said but I told her that she was to return in the morning to the little place where she had lived because she was colored and colored children could not live with white children.

"Are you white?" she said.

"I'm white," I replied, "and my sister is white. And you're colored. And white and colored can't live together because my mother says so."

"Why?" Janie whispered.

"Because they can't," I said. But I knew, though I said it firmly, that something was wrong. I knew my father and mother whom I passionately admired had done that which did not fit in with their teachings. I knew they had betrayed something which they held dear. And I was shamed by their failure and frightened, for I felt that they were no longer as powerful as I had thought. There was something Out There that was stronger than they and I could not bear to believe it. I could not confess that my father, who had always solved the family dilemmas easily and with laughter, could not solve this. I knew that my mother who was so good to children did not believe in her heart that she was being good to this child. There was not a word in my mind that said it but my body knew and my glands, and I was filled with anxiety.

But I felt compelled to believe they were right. It was the only way my world could be held together. And, like a slow poison, it began to seep through me: *I was white. She was colored. We must not be together. It was bad to be together. Though you ate with your nurse when you were little, it was bad to eat with any colored person after that. It was bad just as other things were bad that your mother had told you. It was bad that she was to sleep in the room with me that night. It was bad. . . .*

I was suddenly full of guilt. For three weeks I had done things that white children are not supposed to do. And now I knew these things had been wrong.

I went to the piano and began to play, as I had always done when I was in trouble. I tried to play Paderewski's Minuet and as I stumbled through it, the little girl came over and sat on the bench with me. Feeling lonely, lost in these deep currents that were sweeping through our house that night, she crept closer and put her arms around me and I shrank away as if my body had been uncovered. I had not said a word, I did not say one, but she knew, and tears slowly rolled down her little white face.

And then I forgot it. For more than thirty years the experience was wiped out of my memory. But that night, and the weeks it was tied to, worked its way like a splinter, bit by bit down to the hurt places in my memory and festered there. And as I grew older, as more experiences collected around that faithless time, as memories of earlier, more profound hurts crept closer and closer drawn to that night as if to a magnet, I began to know that people who talked of love and Christianity and democracy did not mean it. That is a hard thing for a child to learn. I still admired my parents, there was so much that was strong and vital and sane and good about them and I never forgot this; I stubbornly believed in their sincerity, as I do to this day, and I loved them. Yet in my heart they were under suspicion. Something was wrong.

Something was wrong with a world that tells you that love is good and people are important and then forces you to deny love and to humiliate people. I knew, though I would not for years confess it aloud, that in trying to shut the Negro race away from us, we have shut ourselves away from so many good, creative, honest, deeply human things in life. I began to understand so slowly at first but more and more clearly as the years passed, that the warped, distorted frame we have put around every Negro child from birth is around every white child also. Each is on a different side of the frame but each is pinioned there. And I knew that what cruelly shapes and cripples the personality of one is as cruelly shaping and crippling the personality of the other. I began to see that though we may, as we acquire new knowledge, live through new experiences, examine old memories, gain the strength to tear the frame from us, yet we are stunted and warped and in our lifetime cannot grow straight again any more than can a tree, put in a steel-like twisting frame when young, grow tall and straight when the frame is torn away at maturity.

As I sit here writing, I can almost touch that little town, so close is the memory of it. There it lies, its main street lined with great oaks, heavy with matted moss that swings softly even now as I remember. A little white town rimmed with Negroes, making a deep shadow on the whiteness. There it lies, broken in two by one strange idea. Minds broken in two. Hearts broken. Conscience torn from acts. A culture split in a thousand pieces. That is segregation. I am remembering: a woman in a mental hospital walking four steps out, four steps in, unable to go further because she has drawn an invisible line around her small world and is terrified to take one step beyond it. . . . A man in a Disturbed Ward assigning "places" to the other patients and violently insisting that each stay in his place. . . . A Negro woman saying to me so quietly, "We cannot ride together on the bus, you know. It is not legal to be human in Georgia."

Memory, walking the streets of one's childhood . . . of the town where one was born.

(1949)

Langston Hughes (1902–1967)

Langston Hughes was one of the most prominent literary voices of the Harlem Renaissance. Born James Langston Mercer Hughes on February 1, 1902, in Joplin, Missouri, to James Nathaniel and Carrie Langston Hughes, the author spent part of his childhood in Lawrence, Kansas, with his grandmother, Mary Langston, whose late husband was involved in John Brown's raid on Harpers Ferry in 1859. Hughes also lived in Topeka, Kansas, and Lincoln, Illinois, before moving with his mother and stepfather to Cleveland, Ohio, at the age of fourteen. In Cleveland, Hughes attended Central High School until 1920, when he graduated and traveled to Mexico to visit his father, who financed Hughes's 1921 move to New York, where he attended Columbia University. After studying at Columbia for a year, Hughes left school to work a series of odd jobs, including employment as a crew member of a freighter to West Africa, and as cook and busboy in Paris and Washington, D.C.

While working, Hughes published poetry in literary magazines, including the *Crisis* and *Opportunity*, and after spending six months in Paris, he returned to the United States in 1924. Two years after his return he enrolled at Lincoln University in Pennsylvania, and published his first collection of poetry, *The Weary Blues* (1926), where the poem, "I, Too," appears. His second volume, *Fine Clothes to the Jew* (1927), including the poem "Song for a Dark Girl" (originally published in the *Crisis*), came out the following year. After graduating from Lincoln, Hughes traveled to Haiti, Cuba, and Russia. In 1930 he published his first novel, *Not without Laughter*, and the following year he collaborated with Zora Neale Hurston on a play, *Mule Bone: A Negro Comedy*.

Throughout the 1930s Hughes toured the South giving poetry readings, and in 1932 he traveled to the Soviet Union to film a movie about race relations in the United States — a trip that sparked his interest in Communism, although he never joined the party. In order to gain more artistic freedom, Hughes ended his relationship with Charlotte Mason, a white patron of several Harlem Renaissance writers, and in 1934 his first collection of short stories, *The Ways of White Folks*, was published to critical acclaim. Although he published several collections, including *Laughing to Keep from Crying* (1952), his most popular stories featured the character Jesse B. Simple (or Semple), whom he introduced during a series of World War II columns for the Chicago *Defender*. Simple appears in several volumes, including *Simple Speaks His Mind* (1950), *Simple Takes a Wife* (1953), *Simple Stakes a Claim* (1957), *Simple's Uncle Sam* (1965), and, posthumously, *The Return of Simple* (1994).

While his Simple stories are well-known, Hughes is typically remembered for his poetry. In addition to volumes previously mentioned he also published *Montage of a Dream Deferred* (1951), where the poem "Harlem" appears, and several other collections as well. Much of Hughes's poetry employs dialect; elements from jazz, blues, and be-bop; and other African American folk traditions, such as the dozens. His writing also demonstrates an interest in Africa and African culture and a keen awareness of economic and other forms of political injustice.

In addition to poetry and short fiction, Hughes published two autobiographies: *The Big Sea* (1940), which many scholars cite as an illustration of the social climate during the Harlem Renaissance, and *I Wonder as I Wander* (1956), and he edited the anthologies *The Poetry of the Negro, 1746 – 1949* (1949) and *An African Treasury* (1960). Hughes also wrote plays and musical dramas, including *Little Ham* (1935); *Mulatto* (1935), which played on Broadway; *Front Porch* (1937); *Tambourines to Glory* (1963), which was adapted from his 1958 novel of the same title; and *Street Scene* (1947). Due to his interest in drama, Hughes founded and supported numerous community theaters, including those in New York, Chicago, and Cleveland.

Hughes died of congestive heart failure in New York on May 22, 1967.

I, Too

I, too, sing America.

I am the darker brother.
They send me to eat in the kitchen
When company comes,
But I laugh,
And eat well,
And grow strong.

Tomorrow,
I'll be at the table
When company comes.
Nobody'll dare
Say to me,
"Eat in the kitchen,"
Then.

Besides,
They'll see how beautiful I am
And be ashamed —

I, too, am America.

(1926)

Song for a Dark Girl

Way Down South in Dixie
(Break the heart of me)
They hung my black young lover
To a cross roads tree.

Way Down South in Dixie
(Bruised body high in air)
I asked the white Lord Jesus
What was the use of prayer?

Way Down South in Dixie
(Break the heart of me)
Love is a gnarled shadow
On a gnarled and naked tree.

(1927)

Harlem

What happens to a dream deferred?

Does it dry up
like a raisin in the sun?
Or fester like a sore —
And then run?
Does it stink like rotten meat?
Or crust and sugar over —
like a syrupy sweet?

Maybe it just sags
like a heavy load.

Or does it explode?

(1951)

Erskine Caldwell   (1903–1987)

Erskine Caldwell was a prolific writer who was deeply committed to social causes. Born on December 17, 1903, in Coweta County, Georgia, Erskine Caldwell was the only son of Ira, a Presbyterian minister, and Caroline Caldwell, a schoolteacher. Due to Ira's profession, the family frequently moved, living in Florida, North and South Carolina, Virginia, and Tennessee, although they later returned to Georgia. Throughout his childhood Caldwell worked with his father, providing assistance to the impoverished population of east Georgia — experiences that greatly influenced Caldwell's later writing. After graduating from high school, Caldwell attended Erskine College in South Carolina, the University of Pennsylvania, and the University of Virginia, where he met Helen Lannigan, whom he married in 1925 but later divorced. The couple had three children. While at the University of Virginia, Caldwell published an essay, "The Georgia Cracker" (1926), dealing with several of the themes, particularly those of racism and social injustice, that appear in his later work.

Caldwell's earliest writing was done as a reporter and literary critic for the *Atlanta Journal*, beginning in 1925. After that he worked at multiple jobs and moved often, publishing several short-story collections, including *American Earth* (1931). His best-known works appeared in the early 1930s. *Tobacco Road* (1932) illustrates the effects of poverty on Georgia's tenant farmers during the Great Depression, and *God's Little Acre* (1933) portrays the economic exploitation of industrial workers. The New York Society for the Prevention of Vice attempted to ban *God's Little Acre* for alleged obscenity, but Caldwell took the highly publicized case to court, and the ruling, in favor of Caldwell, became a landmark in First Amendment litigation. From 1938 to 1941 Caldwell worked as a newspaper and radio correspondent in Mexico, Spain, Czechoslovakia, and the Soviet Union, continuing to publish works of fiction and nonfiction.

While gathering material for a book depicting poverty in the rural South, Caldwell and photographer Margaret Bourke-White fell in love and were married in 1939. In addition to that book, *You Have Seen Their Faces* (1937), the couple collaborated on several others, and then later divorced. After another marriage, to June Johnson (with whom he had one child), Caldwell married Virginia Fletcher in 1957. The two traveled throughout the United States, particularly the South, collaborating on several books, including *Deep South* (1968), which explores regional opposition to integration. Caldwell's extensive list of publications includes a short-story collection, *Kneel to the Rising Sun and Other Stories* (1935), and an autobiography, *With All My Might* (1987). Caldwell died on April 11, 1987, of lung cancer.

The theme that most often pervades Caldwell's fiction and nonfiction is that of social injustice, particularly in terms of class, race, and gender. Caldwell's realistic portrayal of social and economic conditions in the South, such as "The End of Christy Tucker," published in *The Nation* in 1940, provoked criticism from his fellow southerners. Viewing Caldwell's depiction of rural poverty in the South as a betrayal, many accused Caldwell of being a traitor to their region. Nonetheless, seven of Caldwell's stories were included in the *Best American Short Stories* anthology series, and four were collected for the annual O. Henry Memorial Award Prize Stories series. With his work translated into over forty different languages, Caldwell became one of the first authors to be published in mass-market paperback editions, but his cooperation with paperback publishing companies negatively affected his position within the literary establishment. In 1984, however, Caldwell was elected to the fifty-chair body of the American Academy of Arts and Letters. His body of work will be remembered for its significant impact upon southern literature in particular.

The End of Christy Tucker

Christy Tucker rode into the plantation town on muleback late in the afternoon, whistling all the way. He had been hewing new pickets for the fence around his house all morning, and he was feeling good for having got so much done. He did not have a chance to go to the plantation town very often, and when he could go he did not lose any time in getting there.

He tied up the mule at the racks behind the row of stores, and the first thing he noticed was the way the other Negroes out there did not seem anxious to speak to him. Christy had been on friendly terms with all the colored people on the plantation ever since he and his wife had moved there three months before, and he could not understand why they pretended not to see him.

He walked slowly down the road toward the plantation office wondering why nobody spoke to him.

After he had gone a little farther, he met Froggy Miller. He caught Froggy by the arm before Froggy could dodge him.

"What's the matter with you folks today?" he said. Froggy Miller lived only a mile from his house in a straight line across the cotton field, and he knew Froggy better than anyone else on the plantation. "What's the matter, anyway, Froggy?"

Froggy, a big six-foot Negro with close-cropped hair, moved away.

He grabbed Froggy by the arm and shook him.

"Now look here!" Christy said, getting worried. "Why do you and everybody else act so strange?"

"Mr. Lee Grossman sent for you, didn't he?" Froggy said.

"Sure, he sent for me," Christy said. "I reckon he wants to talk to me about the farming. But what's that got to do with — "

Before he could finish, Froggy had pulled away from him and walked hurriedly up the road.

Without wasting any more time, Christy ran toward the plantation office to find out what the trouble was.

The plantation bookkeeper, Hendricks, and Lee Crossman's younger brother, Morgan, were sitting in the front office with their feet on the window sill when he ran inside. Hendricks got up when he saw Christy and went through the door into the back room. While the bookkeeper was in the other room, Morgan Crossman stared sullenly at the Negro.

"Come here, you," Hendricks said, coming through the door. Christy turned around and saw Lee Grossman, the owner and boss of the plantation, standing in the doorway.

"Yes, sir," Christy said.

Lee Grossman was dressed in heavy gray riding breeches and tan shirt, and he wore black boots that laced to his knees. He stood aside while Christy walked into the back room, and closed the door on the outside. Christy walked to the middle of the room and stood there waiting for Lee Grossman.

Christy had moved to the Grossman plantation the first of the year, about three months before. It was the first time he had ever been in Georgia, and he had grown to like it better than Alabama, where he had always lived. He and his wife had decided to come to Georgia because they had heard that the land there was better for sharecropping cotton. Christy said he could not be satisfied merely making a living; he wanted to get ahead in life.

Lee Grossman still had not come, and Christy sat down in one of the chairs. He had no more than seated himself when the door opened. He jumped to his feet.

"Howdy, Mr. Lee," he said, smiling. "I've had a good chance to look at the land, and I'd like to be furnished with another mule and a gang plow. I figure I can raise twice as much cotton on that kind of land with a gang plow, because it's about the best I ever saw. There's not a rock or stump on it, and it's as clear of bushes as the palm of my hand. I haven't even found a gully anywhere on it. If you'll furnish me with another mule and a gang plow, I'll raise more cotton for you than any two sharecroppers on your plantation."

Lee Grossman listened until he had finished, and then he slammed the door shut and strode across the room.

"I sent for you, nigger," he said. "You didn't send for me, did you?"

"That's right, Mr. Lee," he said. "You sent for me."

"Then keep your black face shut until I tell you to open it."

"Yes, sir, Mr. Lee," Christy said, backing across the room until he found himself against the wall. Lee Grossman sat down in a chair and glared at him. "Yes, sir, Mr. Lee," Christy said again.

"You're one of these biggity niggers, ain't you?" Lee said. "Where'd you come from, anyway? You ain't a Georgia nigger, are you?"

"No, sir, Mr. Lee," Christy said, shaking his head. "I was born and raised in Alabama."

"Didn't they teach you any better than this in Alabama?"

"Yes, sir, Mr. Lee."

"Then why did you come over here to Georgia and start acting so biggity?"

"I don't know, Mr. Lee."

Christy wiped his face with the palm of his hand and wondered what Lee Grossman was angry with him about. He began to understand why the other Negroes had gone out of their way to keep from talking to him. They knew he had been sent for, and that meant he had done something to displease Lee Grossman. They did not wish to be seen talking to anyone who was in disfavor with the plantation owner and boss.

"Have you got a radio?" Lee asked.

"Yes, sir."

"Where'd you get it?"

"I bought it on time."

"Where'd you get the money to pay on it?"

"I had a little, and my wife raises a few chickens."

"Why didn't you buy it at the plantation store?"

"I made a better bargain at the other place. I got it a little cheaper."

"Niggers who live on my plantation buy what they need at my plantation store," Lee said.

"I didn't want to go into debt to you, Mr. Lee," Christy said. "I wanted to come out ahead when the accounts are settled at the end of the year."

Lee Grossman leaned back in the chair, crossed his legs, and took out his pocketknife. He began cleaning his fingernails.

There was silence in the room for several minutes. Christy leaned against the wall.

"Stand up straight, nigger!" Lee shouted at him.

"Yes, sir," Christy said, jumping erect.

"Did you split up some of my wood to hew pickets for the fence around the house where you live?"

"Yes, sir, Mr. Lee."

"Why didn't you ask me if I wanted you to do it?"

"I figured the fence needed some new pickets to take the place of some that had rotted, and because I'm living in the house I went ahead and did it."

"You act mighty big, don't you?" Lee said. "You act like you own my house and land, don't you? You act like you think you're as good as a white man, don't you?"

"No sir, Mr. Lee," Christy protested. "I don't try to act any of those ways. I just naturally like to hustle and get things done, that's all. I just can't be satisfied unless I'm fixing a fence or cutting wood or picking cotton, or something. I just naturally like to get things done."

"Do you know what we do with biggity niggers like you in Georgia?"

"No, sir."

"We teach them to mind their own business and stay in their place."

Lee Grossman got up and crossed the room to the closet. He jerked the door open and reached inside. When he turned around, he was holding a long leather strap studded with heavy brass brads. He came back across the room, slapping the strap around his boot tops.

"Who told your wife she could raise chickens on my plantation?" he said to Christy.

"Nobody told her, Mr. Lee," Christy said. "We didn't think you'd mind. There's plenty of yard around the house for them, and I built a little hen house."

"Stop arguing with me, nigger!"

"Yes, sir."

"I don't want chickens scratching up crops on this plantation."

"Yes, sir," Christy said.

"Where did you get money to pay on a radio?"

"I snared a few rabbits and skinned them, and then I sold their hides for a little money."

"I don't want no rabbits touched on my plantation," Lee said. He shook out the heavy strap and cracked it against his boots. "Why haven't you got anything down on the books in the plantation store?" Lee asked.

"I just don't like to go into debt," Christy said. "I want to come out ahead when the accounts are settled at the end of the year."

"That's my business whether you come out owing or owed at the end of the year," Lee said.

He pointed to a crack in the floor.

"Take off that shirt and drop your pants and get down on your knees astraddle that crack," the white man said.

"What are you going to do to me, Mr. Lee?"

"I'll show you what I'm going to do," he replied. "Take off that shirt and pants and get down there like I told you."

"Mr. Lee, I can't let you beat me like that. No, sir, Mr. Lee. I can't let you do that to me. I just can't!"

"You black-skinned, back-talking coon, you!" Lee shouted, his face turning crimson with anger.

He struck Christy with the heavy, brass-studded strap. Christy backed out of reach, and when Lee struck him the second time, the Negro caught the strap and held on to it. Lee glared at him at first, and then he tried to jerk it out of his grip.

"Mr. Lee, I haven't done anything except catch a few rabbits and raise a few chickens and things like that," Christy protested. "I didn't mean any harm at all. I thought you'd be pleased if I put some new pickets in your fence."

"Shut your mouth and get that shirt and pants off like I told you," he said, angrier than ever. "And turn that strap loose before I blast it loose from you."

Christy stayed where he was and held on to the strap with all his might. Lee was so angry he could not speak after that. He ran to the closet and got his pistol. He swung around and fired it at Christy three times. Christy released his grip on the strap and sank to the floor.

Lee's brother, Morgan, and the bookkeeper, Hendricks, came running into the back room.

"What happened, Lee?" his brother asked, seeing Christy Tucker lying on the floor.

"That nigger threatened me," Lee said, blowing hard. He walked to the closet and tossed the pistol on the shelf.

"You and Hendricks heard him threaten to kill me. I had to shoot him down to protect my own life."

They left the back room and went into the front office. Several clerks from the plantation store ran in and wanted to know what all the shooting was about.

"Just a biggity nigger," Lee said, washing his hands at the sink. "He was that Alabama nigger that came over here two or three months ago. I sent for him this morning to ask him what he meant by putting new pickets in the fence around his house without asking me first. When I got him in here, he threatened me. He was a bad nigger."

The clerks went back to the plantation store, and Hendricks opened up his books and went to work on the accounts.

"Open up the back door," Lee told his brother, "and let those niggers out in the back see what happens when one of them gets as biggity as that coon from Alabama got."

His brother opened the back door. When he looked outside into the road, there was not a Negro in sight. The only living thing out there was the mule on which Christy Tucker had ridden into town.

(1940)

Richard Wright (1908–1960)

The first child of Nathanial Wright, a sharecropper, and Ella Wilson Wright, Richard Nathanial Wright was born on September 4, 1908, on a plantation outside of Natchez, Mississippi. After the family's 1912 move to Memphis, Wright lived, along with his brother and mother, who was a domestic worker, with a series of relatives in Mississippi, Arkansas, and Tennessee. In 1925 Wright graduated valedictorian from Smith-Robinson Public School in Jackson, Mississippi, and began working odd jobs, earning enough money to return to Memphis. He moved to Chicago's South Side in 1927 to escape the racial oppression and violence of the South and was followed soon after by his mother and brother, whom Wright supported by working as a postal clerk and an insurance agent. In 1932 he joined the John Reed Society, a Communist organization, and began publishing poems and articles in *Left Front* and *New Masses*.

While employed with the Works Progress Administration's Federal Writers' Project, Wright completed several manuscripts, including a series of short stories, *Lawd Today*, published posthumously in 1963. In 1937 Wright moved to New York to edit Harlem's *Daily Worker*—the largest Communist paper in the United States at the time. The following year he published his critically acclaimed collection of short stories, *Uncle Tom's Children*, which won Wright an award from *Story* magazine as well as a Guggenheim Fellowship. Taken from his childhood experiences in Mississippi, the collection expresses Wright's outrage over the persistence of racial violence. Wright married Rose Dhima Meadman in 1939, and the following year his best-selling novel, *Native Son*, appeared and won the National Association for the Advancement of Colored People's

Spingarn Medal. Wright's social protest novel, which secured his reputation as an accomplished author, criticizes racial injustice and capitalism's effects on the black community. After his first marriage ended, Wright married Ellen Poplar in 1941, and the following year their daughter was born.

The first volume of Wright's autobiography, *Black Boy*, was published in 1945. A chapter from the book, reprinted here, details an experience from his Memphis years, where he forged a note so that he could check out books from an all-white library, and the repercussions that a new perspective had on his life. The larger volume chronicles the first nineteen years of Wright's life and was both critically acclaimed and a commercial success. In 1947, after spending several months in France with his family, Wright permanently moved to Paris because of the disparity in how France and the United States treated African Americans. While there, he joined the literary group *Les Temps Modernes* and the Pan-Africanist organization *Presence Africaine*. From 1955 until 1959 Wright lived in Normandy until he returned to Paris. He continued to write and to travel widely in Europe, Asia, and Africa, and after spending time in Ghana, he published a travel memoir, *Black Power* (1954). Wright published three more novels — *The Outsider* (1953), *Savage Holiday* (1954), and *The Long Dream* (1958) — and two works of nonfiction, *The Color Curtain* (1956) and *White Man Listen!* (1957).

Wright spent the last years of his life lecturing throughout Europe, dying in Paris of heart failure on November 28, 1960. A collection of short stories, *Eight Men* (1961), and a novella, *The Man Who Lived Underground* (1971), were published posthumously. Wright was one of the first black artists to earn a living by writing, and he set the standard for social protest fiction in the United States. Realistically portraying the brutal effects of racism in America, his work argues for racial and economic justice. As such, Wright's work provides a link between writers of the Harlem Renaissance and those of the Black Arts movement.

Selection from *Black Boy*

Chapter 13

One morning I arrived early at work and went into the bank lobby where the Negro porter was mopping. I stood at a counter and picked up the Memphis *Commercial Appeal* and began my free reading of the press. I came finally to the editorial page and saw an article dealing with one H. L. Mencken. I knew by hearsay that he was the editor of the *American Mercury*, but aside from that I knew nothing about him. The article was a furious denunciation of Mencken, concluding with one, hot, short sentence: Mencken is a fool.

I wondered what on earth this Mencken had done to call down upon him the scorn of the South. The only people I had ever heard denounced in the South were Negroes, and this man was not a Negro. Then what ideas did Mencken hold that made a newspaper like the *Commercial Appeal* castigate him publicly? Undoubtedly he must be advocating ideas that the South did not like. Were there, then, people other than Negroes who criticized the South? I knew that during the Civil War the South had hated northern whites, but I had not encountered such hate during my life. Knowing no more of Mencken than I did at that moment, I felt a vague sympathy for him. Had not the South, which had assigned me the role of a non-man, cast at him its hardest words?

Now, how could I find out about this Mencken? There was a huge library near the riverfront, but I knew that Negroes were not allowed to patronize its shelves any more than they were the parks and playgrounds of the city. I had gone into the library several times to get books for the white men on the job. Which of them would now help me to get books? And how could I read them without causing concern to the white men with whom I worked? I had so far been successful in hiding my thoughts and feelings from them, but I knew that I would create hostility if I went about this business of reading in a clumsy way.

I weighed the personalities of the men on the job. There was Don, a Jew; but I distrusted him. His position was not much better than mine and I knew that he was uneasy and insecure; he had always treated me in an offhand, bantering way that barely concealed his contempt. I was afraid to ask him to help me to get books; his frantic desire to demonstrate a racial solidarity with the whites against Negroes might make him betray me.

Then how about the boss? No, he was a Baptist and I had the suspicion that he would not be quite able to comprehend why a black boy would want to read Mencken. There were other white men on the job whose attitudes showed clearly that they were Kluxers or sympathizers, and they were out of the question.

There remained only one man whose attitude did not fit into an anti-Negro category, for I had heard the white men refer to him as a "Pope lover." He was an Irish Catholic and was hated by the white Southerners. I knew that he read books, because I had got him volumes from the library several times. Since he, too, was an object of hatred, I felt that he might refuse me but would hardly betray me. I hesitated, weighing and balancing the imponderable realities.

One morning I paused before the Catholic fellow's desk.

"I want to ask you a favor," I whispered to him.

"What is it?"

"I want to read. I can't get books from the library. I wonder if you'd let me use your card?"

He looked at me suspiciously.

"My card is full most of the time," he said.

"I see," I said and waited, posing my question silently.

"You're not trying to get me into trouble, are you, boy?" he asked, staring at me.

"Oh, no, sir."

"What book do you want?"

"A book by H. L. Mencken."

"Which one?"

"I don't know. Has he written more than one?"

"He has written several."

"I didn't know that."

"What makes you want to read Mencken?"

"Oh, I just saw his name in the newspaper," I said.

"It's good of you to want to read," he said. "But you ought to read the right things."

I said nothing. Would he want to supervise my reading?

"Let me think," he said. "I'll figure out something." I turned from him and he called me back. He stared at me quizzically.

"Richard, don't mention this to the other white men," he said.

"I understand," I said. "I won't say a word."

A few days later he called me to him.

"I've got a card in my wife's name," he said. "Here's mine."

"Thank you, sir."

"Do you think you can manage it?"

"I'll manage fine," I said.

"If they suspect you, you'll get in trouble," he said.

"I'll write the same kind of notes to the library that you wrote when you sent me for books," I told him. "I'll sign your name."

He laughed.

"Go ahead. Let me see what you get," he said.

That afternoon I addressed myself to forging a note. Now, what were the names of books written by H. L. Mencken? I did not know any of them. I finally wrote what I thought would be a foolproof note: *Dear Madam: Will you please let this nigger boy* — I used the word "nigger" to make the librarian feel that I could not possibly be the author of the note — *have some books by H. L. Mencken?* I forged the white man's name.

I entered the library as I had always done when on errands for whites, but I felt that I would somehow slip up and betray myself. I doffed my hat, stood a respectful distance from the desk, looked as unbookish as possible, and waited for the white patrons to be taken care of. When the desk was clear of people, I still waited. The white librarian looked at me.

"What do you want, boy?"

As though I did not possess the power of speech, I stepped forward and simply handed her the forged note, not parting my lips.

"What books by Mencken does he want?" she asked.

"I don't know, ma'am," I said, avoiding her eyes.

"Who gave you this card?"

"Mr. Falk," I said.

"Where is he?"

"He's at work, at the M—— Optical Company," I said. "I've been in here for him before."

"I remember," the woman said. "But he never wrote notes like this."

Oh, God, she's suspicious. Perhaps she would not let me have the books? If she had turned her back at that moment, I would have ducked out the door and never gone back. Then I thought of a bold idea.

"You can call him up, ma'am," I said, my heart pounding.

"You're not using these books, are you?" she asked pointedly.

"Oh, no, ma'am. I can't read."

"I don't know what he wants by Mencken," she said under her breath.

I knew now that I had won; she was thinking of other things and the race question had gone out of her mind. She went to the shelves. Once or twice she looked over her shoulder at me, as though she was still doubtful. Finally she came forward with two books in her hand.

"I'm sending him two books," she said. "But tell Mr. Falk to come in next time, or send me the names of the books he wants. I don't know what he wants to read."

I said nothing. She stamped the card and handed me the books. Not daring to glance at them, I went out of the library, fearing that the woman would call me back for further questioning. A block away from the library I opened one of the books and read a title: *A Book of Prefaces*. I was nearing my nineteenth birthday and I did not know how to pronounce the word "preface." I thumbed the pages and saw strange words and strange names. I shook my head, disappointed. I looked at the other book; it was called *Prejudices*. I knew what that word meant; I had heard it all my life. And right off I was on guard against Mencken's books. Why would a man want to call a book *Prejudices*? The word was so stained with all my memories of racial hate that I could not conceive of anybody using it for a title. Perhaps I had made a mistake about Mencken? A man who had prejudices must be wrong.

When I showed the books to Mr. Falk, he looked at me and frowned.

"That librarian might telephone you," I warned him.

"That's all right," he said. "But when you're through reading those books, I want you to tell me what you get out of them."

That night in my rented room, while letting the hot water run over my can of pork and beans in the sink, I opened *A Book of Prefaces* and began to read. I was jarred and shocked by the style, the clear, clean, sweeping sentences. Why did he write like that? And how did one write like that? I pictured the man as a raging demon, slashing with his pen, consumed with hate, denouncing everything American, extolling everything European or German, laughing at the weaknesses of people, mocking God, authority. What was this? I stood up, trying to realize what reality lay behind the meaning of the words . . . Yes, this man was fighting, fighting with words. He was using words as a weapon, using them as one would use a club. Could words be weapons? Well, yes, for here they were. Then, maybe, perhaps, I could use them as a weapon? No. It frightened me. I read on and what amazed me was not what he said, but how on earth anybody had the courage to say it.

Occasionally I glanced up to reassure myself that I was alone in the room. Who were these men about whom Mencken was talking so passionately? Who was Anatole France? Joseph Conrad? Sinclair Lewis, Sherwood Anderson, Dostoevski, George Moore, Gustave Flaubert, Maupassant, Tolstoy, Frank Harris, Mark Twain, Thomas Hardy, Arnold Bennett, Stephen Crane, Zola, Norris, Gorky, Bergson, Ibsen, Balzac, Bernard Shaw, Dumas, Poe, Thomas Mann, O. Henry, Dreiser, H. G. Wells, Gogol, T. S. Eliot, Gide, Baudelaire, Edgar Lee Masters, Stendhal, Turgenev, Huneker, Nietzsche, and scores of others? Were these men real? Did they exist or had they existed? And how did one pronounce their names?

I ran across many words whose meanings I did not know, and I either looked them up in a dictionary or, before I had a chance to do that, encountered the word in a context that made its meaning clear. But what strange world was this? I concluded the book with the conviction that I had somehow overlooked something terribly important in life. I had once tried to write, had once reveled in feeling, had let my crude imagination roam, but the impulse to dream had been slowly beaten out of me by experience. Now it surged up again and I hungered for books, new ways of looking and seeing. It was not a matter of believing or disbelieving what I read, but of feeling something new, of being affected by something that made the look of the world different.

As dawn broke I ate my pork and beans, feeling dopey, sleepy. I went to work, but the mood of the book would not die; it lingered, coloring everything I saw, heard, did. I now felt that I knew what the white men were feeling. Merely because I had read a book that had spoken of how they lived and thought, I identified myself with that book. I felt vaguely guilty. Would I, filled with bookish notions, act in a manner that would make the whites dislike me?

I forged more notes and my trips to the library became frequent. Reading grew into a passion. My first serious novel was Sinclair Lewis's *Main Street*. It made me see my boss, Mr. Gerald, and identify him as an American type. I would smile when I saw him lugging his golf bags into the office. I had always felt a vast distance separating me from the boss, and now I felt closer to him, though still distant. I felt now that I knew him, that I could feel the very limits of his narrow life. And this had happened because I had read a novel about a mythical man called George F. Babbitt.

The plots and stories in the novels did not interest me so much as the point of view revealed. I gave myself over to each novel without reserve, without trying to criticize it; it was enough for me to see and feel something different. And for me, everything was something different. Reading was like a drug, a dope. The novels created moods in which I lived for days. But I could not conquer my sense of guilt, my feeling that the white men around me knew that I was changing, that I had begun to regard them differently.

Whenever I brought a book to the job, I wrapped it in newspaper — a habit that was to persist for years in other cities and under other circumstances. But some of the white men pried into my packages when I was absent and they questioned me.

"Boy, what are you reading those books for?"

"Oh, I don't know, sir."

"That's deep stuff you're reading, boy."

"I'm just killing time, sir."

"You'll addle your brains if you don't watch out." I read Dreiser's *Jennie Gerhardt* and *Sister Carrie* and they revived in me a vivid sense of my mother's suffering; I was overwhelmed. I grew silent, wondering about the life around me. It would have been impossible for me to have told anyone what I derived from these novels, for it was nothing less than a sense of life itself. All my life had shaped me for the realism, the naturalism of the modern novel, and I could not read enough of them.

Steeped in new moods and ideas, I bought a ream of paper and tried to write; but nothing would come, or what did come was flat beyond telling. I discovered that more than desire and feeling were necessary to write and I dropped the idea. Yet I still wondered how it was possible to know people sufficiently to write about them? Could I ever learn about life and people? To me, with my vast ignorance, my Jim Crow station in life, it seemed a task impossible of achievement. I now knew what being a Negro meant. I could endure the hunger. I had learned to live with hate. But to feel that there were feelings denied me, that the very breath of life itself was beyond my reach, that more than anything else hurt, wounded me. I had a new hunger.

In buoying me up, reading also cast me down, made me see what was possible, what I had missed. My tension returned, new, terrible, bitter, surging, almost too great to be contained. I no longer *felt* that the world about me was hostile, killing; I *knew* it. A million times I asked myself what I could do to save myself, and there were no answers. I seemed forever condemned, ringed by walls.

I did not discuss my reading with Mr. Falk, who had lent me his library card; it would have meant talking about myself and that would have been too painful. I smiled each day, fighting desperately to maintain my old behavior, to keep my disposition seemingly sunny. But some of the white men discerned that I had begun to brood.

"Wake up there, boy!" Mr. Olin said one day.

"Sir!" I answered for the lack of a better word.

"You act like you've stolen something," he said. I laughed in the way I knew he expected me to laugh, but I resolved to be more conscious of myself, to watch my every act, to guard and hide the new knowledge that was dawning within me.

If I went north, would it be possible for me to build a new life then? But how could a man build a life upon vague, unformed yearnings? I wanted to write and I did not even know the English language. I bought English grammars and found them dull. I felt that I was getting a better sense of the language from novels than from grammars. I read hard, discarding a writer as soon as I felt that I had grasped his point of view. At night the printed page stood before my eyes in sleep.

Mrs. Moss, my landlady, asked me one Sunday morning:

"Son, what is this you keep on reading?"

"Oh, nothing. Just novels."

"What you get out of 'em?"

"I'm just killing time," I said.

"I hope you know your own mind," she said in a tone which implied that she doubted if I had a mind.

I knew of no Negroes who read the books I liked and I wondered if any Negroes ever thought of them. I knew that there were Negro doctors, lawyers, newspapermen, but I never saw any of them. When I read a Negro newspaper I never caught the faintest echo of my preoccupation in its pages. I felt trapped and occasionally, for a few days, I would stop reading. But a vague hunger would come over me for books, books that opened up new avenues of feeling and seeing, and again I would forge another note to the white librarian. Again I would read and wonder as only the naïve and unlettered can read and wonder, feeling that I carried a secret, criminal burden about with me each day.

That winter my mother and brother came and we set up housekeeping, buying furniture on the installment plan, being cheated and yet knowing no way to avoid it. I began to eat warm food and to my surprise found that regular meals enabled me to read faster. I may have lived through many illnesses and survived them, never suspecting that I was ill. My brother obtained a job and we began to save toward the trip north, plotting our time, setting tentative dates for departure. I told none of the white men on the job that I was planning to go north; I knew that the moment they felt I was thinking of the North they would change toward me. It would have made them feel that I did not like the life I was living, and because my life was completely conditioned by what they said or did, it would have been tantamount to challenging them.

I could calculate my chances for life in the South as a Negro fairly clearly now.

I could fight the southern whites by organizing with other Negroes, as my grandfather had done. But I knew that I could never win that way; there were many whites and there were but few blacks. They were strong and we were weak. Outright black rebellion could never win. If I fought openly I would die and I did not want to die. News of lynchings were frequent.

I could submit and live the life of a genial slave, but that was impossible. All of my life had shaped me to live by my own feelings and thoughts. I could make up to Bess and marry her and inherit the house. But that, too, would be the life of a slave; if I did that, I would crush to death something within me, and I would hate myself as much as I knew the whites already hated those who had submitted. Neither could I ever willingly present myself to be kicked, as Shorty had done. I would rather have died than do that.

I could drain off my restlessness by fighting with Shorty and Harrison. I had seen many Negroes solve the problem of being black by transferring their hatred of themselves to others with a black skin and fighting them. I would have to be cold to do that, and I was not cold and I could never be.

I could, of course, forget what I had read, thrust the whites out of my mind, forget them; and find release from anxiety and longing in sex and alcohol. But the memory of how my father had conducted himself made that course repugnant. If I did not want others to violate my life, how could I voluntarily violate it myself?

I had no hope whatever of being a professional man. Not only had I been so conditioned that I did not desire it, but the fulfillment of such an ambition was beyond my capabilities. Well-to-do Negroes lived in a world that was almost as alien to me as the world inhabited by whites.

What, then, was there? I held my life in my mind, in my consciousness each day, feeling at times that I would stumble and drop it, spill it forever. My reading had created a vast sense of distance between me and the world in which I lived and tried to make a living, and that sense of distance was increasing each day. My days and nights were one long, quiet, continuously contained dream of terror, tension and anxiety. I wondered how long I could bear it.

(1945)

Ralph Ellison (1914–1994)

alph Waldo Ellison was born on March 1, 1914, in Oklahoma City, Oklahoma, to Ida and Lewis Alfred Ellison, who moved from their native South Carolina to provide a less oppressive environment for Ralph and his brother. Ellison attended Frederick Douglass High School before enrolling at Tuskegee Institute in 1933 to study music composition and literature. After financial difficulties forced Ellison to leave school in 1936, he moved to

New York, where he befriended Richard Wright. Ellison worked for the Works Progress Administration compiling African American folklore, edited the *Negro Quarterly*, and served in the U.S. Merchant Marine before returning to New York. In 1946 he married Fanny McConnell.

Ellison received a Rosenwald Fellowship to work on his first novel, *Invisible Man* (1952), but during the seven years he spent writing the novel, he published reviews and short stories to support himself and his wife. The novel, which won the National Book Award in 1953 and garnered international acclaim, follows a young African American man through his struggles with identity, racism, and alienation. A classic of modernist experimentation, it contains elements of a protest novel while also satirizing various entities involved in the civil rights struggle. The chapter included here, "The Battle Royal," published separately as a short story in 1947, reveals the novel's protagonist at the early stages of his journey, when he is still naïve about what lies before him. In addition to fiction, Ellison published two collections of essays, *Shadow and Act* (1964) and *Going to the Territory* (1986).

Ellison lectured throughout the United States and Europe and taught at a number of institutions of higher education, including New York University, Rutgers University, the University of Chicago, and Yale. He also served as an editorial board member for *American Scholar* and as a trustee for the John F. Kennedy Center for the Performing Arts. Ellison died of cancer on April 16, 1994, in New York City. A collection of short stories, *Flying Home and Other Stories* (1996), and a second novel, *Juneteenth* (1999), were published posthumously. In 2003 the city of New York unveiled a monument honoring Ellison, a writer who was important to civil rights literature and to the development of literary modernism worldwide.

Selection from *Invisible Man*

Chapter 1, The Battle Royal

It goes a long way back, some twenty years. All my life I had been looking for something, and everywhere I turned someone tried to tell me what it was. I accepted their answers too, though they were often in contradiction and even self-contradictory. I was naive. I was looking for myself and asking everyone except myself questions which I, and only I, could answer. It took me a long time and much painful boomeranging of my expectations to achieve a realization everyone else appears to have been born with: That I am nobody but myself. But first I had to discover that I am an invisible man!

And yet I am no freak of nature, nor of history. I was in the cards, other things having been equal (or unequal) eighty-five years ago. I am not ashamed of my grandparents for having been slaves. I am only ashamed of myself for having at one time been ashamed. About eighty-five years ago they were told that they were free, united with others of our country in everything pertaining to the common good, and, in everything social, separate like the fingers of the hand. And they believed it. They exulted in it. They stayed in their place, worked hard, and brought up my father to do the same. But my grandfather is the one. He was an odd old guy, my grandfather, and I am told I take after him. It was he who caused the trouble. On his deathbed he called my father to him and said, "Son, after I'm gone I want you to keep up the good fight. I never told you, but our life is a war and I have been a traitor all my born days, a spy in the enemy's country ever since I give up my gun back in the Reconstruction. Live with your head in the lion's mouth. I want you to overcome 'em with yeses, undermine 'em with grins, agree 'em to death and destruction, let 'em swoller you till they vomit or bust wide open." They thought the old man had gone out of his mind. He had been the meekest of men. The younger children were rushed from the room, the shades drawn and the flame of the lamp turned so low that it sputtered on the wick like the old man's breathing. "Learn it to the younguns," he whispered fiercely; then he died.

But my folks were more alarmed over his last words than over his dying. It was as though he had not died at all, his words caused so much anxiety. I was warned emphatically to forget what he had said and, indeed, this is the first time it has been mentioned outside the family circle. It had a tremendous effect upon me, however. I could never be sure of what he meant. Grandfather had been a quiet old man who never made any trouble, yet on his deathbed he had called himself a traitor and a spy, and he had spoken of his meekness as a dangerous activity. It became a constant puzzle which lay unanswered in the back of my mind. And whenever things went well for me I remembered my grandfather and felt guilty and uncomfortable. It was as though I was carrying out his advice in spite of myself. And to make it worse, everyone loved me for it. I was praised by the most lily-white men of the town. I was considered an example of desirable conduct—just as my grandfather had been. And what puzzled me was that the old man had defined it as treachery. When I was praised for my conduct I felt a guilt that in some way I was doing something that was really against the wishes of the white folks, that if they had understood they would have desired me to act just the opposite, that I should have been sulky and mean, and that that really would have been what they wanted, even though they were fooled and thought they wanted me to act as I did. It made me afraid that some day they would look upon me as a traitor and I would be lost. Still I was more afraid to act any other way because they didn't like that at all. The old man's words were like a curse. On my graduation day I delivered an oration in which I showed that humility was the secret, indeed, the very essence of progress. (Not that I believed this—how could I, remembering my grandfather?—I only believed that it worked.) It was a great success. Everyone praised me and I was invited to give the speech at a gathering of the town's leading white citizens. It was a triumph for our whole community.

It was in the main ballroom of the leading hotel. When I got there I discovered that it was on the occasion of a smoker, and I was told that since I was to be there anyway I might as well take part in the battle royal to be fought by some of my schoolmates as part of the entertainment. The battle royal came first.

All of the town's big shots were there in their tuxedoes, wolfing down the buffet foods, drinking beer and whiskey and smoking black cigars. It was a large room with a high ceiling. Chairs were arranged in neat rows around three sides of a portable boxing ring. The fourth side was clear, revealing a gleaming space of polished floor. I had some misgivings over the battle royal, by the way. Not from a distaste for fighting, but because I didn't care too much for the other fellows who were to take part. They were tough guys who seemed to have no grandfather's curse worrying their minds. No one could mistake their toughness. And besides, I suspected that fighting a battle royal might detract from the dignity of my speech. In those pre-invisible days I visualized myself as a potential Booker T. Washington. But the other fellows didn't care too much for me either, and there were nine of them. I felt superior to them in my way, and I didn't like the manner in which we were all crowded together into the servants' elevator. Nor did they like my being there. In fact, as the warmly lighted floors flashed past the elevator we had words over the fact that I, by taking part in the fight, had knocked one of their friends out of a night's work.

We were led out of the elevator through a rococo hall into an anteroom and told to get into our fighting togs. Each of us was issued a pair of boxing gloves and ushered out into the big mirrored hall, which we entered looking cautiously about us and whispering, lest we might accidentally be heard above the noise of the room. It was foggy with cigar smoke. And already the whiskey was taking effect. I was shocked to see some of the most important men of the town quite tipsy. They were all there — bankers, lawyers, judges, doctors, fire chiefs, teachers, merchants. Even one of the more fashionable pastors. Something we could not see was going on up front. A clarinet was vibrating sensuously and the men were standing up and moving eagerly forward, We were a small tight group, clustered together, our bare upper bodies touching and shining with anticipatory sweat; while up front the big shots were becoming increasingly excited over something we still could not see. Suddenly I heard the school superintendent, who had told me to come, yell, "Bring up the shines, gentlemen! Bring up the little shines!"

We were rushed up to the front of the ballroom, where it smelled even more strongly of tobacco and whiskey. Then we were pushed into place. I almost wet my pants. A sea of faces, some hostile, some amused, ringed around us, and in the center, facing us, stood a magnificent blonde — stark naked. There was dead

silence. I felt a blast of cold air chill me. I tried to back away, but they were behind me and around me. Some of the boys stood with lowered heads, trembling.
I felt a wave of irrational guilt and fear. My teeth chattered, my skin turned to
goose flesh, my knees knocked. Yet I was strongly attracted and looked in spite
of myself. Had the price of looking been blindness, I would have looked. The
hair was yellow like that of a circus kewpie doll, the face heavily powdered and
rouged, as though to form an abstract mask, the eyes hollow and smeared a
cool blue, the color of a baboon's butt. I felt a desire to spit upon her as my eyes
brushed slowly over her body. Her breasts were firm and round as the domes
of East Indian temples, and I stood so close as to see the fine skin texture and
beads of pearly perspiration glistening like dew around the pink and erected
buds of her nipples. I wanted at one and the same time to run from the room,
to sink through the floor, or go to her and cover her from my eyes and the eyes
of the others with my body; to feel the soft thighs, to caress her and destroy her,
to love her and murder her, to hide from her, and yet to stroke where below the
small American flag tattooed upon her belly her thighs formed a capital V. I had
a notion that of all in the room she saw only me with her impersonal eyes.

And then she began to dance, a slow sensuous movement; the smoke of a
hundred cigars clinging to her like the thinnest of veils. She seemed like a fair
bird-girl girdled in veils calling to me from the angry surface of some gray and
threatening sea. I was transported. Then I became aware of the clarinet playing
and the big shots yelling at us. Some threatened us if we looked and others if
we did not. On my right I saw one boy faint. And now a man grabbed a silver
pitcher from a table and stepped close as he dashed ice water upon him and
stood him up and forced two of us to support him as his head hung and moans
issued from his thick bluish lips. Another boy began to plead to go home. He
was the largest of the group, wearing dark red fighting trunks much too small
to conceal the erection which projected from him as though in answer to the
insinuating low-registered moaning of the clarinet. He tried to hide himself
with his boxing gloves.

And all the while the blonde continued dancing, smiling faintly at the big
shots who watched her with fascination, and faintly smiling at our fear. I noticed a certain merchant who followed her hungrily, his lips loose and drooling.
He was a large man who wore diamond studs in a shirtfront which swelled with
the ample paunch underneath, and each time the blonde swayed her undulating
hips he ran his hand through the thin hair of his bald head and, with his arms
upheld, his posture clumsy like that of an intoxicated panda, wound his belly in
a slow and obscene grind. This creature was completely hypnotized. The music
had quickened. As the dancer flung herself about with a detached expression on
her face, the men began reaching out to touch her. I could see their beefy fingers
sink into the soft flesh. Some of the others tried to stop them and she began to
move around the floor in graceful circles, as they gave chase, slipping and slid-

ing over the polished floor. It was mad. Chairs went crashing, drinks were spilt, as they ran laughing and howling after her. They caught her just as she reached a door, raised her from the floor, and tossed her as college boys are tossed at a hazing, and above her red, fixed-smiling lips I saw the terror and disgust in her eyes, almost like my own terror and that which I saw in some of the other boys. As I watched, they tossed her twice and her soft breasts seemed to flatten against the air and her legs flung wildly as she spun. Some of the more sober ones helped her to escape. And I started off the floor, heading for the anteroom with the rest of the boys.

Some were still crying and in hysteria. But as we tried to leave we were stopped and ordered to get into the ring. There was nothing to do but what we were told. All ten of us climbed under the ropes and allowed ourselves to be blindfolded with broad bands of white cloth. One of the men seemed to feel a bit sympathetic and tried to cheer us up as we stood with our backs against the ropes. Some of us tried to grin. "See that boy over there?" one of the men said. "I want you to run across at the bell and give it to him right in the belly. If you don't get him, I'm going to get you. I don't like his looks." Each of us was told the same. The blindfolds were put on. Yet even then I had been going over my speech. In my mind each word was as bright as flame. I felt the cloth pressed into place, and frowned so that it would be loosened when I relaxed.

But now I felt a sudden fit of blind terror. I was unused to darkness. It was as though I had suddenly found myself in a dark room filled with poisonous cottonmouths. I could hear the bleary voices yelling insistently for the battle royal to begin.

"Get going in there!"

"Let me at that big nigger!"

I strained to pick up the school superintendent's voice, as though to squeeze some security out of that slightly more familiar sound.

"Let me at those black sonsabitches!" someone yelled.

"No, Jackson, no!" another voice yelled. "Here, somebody, help me hold Jack."

"I want to get at that ginger-colored nigger. Tear him limb from limb," the first voice yelled.

I stood against the ropes trembling. For in those days I was what they called ginger-colored, and he sounded as though he might crunch me between his teeth like a crisp ginger cookie.

Quite a struggle was going on. Chairs were being kicked about and I could hear voices grunting as with a terrific effort. I wanted to see, to see more desperately than ever before. But the blindfold was tight as a thick skin-puckering scab and when I raised my gloved hands to push the layers of white aside a voice yelled, "Oh, no you don't, black bastard! Leave that alone!"

"Ring the bell before Jackson kills him a coon!" someone boomed in the sudden silence. And I heard the bell clang and the sound of the feet scuffling forward.

A glove smacked against my head. I pivoted, striking out stiffly as someone went past, and felt the jar ripple along the length of my arm to my shoulder. Then it seemed as though all nine of the boys had turned upon me at once. Blows pounded me from all sides while I struck out as best I could. So many blows landed upon me that I wondered if I were not the only blindfolded fighter in the ring, or if the man called Jackson hadn't succeeded in getting me after all.

Blindfolded, I could no longer control my motions. I had no dignity. I stumbled about like a baby or a drunken man. The smoke had become thicker and with each new blow it seemed to sear and further restrict my lungs. My saliva became like hot bitter glue. A glove connected with my head, filling my mouth with warm blood. It was everywhere. I could not tell if the moisture I felt upon my body was sweat or blood. A blow landed hard against the nape of my neck. I felt myself going over, my head hitting the floor. Streaks of blue light filled the black world behind the blindfold. I lay prone, pretending that I was knocked out, but felt myself seized by hands and yanked to my feet. "Get going, black boy! Mix it up!" My arms were like lead, my head smarting from blows. I managed to feel my way to the ropes and held on, trying to catch my breath. A glove landed in my mid-section and I went over again, feeling as though the smoke had become a knife jabbed into my guts. Pushed this way and that by the legs milling around me, I finally pulled erect and discovered that I could see the black, sweat-washed forms weaving in the smoky-blue atmosphere like drunken dancers weaving to the rapid drumlike thuds of blows.

Everyone fought hysterically. It was complete anarchy. Everybody fought everybody else. No group fought together for long. Two, three, four, fought one, then turned to fight each other, were themselves attacked. Blows landed below the belt and in the kidney, with the gloves open as well as closed, and with my eye partly opened now there was not so much terror. I moved carefully, avoiding blows, although not too many to attract attention, fighting from group to group. The boys groped about like blind, cautious crabs crouching to protect their mid-sections, their heads pulled in short against their shoulders, their arms stretched nervously before them, with their fists testing the smoke-filled air like the knobbed feelers of hypersensitive snails. In one corner I glimpsed a boy violently punching the air and heard him scream in pain as he smashed his hand against a ring post. For a second I saw him bent over holding his hand, then going down as a blow caught his unprotected head. I played one group against the other, slipping in and throwing a punch then stepping out of range while pushing the others into the melee to take the blows blindly aimed at me. The smoke was agonizing and there were no rounds, no bells at three-minute intervals to relieve our exhaustion. The room spun round me, a swirl of lights, smoke, sweating bodies surrounded by tense white faces. I bled from both nose and mouth, the blood spattering upon my chest.

The men kept yelling, "Slug him, black boy! Knock his guts out!"

"Uppercut him! Kill him! Kill that big boy!"

Taking a fake fall, I saw a boy going down heavily beside me as though we were felled by a single blow, saw a sneaker-clad foot shoot into his groin as the two who had knocked him down stumbled upon him. I rolled out of range, feeling a twinge of nausea.

The harder we fought the more threatening the men became. And yet, I had begun to worry about my speech again. How would it go? Would they recognize my ability? What would they give me?

I was fighting automatically when suddenly I noticed that one after another of the boys was leaving the ring. I was surprised, filled with panic, as though I had been left alone with an unknown danger. Then I understood. The boys had arranged it among themselves. It was the custom for the two men left in the ring to slug it out for the winner's prize. I discovered this too late. When the bell sounded two men in tuxedoes leaped into the ring and removed the blindfold. I found myself facing Tatlock, the biggest of the gang. I felt sick at my stomach. Hardly had the bell stopped ringing in my ears than it clanged again and I saw him moving swiftly toward me. Thinking of nothing else to do I hit him smash on the nose. He kept coming, bringing the rank sharp violence of stale sweat. His face was a black blank of a face, only his eyes alive — with hate of me and aglow with a feverish terror from what had happened to us all. I became anxious. I wanted to deliver my speech and he came at me as though he meant to beat it out of me. I smashed him again and again, taking his blows as they came. Then on a sudden impulse I struck him lightly and as we clinched, I whispered, "Fake like I knocked you out, you can have the prize."

"I'll break your behind," he whispered hoarsely.

"For *them?*"

"For *me,* sonofabitch!"

They were yelling for us to break it up and Tatlock spun me half around with a blow, and as a joggled camera sweeps in a reeling scene, I saw the howling red faces crouching tense beneath the cloud of blue-gray smoke. For a moment the world wavered, unraveled, flowed, then my head cleared and Tatlock bounced before me. That fluttering shadow before my eyes was his jabbing left hand. Then falling forward, my head against his damp shoulder, I whispered,

"I'll make it five dollars more."

"Go to hell!"

But his muscles relaxed a trifle beneath my pressure and I breathed, "Seven?"

"Give it to your ma," he said, ripping me beneath the heart.

And while I still held him I butted him and moved away. I felt myself bombarded with punches. I fought back with hopeless desperation. I wanted to deliver my speech more than anything else in the world, because I felt that only these men could judge truly my ability, and now this stupid clown was ruining my chances. I began fighting carefully now, moving in to punch him and out again with my greater speed. A lucky blow to his chin and I had him going too — until I heard a loud voice yell, "I got my money on the big boy."

Hearing this, I almost dropped my guard. I was confused.

Should I try to win against the voice out there? Would not this go against my speech, and was not this a moment for humility, for nonresistance? A blow to my head as I danced about sent my right eye popping like a jack-in-the-box and settled my dilemma. The room went red as I fell. It was a dream fall, my body languid and fastidious as to where to land, until the floor became impatient and smashed up to meet me. A moment later I came to. An hypnotic voice said FIVE emphatically. And I lay there, hazily watching a dark red spot of my own blood shaping itself into a butterfly, glistening and soaking into the soiled gray world of the canvas.

When the voice drawled TEN I was lifted up and dragged to a chair. I sat dazed. My eye pained and swelled with each throb of my pounding heart and I wondered if now I would be allowed to speak. I was wringing wet, my mouth still bleeding. We were grouped along the wall now. The other boys ignored me as they congratulated Tatlock and speculated as to how much they would be paid. One boy whimpered over his smashed hand. Looking up front, I saw attendants in white jackets rolling the portable ring away and placing a small square rug in the vacant space surrounded by chairs. Perhaps, I thought, I will stand on the rug to deliver my speech.

Then the M.C. called to us, "Come on up here boys and get your money."

We ran forward to where the men laughed and talked in their chairs, waiting. Everyone seemed friendly now.

"There it is on the rug," the man said. I saw the rug covered with coins of all dimensions and a few crumpled bills. But what excited me, scattered here and there, were the gold pieces.

"Boys, it's all yours," the man said. "You get all you grab."

"That's right, Sambo," a blond man said, winking at me confidentially.

I trembled with excitement, forgetting my pain. I would get the gold and the bills, I thought. I would use both hands. I would throw my body against the boys nearest me to block them from the gold.

"Get down around the rug now," the man commanded, "and don't anyone touch it until I give the signal."

"This ought to be good," I heard.

As told, we got around the square rug on our knees. Slowly the man raised his freckled hand as we followed it upward with our eyes.

I heard, "These niggers look like they're about to pray."

Then, "Ready," the man said, "Go."

I lunged for a yellow coin lying on the blue design of the carpet, touching it and sending a surprised shriek to join those rising around me. I tried frantically to remove my hand but could not let go. A hot, violent force tore through my body, shaking me like a wet rat. The rug was electrified. The hair bristled up on my head as I shook myself free. My muscles jumped, my nerves jangled, writhed. But I saw that this was not stopping the other boys. Laughing in fear and embarrassment, some were holding back and scooping up the coins knocked off by the painful contortions of the others. The men roared above us as we struggled.

"Pick it up, goddamnit, pick it up!" someone called like a bass-voiced parrot. "Go on, get it!"

I crawled rapidly around the floor, picking up the coins, trying to avoid the coppers and to get greenbacks and the gold. Ignoring the shock by laughing, as I brushed the coins off quickly, I discovered that I could contain the electricity —a contradiction, but it works. Then the men began to push us onto the rug. Laughing embarrassedly, we struggled out of their hands and kept after the coins. We were all wet and slippery and hard to hold. Suddenly I saw a boy lifted into the air, glistening with sweat like a circus seal, and dropped, his wet back landing flush upon the charged rug, heard him yell and saw him literally dance upon his back, his elbows beating a frenzied tattoo upon the floor, his muscles twitching like the flesh of a horse stung by many flies. When he finally rolled off, his face was gray and no one stopped him when he ran from the floor amid booming laughter.

"Get the money," the M.C. called. "That's good hard American cash!"

And we snatched and grabbed, snatched and grabbed. I was careful not to come too close to the rug now, and when I felt the hot whiskey breath descend upon me like a cloud of foul air I reached out and grabbed the leg of a chair. It was occupied and I held on desperately.

"Leggo, nigger! Leggo!"

The huge face wavered down to mine as he tried to push me free. But my body was slippery and he was too drunk. It was Mr. Colcord, who owned a chain of movie houses and "entertainment palaces." Each time he grabbed me I slipped out of his hands. It became a real struggle. I feared the rug more than I did the drunk, so I held on, surprising myself for a moment by trying to topple him upon the rug. It was such an enormous idea that I found myself actually carrying it out. I tried not to be obvious, yet when I grabbed his leg, trying to tumble him out of the chair, he raised up roaring with laughter, and, looking at me with soberness dead in the eye, kicked me viciously in the chest. The chair leg flew out of my hand and I felt myself going and rolled. It was as though I had rolled through a bed of hot coals. It seemed a whole century would pass before

I would roll free, a century in which I was seared through the deepest levels of my body to the fearful breath within me and the breath seared and heated to the point of explosion. It'll all be over in a flash, I thought as I rolled clear. It'll all be over in a flash.

But not yet, the men on the other side were waiting, red faces swollen as though from apoplexy as they bent forward in their chairs. Seeing their fingers coming toward me I rolled away as a fumbled football rolls off the receiver's fingertips, back into the coals. That time I luckily sent the rug sliding out of place and heard the coins ringing against the floor and the boys scuffling to pick them up and the M.C. calling, "All right, boys, that's all. Go get dressed and get your money."

I was limp as a dish rag. My back felt as though it had been beaten with wires.

When we had dressed the M.C. came in and gave us each five dollars, except Tatlock, who got ten for being last in the ring. Then he told us to leave. I was not to get a chance to deliver my speech, I thought. I was going out into the dim alley in despair when I was stopped and told to go back. I returned to the ballroom, where the men were pushing back their chairs and gathering in groups to talk.

The M.C. knocked on a table for quiet. "Gentlemen," he said, "we almost forgot an important part of the program. A most serious part, gentlemen. This boy was brought here to deliver a speech which he made at his graduation yesterday."

"Bravo!"

"I'm told that he is the smartest boy we've got out there in Greenwood. I'm told that he knows more big words than a pocket-sized dictionary."

Much applause and laughter.

"So now, gentlemen, I want you to give him your attention."

There was still laughter as I faced them, my mouth dry, my eye throbbing. I began slowly, but evidently my throat was tense, because they began shouting, "Louder! Louder!"

"We of the younger generation extol the wisdom of that great leader and educator," I shouted, "who first spoke these flaming words of wisdom: 'A ship lost at sea for many days suddenly sighted a friendly vessel. From the mast of the unfortunate vessel was seen a signal: "Water, water; we die of thirst!" The answer from the friendly vessel came back: "Cast down your bucket where you are." The captain of the distressed vessel, at last heeding the injunction, cast down his bucket, and it came up full of fresh sparkling water from the mouth of the Amazon River.' And like him I say, and in his words, 'To those of my race who depend upon bettering their condition in a foreign land, or who underestimate the importance of cultivating friendly relations with the Southern white man, who is his next-door neighbor, I would say: "Cast down your bucket where you are" — cast it down in making friends in every manly way of the people of all races by whom we are surrounded.'"

I spoke automatically and with such fervor that I did not realize that the men were still talking and laughing until my dry mouth, filling up with blood from the cut, almost strangled me. I coughed, wanting to stop and go to one of the tall brass, sand-filled spittoons to relieve myself, but a few of the men, especially the superintendent, were listening and I was afraid. So I gulped it down, blood, saliva and all, and continued. (What powers of endurance I had during those days! What enthusiasm! What a belief in the rightness of things!) I spoke even louder in spite of the pain. But still they talked and still they laughed, as though deaf with cotton in dirty ears. So I spoke with greater emotional emphasis. I closed my ears and swallowed blood until I was nauseated. The speech seemed a hundred times as long as before, but I could not leave out a single word. All had to be said, each memorized nuance considered, rendered. Nor was that all. Whenever I uttered a word of three or more syllables a group of voices would yell for me to repeat it. I used the phrase "social responsibility" and they yelled:

"What's that word you say, boy?" "Social responsibility," I said. "What?"

"Social."

"Louder."

". . . responsibility."

"More!"

"Respon — "

"Repeat!"

" — sibility."

The room filled with the uproar of laughter until, no doubt distracted by having to gulp down my blood, I made a mistake and yelled a phrase I had often seen denounced in newspaper editorials, heard debated in private.

"Social"

"What?" they yelled.

"Equality."

The laughter hung smokelike in the sudden stillness. I opened my eyes, puzzled. Sounds of displeasure filled the room. The M.C. rushed forward. They shouted hostile phrases at me. But I did not understand

A small dry mustached man in the front row blared out, "Say that slowly, son!"

"What, sir?"

"What you just said!"

"Social responsibility, sir," I said.

"You weren't being smart, were you, boy?" he said, not unkindly.

"No, sir!"

"You sure that about 'equality' was a mistake?"

"Oh, yes, sir," I said. "I was swallowing blood."

"Well, you had better speak more slowly so we can understand. We mean to do right by you, but you've got to know your place at all times. All right, now, go on with your speech."

I was afraid. I wanted to leave but I wanted also to speak and I was afraid they'd snatch me down.

"Thank you, sir," I said, beginning where I had left off, and having them ignore me as before.

Yet when I finished there was a thunderous applause. I was surprised to see the superintendent come forth with a package wrapped in white tissue paper, and, gesturing for quiet, address the men.

"Gentlemen, you see that I did not overpraise this boy. He makes a good speech and some day he'll lead his people in the proper paths. And I don't have to tell you that that is important in these days and times. This is a good, smart boy, and so to encourage him in the right direction, in the name of the Board of Education I wish to present him a prize in the form of this . . ."

He paused, removing the tissue paper and revealing a gleaming calfskin brief case.

". . . in the form of this first-class article from Shad Whitmore's shop."

"Boy," he said, addressing me, "take this prize and keep it well. Consider it a badge of office. Prize it. Keep developing as you are and some day it will be filled with important papers that will help shape the destiny of your people."

I was so moved that I could hardly express my thanks. A rope of bloody saliva forming a shape like an undiscovered continent drooled upon the leather and I wiped it quickly away. I felt an importance that I had never dreamed.

"Open it and see what's inside," I was told.

My fingers a-tremble, I complied, smelling the fresh leather and finding an official-looking document inside. It was a scholarship to the state college for Negroes. My eyes filled with tears and I ran awkwardly off the floor.

I was overjoyed; I did not even mind when I discovered that the gold pieces I had scrambled for were brass pocket tokens advertising a certain make of automobile.

When I reached home everyone was excited. Next day the neighbors came to congratulate me. I even felt safe from grandfather, whose deathbed curse usually spoiled my triumphs. I stood beneath his photograph with my brief case in hand and smiled triumphantly into his stolid black peasant's face. It was a face that fascinated me. The eyes seemed to follow everywhere I went.

That night I dreamed I was at a circus with him and that he refused to laugh at the clowns no matter what they did. Then later he told me to open my brief case and read what was inside and I did, finding an official envelope stamped with the state seal; and inside the envelope I found another and another, endlessly, and I thought I would fall of weariness. "Them's years," he said. "Now

open that one." And I did and in it I found an engraved document containing
a short message in letters of gold. "Read it," my grandfather said.

"Out loud!"

"To Whom It May Concern," I intoned. "Keep This Nigger-Boy Running."

I awoke with the old man's laughter ringing in my ears.

(It was a dream I was to remember and dream again for many years after. But
at that time I had no insight into its meaning. First I had to attend college.)

(1947)

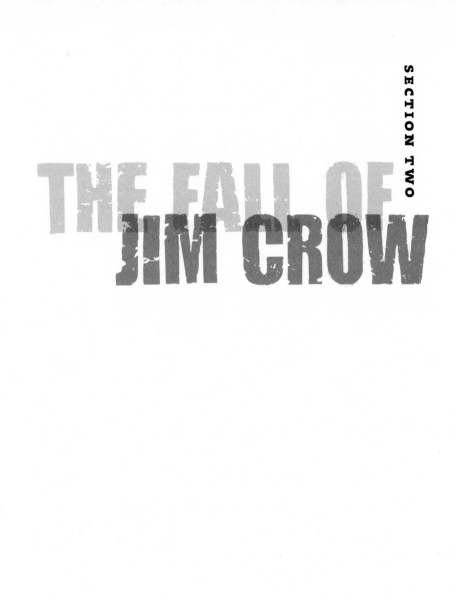

THE FALL OF JIM CROW

T he Fall of Jim Crow" covers literature from the mid-1950s to the mid-1970s, a pivotal time in civil rights history. Some scholars divide this period into two roughly ten-year spans. During the movement's "southern phase," the national spotlight turned on the Deep South, where the forces of oppression and resistance battled from the streets to the courts. After student activist Stokely Carmichael coined the term "Black Power" in 1966, the spotlight turned north and west. Racial unrest, the rise of related struggles, and an emerging backlash against civil rights groups and gains made clear that Jim Crow was dead, but racism was like the mythical Hydra monster. Just when the "problem of the color-line" that Du Bois had identified in 1903 seemed solved, more problems seemed to spring from Jim Crow's remains. Literature was intrinsic to both parts of this period. As many of the nation's best writers accurately point out, the trial of consciousness that started in 1954 was not just a southern phenomenon, even though the states of the former Confederacy became the initial stage upon which that drama played itself out. As the spotlight turned national, Black Power found creative expression in the Black Arts movement, a second cultural renaissance (after the Harlem, or New Negro, Renaissance of the 1920s) that was decidedly grassroots and explicitly political.

During these pivotal years, old characters underwent further transformation, and new ones were added. As section 1's introduction discusses, Jim Crow was always a caricature, but something strange happened to him between birth and death: he changed his race. Jim Crow started out as a stereotypical portrayal of a black man, common to minstrel shows of the nineteenth century, who dressed in tattered clothing, spoke in broken English, and danced to a syncopated beat. By the middle of the twentieth century, however, "Jim Crow" had become code for segregation and violent oppression, with the name conjuring up a stereotypical portrait of a white southern racist. This Jim Crow peppered his speech with racial epithets, often carried a Confederate flag, and usually wielded some kind of weapon. During the middle decades of the twentieth century, Jim Crow's nemesis, previously referred to as the New Negro, underwent a metamorphosis too. Early civil rights activists conducted their campaigns behind the shield of middle-class respectability. Given the brutally negative racial stereotypes of the times, it was important that spokespersons for the cause be articulate, well educated, well mannered, and well groomed. Protestors went out in their Sunday best: suits and ties for men, dresses for women, and freshly polished shoes for all. As Black Power gained momentum, amid more wide-spread 1960s countercultural upheavals, the New Negro persona seemed too stuffy to fight a revolution. In its place appeared the "Brotha" and the "Sista," guerrilla warriors better prepared for battle with the Hydra monster, known now as "the Man." Brotha and Sista rejected the Man's standard written English in favor of urban slang, traded in his "slave names" for Afrocentric ones, wore their hair "natural," and exchanged his suits and dresses for dashikis and kente cloth. These were not merely fashions, but fashion statements. And these statements also recognized that the color-line problem was not only about legislation, but also about the ways in which racial constructions influence even the most personal aspects of one's daily life.

Historical Overview

Pinpointing Jim Crow's exact time of death is difficult, but in 1954 he was clearly dealt a fatal blow. The U.S. Supreme Court ruled in *Brown v. Board of Education* that segregation in public schools was unconstitutional, culminating decades-long legal work to reverse the 1896 *Plessy v. Ferguson* ruling and paving the way to dismantle other supposedly separate but equal accommodations in public facilities. One could argue that a domino effect of civil rights gains followed soon after, with bastions of segregation toppling one by one. In 1955 the Montgomery Bus Boycott, and in 1960 the Greensboro Sit-Ins, showed how powerfully successful nonviolent direct action could be at effecting change. The federal government showed a willingness to help (even though it needed occasional prodding) with school integration in Little Rock in 1957, with the desegregation of public transportation during the Freedom Rides of 1961, and through a series of Civil Rights and Voting Rights Acts in the early 1960s. Of particular importance was the enormous, interracial grassroots support from within and outside the South, as hundreds of thousands gathered in places like Washington, D.C., for the march led by Dr. Martin Luther King Jr. in 1963, or Mississippi for Freedom Summer's voter registration drives in 1964. Although no official announcements were made nor autopsies performed, Jim Crow had certainly expired by the following year.

He did not go out without a violent, dirty fight, however, which makes any argument about a domino effect of civil rights gains hard to sustain. As with the turn of the twentieth century, this period was one of great gains and losses. The *Brown* decision led to backlash on an official level, through the formation of groups such as White Citizens' Councils, and on an unofficial one, through activities of groups such as the Ku Klux Klan (both, it must be noted, often shared members and goals). Attempted integration at the University of Mississippi met rioting and gunfire, Freedom Riders in Alabama met baseball-bat-wielding mobs, and protestors in Birmingham met police dogs and fire hoses. Being a civil rights worker meant risking one's life, as the deaths of people like King,

Medgar Evers, James Chaney, Andrew Goodman, and Michael Schwerner sadly demonstrate. Perhaps the most devastating losses of all were those of innocent bystanders, many of whom were children. Fourteen-year-old Emmett Till was lynched in 1955, not long after the *Brown* decision and some say because of it, when he flirted with a white woman in Money, Mississippi. Addie Mae Collins, Denise McNair, Carole Robertson, and Cynthia Wesley were killed in 1963 when Klan members blew up a Birmingham church that had been the site of several civil rights organizational meetings. Prosecutions and convictions were nearly impossible to obtain in most white-on-black crimes during this era, offering powerful testimony to the hold that Jim Crow maintained on the nation, even in his dying moments. Some consolation can be found in the way that these tragic events galvanized activists for years to follow.

The life and death of Malcolm X was clearly a driving force for the Black Power movement. Rather than focusing on integration and voting rights, this phase concentrated on political and economic self-sufficiency within the black community. Instead of advocating nonviolent direct action, Black Power highlighted the need for armed self-defense against a white aggression that seemed to know few limits. Malcolm X's fiery rhetoric, the Black Panthers' paramilitary dress and equally confrontational style, and the outbreaks of urban anger in places like Watts, Newark, Detroit, and elsewhere led many Americans to equate Black Power with violence and to obscure its focus on self-help. An aggressive campaign of surveillance and arrests by the Federal Bureau of Investigation (FBI), assisted by local law enforcement officials, eventually undermined the Panthers and other radical groups that emerged during the late 1960s. That the federal government could be both help and hindrance during such turbulent times is not hard to comprehend, especially where groups like the Panthers were concerned. The FBI (fearing that civil rights groups might have Communist ties) had been secretly spying on King and his associates while supposedly helping them against the Klan, but with the Panthers, the federal government gave no pretense of assistance. Malcolm X and the Black Power activists who followed him offered pointed critiques that mainstream Americans, especially whites, did not want to hear. Before his 1965 assassination, Malcolm X had been saying for years that civil rights issues were not just regional problems that could be solved through legislation. Jim Crow was not the only enemy. The real enemies were the racism, economic inequality, and injustice permeating *American*, not just southern, institutions and history. Black Power's solution was to focus on black institutions and history at the expense of white, implicitly racist ones — a solution that some Americans received as near-gospel and others as near-treason. The rise and fall of Black Power took place within the context of escalating protests over U.S. participation in the Vietnam conflict, and the height of Cold War paranoia, when critiques of the nation were easily perceived as threats. Anyone who cut short the celebration over Jim Crow's death to say that there was an American Hydra monster in the nation's midst got the blame, not the monster itself.

Despite the recognition of a new, multiheaded monster, a revolutionary spirit had also taken hold across the country by this period's end. Multiple groups, inspired by the successes of the southern phase, the critiques of Black Power, or their own contributions to the monumental changes taking place, renewed old struggles and began expanding the notion of the civil rights movement. The National Organization for Women formed in 1966, many of its early members veterans of Freedom Summer. The American Indian movement was founded in 1968. In 1969 the Stonewall Riots in New York inaugurated the Gay Liberation movement. That same year La Raza Unida formed to support Mexican American causes and candidates. These organizations and others like them have transformed the nation's sense of itself in immeasurable ways. The 1960s and 1970s saw similar transformations happening worldwide. Some revolutions were sexual, some were religious, some were economic, and some were cultural. All were political in a sense, and most met a form of backlash. What was true across the globe was true for the Panthers and true for the civil rights movement more generally. Oppression generates resistance, which meets opposition, which in turn creates new forms of struggle.

Literary Developments and Themes

Modernist aesthetics continued to dominate the literature of the mid-1950s through the mid-1970s, but Cold War sensibilities caused some writers to retreat from the overtly political stances taken by those in the 1930s and 1940s. Writers of the New Critical school, using the terminology of literary scholar Cleanth Brooks, saw texts as "well-wrought urns," complete in themselves, somehow separate from (and implicitly superior to) the sociopolitical realities of the day. New Critics judged literature on its ability to reflect "timeless," "universal" values, and praised in particular those works that were stylistically complex, rich in literary allusion, densely layered with symbolism, and ambiguous in meaning. Literature, and literary study, was for New Critics its own domain, with rules and traditions that required mastery, maybe not for admission but certainly for comprehension. Not every writer and scholar of the time followed this line of thinking, of course, and by the late 1960s reaction against New Critical dictates had begun to set in. Feminists and other radical scholars who saw all engagement with the world, even one's personal choices, as inherently political, refused to see literature as a separate sphere. Literature, and art more generally, cannot help but shape and be shaped by the values of its place, time, and author. Detractors were also quick to point out that New Criticism had its roots in the very white, male, southern agrarianism that contemporary social movements were threatening, so it was no coincidence that scholars and authors such as

Brooks, Robert Penn Warren, Allen Tate, and John Crowe Ransom would advocate styles of writing and forms of analysis with an "old boys' club" sensibility.

New Critics wielded a great deal of power over how literature was published, circulated, anthologized, and taught. But the spirit of change, especially through grassroots, do-it-yourself efforts, that was afoot everywhere was moving through writers and artists as well. If the literary establishment slammed the door in your face, the feeling went, then scrounge up the materials to build your own house. During the 1960s, the Black Arts movement captured this feeling for the civil rights struggle. Poets like Nikki Giovanni initially published their own works. Others like Audre Lorde went through small, locally owned black or feminist cooperatives. Some founded their own companies, like Haki Madhubuti's Third World Press and Dudley Randall's Broadside Press, that went on to publish some of the most important works of the day. Journals like *Negro Digest* were essential to the circulation of individual works, just as publications like the *Crisis* and *Opportunity* had been during the Harlem Renaissance. In Harlem, the Black Arts Repertory Theater School (BART), founded by Amiri Baraka and others, became a model performance and arts space for other communities. Such developments barely touch upon the explosion in black literature and art that was happening all over the country. The Black Arts movement took its philosophy of self-help and self-empowerment directly from Black Power. Its philosophy of direct confrontation with sociopolitical reality came from the times themselves, in direct opposition to New Critical tenets. For Black Arts movement practitioners, literature was not meant to be a world apart, but a means through which the world could be transformed. While Brooks thought a poem should be a well-wrought urn, for Baraka a poem worked best when used as a tool or a weapon. Like Frances E. W. Harper, W. E. B. Du Bois, and Richard Wright from section 1, Black Arts movement writers believed that their art not only had the power to change the world, but also an obligation to do so.

That authors from the mid-1950s through the mid-1970s often defied New Critical norms to focus on timely topics is apparent from the wealth of literature dealing with significant people, places, and events of the civil rights movement. Tributes to heroes and martyrs especially abound, with Malcolm X and Martin Luther King Jr. the most frequent topics. The two slain leaders came to symbolize, respectively, the philosophies of Black Power and nonviolent direct action, and their untimely deaths occasioned works of public mourning and reflection by Baraka, Lucille Clifton, Nikki Giovanni, Michael S. Harper, Robert Hayden, June Jordan, Audre Lorde, Haki Madhubuti, Margaret Walker, and others. Another leader, Medgar Evers, is alternatively eulogized as prophet in Walker's "Micah," and demonized by the speaker of Eudora Welty's chilling "Where Is the Voice Coming From?" a fictional tour-de-force that probes the heart of a racist murderer. Other events that showed the nation just how far

Jim Crow was willing to go are remembered in Gwendolyn Brooks's poems about Little Rock and Emmett Till; Harper's, Lorde's, and Randall's selections on the 1963 Birmingham church bombings; and Walker's grouping of poems on Mississippi. Not all the literature of this time focused on death and mourning, however, as Clifton's, Giovanni's, and Jordan's celebrations of black empowerment clearly demonstrate. Literature of the period could relate to the civil rights movement without directly engaging contemporary newspaper headlines. Sometimes authors take their subject matter from recognizable situations but situate their characters within fictional spaces for maximum artistic leeway. Flannery O'Connor probes the comic possibilities in what happens when white people who think they are not racist ride on a recently integrated bus. For the black man and white woman on the subway in Baraka's *Dutchman*, who embody racial forces beyond their knowing or control, the situation is far from comic. Howard Sackler's *The Great White Hope* finds tragedy and heroism in a story based upon real-life events from earlier in the century, offering a painful reminder of how slowly attitudes about race can change. As these and other literary works move beyond the headlines, they support Black Power arguments about racism being a persistent, pervasive national problem—rather than a uniquely southern narrative about the antics of Jim Crow.

Other important themes in the literature from this period are the political and philosophical debates that appear both in documentary and creative writing. King's 1963 "Letter from a Birmingham Jail" argues for the legitimacy of nonviolent direct action in an essay directed primarily at a group of white clergymen who had criticized civil rights protests, rather than the absence of civil rights, as a threat to social order. Malcolm X's *Autobiography*, published just one year later, targets U.S. civil rights struggles as naïve, saying that black people must control and defend black economic resources worldwide rather than trust any oppressive, deceptive white government to provide anything closely resembling rights or justice. At issue, he says in chapter 11 of the book, are black *human rights* on a global scale. Because King was a proponent of integration, and Malcolm X of nationalism, and because King advocated nonviolent strategies such as boycotts, marches, and sit-ins, while Malcolm X supported self-defense and did not shy away from provocative phrases like "the white man is the devil," the two are often cast as opposites. In reality, and especially near the end of both their lives, their insights about race, economics, and rights were not so far apart. Complicated problems demand equally complicated solutions, a truth made concrete in fiction and nonfiction writings from the period, where internal struggles with the day's debates play themselves out on the page. James Baldwin's "Notes of a Native Son" and Eldridge Cleaver's "On Becoming" poise precariously between love and rage. The question is where they will fall, and what action will result.

Most importantly, the literature from this period reveals the distinctive spirit of the times, which sometimes manifested itself as mourning, sometimes as defiance, and sometimes as hope, but most often focused on change. Margaret Walker spoke of King as Moses, leading his people to the promised land of freedom. King envisioned a beloved community, where justice would prevail through peaceful methods. Malcolm X envisioned a nation where justice would exist in reality, and not just in rhetoric. Baraka attempted to chant that future world into being in his poem "It's Nation Time." Nikki Giovanni's poem "Adulthood" provides a different perspective on change, looking back to an earlier period before violent events of the 1960s made her lose her innocence. The poem's speaker does not really want to turn back the clock, although many people during this period certainly did, as the forces of backlash that "Adulthood" refers to clearly demonstrate. If the defining theme of section 1's history and literature was the battle between Jim Crow and the New Negro, then a key question in the wake of Jim Crow's death was how to sustain the social transformations that did occur against forces that never wanted them in the first place. Jim Crow was an easily identifiable target, living in a particular place at a particular time. "The Man," or whatever name the Hydra monster of racism might go by in the future, was anywhere and everywhere — a much more subtle, elusive enemy.

Eudora Welty

Born on April 3, 1909, in Jackson, Mississippi, Eudora Welty was the oldest of three children of Christian Webb Welty, an insurance executive, and Mary Chestina Andrews. Eudora Welty graduated from high school in 1925 and attended the Mississippi State College for Women before transferring to the University of Wisconsin, where she earned her bachelor's degree in English in 1929. She then did some graduate work in advertising at the School of Business at Columbia University. After her father's death in 1931 Welty returned to Jackson, where she remained for most of her life, although she traveled abroad throughout the 1940s and 1950s. She worked for a local radio station, as well as part-time for the Memphis *Commercial Appeal*. Welty also worked as a photographer and junior publicity agent for the Works Progress Administration (WPA) in the 1930s, photographing life in rural Mississippi during the Depression.

In 1936 Welty published her first short story, "Death of a Traveling Salesman," and in 1946 she published her first full-length novel, *Delta Wedding*. Many of her early stories appeared in the *Southern Review*, and her literary criticism was printed in various magazines and journals. She served as an honorary consultant in letters for the Library of Congress (1958) and received two Guggenheim fellowships in addition to grants from the Rockefeller Foundation and the National Institute of Arts and Letters. Welty was elected to the American Academy of Arts and Letters and was awarded a number of honorary degrees. She won the first of five O. Henry Prizes in 1941, and in 1972 she won a Pulitzer Prize for *The Optimist's Daughter*. She won an American Book Award, the National Medal of Literature, and the Presidential Medal of Freedom. At the time of her death in 2001 Welty was regarded as one of American literature's most significant fictional stylists.

After receiving the news of Medgar Evers's murder (on June 12, 1963), Welty wrote "Where Is the Voice Coming From?" that very night and published the piece in *The New Yorker* a few weeks later. She claimed that she was deeply disturbed by the event, yet she understood how the murderer felt. Like much of her other work dedicated to showing the reader the truth no matter how painful it may be, the story illustrates the cultural environment that allowed and encouraged white southerners to complacently accept or to ardently embrace racism. Though Welty is not typically characterized as a protest writer or as a vocal advocate for social justice, her work contains subtle criticisms that reviewers often miss. Critiquing the sexism, pervasive poverty, and violence that support Jim Crow oppression, her work as a whole disrupts stereotypes of race and of white southern femininity by undermining the plantation romance of the Old South. Some of Welty's most celebrated works include *A Curtain of Green and*

Other Stories (1941), *The Robber Bridegroom* (1942), *The Wide Net* (1943), *Delta Wedding* (1946), *The Golden Apples* (1949), *The Ponder Heart* (1954), *The Bride of Innisfallen and Other Stories* (1955), *The Optimist's Daughter* (1972), and *The Collected Stories of Eudora Welty* (1980).

Where Is the Voice Coming From?

I says to my wife, "You can reach and turn it off. You don't have to set and look at a black nigger face no longer than you want to, or listen to what you don't want to hear. It's still a free county."

I reckon that's how I give myself the idea.

I says, I could find right exactly where in Thermopylae that nigger's living and ask for equal time. And without a bit of trouble to me.

And I ain't saying it might not be because that's pretty close to where *I* live. The other hand, there could be reasons you might have yourself for knowing how to get there in the dark. It's where you all go for the thing you want when you want it the most. Ain't that right?

The Branch Bank sign tells you in lights, all night long even, what time it is and how hot. When it was quarter to four, and 92, that was me going by in my brother-in-law's truck. He don't deliver nothing at that hour of the morning.

So you leave Four Corners and head west on Nathan B. Forrest Road, past the Surplus & Salvage, not much beyond the Kum Back Drive-In and Trailer Camp, not as far as where the signs starts saying "Live Bait," "Used Parts," "Fireworks," "Peaches," and "Sister Peebles Reader and Adviser." Turn before you hit the city limits and duck back towards the I.C. tracks. And his street's been paved.

And there was his light on, waiting for me. In his garage, if you please. His car's gone. He's out planning still some other ways to do what we tell 'em they can't. I *thought* I'd beat him home. All I had to do was pick my tree and walk in close behind it.

I didn't come expecting not to wait. But it was so hot, all I did was hope and pray one or the other of us wouldn't melt before it was over.

Now, it wasn't no bargain I'd struck.

I've heard what you've heard about Goat Dykeman, in Mississippi. Sure, everybody knows about Goat Dykeman. Goat he got word to the Governor's Mansion he'd go up yonder and shoot that Nigger Meredith clean out of school, if he's let out of the pen to do it. Old Ross turned *that* over in his mind before saying him nay, it stands to reason.

I ain't no Goat Dykeman, I ain't in no pen, and I ain't ask no Governor Barnett to give me one thing. Unless he wants to give me a pat on the back for the trouble I took this morning. But he don't have to if he don't want to. I done what I done for my own pure-D satisfaction.

As soon as I heard wheels, I knowed who was coming. That was him and bound to be him. It was the right nigger heading in a new white car up his drive-way towards his garage with the light shining, but stopping before he got there, maybe not to wake 'em. That was him. I knowed it when he cut off the car lights and put his foot out and I knowed him standing dark against the light. I knowed him then like I know me now. I knowed him even by his still, listening back.

Never seen him before, never seen him since, never seen anything of his black face but his picture, never seen his face alive, any time at all, or any-wheres, and didn't want to, need to, never hope to see that face and never will. As long as there was no question in my mind.

He had to be the one. He stood right still and waited against the light, his back was fixed, fixed on me like a preacher's eyeballs when he's yelling "Are you saved?" He's the one.

I'd already brought up my rifle, I'd already taken my sights. And I'd already got him, because it was too late then for him or me to turn by one hair.

Something darker than him, like the wings of a bird, spread on his back and pulled him down. He climbed up once, like a man under bad claws, and like just blood could weigh a ton he walked with it on his back to better light. Didn't get no further than his door. And fell to stay.

He was down. He was down, and a ton load of bricks on his back wouldn't have laid any heavier. There on his paved driveway, yes sir.

And it wasn't till the minute before that the mockingbird had quit singing. He'd been singing up my sassafras tree. Either he was up early, or he hadn't never gone to bed, he was like me. And the mocker he'd stayed right with me, filling the air till come the crack, till I turned loose of my load. I was like him. I was on top of the world myself. For once.

I stepped to the edge of his light there, where he's laying flat, I says, "Roland? There was one way left, for me to be ahead of you and stay ahead of you, by Dad, and I just taken it, Now I'm alive and you ain't. We ain't never now, never going to be equals and you know why? One of us is dead. What about that, Roland?" I said, "Well, you seen to it, didn't you?"

I stood a minute — just to see would somebody inside come out long enough to pick him up. And there she comes, the woman. I doubt she'd been to sleep. Because it seemed to me she'd been in there keeping awake all along.

It was mighty green where I skint over the yard getting back. That nigger wife of his, she wanted nice grass! I bet my wife would hate to pay her water bill. And for burning her electricity. And there's my brother-in-law's truck, still waiting with the door open. "No Riders" — that didn't mean me.

There wasn't a thing I been able to think of since would have made it go any nicer. Except a chair to my back while I was putting in my waiting. But going home, I seen what little times it takes after a while to get a thing done like you really want it. It was 4:34, and while I was looking it moved to 35. And the temperature stuck where it was. All that night I guarantee you it had stood without dropping, a good 92.

My wife says, "What? Didn't the skeeters bite you?" She said, "Well, they been asking that — why somebody didn't trouble to load a rifle and get some of these agitators out of Thermopylae. Didn't the fella keep drumming it in, what a good idea? The one that writes a column ever' day?"

I says to my wife, "Find *some* way I don't get the credit."

"He says do it for Thermopylae," she says. "Don't you ever skim the paper?"

I says, "Thermopylae never done nothing for me. And I don't owe nothing to Thermopylae. Didn't do it for you. Hell, any more'n I'd do something for them Kennedys! I done it for my own pure-D satisfaction."

"It's going to get him right back on TV," says my wife. "You watch for the funeral."

I says, "You didn't even leave a light burning when you went to bed. So how was I supposed to even get home or pull Buddy's truck up safe in our front yard?"

"Well, hear another good joke on you," my wife says next. "Didn't you hear the news? The N. double A. C. P. is fixing to send somebody to Thermopylae. Why couldn't you waited? You might could have got you somebody better. Listen and hear 'em say so."

I ain't but one. I reckon you have to tell somebody.

"Where's the gun, then?" my wife says. "What did you do with our protection?"

I says, "It was scorching! It was scorching!" I told her, "It's laying out on the ground in rank weeds, trying to cool off, that's what it's doing now."

"You dropped it," she says. "Back there."

And I told her, "Because I'm so tired of ever'thing in the world being just that hot to the touch! The keys to the truck, the doorknob, the bed sheet, ever'thing, it's all like a stove lid. There just ain't much going that's worth holding on to it no more," I says, "when it's a hundred and two in the shade by day and by night not too much difference. I wish you'd laid your finger to that gun."

"Trust you to come off and leave it," my wife says.

"Is that how no-'count I am?" she makes me ask. "You want to go back and get it?"

"You're the one they'll catch. I say it's so hot that even if you get to sleep you wake up feeling like you cried all night!" says my wife. "Cheer up, here's one more joke before time to get up. Heard what *Caroline* said? Caroline said, 'Daddy, I just can't wait to grow up big, so I can marry *James Meredith*.' I heard that where I work. One rich-bitch to another one, to make her cackle."

"At least I kept some dern teen-ager from North Thermopylae getting there and doing it first," I says. "Driving his own car."

ON TV AND IN THE PAPER, they don't know but half of it. They know who Roland Summers was without knowing who I am. His face was in front of the public before I got rid of him, and after I got rid of him there it is again — the same picture. And none of me. I ain't ever had one made. Not ever! The best that newspaper could do for me was offer a five-hundred-dollar reward for finding out who I am. For as long as they don't know who that is, whoever shot Roland is worth a good deal more right now than Roland is.

But by the time I was moving around uptown, it was hotter still. That pavement in the middle of Main Street was so hot to my feet I might've been walking the barrel of my gun. If the whole world could've just felt Main Street this morning through the soles of my shoes, maybe it would've helped some.

Then the first thing I heard 'em say was the N. double A. C. P. done it themselves, killed Roland Summers, and proved it by saying the shooting was done by a expert (I hope to tell you it was!) and at just the right hour and minute to get the whites in trouble.

You can't win.

"They'll never find him," the old man trying to sell roasted peanuts tells me to my face.

And it's so hot.

It looks like the town's on fire already, whichever ways you turn, ever' street you strike, because there's those trees hanging them pones of bloom like split watermelon. And a thousand cops crowding ever'where you go, half of 'em too young to start shaving, but all streaming sweat alike. I'm getting tired of 'em.

I was already tired of seeing a hundred cops getting us white people nowheres. Back at the beginning, I stood on the corner and I watched them new babyface cops loading nothing but nigger children into the paddy wagon and they come marching out of a little parade and into the paddy wagon singing. And they got in and sat down without providing a speck of trouble, and their hands held little new American flags, and all the cops could do was knock them flagsticks a-loose from their hands, and not let 'em pick 'em up, that was all, and give 'em a free ride. And children can just get 'em more flags.

Everybody: It don't get you nowhere to take nothing from nobody unless you make sure it's for keeps, for good and all, for ever and amen.

I won't be sorry to see them brickbats hail down on us for a change. Pop bottles too, they can come flying whenever they want to. Hundreds, all to smash, like Birmingham. I'm waiting on 'em to bring out them switchblade knives, like Harlem and Chicago. Watch TV long enough and you'll see it all to happen on Deacon Street in Thermopylae. What's holding it back, that's all? — Because it's *in* 'em.

I'm ready myself for that funeral.

Oh, they may find me. May catch me one day in spite of 'emselves. (But I grew up in the country.) May try to railroad me into the electric chair, and what that amounts to is something hotter than yesterday and today put together.

But I advise 'em to go careful. Ain't it about time us taxpayers starts to calling the moves? Starts to telling the teachers *and* the preachers *and* the judges of our so-called courts how far they can go?

Even the President so far, he can't walk in my house without being invited, like he's my daddy, just to say whoa. Not yet!

Once, I run away from my home. And there was a ad for me, come to be printed in our county weekly. My mother paid for it. It was from her. It says: "SON: You are not being hunted for anything but to find you." That time, I come on back home.

But people are dead now.

And it's so hot. Without it even being August yet.

Anyways, I seen him fall. I was evermore the one.

So I reach me down my old guitar off the nail in the wall. 'Cause I've got my guitar, what I've held on to from way back when, and I never dropped that, never lost or forgot it, never hocked it but to get it again, never give it away, and I set in my chair, with nobody home but me, and I start to play, and sing a-Down. And sing a-down, down, down, down. Sing a-down, down, down, down. Down.

(1963)

Robert Hayden (1913–1980)

Born Asa Bundy Sheffey on August 4, 1913, to Asa and Gladys Sheffey, Robert Hayden spent his childhood in Detroit, Michigan, in the home of his foster parents, Sue Ellen Westerfield and William Hayden. He graduated from Detroit High School in 1932 and went to Detroit City College (now Wayne State University) on a scholarship. While there he earned a bachelor's degree in Spanish with a minor in English, and he met Langston Hughes, an important influence on his writing. From 1936 until 1938 Hayden worked with Detroit's Federal Writers Project, researching local black history and folklore. Also during that time Hayden wrote theater and music reviews for the *Michigan Chronicle*, a local black paper.

In 1940 Hayden married concert pianist Erma Morris. The couple then moved to New York, and in 1942, their only child was born. That same year Hayden began graduate work in English under W. H. Auden at the University of Michigan. He won the Hopwood Prize for Student Poetry twice and graduated in 1944, when he began teaching, becoming the first black member of the university's English department. In 1946 he took a professorship of English at Fisk University in Nashville, Tennessee, where he taught for over twenty years before returning to the University of Michigan in 1969.

During the 1960s Hayden achieved international attention and acclaim for his writing. He won the grand prize for poetry in 1966 at the First World Festival of Negro Arts in Dakur for his 1962 collection, *A Ballad of Remembrance*, which was published in the United States under the title *Selected Poems* (1966). Two of his collections, *Words in the Mourning Time* (1970), where the poem "El-Hajj Malik El-Shabazz" appeared, and *American Journal* (1978), were nominated for National Book Awards. In 1970 he was awarded the Russell Loines Award from the National Institute of Arts and Letters, and in 1976 he was appointed as the poetry consultant to the Library of Congress (now the poet laureate) and was the first African American artist to hold the position. He received a fellowship in 1977 from the American Academy of Poets. On February 25, 1980, Hayden died in Ann Arbor, Michigan. His many published collections speak to his legacy as a significant modernist poet. Some of his most celebrated works include *The Lion and the Archer* (1948), *Figure of Time: Poems* (1955), *The Night Blooming Cereus* (1972), *Angle of Ascent: New and Selected Poems* (1975), and *Collected Poems* (1985).

Hayden's poetry emphasizes the importance of African and African American history, sometimes addressing specific people and events, such as the Scottsboro boys, slave revolts, and the life and death of Malcolm X. Although his work has been criticized by more militant black scholars and artists, it also expresses the need for radical politics to achieve racial equality. Hayden believed that modern conditions of human life can be seen most clearly in black experience.

El-Hajj Malik El-Shabazz

(Malcolm X)

O masks and metamorphoses of Ahab, Native Son

I
The icy evil that struck his father down
and ravished his mother into madness
trapped him in violence of a punished self
struggling to break free.

As Home Boy, as Dee-troit Red,
he fled his name, became the quarry
of his own obsessed pursuit.

He conked his hair and Lindy-hopped,
zoot-suited jiver, swinging those chicks
in the hot rose and reefer glow.

His injured childhood bullied him.
He skirmished in the Upas trees
and cannibal flowers of the American Dream —

but could not hurt the enemy
powered against him there.

II
Sometimes the dark that gave his life
its cold satanic sheen would shift
a little, and he saw himself
floodlit and eloquent;

yet how could he, "Satan" in The Hole,
guess what the waking dream foretold?

Then false dawn of vision came;
he fell upon his face before
a racist Allah pledged to wrest him from
the hellward-thrusting hands of Calvin's Christ —

to free him and his kind
from Yakub's white-faced treachery.
He rose redeemed from all but prideful anger,

though adulterate attars could not cleanse
him of the odors of the pit.

III
Asalam alaikum!

He X'd his name, became his people's anger,
exhorted them to vengeance for their past;
rebuked, admonished them,

their scourger who
would shame them, drive them from
the lush ice gardens of their servitude.

Asalam alaikum!

Rejecting Ahab, he was of Ahab's tribe.
"Strike through the mask!"

IV
Time. "The martyr's time," he said.
Time and the karate killer,

knifer, gunman. Time that brought
ironic trophies as his faith

twined sparking round the bole,
the fruit of neo-Islam.
"The martyr's time."

But first, the ebb time pilgrimage
toward revelation, hejira to
his final metamorphosis;

Labbayk! Labbayk!

He fell upon his face before
Allah the raceless in whose blazing Oneness all
were one. He rose renewed renamed, became
much more than there was time for him to be.

(1970)

Dudley Randall   (1914–2000)

orn in Washington, D.C., on January 14, 1914, Dudley Randall moved
with his parents and his four siblings first to East St. Louis, Illinois,
and then to Detroit, Michigan, in 1920, when his father was hired by
an automobile plant. At the age of thirteen, Randall published his first
poem after winning a *Detroit Free Press* poetry contest. After graduating from
high school, Randall worked in a Ford automobile plant and for the U.S. Post
Office before serving in the army during World War II. He earned a bachelor's
degree in English in 1949 from Wayne State University, and then he attended
the University of Michigan, where he earned a master's degree in library science
in 1951. In 1957 Randall married Vivian Barnett Spencer.

After working in libraries for numerous institutions, Randall founded Broadside Press in 1965. As an independent press, Broadside published a number of
African American poets who were being rejected by mainstream white presses
and may not otherwise have found an audience. Randall published the early
work of many Black Arts movement poets who remain critically acclaimed,
including Sonia Sanchez, Gwendolyn Brooks, Nikki Giovanni, Lucille Clifton,
Haki Madhubuti, June Jordan, Amiri Baraka, Alice Walker, and Audre Lorde.
Randall sold Broadside Press in 1985.

Through the press, Randall also published his own work, including the
broadside "Ballad of Birmingham," which deals with a 1963 Birmingham, Ala-

bama, church bombing that killed four girls. His next publication, a chapbook, *Poem Counterpoem*, is a collaboration between himself and Margaret Danner. Published in 1966 *Poem Counterpoem* was the press's first printed collection. After the 1967 Detroit riot, Randall published his collection *Cities Burning* (1968) with Broadside, but since then, Third World Press and others have published his work.

Randall's writing often engages events, people, and philosophies that were part of the civil rights movement, as well as other significant aspects of African and African American history and culture. Randall taught English at the University of Michigan and served as a poet-in-residence for the University of Detroit. He was named Detroit's first poet laureate in 1981, and he received fellowships from the National Endowment for the Arts, which presented him with a Lifetime Achievement Award in 1996. Dudley Randall died on August 5, 2000.

Ballad of Birmingham

"Mother dear, may I go downtown
Instead of out to play,
And march the streets of Birmingham
In a Freedom March today?"

"No, baby, no, you may not go,
For the dogs are fierce and wild,
And clubs and hoses, guns and jails
Aren't good for a little child."

"But, mother, I won't be alone.
Other children will go with me
And march the streets of Birmingham
To make our country free."

"No, baby, no, you may not go,
For I fear those guns will fire.
But you may go to church instead
And sing in the children's choir."

She has combed and brushed her night-dark hair,
And bathed rose petal sweet,
And drawn white gloves on her small brown hands,
And white shoes on her feet.

The mother smiled to know that her child
Was in the sacred place,
But that smile was the last smile
To come upon her face.

For when she heard the explosion,
Her eyes grew wet and wild.
She raced through the streets of Birmingham
Calling for her child.

She clawed through bits of glass and brick,
Then lifted out a shoe.
"O, here's the shoe my baby wore,
But, baby, where are you?"

(1965)

Margaret Walker   (1915–1998)

argaret Abigail Walker was born on July 7, 1915, in Birmingham, Alabama, to Rev. Sigismund C. Walker, a minister from Jamaica, and Marion Dozier Walker, a music teacher. When Walker was ten the family moved to New Orleans, where Walker attended Gilbert Academy until she graduated at age fourteen. She then attended New Orleans University (now Dillard University) until her sophomore year, when she met Langston Hughes, who, along with Zora Neale Hurston, was a major literary influence on her. Hughes encouraged Walker to transfer to a more prestigious school outside the South, and she took his advice and transferred to Northwestern University in Chicago, earning her bachelor's degree in 1935. That same year, Walker's first poem appeared in the *Crisis*, a literary magazine published by the National Association for the Advancement of Colored People (NAACP).

After graduating, Walker worked with the Works Progress Administration (WPA), helping disadvantaged women in Chicago's North Side. Then the WPA's Federal Writers' Project hired her as a junior writer along with Gwendolyn Brooks and Richard Wright, who became a close friend of Walker's. In 1939 Walker enrolled in the University of Iowa's Writers' Workshop, earning a master's degree in 1940. Her master's thesis later became the first work by an African American woman to be published by Yale University Press. Her later collection, *For My People* (1942), received the Yale Younger Poets Award.

In 1941 Walker took a teaching position at Livingstone College in Salisbury, North Carolina, and while there, she met Firnist James Alexander, whom she married in 1943. The next year, the couple had the first of their four children. Walker began teaching at Jackson State College in Mississippi in 1949 and remained there until she retired thirty years later. She founded the Institute for the Study of History, Life and Culture of Black People in 1968 (now the Margaret Walker Alexander National Research Center). Located on Jackson State's campus, the center is dedicated to the preservation of African American history and culture.

In 1963 Walker returned to the Writers' Workshop at the University of Iowa, earning a doctorate in English in 1965. Her dissertation was later published as her only novel, *Jubilee* (1966). She published a volume of poetry with Dudley Randall's Broadside Press, *Prophets for a New Day* (1970), which speaks to events in Mississippi and beyond. Throughout the volume, Walker invokes biblical prophets to illustrate the significance of civil rights leaders' work. As she does in other writings, Walker uses black dialect, spirituals, and folk proverbs to celebrate African and African American cultural traditions, especially when they are used to fight racism and other forms of social injustice. *Prophets for a New Day* was reprinted, along with Walker's later poetry, in *This Is My Century: New and Collected Poems* (1989). The poetry selections below (from *Prophets*) consider the 1962 riots occasioned by James Meredith's integration of the University of Mississippi, commemorate the famous 1963 March on Washington, and elegize civil rights activists who lost their lives: NAACP leader Medgar Evers and three civil rights workers killed during Freedom Summer of 1964.

Walker died on November 30, 1998, in Chicago, Illinois, while she was still working on several manuscripts.

At the Lincoln Monument in Washington, August 28, 1963

There they stand together, like Moses standing with Aaron;
Whose rod is in his hand,
The old man Moses standing with his younger brother, Aaron,
Old man with a dream he has lived to see come true.
And that firebrand standing close at hand,
Stretching forth a rod across the land,
Leading his people forth with Aaron at his side
In their marching out of Egypt,
To — the Red Sea
With the East wind sweeping back a Tide
Of the hosts of Pharaoh.
We woke up one morning in Egypt
And the river ran red with blood;
We woke up one morning in Egypt
And the houses of death were afraid.
Now the leaders of the marchers
Stand and count the uncountable;
Jacob's house has grown into a Nation.
The slaves break forth from bondage,

And there are with them intermingled
All the wives and children of other nations,
All the heathen marriages with the peoples of the land;
They march out of Goshen
They overflow out of Egypt
The Red Sea cannot stop them
And here in the wilderness of a century of wandering
Where shall we lead them
If not to freedom?

So the leaders of the marchers
Stand and catechize the people
Write this word upon your hearts
And mark this message on the doors of your houses
See that you do not forget
How this day the Lord has set our faces toward Freedom
Teach these words to your children
And see that they do not forget them.
Recite them in your going out and your coming in
And speak them in the silence of the night.
Remember the covenant we have made together
Here in the eyes of our Liberator
Here in the witnessing presence of our God and fellowman.
Where shall we march
If not to Freedom
And to our Promised Land?

(1970)

For Andy Goodman, Michael Schwerner, and James Chaney

Three Civil Rights Workers Murdered in Mississippi on June 21, 1964

Poem Written After Seeing the Movie, *Andy in the A.M.*

Three faces . . .
    mirrored in the muddy stream of living. . . .
young and tender like
quiet beauty of still water,
    sensitive as the mimosa leaf,
    intense as the stalking cougar
    and impassive as the face of rivers;
The sensitive face of Andy

The intense face of Michael
The impassive face of Chaney.

Three leaves . . .
 Floating in the melted snow
 Flooding the Spring
 oak leaves
 one by one
 moving like a barge
 across the seasons
 moving like a breeze across the windowpane
 winter . . . summer . . . spring
When is the evil year of the cricket?
When comes the violent day of the stone?
In which month
do the dead ones appear at the cistern?

Three lives . . .
 turning on the axis of our time
 Black and white together
 turning on the wheeling compass
 of a decade and a day
 The concerns of a century of time
. . . an hourglass of destiny

Three lives . . .
 ripe for immortality of daisies and wheat
 for the simple beauty of a hummingbird
 and dignity of a sequoia
 of renunciation and
 resurrection
For the Easter morning of our Meridians.

Why should another die for me?
Why should there be a calvary
A subterranean hell for three?
In the miry clay?
In the muddy stream?
In the red misery?
In mutilating hatred and in fear?
The brutish and the brazen
without brain
without blessing
without beauty . . .

They have killed these three.
They have killed them for me.

Sunrise and sunset . . .
Spring rain and winter windowpane . . .
I see the first leaves budding
The green Spring returning
I mark the falling of golden Autumn leaves
and three lives floating down the quiet stream
Till they come to the surging falls. . . .

The burned blossoms of the dogwood tree
tremble in the Mississippi morning
The wild call of the cardinal bird
troubles the Mississippi morning
I hear the morning singing
larks, robins, and the mockingbird
while the mourning dove broods over the meadow
Summer leaf falls never turning brown

Deep in a Mississippi thicket
I hear that mourning dove
Bird of death singing in the swamp
Leaves of death floating in their watery grave

Three faces turn their ears and eyes sensitive
intense
impassive
to see the solemn sky of summer
to hear the brooding cry
of the mourning dove

Mississippi bird of sorrow
O mourning bird of death
Sing their sorrow
Mourn their pain
And teach us death,
To love and live with them again!

(1970)

Micah

In Memory of Medgar Evers of Mississippi

Micah was a young man of the people
Who came up from the streets of Mississippi
And cried out his Vision to his people;
Who stood fearless before the waiting throng
Like an astronaut shooting into space.
Micah was a man who spoke against Oppression
Crying: Woe to you Workers of iniquity!
Crying: Woe to you doers of violence!
Crying: Woe to you breakers of the peace!
Crying: Woe to you, my enemy!
For when I fall I shall rise in deathless dedication.
When I stagger under the wound of your paid assassins
I shall be whole again in deathless triumph!
For your rich men are full of violence
And your mayors of your cities speak lies.
They are full of deceit.
We do not fear them.
They shall not enter the City of good-will.
We shall dwell under our own vine and fig tree in peace.
And they shall not be remembered in the Book of Life.
Micah was a man.

(1970)

Oxford Is a Legend

OXFORD is a legend
Where battlements were placed
One flaming night
And they fought the civil war all over again
With a rebel yell, and rebel flag, and scholars yelling "nigger,"
A Confederate general,
And the Union army;
Where innocent bystanders
Were killed.

OXFORD is a legend
Only a state of mind
And a place in Yoknapatawpha
Too bad the old man from Jefferson County

Died before he saw the fighting in his streets
Before he had to bear arms for Mississippi
And shoot the Negroes in the streets.

OXFORD is a legend
Name of a town in England
University town in England and Ohio and Mississippi
Where all the bygone years of chivalry and poetry and crinoline
Are dead.

OXFORD is a legend
Out of time more than battle place, or a name
With the figure of one brave and smiling little man
Smiling that courageous, ironic, bright, grim smile
Smile of a black American.

(1970)

Gwendolyn Brooks   (1917–2000)

G wendolyn Brooks was a widely known, well-respected poet whose work forms a bridge between two significant literary developments, the Harlem Renaissance and the Black Arts movement. Born June 17, 1917, to Keyiah Corrine Winns and David Anderson Brooks in Topeka, Kansas, Brooks moved with her family five weeks after her birth to the South Side of Chicago, where she lived for most of her life. During her childhood Brooks's parents encouraged her literary ambitions. At sixteen she met Langston Hughes and James Weldon Johnson, both of whom became mentors to her. At age thirteen Brooks published her first poem in *American Child* magazine, and by the time she graduated from high school, she was already a regular contributor to the Chicago *Defender*. After majoring in English, Brooks graduated from Wilson Junior College in 1936 with an associate degree and then began working as a maid and as a secretary. In 1938 she joined Chicago's National Association for the Advancement of Colored People (NAACP) Youth Council, where she met her future husband, Henry Lowington Blakely (whom she married in 1939).

Brooks attended a poetry workshop in 1940 and was exposed to the modernist verse that would influence her subsequent writing. She enjoyed a long career punctuated by many awards and distinctions. Brooks won the Midlands Writer's Conference poetry award in 1943 and in 1950 was the first African American to win the Pulitzer Prize, for *Annie Allen* (1949). In 1945 Brooks was picked as one of ten Women of the Year by *Mademoiselle* magazine, and she was awarded a Guggenheim Fellowship in 1946. She was named poet laureate for the state of Illinois in 1968. Brooks also received the Poetry Society of America's Frost Medal, the Lifetime Achievement Award from the National Endowment for the Humanities, the First Woman Award from the National First Ladies' Library, and the Anisfield-Wolf Award. She was the first African American to serve as the poetry consultant for the Library of Congress, and in 1995 President Bill Clinton awarded her the National Medal of Art.

Brooks taught at several universities, including the City University of New York and Chicago State University, which established the Gwendolyn Brooks Center for Black Literature and Creative Writing in 1993. Additionally, she combined her artistic and pedagogic endeavors with her political activism when she taught a creative writing class to Chicago's Blackstone Rangers, a teenage gang.

Many of Brooks's poems depict scenes of everyday life, particularly that of urban blacks, but some of her poems deal with memorable public events. Brooks's main goal in her writing was to portray African Americans *for* African Americans, and much of her writing deals with issues of racism, classism, and sexism in America. *The Bean Eaters* (1960), published at the height of the civil rights movement, deals with very specific racial issues. The two selections reprinted here focus on individuals involved in the 1955 Emmett Till case and the 1957 integration of Central High School in Little Rock, Arkansas. Brooks's other widely acclaimed books include *A Street in Bronzeville* (1945), *Maud Martha* (1953), and *We Real Cool* (1966). While Langston Hughes was a mentor to her, younger artists influenced her as well, particularly those who were part of the new black nationalism. In 1967 she attended the second Black Writers' Conference at Fisk University where she met many such artists, including Amiri Baraka, who inspired her to take a more radical social perspective. One concrete step involved making sure that her volumes were affordable for her primary readers and not just for a privileged elite. Beginning in 1969 all of Brooks's works were published by Broadside Press, an all-black publishing company founded by Dudley Randall.

Diagnosed with cancer, Brooks passed away on December 3, 2000, while living in Chicago. Throughout her long career Brooks published numerous collections of poetry, and though she enjoyed many distinctions for her literary merit, she never lost sight of her vision for social equality, remaining committed to the struggle for it both in her life and in her literature.

A Bronzeville Mother Loiters in Mississippi. Meanwhile, a Mississippi Mother Burns Bacon.

From the first it had been like a
Ballad. It had the beat inevitable. It had the blood.

A wildness cut up, and tied in little bunches,
Like the four-line stanzas of the ballads she had never quite
Understood — the ballads they had set her to, in school.

Herself: the milk-white maid, the "maid mild"
Of the ballad. Pursued
By the Dark Villain. Rescued by the Fine Prince.
The Happiness-Ever-After.
That was worth anything.
It was good to be a "maid mild."
That made the breath go fast.

Her bacon burned. She
Hastened to hide it in the step-on can, and
Drew more strips from the meat case. The eggs and sour-milk biscuits
Did well. She set out a jar
Of her new quince preserve.

. . . But there was a something about the matter of the Dark Villain.
He should have been older, perhaps.
The hacking down of a villain was more fun to think about
When his menace possessed undisputed breadth, undisputed height,
And a harsh kind of vice.
And best of all, when his history was cluttered
With the bones of many eaten knights and princesses.

The fun was disturbed, then all but nullified
When the Dark Villain was a blackish child
Of fourteen, with eyes still too young to be dirty,
And a mouth too young to have lost every reminder
Of its infant softness.

That boy must have been surprised! For
These were grown-ups. Grown-ups were supposed to be wise.
And the Fine Prince — and that other — so tall, so broad, so
Grown! Perhaps the boy had never guessed
That the trouble with grown-ups was that under the magnificent shell of
    adulthood, just under,
Waited the baby full of tantrums.
It occurred to her that there may have been something
Ridiculous in the picture of the Fine Prince
Rushing (rich with the breadth and height and
Mature solidness whose lack, in the Dark Villain, was impressing her,
Confronting her more and more as this first day after the trial

And acquittal wore on) rushing
With his heavy companion to hack down (unhorsed)
That little foe.
So much had happened, she could not remember now what that foe had done
Against her, or if anything had been done.
The one thing in the world that she did know and knew
With terrifying clarity was that her composition
Had disintegrated. That, although the pattern prevailed,
The breaks were everywhere. That she could think
Of no thread capable of the necessary
Sew-work.

She made the babies sit in their places at the table.
Then, before calling Him, she hurried
To the mirror with her comb and lipstick. It was necessary
To be more beautiful than ever.
The beautiful wife.
For sometimes she fancied he looked at her as though
Measuring her. As if he considered, Had she been worth It?
Had *she* been worth the blood, the cramped cries, the little stuttering bravado,
The gradual dulling of those Negro eyes,
The sudden, overwhelming *little-boyness* in that barn?
Whatever she might feel or half-feel, the lipstick necessity was something
    apart. He must never conclude
That she had not been worth It.

He sat down, the Fine Prince, and
Began buttering a biscuit. He looked at his hands.
He twisted in his chair, he scratched his nose.
He glanced again, almost secretly, at his hands.
More papers were in from the North, he mumbled. More meddling headlines.
With their pepper-words, "bestiality," and "barbarism," and "Shocking."
The half-sneers he had mastered for the trial worked across
His sweet and pretty face.

What he'd like to do, he explained, was kill them all.
The time lost. The unwanted fame.
Still, it had been fun to show those intruders
A thing or two. To show that snappy-eyed mother,
That sassy, Northern, brown-black —

Nothing could stop Mississippi. He knew that. Big Fella
Knew that.
And, what was so good, Mississippi knew that.

Nothing and nothing could stop Mississippi.
They could send in their petitions, and scar
Their newspapers with bleeding headlines. Their governors
Could appeal to Washington . . .

"What I want," the older baby said, "is 'lasses on my jam."
Whereupon the younger baby
Picked up the molasses pitcher and threw
The molasses in his brother's face. Instantly
The Fine Prince leaned across the table and slapped
The small and smiling criminal.
She did not speak. When the Hand
Came down and away, and she could look at her child,
At her baby-child,
She could think only of blood.
Surely her baby's cheek
Had disappeared, and in its place, surely,
Hung a heaviness, a lengthening red, a red that had no end.
She shook her head. It was not true, of course.
It was not true at all. The
Child's face was as always, the
Color of the paste in her paste-jar.

She left the table, to the tune of the children's lamentations, which were
    shriller
Than ever. She
Looked out of a window. She said not a word. *That*
Was one of the new Somethings —
The fear,
Tying her as with iron.

Suddenly she felt his hands upon her. He had followed her
To the window. The children were whimpering now.
Such bits of tots. And she, their mother,
Could not protect them. She looked at her shoulders, still
Gripped in the claim of his hands. She tried, but could not resist the idea
That a red ooze was seeping, spreading darkly, thickly, slowly,
Over her white shoulders, her own shoulders,
And over all of Earth and Mars.

He whispered something to her, did the Fine Prince, something
About love, something about love and night and intention.
She heard no hoof-beat of the horse and saw no flash of the shining steel.

He pulled her face around to meet
His, and there it was, close close,
For the first time in all those days and nights.
His mouth, wet and red,
So very, very, very red,
Closed over hers.

Then a sickness heaved within her. The courtroom Coca-Cola,
The courtroom beer and hate and sweat and drone,
Pushed like a wall against her. She wanted to bear it.
But his mouth would not go away and neither would the
Decapitated exclamation points in that Other Woman's eyes.

She did not scream.
She stood there.
But a hatred for him burst into glorious flower,
And its perfume enclasped them — big,
Bigger than all magnolias.

The last bleak news of the ballad.
The rest of the rugged music.
The last quatrain.

(1960)

The Chicago Defender Sends a Man to Little Rock

Fall, 1957

In Little Rock the people bear
Babes, and comb and part their hair
And watch the want ads, put repair
To roof and latch. While wheat toast burns
A woman waters multiferns.

Time upholds or overturns
The many, tight, and small concerns.

In Little Rock the people sing
Sunday hymns like anything,
Through Sunday pomp and polishing.

And after testament and tunes,
Some soften Sunday afternoons
With lemon tea and Lorna Doones.

I forecast
And I believe
Come Christmas Little Rock will cleave
To Christmas tree and trifle, weave,
From laugh and tinsel, texture fast.

In Little Rock is baseball; Barcarolle.
That hotness in July . . . the uniformed figures raw and implacable
And not intellectual,
Batting the hotness or clawing the suffering dust.
The Open Air Concert, on the special twilight green. . . .
When Beethoven is brutal or whispers to lady-like air.
Blanket-sitters are solemn, as Johann troubles to lean
To tell them what to mean. . . .

There is love, too, in Little Rock. Soft women softly
Opening themselves in kindness,
Or, pitying one's blindness,
Awaiting one's pleasure
In azure
Glory with anguished rose at the root . . .
To wash away old semi-discomfitures.
They re-teach purple and unsullen blue.
The wispy soils go. And uncertain
Half-havings have they clarified to sures.

In Little Rock they know
Not answering the telephone is a way of rejecting life,
That it is our business to be bothered, is our business
To cherish bores or boredom, be polite
To lies and love and many-faceted fuzziness.

I scratch my head, massage the hate-I-had.
I blink across my prim and pencilled pad.
The saga I was sent for is not down.
Because there is a puzzle in this town.
The biggest News I do not dare
Telegraph to the Editor's chair:
"They are like people everywhere."

The angry Editor would reply
In hundred harryings of Why.

And true, they are hurling spittle, rock,
Garbage and fruit in Little Rock.

And I saw coiling storm a-writhe
On bright madonnas. And a scythe
Of men harassing brownish girls.
(The bows and barrettes in the curls
And braids declined away from joy.)

I saw a bleeding brownish boy. . . .

The lariat lynch-wish I deplored.

The loveliest lynchee was our Lord.

(1960)

James Baldwin   (1924–1987)

ne of the most powerful literary figures in the struggle for civil rights, James Baldwin was born in Harlem on August 2, 1924, to Emma Berdis Jones. Three years later, he was adopted by his stepfather, David Baldwin, whose religious fundamentalism set the stage for much of his stepson's writing. James Baldwin himself spent a brief period as a child evangelist, but later left the church. Still, a consciousness of right and wrong, sin and redemption remain strong in his work. Baldwin also showed interest in a literary career from an early age. An avid reader from the start, Baldwin claimed that by thirteen, he had read most of the books in Harlem's two libraries. At twelve, Baldwin had a short story published in his church newspaper. In high school he was part of a literary club and the editor of the school paper.

His literary apprenticeship began in earnest in 1943, when he moved to Greenwich Village and met Richard Wright, who became his mentor. The two later became estranged after Baldwin published a critique of Wright's *Native Son* titled "Everybody's Protest Novel" (1949), but the essay cemented his reputation as a major American writer. The pattern of Oedipal struggle between father and son, mentor and apprentice that had characterized Baldwin's life up to this point appeared as a major theme in his first full-length work, *Go Tell It on the Mountain* (1953). Baldwin produced the book while living in Paris, where he had moved in 1948 after struggling with racism and homophobia in the United States. He eventually returned from France in 1957 in order to join the struggle for civil rights. After touring the South, Baldwin went back to France, where he lived until his death on November 30, 1987.

In his writing Baldwin consistently links his personal experiences, particularly those of poverty, police brutality, abuse, racism, and religious indoctrination, to questions of national and global destiny. Articulating the painful legacy of slavery and racism in modern America, Baldwin produced an honest and passionate racial discourse that challenged the nation to deal head-on with issues of social justice. Through the 1950s and 1960s Baldwin specifically addressed the issues of desegregation and black separatism. Some of the major themes in his writing are social injustice, especially that of racial and sexual intolerance, and the failed democracy of America. He also deals with prevalent stereotypes about the sexuality of black men, who, Baldwin argued, bear the brunt of America's sexual anxiety.

Baldwin not only affected African American literature but also American culture as a whole. He wrote essays, novels, plays, poems, short stories, and children's books, and held several short teaching appointments during the 1970s and 1980s, including those at the University of Massachusetts at Amherst, Bowling Green State University, Mount Holyoke College, and the University of California at Berkeley. The many important literary works Baldwin left behind demonstrate his enduring legacy; these include *Notes of a Native Son* (1955) — the title essay of which is reprinted here, *Giovanni's Room* (1956), *Another Country* (1962), *The Fire Next Time* (1963), *Blues for Mr. Charlie* (1964), *Going to Meet the Man* (1965), and *Tell Me How Long This Train's Been Gone* (1968).

Notes of a Native Son

On the 29th of July, in 1943, my father died. On the same day, a few hours later, his last child was born. Over a month before this, while all our energies were concentrated in waiting for these events, there had been, in Detroit, one of the bloodiest race riots of the century. A few hours after my father's funeral, while he lay in state in the undertaker's chapel, a race riot broke out in Harlem. On the morning of the 3rd of August, we drove my father to the graveyard through a wilderness of smashed plate glass.

The day of my father's funeral had also been my nineteenth birthday. As we drove him to the graveyard, the spoils of injustice, anarchy, discontent, and hatred were all around us. It seemed to me that God himself had devised, to mark my father's end, the most sustained and brutally dissonant of codas. And it seemed to me, too, that the violence which rose all about us as my father left the world had been devised as a corrective for the pride of his eldest son. I had declined to believe in that apocalypse which had been central to my father's vision; very well, life seemed to be saying, here is something that will certainly pass for an apocalypse until the real thing comes along. I had inclined to be contemptuous of my father for the conditions of his life, for the conditions of our lives. When his life had ended I began to wonder about that life and also, in a new way, to be apprehensive about my own.

I had not known my father very well. We had got on badly, partly because we shared, in our different fashions, the vice of stubborn pride. When he was dead I realized that I had hardly ever spoken to him. When he had been dead a long time I began to wish I had. It seems to be typical of life in America, where opportunities, real and fancied, are thicker than anywhere else on the globe, that the second generation has no time to talk to the first. No one, including my father, seems to have known exactly how old he was, but his mother had been born during slavery. He was of the first generation of free men. He, along with thousands of other Negroes, came North after 1919 and I was part of that generation which had never seen the landscape of what Negroes sometimes call the Old Country.

He had been born in New Orleans and had been a quite young man there during the time that Louis Armstrong, a boy, was running errands for the dives and honky-tonks of what was always presented to me as one of the most wicked of cities — to this day, whenever I think of New Orleans, I also helplessly think of Sodom and Gomorrah. My father never mentioned Louis Armstrong, except to forbid us to play his records; but there was a picture of him on our wall for a long time. One of my father's strong-willed female relatives had placed it there and forbade my father to take it down. He never did, but he eventually maneuvered her out of the house and when, some years later, she was in trouble and near death, he refused to do anything to help her.

He was, I think, very handsome. I gather this from photographs and from my own memories of him, dressed in his Sunday best and on his way to preach a sermon somewhere, when I was little. Handsome, proud, and ingrown, "like a toe-nail," somebody said. But he looked to me, as I grew older, like pictures I had seen of African tribal chieftains: he really should have been naked, with war-paint on and barbaric mementos, standing among spears. He could be chilling in the pulpit and indescribably cruel in his personal life and he was certainly the most bitter man I have ever met; yet it must be said that there was something else in him, buried in him, which lent him his tremendous power and, even, a rather crushing charm. It had something to do with his blackness, I think — he was very black — with his blackness and his beauty, and with the fact that he knew that he was black but did not know that he was beautiful. He claimed to be proud of his blackness but it had also been the cause of much humiliation and it had fixed bleak boundaries to his life. He was not a young man when we were growing up and he had already suffered many kinds of ruin; in his outrageously demanding and protective way he loved his children, who were black like him and menaced, like him; and all these things sometimes showed in his face when he tried, never to my knowledge with any success, to establish contact with any of us. When he took one of his children on his knee to play, the child always became fretful and began to cry; when he tried to help one of us with our homework the absolutely unabating tension which emanated from him caused our minds and our tongues to become paralyzed, so that he, scarcely knowing why, flew into a rage and the child, not knowing why, was punished. If it ever entered his head to bring a surprise home for his children, it was, almost unfailingly, the wrong surprise and even the big watermelons he often brought home on his back in the summertime led to the most appalling scenes. I do not remember, in all those years, that one of his children was ever glad to see him come home. From what I was able to gather of his early life, it seemed that this inability to establish contact with other people had always marked him and had been one of the things which had driven him out of New Orleans. There was something in him, therefore, groping and tentative, which was never expressed and which was buried with him. One saw it most clearly when he was facing new people and hoping to impress them. But he never did, not for long. We went from church to smaller and more improbable church, he found himself in less and less demand as a minister, and by the time he died none of his friends had come to see him for a long time. He had lived and died in an intolerable bitterness of spirit and it frightened me, as we drove him to the graveyard through those unquiet, ruined streets, to see how powerful and overflowing this bitterness could be and to realize that this bitterness now was mine.

When he died I had been away from home for a little over a year. In that year I had had time to become aware of the meaning of all my father's bitter warnings, had discovered the secret of his proudly pursed lips and rigid carriage: I had discovered the weight of white people in the world, I saw that this had been for my ancestors and now would be for me an awful thing to live with and that the bitterness which had helped to kill my father could also kill me.

He had been ill a long time — in the mind, as we now realized, reliving instances of his fantastic intransigence in the new light of his affliction and endeavoring to feel a sorrow for him which never, quite, came true. We had not known that he was being eaten up by paranoia, and the discovery that his cruelty, to our bodies and our minds, had been one of the symptoms of his illness was not, then, enough to enable us to forgive him. The younger children felt, quite simply, relief that he would not be coming home anymore. My mother's observation that it was he, after all, who had kept them alive all these years meant nothing because the problems of keeping children alive are not real for children. The older children felt, with my father gone, that they could invite their friends to the house without fear that their friends would be insulted or, as had sometimes happened with me, being told that their friends were in league with the devil and intended to rob our family of everything we owned. (I didn't fail to wonder, and it made me hate him, what on earth we owned that anybody else would want.)

His illness was beyond all hope of healing before anyone realized that he was ill. He had always been so strange and had lived, like a prophet, in such unimaginably close communion with the Lord that his long silences which were punctuated by moans and hallelujahs and snatches of old songs while he sat at the living-room window never seemed odd to us. It was not until he refused to eat because, he said, his family was trying to poison him that my mother was forced to accept as a fact what had, until then, been only an unwilling suspicion. When he was committed, it was discovered that he had tuberculosis and, as it turned out, the disease of his mind allowed the disease of his body to destroy him. For the doctors could not force him to eat, either, and, though he was fed intravenously, it was clear from the beginning that there was no hope for him.

In my mind's eye I could see him, sitting at the window, locked up in his terrors; hating and fearing every living soul including his children who had betrayed him, too, by reaching towards the world which had despised him. There were nine of us. I began to wonder what it could have felt like for such a man to have had nine children whom he could barely feed. He used to make little jokes about our poverty, which never, of course, seemed very funny to us; they could not have seemed very funny to him, either, or else our all too feeble response to them would never have caused such rages. He spent great energy and achieved, to our chagrin, no small amount of success in keeping us away from the people who surrounded us, people who had all-night rent parties to which we listened when we should have been sleeping, people who cursed and drank and flashed razor blades on Lenox Avenue. He could not understand why, if they had so much energy to spare, they could not use it to make their lives better. He treated almost everybody on our block with a most uncharitable asperity and neither they, nor, of course, their children were slow to reciprocate.

The only white people who came to our house were welfare workers and bill collectors. It was almost always my mother who dealt with them, for my father's temper, which was at the mercy of his pride, was never to be trusted. It was clear that he felt their very presence in his home to be a violation: this was conveyed by his carriage, almost ludicrously stiff, and by his voice, harsh and vindictively polite. When I was around nine or ten I wrote a play which was directed by a young, white schoolteacher, a woman, who then took an interest in me, and gave me books to read and, in order to corroborate my theatrical bent, decided to take me to see what she somewhat tactlessly referred to as "real" plays. Theater-going was forbidden in our house, but, with the really cruel intuitiveness of a child, I suspected that the color of this woman's skin would carry the day for me. When, at school, she suggested taking me to the theater, I did not, as I might have done if she had been a Negro, find a way of discouraging her, but agreed that she should pick me up at my house one evening. I then, very cleverly, left all the rest to my mother, who suggested to my father, as I knew she would, that it would not be very nice to let such a kind woman make the trip for nothing. Also, since it was a schoolteacher, I imagine that my mother countered the idea of sin with the idea of "education," which word, even with my father, carried a kind of bitter weight.

Before the teacher came my father took me aside to ask why she was coming, what *interest* she could possibly have in our house, in a boy like me. I said I didn't know but I, too, suggested that it had something to do with education. And I understood that my father was waiting for me to say something — I didn't quite know what; perhaps that I wanted his protection against this teacher and her "education." I said none of these things and the teacher came and we went out. It was clear, during the brief interview in our living room, that my father was agreeing very much against his will and that he would have refused permission if he had dared. The fact that he did not dare caused me to despise him: I had no way of knowing that he was facing in that living room a wholly unprecedented and frightening situation.

Later, when my father had been laid off from his job, this woman became very important to us. She was really a very sweet and generous woman and went to a great deal of trouble to be of help to us, particularly during one awful winter. My mother called her by the highest name she knew: she said she was a "christian." My father could scarcely disagree but during the four or five years of our relatively close association he never trusted her and was always trying to surprise in her open, Midwestern face the genuine, cunningly hidden, and hideous motivation. In later years, particularly when it began to be clear that this "education" of mine was going to lead me to perdition, he became more explicit and warned me that my white friends in high school were not really my friends and that I would see, when I was older, how white people would do anything to keep a Negro down. Some of them could be nice, he admitted, but none of them were to be trusted and most of them were not even nice. The best thing was to have as little to do with them as possible. I did not feel this way and I was certain, in my innocence, that I never would.

But the year which preceded my father's death had made a great change in my life. I had been living in New Jersey, working in defense plants, working and living among southerners, white and black. I knew about the south, of course, and about how southerners treated Negroes and how they expected them to behave, but it had never entered my mind that anyone would look at me and expect *me* to behave that way. I learned in New Jersey that to be a Negro meant, precisely, that one was never looked at but was simply at the mercy of the reflexes the color of one's skin caused in other people. I acted in New Jersey as I had always acted, that is as though I thought a great deal of myself — I had to *act* that way — with results that were, simply, unbelievable. I had scarcely arrived before I had earned the enmity, which was extraordinarily ingenious, of all my superiors and nearly all my co-workers. In the beginning, to make matters worse, I simply did not know what was happening. I did not know what I had done, and I shortly began to wonder what *anyone* could possibly do, to bring about such unanimous, active, and unbearably vocal hostility. I knew about jim-crow but I had never experienced it. I went to the same self-service restaurant three times and stood with all the Princeton boys before the counter, waiting for a hamburger and coffee; it was always an extraordinarily long time before anything was set before me; but it was not until the fourth visit that I learned that, in fact, nothing had ever been set before me: I had simply picked something up. Negroes were not served there, I was told, and they had been waiting for me to realize that I was always the only Negro present. Once I was told this, I determined to go there all the time. But now they were ready for me and, though some dreadful scenes were subsequently enacted in that restaurant, I never ate there again.

It was the same story all over New Jersey, in bars, bowling alleys, diners, places to live. I was always being forced to leave, silently, or with mutual imprecations. I very shortly became notorious and children giggled behind me when I passed and their elders whispered or shouted — they really believed that I was mad. And it did begin to work on my mind, of course; I began to be afraid to go anywhere and to compensate for this I went places to which I really should not have gone and where, God knows, I had no desire to be. My reputation in town naturally enhanced my reputation at work and my working day became one long series of acrobatics designed to keep me out of trouble. I cannot say that these acrobatics succeeded. It began to seem that the machinery of the organization I worked for was turning over, day and night, with but one aim: to eject me. I was fired once, and contrived, with the aid of a friend from New York, to get back on the payroll; was fired again, and bounced back again. It took a while to fire me for the third time, but the third time took. There were no loopholes anywhere. There was not even any way of getting back inside the gates.

That year in New Jersey lives in my mind as though it were the year during which, having an unsuspected predilection for it, I first contracted some dread, chronic disease, the unfailing symptom of which is a kind of blind fever, a pounding in the skull and fire in the bowels. Once this disease is contracted, one can never be really carefree again, for the fever, without an instant's warning, can recur at any moment. It can wreck more important things than race relations. There is not a Negro alive who does not have this rage in his blood — one has the choice, merely, of living with it consciously or surrendering to it. As for me, this fever has recurred in me, and does, and will until the day I die.

My last night in New Jersey, a white friend from New York took me to the nearest big town, Trenton, to go to the movies and have a few drinks. As it turned out, he also saved me from, at the very least, a violent whipping. Almost every detail of that night stands out very clearly in my memory. I even remember the name of the movie we saw because its title impressed me as being so patly ironical. It was a movie about the German occupation of France, starring Maureen O'Hara and Charles Laughton and called *This Land Is Mine*. I remember the name of the diner we walked into when the movie ended: it was the "American Diner." When we walked in the counterman asked what we wanted and I remember answering with the casual sharpness which had become my habit: "We want a hamburger and a cup of coffee, what do you think we want?" I do not know why, after a year of such rebuffs, I so completely failed to anticipate his answer, which was, of course, "We don't serve Negroes here." This reply failed to discompose me, at least for the moment. I made some sardonic comment about the name of the diner and we walked out into the streets.

This was the time of what was called the "brownout," when the lights in all American cities were very dim. When we re-entered the streets something happened to me which had the force of an optical illusion, or a nightmare. The streets were very crowded and I was facing north. People were moving in every direction but it seemed to me, in that instant, that all of the people I could see, and many more than that, were moving toward me, against me, and that everyone was white. I remember how their faces gleamed. And I felt, like a physical sensation, a *click* at the nape of my neck as though some interior string connecting my head to my body had been cut. I began to walk. I heard my friend call after me, but I ignored him. Heaven only knows what was going on in his mind, but he had the good sense not to touch me — I don't know what would have happened if he had — and to keep me in sight. I don't know what was going on in my mind, either; I certainly had no conscious plan. I wanted to do something to crush these white faces, which were crushing me. I walked for perhaps a block or two until I came to an enormous, glittering, and fashionable restaurant in which I knew not even the intercession of the Virgin would cause me to be served. I pushed through the doors and took the first vacant seat I saw, at a table for two, and waited.

I do not know how long I waited and I rather wonder, until today, what I could possibly have looked like. Whatever I looked like, I frightened the waitress who shortly appeared, and the moment she appeared all of my fury flowed towards her. I hated her for her white face, and for her great, astounded, frightened eyes. I felt that if she found a black man so frightening I would make her fright worth-while.

She did not ask me what I wanted, but repeated, as though she had learned it somewhere, "We don't serve Negroes here." She did not say it with the blunt, derisive hostility to which I had grown so accustomed, but, rather, with a note of apology in her voice, and fear. This made me colder and more murderous than ever. I felt I had to do something with my hands. I wanted her to come close enough for me to get her neck between my hands.

So I pretended not to have understood her, hoping to draw her closer. And she did step a very short step closer, with her pencil poised incongruously over her pad, and repeated the formula: ". . . don't serve Negroes here."

Somehow, with the repetition of that phrase, which was already ringing in my head like a thousand bells of a nightmare, I realized that she would never come any closer and that I would have to strike from a distance. There was nothing on the table but an ordinary water-mug half full of water, and I picked this up and hurled it with all my strength at her. She ducked and it missed her and shattered against the mirror behind the bar. And, with that sound, my frozen blood abruptly thawed, I returned from wherever I had been, I saw, for the first time, the restaurant, the people with their mouths open, already, as it seemed to me, rising as one man, and I realized what I had done, and where I was, and I was frightened. I rose and began running for the door. A round, potbellied man grabbed me by the nape of the neck just as I reached the doors and began to beat me about the face. I kicked him and got loose and ran into the streets. My friend whispered, *"Run!"* and I ran.

My friend stayed outside the restaurant long enough to misdirect my pursuers and the police, who arrived, he told me, at once. I do not know what I said to him when he came to my room that night. I could not have said much. I felt, in the oddest, most awful way, that I had somehow betrayed him. I lived it over and over and over again, the way one relives an automobile accident after it has happened and one finds oneself alone and safe. I could not get over two facts, both equally difficult for the imagination to grasp, and one was that I could have been murdered. But the other was that I had been ready to commit murder. I saw nothing very clearly but I did see this: that my life, my *real* life, was in danger, and not from anything other people might do but from the hatred I carried in my own heart.

II

I had returned home around the second week in June — in great haste because it seemed that my father's death and my mother's confinement were both but a matter of hours. In the case of my mother, it soon became clear that she had simply made a miscalculation. This had always been her tendency and I don't believe that a single one of us arrived in the world, or has since arrived anywhere else, on time. But none of us dawdled so intolerably about the business of being born as did my baby sister. We sometimes amused ourselves, during those endless, stifling weeks, by picturing the baby sitting within in the safe, warm dark, bitterly regretting the necessity of becoming a part of our chaos and stubbornly putting it off as long as possible. I understood her perfectly and congratulated her on showing such good sense so soon. Death, however, sat as purposefully at my father's bedside as life stirred within my mother's womb and it was harder to understand why he so lingered in that long shadow. It seemed that he had bent, and for a long time, too, all of his energies towards dying. Now death was ready for him but my father held back.

All of Harlem, indeed, seemed to be infected by waiting. I had never before known it to be so violently still. Racial tensions throughout this country were exacerbated during the early years of the war, partly because the labor market brought together hundreds of thousands of ill-prepared people and partly because Negro soldiers, regardless of where they were born, received their military training in the south. What happened in defense plants and army camps had repercussions, naturally, in every Negro ghetto. The situation in Harlem had grown bad enough for clergymen, policemen, educators, politicians, and social workers to assert in one breath that there was no "crime wave" and to offer, in the very next breath, suggestions as to how to combat it. These suggestions always seemed to involve playgrounds, despite the fact that racial skirmishes were occurring in the playgrounds, too. Playground or not, crime wave or not, the Harlem police force had been augmented in March, and the unrest grew — perhaps, in fact, partly as a result of the ghetto's instinctive hatred of policemen. Perhaps the most revealing news item, out of the steady parade of reports of muggings, stabbings, shootings, assaults, gang wars, and accusations of police brutality, is the item concerning six Negro girls who set upon a white girl in the subway because, as they all too accurately put it, she was stepping on their toes. Indeed she was, all over the nation.

I had never before been so aware of policemen, on foot, on horseback, on corners, everywhere, always two by two. Nor had I ever been so aware of small knots of people. They were on stoops and on corners and in doorways, and what was striking about them, I think, was that they did not seem to be talking. Never, when I passed these groups, did the usual sound of a curse or a laugh ring out and neither did there seem to be any hum of gossip. There was certainly, on the other hand, occurring between them communication extraordinarily intense. Another thing that was striking was the unexpected diversity of the people who made up these groups. Usually, for example, one would see a group of sharpies standing on the street corner, jiving the passing chicks; or a group of older men, usually, for some reason, in the vicinity of a barber shop, discussing baseball scores, or the numbers, or making rather chilling observations about women they had known. Women, in a general way, tended to be seen less often together — unless they were church women, or very young girls, or prostitutes met together for an unprofessional instant. But that summer I saw the strangest combinations: large, respectable, churchly matrons standing on the stoops or the corners with their hair tied up, together with a girl in sleazy satin whose face bore the marks of gin and the razor, or heavy-set, abrupt, no-nonsense older men, in company with the most disreputable and fanatical "race" men, or these same "race" men with the sharpies, or these sharpies with the churchly women. Seventh Day Adventists and Methodists and Spiritualists seemed to be hobnobbing with Holyrollers and they were all, alike, entangled with the most flagrant disbelievers; something heavy in their stance seemed to indicate that they had all, incredibly, seen a common vision, and on each face there seemed to be the same strange, bitter shadow.

The churchly women and the matter-of-fact, no-nonsense men had children in the Army. The sleazy girls they talked to had lovers there, the sharpies and the "race" men had friends and brothers there. It would have demanded an unquestioning patriotism, happily as uncommon in this country as it is undesirable, for these people not to have been disturbed by the bitter letters they received, by the newspaper stories they read, not to have been enraged by the posters, then to be found all over New York, which described the Japanese as "yellow-bellied Japs." It was only the "race" men, to be sure, who spoke ceaselessly of being revenged — how this vengeance was to be exacted was not clear — for the indignities and dangers suffered by Negro boys in uniform; but everybody felt a directionless, hopeless bitterness, as well as that panic which can scarcely be suppressed when one knows that a human being one loves is beyond one's reach, and in danger. This helplessness and this gnawing uneasiness does something, at length, to even the toughest mind. Perhaps the best way to sum all this up is to say that the people I knew felt, mainly, a peculiar kind of relief when they knew that their boys were being shipped out of the south, to do battle overseas. It was, perhaps, like feeling that the most dangerous part of a dangerous journey had been passed and that now, even if death should come, it would come with honor and without the complicity of their countrymen. Such a death would be, in short, a fact with which one could hope to live.

It was on the 28th of July, which I believe was a Wednesday, that I visited my father for the first time during his illness and for the last time in his life. The moment I saw him I knew why I had put off this visit so long. I had told my mother that I did not want to see him because I hated him. But this was not true. It was only that I *had* hated him and I wanted to hold on to this hatred. I did not want to look on him as a ruin: it was not a ruin I had hated. I imagine that one of the reasons people cling to their hates so stubbornly is because they sense, once hate is gone, that they will be forced to deal with pain.

We traveled out to him, his older sister and myself, to what seemed to be the very end of a very Long Island. It was hot and dusty and we wrangled, my aunt and I, all the way out, over the fact that I had recently begun to smoke and, as she said, to give myself airs. But I knew that she wrangled with me because she could not bear to face the fact of her brother's dying. Neither could I endure the reality of her despair, her unstated bafflement as to what had happened to her brother's life, and her own. So we wrangled and I smoked and from time to time she fell into a heavy reverie. Covertly, I watched her face, which was the face of an old woman; it had fallen in, the eyes were sunken and lightless; soon she would be dying, too. In my childhood — it had not been so long ago — I had thought her beautiful. She had been quick-witted and quick-moving and very generous with all the children and each of her visits had been an event. At one time one of my brothers and myself had thought of running away to live with her. Now she could no longer produce out of her handbag some unexpected and yet familiar delight. She made me feel pity and revulsion and fear. It was awful to realize that she no longer caused me to feel affection. The closer we came to the hospital the more querulous she became and at the same time, naturally, grew more dependent on me. Between pity and guilt and fear I began to feel that there was another me trapped in my skull like a jack-in-the-box who might escape my control at any moment and fill the air with screaming.

She began to cry the moment we entered the room and she saw him lying there, all shriveled and still, like a little black monkey. The great, gleaming apparatus which fed him and would have compelled him to be still even if he had been able to move brought to mind, not beneficence, but torture; the tubes entering his arm made me think of pictures I had seen when a child, of Gulliver, tied down by the pygmies on that island. My aunt wept and wept, there was a whistling sound in my father's throat; nothing was said; he could not speak. I wanted to take his hand, to say something. But I do not know what I could have said, even if he could have heard me. He was not really in that room with us, he had at last really embarked on his journey; and though my aunt told me that he said he was going to meet Jesus, I did not hear anything except that whistling in his throat. The doctor came back and we left, into that unbearable train again, and home. In the morning came the telegram saying that he was dead. Then the house was suddenly full of relatives, friends, hysteria, and confusion and I quickly left my mother and the children to the care of those impressive women, who, in Negro communities at least, automatically appear at times of bereavement armed with lotions, proverbs, and patience, and an ability to cook. I went downtown. By the time I returned, later the same day, my mother had been carried to the hospital and the baby had been born.

III

For my father's funeral I had nothing black to wear and this posed a nagging problem all day long. It was one of those problems, simple, or impossible of solution, to which the mind insanely clings in order to avoid the mind's real trouble. I spent most of that day at the downtown apartment of a girl I knew, celebrating my birthday with whiskey and wondering what to wear that night. When planning a birthday celebration one naturally does not expect that it will be up against competition from a funeral and this girl had anticipated taking me out that night, for a big dinner and a night club afterwards. Sometime during the course of that long day we decided that we would go out anyway, when my father's funeral service was over. I imagine I decided it, since, as the funeral hour approached, it became clearer and clearer to me that I would not know what to do with myself when it was over. The girl, stifling her very lively concern as to the possible effects of the whiskey on one of my father's chief mourners, concentrated on being conciliatory and practically helpful. She found a black shirt for me somewhere and ironed it and, dressed in the darkest pants and jacket I owned, and slightly drunk, I made my way to my father's funeral.

The chapel was full, but not packed, and very quiet. There were, mainly, my father's relatives, and his children, and here and there I saw faces I had not seen since childhood, the faces of my father's one-time friends. They were very dark and solemn now, seeming somehow to suggest that they had known all along that something like this would happen. Chief among the mourners was my aunt, who had quarreled with my father all his life; by which I do not mean to suggest that her mourning was insincere or that she had not loved him. I suppose that she was one of the few people in the world who had, and their incessant quarreling proved precisely the strength of the tie that bound them. The only other person in the world, as far as I knew, whose relationship to my father rivaled my aunt's in depth was my mother, who was not there.

It seemed to me, of course, that it was a very long funeral. But it was, if anything, a rather shorter funeral than most, nor, since there were no overwhelming, uncontrollable expressions of grief, could it be called — if I dare to use the word — successful. The minister who preached my father's funeral sermon was one of the few my father had still been seeing as he neared his end. He presented to us in his sermon a man whom none of us had ever seen — a man thoughtful, patient, and forbearing, a Christian inspiration to all who knew him, and a model for his children. And no doubt the children, in their disturbed and guilty state, were almost ready to believe this; he had been remote enough to be anything and, anyway, the shock of the incontrovertible, that it was really our father lying up there in that casket, prepared the mind for anything. His sister moaned and this grief-stricken moaning was taken as corroboration. The other faces held a dark, non-committal thoughtfulness. This was not the man they had known, but they had scarcely expected to be confronted with *him*; this was, in a sense deeper than questions of fact, the man they had not known, and the man they had not known may have been the real one. The real man, whoever he had been, had suffered and now he was dead: this was all that was sure and all that mattered now. Every man in the chapel hoped that when his hour came he, too, would be eulogized, which is to say forgiven, and that all of his lapses, greeds, errors, and strayings from the truth would be invested with coherence and looked upon with charity. This was perhaps the last thing human beings could give each other and it was what they demanded, after all, of the Lord. Only the Lord saw the midnight tears, only He was present when one of His children, moaning and wringing hands, paced up and down the room. When one slapped one's child in anger the recoil in the heart reverberated through heaven and became part of the pain of the universe. And when the children were hungry and sullen and distrustful and one watched them, daily, growing wilder, and further away, and running headlong into danger, it was the Lord who knew what the charged heart endured as the strap was laid to the backside; the Lord alone who knew what one would have said if one had had, like the Lord, the gift of the living word. It was the Lord who knew of the impossibility every parent in that room faced: how to prepare the child for the day when the child would be despised and how to create in the child — by what means? — a stronger antidote to this poison than one had found for oneself. The avenues, side streets, bars, billiard halls, hospitals, police stations, and even the playgrounds of Harlem — not to mention the houses of correction, the jails, and the morgue — testified to the potency of the poison while remaining silent as to the efficacy of whatever antidote, irresistibly raising the question of whether or not such an antidote existed; raising, which was worse, the question of whether or not an antidote was desirable; perhaps poison should be fought with poison. With these several schisms in the mind and with more terrors in the heart than could be named, it was better not to judge the man who had gone down under an impossible burden. It was better to remember: *Thou knowest this man's fall; but thou knowest not his wrassling.*

While the preacher talked and I watched the children — years of changing their diapers, scrubbing them, slapping them, taking them to school, and scolding them had had the perhaps inevitable result of making me love them, though I am not sure I knew this then — my mind was busily breaking out with a rash of disconnected impressions. Snatches of popular songs, indecent jokes, bits of books I had read, movie sequences, faces, voices, political issues — I thought I was going mad; all these impressions suspended, as it were, in the solution of the faint nausea produced in me by the heat and liquor. For a moment I had the impression that my alcoholic breath, inefficiently disguised with chewing gum, filled the entire chapel. Then someone began singing one of my father's favorite songs and, abruptly, I was with him, sitting on his knee, in the hot, enormous, crowded church which was the first church we attended. It was the Abyssinia Baptist Church on 138th Street. We had not gone there long. With this image, a host of others came. I had forgotten, in the rage of my growing up, how proud my father had been of me when I was little. Apparently, I had had a voice and my father had liked to show me off before the members of the church. I had forgotten what he had looked like when he was pleased but now I remembered that he had always been grinning with pleasure when my solos ended. I even remembered certain expressions on his face when he teased my mother — had he loved her? I would never know. And when had it all begun to change? For now it seemed that he had not always been cruel. I remembered being taken for a haircut and scraping my knee on the footrest of the barber's chair and I remembered my father's face as he soothed my crying and applied the stinging iodine. Then I remembered our fights, fights which had been of the worst possible kind because my technique had been silence.

I remembered the one time in all our life together when we had really spoken to each other.

It was on a Sunday and it must have been shortly before I left home. We were walking, just the two of us, in our usual silence, to or from church. I was in high school and had been doing a lot of writing and I was, at about this time, the editor of the high school magazine. But I had also been a Young Minister and had been preaching from the pulpit. Lately, I had been taking fewer engagements and preached as rarely as possible. It was said in the church, quite truthfully, that I was "cooling off."

My father asked me abruptly, "You'd rather write than preach, wouldn't you?"

I was astonished at his question — because it was a real question. I answered, "Yes."

That was all we said. It was awful to remember that that was all we had ever said.

The casket now was opened and the mourners were being led up the aisle to look for the last time on the deceased. The assumption was that the family was too overcome with grief to be allowed to make this journey alone and I watched while my aunt was led to the casket and, muffled in black, and shaking, led back to her seat. I disapproved of forcing the children to look on their dead father, considering that the shock of his death, or, more truthfully, the shock of death as a reality, was already a little more than a child could bear, but my judgment in this matter had been overruled and there they were, bewildered and frightened and very small, being led, one by one, to the casket. But there is also something very gallant about children at such moments. It has something to do with their silence and gravity and with the fact that one cannot help them. Their legs, somehow, seem *exposed*, so that it is at once incredible and terribly clear that their legs are all they have to hold them up.

I had not wanted to go to the casket myself and I certainly had not wished to be led there, but there was no way of avoiding either of these forms. One of the deacons led me up and I looked on my father's face. I cannot say that it looked like him at all. His blackness had been equivocated by powder and there was no suggestion in that casket of what his power had or could have been. He was simply an old man dead, and it was hard to believe that he had ever given any-one either joy or pain. Yet, his life filled that room. Further up the avenue his wife was holding his newborn child. Life and death so close together, and love and hatred, and right and wrong, said something to me which I did not want to hear concerning man, concerning the life of man.

After the funeral, while I was downtown desperately celebrating my birth-day, a Negro soldier, in the lobby of the Hotel Braddock, got into a fight with a white policeman over a Negro girl. Negro girls, white policemen, in or out of uniform, and Negro males — in or out of uniform — were part of the furniture of the lobby of the Hotel Braddock and this was certainly not the first time such an incident had occurred. It was destined, however, to receive an unprece-dented publicity, for the fight between the policeman and the soldier ended with the shooting of the soldier. Rumor, flowing immediately to the streets outside, stated that the soldier had been shot in the back, an instantaneous and revealing invention, and that the soldier had died protecting a Negro woman. The facts were somewhat different — for example, the soldier had not been shot in the back, and was not dead, and the girl seems to have been as dubious a symbol of womanhood as her white counterpart in Georgia usually is, but no one was interested in the facts. They preferred the invention because this invention expressed and corroborated their hates and fears so perfectly. It is just as well to remember that people are always doing this. Perhaps many of those legends, including Christianity, to which the world clings began their conquest of the world with just some such concerted surrender to distortion. The effect, in Harlem, of this particular legend was like the effect of a lit match in a tin of gasoline. The mob gathered before the doors of the Hotel Braddock simply began to swell and to spread in every direction, and Harlem exploded.

The mob did not cross the ghetto lines. It would have been easy, for example, to have gone over Morningside Park on the west side or to have crossed the Grand Central railroad tracks at 125th Street on the east side, to wreak havoc in white neighborhoods. The mob seems to have been mainly interested in something more potent and real than the white face, that is, in white power, and the principal damage done during the riot of the summer of 1943 was to white business establishments in Harlem. It might have been a far bloodier story, of course, if, at the hour the riot began, these establishments had still been open. From the Hotel Braddock the mob fanned out, east and west along 125th Street, and for the entire length of Lenox, Seventh, and Eighth avenues. Along each of these avenues, and along each major side street — 116th, 125th, 135th, and so on — bars, stores, pawnshops, restaurants, even little luncheonettes had been smashed open and entered and looted — looted, it might be added, with more haste than efficiency. The shelves really looked as though a bomb had struck them. Cans of beans and soup and dog food, along with toilet paper, corn flakes, sardines and milk tumbled every which way, and abandoned cash registers and cases of beer leaned crazily out of the splintered windows and were strewn along the avenues. Sheets, blankets, and clothing of every description formed a kind of path, as though people had dropped them while running. I truly had not realized that Harlem *had* so many stores until I saw them all smashed open; the first time the word *wealth* ever entered my mind in relation to Harlem was when I saw it scattered in the streets. But one's first, incongruous impression of plenty was countered immediately by an impression of waste. None of this was doing anybody any good. It would have been better to have left the plate glass as it had been and the goods lying in the stores.

It would have been better, but it would also have been intolerable, for Harlem had needed something to smash. To smash something is the ghetto's chronic need. Most of the time it is the members of the ghetto who smash each other, and themselves. But as long as the ghetto walls are standing there will always come a moment when these outlets do not work. That summer, for example, it was not enough to get into a fight on Lenox Avenue, or curse out one's cronies in the barber shops. If ever, indeed, the violence which fills Harlem's churches, pool halls, and bars erupts outward in a more direct fashion, Harlem and its citizens are likely to vanish in an apocalyptic flood. That this is not likely to happen is due to a great many reasons, most hidden and powerful among them the Negro's real relation to the white American. This relation prohibits, simply, anything as uncomplicated and satisfactory as pure hatred. In order really to hate white people, one has to blot so much out of the mind — and the heart — that this hatred itself becomes an exhausting and self-destructive pose. But this does not mean, on the other hand, that love comes easily; the white world is too powerful, too complacent, too ready with gratuitous humiliation, and, above all, too ignorant and too innocent for that. One is absolutely forced to make perpetual qualifications and one's own reactions are always canceling each other out. It is this, really, which has driven so many people mad, both white and black. One is always in the position of having to decide between amputation and gangrene. Amputation is swift but time may prove that the amputation was not necessary — or one may delay the amputation too long. Gangrene is slow, but it is impossible to be sure that one is reading one's symptoms right. The idea of going through life as a cripple is more than one can bear, and equally unbearable is the risk of swelling up slowly, in agony, with poison. And the trouble, finally, is that the risks are real even if the choices do not exist.

"But as for me and my house," my father had said, "we will serve the Lord." I wondered, as we drove him to his resting place, what this line had meant for him. I had heard him preach it many times. I had preached it once myself, proudly giving it an interpretation different from my father's. Now the whole thing came back to me, as though my father and I were on our way to Sunday school and I were memorizing the golden text: *And if it seem evil unto you to serve the Lord, choose you this day whom you will serve; whether the gods which your fathers served that were on the other side of the flood, or the gods of the Amorites, in whose land ye dwell: but as for me and my house, we will serve the Lord.* I suspected in these familiar lines a meaning which had never been there for me before. All of my father's texts and songs, which I had decided were meaningless, were arranged before me at his death like empty bottles, waiting to hold the meaning which life would give them for me. This was his legacy: nothing is ever escaped. That bleakly memorable morning I hated the unbelievable streets and the Negroes and whites who had, equally, made them that way. But I knew that it was folly, as my father would have said, this bitterness was folly. It was necessary to hold on to the things that mattered. The dead man mattered, the new life mattered; blackness and whiteness did not matter; to believe that they did was to acquiesce in one's own destruction. Hatred, which could destroy so much, never failed to destroy the man who hated and this was an immutable law.

It began to seem that one would have to hold in the mind forever two ideas which seemed to be in opposition. The first idea was acceptance, the acceptance, totally without rancor, of life as it is, and men as they are: in the light of this idea, it goes without saying that injustice is a commonplace. But this did not mean that one could be complacent, for the second idea was of equal power: that one must never, in one's own life, accept these injustices as commonplace but must fight them with all one's strength. This fight begins, however, in the heart and it now had been laid to my charge to keep my own heart free of hatred and despair. This intimation made my heart heavy and, now that my father was irrecoverable, I wished that he had been beside me so that I could have searched his face for the answers which only the future would give me now.

(1955)

Flannery O'Connor (1925–1964)

M ary Flannery O'Connor was born to Regina Cline and Edward Francis O'Connor Jr. on March 25, 1925, in Savannah, Georgia. As a teenager she moved with her family to Milledgeville, where she later attended Georgia State College for Women (now Georgia College). The satiric eye and keen ear for southern idioms that she honed as a cartoonist and writer in college helped her gain admittance to the University of Iowa's prestigious Writers' Workshop, where she graduated with an M.F.A. in 1947. The early 1950s brought both fame and bad news to O'Connor. In 1951 she was diagnosed with lupus, the same disease that had killed her father ten years earlier. Although crippling pain and frequent hospital visits kept her from working as much she liked, she published her first novel, *Wise Blood*, in 1952 and several highly acclaimed short stories over the next few years. Her first collection, *A Good Man Is Hard to Find*, appeared in 1955; she published a second novel, *The Violent Bear It Away*, in 1960; and her final book of short stories, *Everything That Rises Must Converge*, came out in 1965, one year after she died from kidney failure.

Although O'Connor's illness kept her close to home and under Regina's care for most of her adult years, she lived a spiritually and intellectually engaged life filled with frequent visitors, occasional lecture trips, and rich correspondence with leading writers and thinkers of her day. Rather than limiting O'Connor's fiction, Milledgeville's Deep South manners and modes of expression provided plenty of material for the author's sardonic wit and devoutly Catholic vision. Her primary targets were the narrow-minded and self-righteous, who get their comeuppance, and an opportunity to receive God's grace, in unexpected —

often grotesquely violent — ways. A prattling, narcissistic grandmother finds real human connection for the first time, ironically with the serial killer who murders her family. A Ph.D. who claims to believe in nothing has her wooden leg, and her figuratively wooden heart, stolen by a traveling Bible salesman. In the story reprinted here, the white mother's racial clichés and her son's false liberalism meet their match in a black woman who has had enough of both.

Because O'Connor often deals with racist characters, and her views of the civil rights movement were more conservative than progressive, some contemporary readers have argued that her work supported rather than challenged the late 1950s' and early 1960s' racial status quo. Black figures appear in her fiction primarily as comic relief or to facilitate white characters' spiritual confrontations, never as fully rounded characters in their own right. Still, few writers have managed to satirize white racism with as much wit and wisdom as Flannery O'Connor. Racism in her work is both an object of ridicule and the mark of a human being's spiritual failure.

Everything That Rises Must Converge

Her doctor had told Julian's mother that she must lose twenty pounds on account of her blood pressure, so on Wednesday nights Julian had to take her downtown on the bus for a reducing class at the Y. The reducing class was designed for working girls over fifty, who weighed from 165 to 200 pounds. His mother was one of the slimmer ones, but she said ladies did not tell their age or weight. She would not ride the buses by herself at night since they had been integrated, and because the reducing class was one of her few pleasures, necessary for her health, and *free*, she said Julian could at least put himself out to take her, considering all she did for him. Julian did not like to consider all she did for him, but every Wednesday night he braced himself and took her.

She was almost ready to go, standing before the hall mirror, putting on her hat, while he, his hands behind him, appeared pinned to the door frame, waiting like Saint Sebastian for the arrows to begin piercing him. The hat was new and had cost her seven dollars and a half. She kept saying, "Maybe I shouldn't have paid that for it. No, I shouldn't have. I'll take it off and return it tomorrow. I shouldn't have bought it."

Julian raised his eyes to heaven. "Yes, you should have bought it," he said. "Put it on and let's go." It was a hideous hat. A purple velvet flap came down on one side of it and stood up on the other; the rest of it was green and looked like a cushion with the stuffing out. He decided it was less comical than jaunty and pathetic. Everything that gave her pleasure was small and depressed him.

She lifted the hat one more time and set it down slowly on top of her head. Two wings of gray hair protruded on either side of her florid face, but her eyes, sky-blue, were as innocent and untouched by experience as they must have been when she was ten. Were it not that she was a widow who had struggled fiercely to feed and clothe and put him through school and who was supporting him still, "until he got on his feet," she might have been a little girl that he had to take to town.

"It's all right, it's all right," he said. "Let's go." He opened the door himself and started down the walk to get her going. The sky was a dying violet and the houses stood out darkly against it, bulbous liver-colored monstrosities of a uniform ugliness though no two were alike. Since this had been a fashionable neighborhood forty years ago, his mother persisted in thinking they did well to have an apartment in it. Each house had a narrow collar of dirt around it in which sat, usually, a grubby child. Julian walked with his hands in his pockets, his head down and thrust forward and his eyes glazed with the determination to make himself completely numb during the time he would be sacrificed to her pleasure.

The door closed and he turned to find the dumpy figure, surmounted by the atrocious hat, coming toward him. "Well," she said, "you only live once and paying a little more for it, I at least won't meet myself coming and going."

"Some day I'll start making money," Julian said gloomily — he knew he never would — "and you can have one of those jokes whenever you take the fit." But first they would move. He visualized a place where the nearest neighbors would be three miles away on either side.

"I think you're doing fine," she said, drawing on her gloves. "You've only been out of school a year. Rome wasn't built in a day."

She was one of the few members of the Y reducing class who arrived in hat and gloves and who had a son who had been to college. "It takes time," she said, "and the world is in such a mess. This hat looked better on me than any of the others, though when she brought it out I said, 'Take that thing back. I wouldn't have it on my head,' and she said, 'Now wait till you see it on,' and when she put it on me, I said, 'We-ull,' and she said, 'If you ask me, that hat does something for you and you do something for the hat, and besides,' she said, 'with that hat, you won't meet yourself coming and going.'"

Julian thought he could have stood his lot better if she had been selfish, if she had been an old hag who drank and screamed at him. He walked along, saturated in depression, as if in the midst of his martyrdom he had lost his faith. Catching sight of his long, hopeless, irritated face, she stopped suddenly with a grief-stricken look, and pulled back on his arm. "Wait on me," she said. "I'm going back to the house and take this thing off and tomorrow I'm going to return it. I was out of my head. I can pay the gas bill with the seven-fifty."

He caught her arm in a vicious grip. "You are not going to take it back," he said. "I like it."

"Well," she said, "I don't think I ought . . ."

"Shut up and enjoy it," he muttered, more depressed than ever.

"With the world in the mess it's in," she said, "it's a wonder we can enjoy anything. I tell you, the bottom rail is on the top."

Julian sighed.

"Of course," she said, "if you know who you are, you can go anywhere." She said this every time he took her to the reducing class. "Most of them in it are not our kind of people," she said, "but I can be gracious to anybody. I know who I am."

"They don't give a damn for your graciousness," Julian said savagely. "Knowing who you are is good for one generation only. You haven't the foggiest idea where you stand now or who you are."

She stopped and allowed her eyes to flash at him. "I most certainly do know who I am," she said, "and if you don't know who you are, I'm ashamed of you."

"Oh hell," Julian said.

"Your great-grandfather was a former governor of this state," she said. "Your grandfather was a prosperous landowner. Your grandmother was a Godhigh."

"Will you look around you," he said tensely, "and see where you are now?" and he swept his arm jerkily out to indicate the neighborhood, which the growing darkness at least made less dingy.

"You remain what you are," she said. "Your great-grandfather had a plantation and two hundred slaves."

"There are no more slaves," he said irritably.

"They were better off when they were," she said. He groaned to see that she was off on that topic. She rolled onto it every few days like a train on an open track. He knew every stop, every junction, every swamp along the way, and knew the exact point at which her conclusion would roll majestically into the station: "It's ridiculous. It's simply not realistic. They should rise, yes, but on their own side of the fence."

"Let's skip it," Julian said.

"The ones I feel sorry for," she said, "are the ones that are half white. They're tragic."

"Will you skip it?"

"Suppose we were half white. We would certainly have mixed feelings."

"I have mixed feelings now," he groaned.

"Well let's talk about something pleasant," she said. "I remember going to Grandpa's when I was a little girl. Then the house had double stairways that went up to what was really the second floor — all the cooking was done on the first. I used to like to stay down in the kitchen on account of the way the walls smelled. I would sit with my nose pressed against the plaster and take deep breaths. Actually the place belonged to the Godhighs but your grandfather Chestny paid the mortgage and saved it for them. They were in reduced circumstances," she said, "but reduced or not, they never forgot who they were."

"Doubtless that decayed mansion reminded them," Julian muttered. He never spoke of it without contempt or thought of it without longing. He had seen it once when he was a child before it had been sold. The double stairways had rotted and been torn down. Negroes were living in it. But it remained in his mind as his mother had known it. It appeared in his dreams regularly. He would stand on the wide porch, listening to the rustle of oak leaves, then wander through the high-ceilinged hall into the parlor that opened onto it and gaze at the worn rugs and faded draperies. It occurred to him that it was he, not she, who could have appreciated it. He preferred its threadbare elegance to anything he could name and it was because of it that all the neighborhoods they had lived in had been a torment to him — whereas she had hardly known the difference. She called her insensitivity "being adjustable."

"And I remember the old darky who was my nurse, Caroline. There was no better person in the world. I've always had a great respect for my colored friends," she said. "I'd do anything in the world for them and they'd . . ."

"Will you for God's sake get off that subject?" Julian said. When he got on a bus by himself, he made it a point to sit down beside a Negro, in reparation as it were for his mother's sins.

"You're mighty touchy tonight," she said. "Do you feel all right?"

"Yes I feel all right," he said. "Now lay off."

She pursed her lips. "Well, you certainly are in a vile humor," she observed. "I just won't speak to you at all."

They had reached the bus stop. There was no bus in sight and Julian, his hands still jammed in his pockets and his head thrust forward, scowled down the empty street. The frustration of having to wait on the bus as well as ride on it began to creep up his neck like a hot hand. The presence of his mother was borne in upon him as she gave a pained sigh. He looked at her bleakly. She was holding herself very erect under the preposterous hat, wearing it like a banner of her imaginary dignity. There was in him an evil urge to break her spirit. He suddenly unloosened his tie and pulled it off and put it in his pocket.

She stiffened. "Why must you look like that when you take me to town?" she said. "Why must you deliberately embarrass me?"

"If you'll never learn where you are," he said, "you can at least learn where I am."

"You look like a — thug," she said.

"Then I must be one," he murmured.

"I'll just go home," she said. "I will not bother you. If you can't do a little thing like that for me . . ."

Rolling his eyes upward, he put his tie back on. "Restored to my class," he muttered. He thrust his face toward her and hissed, "True culture is in the, mind, the *mind*," he said, and tapped his head, "the mind."

"It's in the heart," she said, "and in how you do things and how you do things is because of who you are."

"Nobody in the damn bus cares who you *are*."

"I care who I am," she said icily.

The lighted bus appeared on top of the next hill and as it approached, they moved out into the street to meet it. He put his hand under her elbow and hoisted her up on the creaking step. She entered with a little smile, as if she were going into a drawing room where everyone had been waiting for her. While he put in the tokens, she sat down on one of the broad front seats for three which faced the aisle. A thin woman with protruding teeth and long yellow hair was sitting on the end of it. His mother moved up beside her and left room for Julian beside herself. He sat down and looked at the floor across the aisle where a pair of thin feet in red and white canvas sandals were planted.

His mother immediately began a general conversation meant to attract anyone who felt like talking. "Can it get any hotter?" she said and removed from her purse a folding fan, black with a Japanese scene on it, which she began to flutter before her.

"I reckon it might could," the woman with the protruding teeth said, "but I know for a fact my apartment couldn't get no hotter."

"It must get the afternoon sun," his mother said. She sat forward and looked up and down the bus. It was half filled. Everybody was white. "I see we have the bus to ourselves," she said. Julian cringed.

"For a change," said the woman across the aisle, the owner of the red and white canvas sandals. "I come on one the other day and they were thick as fleas — up front and all through."

"The world is in a mess everywhere," his mother said. "I don't know how we've let it get in this fix."

"What gets my goat is all those boys from good families stealing automobile tires," the woman with the protruding teeth said. "I told my boy, I said you may not be rich but you been raised right and if I ever catch you in any such mess, they can send you on to the reformatory. Be exactly where you belong."

"Training tells," his mother said. "Is your boy in high school?"

"Ninth grade," the woman said.

"My son just finished college last year. He wants to write but he's selling typewriters until he gets started," his mother said.

The woman leaned forward and peered at Julian. He threw her such a malevolent look that she subsided against the seat. On the floor across the aisle there was an abandoned newspaper. He got up and got it and opened it out in front of him. His mother discreetly continued the conversation in a lower tone but the woman across the aisle said in a loud voice, "Well that's nice. Selling typewriters is close to writing. He can go right from one to the other."

"I tell him," his mother said, "that Rome wasn't built in a day." Behind the newspaper Julian was withdrawing into the inner compartment of his mind where he spent most of his time. This was a kind of mental bubble in which he established himself when he could not bear to be a part of what was going on around him. From it he could see out and judge but in it he was safe from any kind of penetration from without. It was the only place where he felt free of the general idiocy of his fellows. His mother had never entered it but from it he could see her with absolute clarity.

The old lady was clever enough and he thought that if she had started from any of the right premises, more might have been expected of her. She lived according to the laws of her own fantasy world, outside of which he had never seen her set foot. The law of it was to sacrifice herself for him after she had first created the necessity to do so by making a mess of things. If he had permitted her sacrifices, it was only because her lack of foresight had made them necessary. All of her life had been a struggle to act like a Chestny without the Chestny goods, and to give him everything she thought a Chestny ought to have; but since, said she, it was fun to struggle, why complain? And when you had won, as she had won, what fun to look back on the hard times! He could not forgive her that she had enjoyed the struggle and that she thought she had won.

What she meant when she said she had won was that she had brought him up successfully and had sent him to college and that he had turned out so well — good looking (her teeth had gone unfilled so that his could be straightened), intelligent (he realized he was too intelligent to be a success), and with a future ahead of him (there was of course no future ahead of him). She excused his gloominess on the grounds that he was still growing up and his radical ideas on his lack of practical experience. She said he didn't yet know a thing about "life," that he hadn't even entered the real world — when already he was as disenchanted with it as a man of fifty.

The further irony of all this was that in spite of her, he had turned out so well. In spite of going to only a third-rate college, he had, on his own initiative, come out with a first-rate education; in spite of growing up dominated by a small mind, he had ended up with a large one; in spite of all her foolish views, he was free of prejudice and unafraid to face facts. Most miraculous of all, instead of being blinded by love for her as she was for him, he had cut himself emotionally free of her and could see her with complete objectivity. He was not dominated by his mother.

The bus stopped with a sudden jerk and shook him from his meditation. A woman from the back lurched forward with little steps and barely escaped falling in his newspaper as she righted herself. She got off and a large Negro got on. Julian kept his paper lowered to watch. It gave him a certain satisfaction to see injustice in daily operation. It confirmed his view that with a few exceptions there was no one worth knowing within a radius of three hundred miles. The Negro was well dressed and carried a briefcase. He looked around and then sat down on the other end of the seat where the woman with the red and white canvas sandals was sitting. He immediately unfolded a newspaper and obscured himself behind it. Julian's mother's elbow at once prodded insistently into his ribs. "Now you see why I won't ride on these buses by myself," she whispered.

The woman with the red and white canvas sandals had risen at the same time the Negro sat down and had gone further back in the bus and taken the seat of the woman who had got off. His mother leaned forward and cast her an approving look.

Julian rose, crossed the aisle, and sat down in the place of the woman with the canvas sandals. From this position, he looked serenely across at his mother. Her face had turned an angry red. He stared at her, making his eyes the eyes of a stranger. He felt his tension suddenly lift as if he had openly declared war on her.

He would have liked to get in conversation with the Negro and to talk with him about art or politics or any subject that would be above the comprehension of those around them, but the man remained entrenched behind his paper. He was either ignoring the change of seating or had never noticed it. There was no way for Julian to convey his sympathy.

His mother kept her eyes fixed reproachfully on his face. The woman with the protruding teeth was looking at him avidly as if he were a type of monster new to her.

"Do you have a light?" he asked the Negro.

Without looking away from his paper, the man reached in his pocket and handed him a packet of matches.

"Thanks," Julian said. For a moment he held the matches foolishly. A NO SMOKING sign looked down upon him from over the door. This alone would not have deterred him; he had no cigarettes. He had quit smoking some months before because he could not afford it. "Sorry," he muttered and handed back the matches. The Negro lowered the paper and gave him an annoyed look. He took the matches and raised the paper again.

His mother continued to gaze at him but she did not take advantage of his momentary discomfort. Her eyes retained their battered look. Her face seemed to be unnaturally red, as if her blood pressure had risen. Julian allowed no glimmer of sympathy to show on his face. Having got the advantage, he wanted desperately to keep it and carry it through. He would have liked to teach her a lesson that would last her a while, but there seemed no way to continue the point. The Negro refused to come out from behind his paper.

Julian folded his arms and looked stolidly before him, facing her but as if he did not see her, as if he had ceased to recognize her existence. He visualized a scene in which, the bus having reached their stop, he would remain in his seat and when she said, "Aren't you going to get off?" he would look at her as at a stranger who had rashly addressed him. The corner they got off on was usually deserted, but it was well lighted and it would not hurt her to walk by herself the four blocks to the Y. He decided to wait until the time came and then decide whether or not he would let her get off by herself. He would have to be at the Y at ten to bring her back, but he could leave her wondering if he was going to show up. There was no reason for her to think she could always depend on him.

He retired again into the high-ceilinged room sparsely settled with large pieces of antique furniture. His soul expanded momentarily but then he became aware of his mother across from him and the vision shriveled. He studied her coldly. Her feet in little pumps dangled like a child's and did not quite reach the floor. She was training on him an exaggerated look of reproach. He felt completely detached from her. At that moment he could with pleasure have slapped her as he would have slapped a particularly obnoxious child in his charge.

He began to imagine various unlikely ways by which he could teach her a lesson. He might make friends with some distinguished Negro professor or lawyer and bring him home to spend the evening. He would be entirely justified but her blood pressure would rise to 300. He could not push her to the extent of making her have a stroke, and moreover, he had never been successful at making any Negro friends. He had tried to strike up an acquaintance on the bus with some of the better types, with ones that looked like professors or ministers or lawyers. One morning he had sat down next to a distinguished-looking dark brown man who had answered his questions with a sonorous solemnity but who had turned out to be an undertaker. Another day he had sat down beside a cigar-smoking Negro with a diamond ring on his finger, but after a few stilted pleasantries, the Negro had rung the buzzer and risen, slipping two lottery tickets into Julian's hand as he climbed over him to leave.

He imagined his mother lying desperately ill and his being able to secure only a Negro doctor for her. He toyed with that idea for a few minutes and then dropped it for a momentary vision of himself participating as a sympathizer in a sit-in demonstration. This was possible but he did not linger with it. Instead, he approached the ultimate horror. He brought home a beautiful suspiciously Negroid woman. Prepare yourself, he said. There is nothing you can do about it. This is the woman I've chosen. She's intelligent, dignified, even good, and she's suffered and she hasn't thought it *fun*. Now persecute us, go ahead and persecute us. Drive her out of here, but remember, you're driving me too. His eyes were narrowed and through the indignation he had generated, he saw his mother across the aisle, purple-faced, shrunken to the dwarf-like proportions of her moral nature, sitting like a mummy beneath the ridiculous banner of her hat.

He was tilted out of his fantasy again as the bus stopped. The door opened with a sucking hiss and out of the dark a large, gaily dressed, sullen-looking colored woman got on with a little boy. The child, who might have been four, had on a short plaid suit and a Tyrolean hat with a blue feather in it. Julian hoped that he would sit down beside him and that the woman would push in beside his mother. He could think of no better arrangement.

As she waited for her tokens, the woman was surveying the seating possibilities — he hoped with the idea of sitting where she was least wanted. There was something familiar-looking about her but Julian could not place what it was. She was a giant of a woman. Her face was set not only to meet opposition but to seek it out. The downward tilt of her large lower lip was like a warning sign DON'T TAMPER WITH ME. Her bulging figure was encased in a green crepe dress and her feet overflowed in red shoes. She had on a hideous hat. A purple velvet flap came down on one side of it and stood up on the other; the rest of it was green and looked like a cushion with the stuffing out. She carried a mammoth red pocketbook that bulged throughout as if it were stuffed with rocks.

To Julian's disappointment, the little boy climbed up on the empty seat beside his mother. His mother lumped all children, black and white, into the common category, "cute," and she thought little Negroes were on the whole cuter than little white children. She smiled at the little boy as he climbed on the seat.

Meanwhile the woman was bearing down upon the empty seat beside Julian. To his annoyance, she squeezed herself into it. He saw his mother's face change as the woman settled herself next to him and he realized with satisfaction that this was more objectionable to her than it was to him. Her face seemed almost gray and there was a look of dull recognition in her eyes, as if suddenly she had sickened at some awful confrontation. Julian saw that it was because she and the woman had, in a sense, swapped sons. Though his mother would not realize the symbolic significance of this, she would feel it. His amusement showed plainly on his face.

The woman next to him muttered something unintelligible to herself. He was conscious of a kind of bristling next to him, muted growling like that of an angry cat. He could not see anything but the red pocketbook upright on the bulging green thighs. He visualized the woman as she had stood waiting for her tokens — the ponderous figure, rising from the red shoes upward over the solid hips, the mammoth bosom, the haughty face, to the green and purple hat.

His eyes widened.

The vision of the two hats, identical, broke upon him with the radiance of a brilliant sunrise. His face was suddenly lit with joy. He could not believe that Fate had thrust upon his mother such a lesson. He gave a loud chuckle so that she would look at him and see that he saw. She turned her eyes on him slowly. The blue in them seemed to have turned a bruised purple. For a moment he had an uncomfortable sense of her innocence, but it lasted only a second before principle rescued him. Justice entitled him to laugh. His grin hardened until it said to her as plainly as if he were saying aloud: Your punishment exactly fits your pettiness. This should teach you a permanent lesson.

Her eyes shifted to the woman. She seemed unable to bear looking at him and to find the woman preferable. He became conscious again of the bristling presence at his side. The woman was rumbling like a volcano about to become active. His mother's mouth began to twitch slightly at one corner. With a sinking heart, he saw incipient signs of recovery on her face and realized that this was going to strike her suddenly as funny and was going to be no lesson at all. She kept her eyes on the woman and an amused smile came over her face as if the woman were a monkey that had stolen her hat. The little Negro was looking up at her with large fascinated eyes. He had been trying to attract her attention for some time.

"Carver!" the woman said suddenly. "Come heah!"

When he saw that the spotlight was on him at last, Carver drew his feet up and turned himself toward Julian's mother and giggled.

"Carver!" the woman said. "You heah me? Come heah!"

Carver slid down from the seat but remained squatting with his back against the base of it, his head turned slyly around toward Julian's mother, who was smiling at him. The woman reached a hand across the aisle and snatched him to her. He righted himself and hung backwards on her knees, grinning at Julian's mother. "Isn't he cute?" Julian's mother said to the woman with the protruding teeth.

"I reckon he is," the woman said without conviction.

The Negress yanked him upright but he eased out of her grip and shot across the aisle and scrambled, giggling wildly, onto the seat beside his love.

"I think he likes me," Julian's mother said, and smiled at the woman. It was the smile she used when she was being particularly gracious to an inferior. Julian saw everything lost. The lesson had rolled off her like rain on a roof.

The woman stood up and yanked the little boy off the seat as if she were snatching him from contagion. Julian could feel the rage in her at having no weapon like his mother's smile. She gave the child a sharp slap across his leg. He howled once and then thrust his head into her stomach and kicked his feet against her shins. "Behave," she said vehemently.

The bus stopped and the Negro who had been reading the newspaper got off. The woman moved over and set the little boy down with a thump between herself and Julian. She held him firmly by the knee. In a moment he put his hands in front of his face and peeped at Julian's mother through his fingers.

"I see yoooooooo!" she said and put her hand in front of her face and peeped at him.

The woman slapped his hand down. "Quit yo' foolishness," she said, "before I knock the living Jesus out of you!"

Julian was thankful that the next stop was theirs. He reached up and pulled the cord. The woman reached up and pulled it at the same time. Oh my God, he thought. He had the terrible intuition that when they got off the bus together, his mother would open her purse and give the little boy a nickel. The gesture would be as natural to her as breathing. The bus stopped and the woman got up and lunged to the front, dragging the child, who wished to stay on, after her.

Julian and his mother got up and followed. As they neared the door, Julian tried to relieve her of her pocketbook.

"No," she murmured, "I want to give the little boy a nickel."

"No!" Julian hissed. "No!"

She smiled down at the child and opened her bag. The bus door opened and the woman picked him up by the arm and descended with him, hanging at her hip. Once in the street she set him down and shook him.

Julian's mother had to close her purse while she got down the bus step but as soon as her feet were on the ground, she opened it again and began to rummage inside. "I can't find but a penny," she whispered, "but it looks like a new one."

"Don't do it!" Julian said fiercely between his teeth. There was a streetlight on the corner and she hurried to get under it so that she could better see into her pocketbook. The woman was heading off rapidly down the street with the child still hanging backward on her hand.

"Oh little boy!" Julian's mother called and took a few quick steps and caught up with them just beyond the lamppost. "Here's a bright new penny for you," and she held out the coin, which shone bronze in the dim light.

The huge woman turned and for a moment stood, her shoulders lifted and her face frozen with frustrated rage, and stared at Julian's mother. Then all at once she seemed to explode like a piece of machinery that had been given one ounce of pressure too much. Julian saw the black fist swing out with the red pocketbook. He shut his eyes and cringed as he heard the woman shout, "He don't take nobody's pennies!" When he opened his eyes, the woman was disappearing down the street with the little boy staring wide-eyed over her shoulder. Julian's mother was sitting on the sidewalk.

"I told you not to do that," Julian said angrily. "I told you not to do that!"

He stood over her for a minute, gritting his teeth. Her legs were stretched out in front of her and her hat was on her lap. He squatted down and looked her in the face. It was totally expressionless. "You got exactly what you deserved," he said. "Now get up."

He picked up her pocketbook and put what had fallen out back in it. He picked the hat up off her lap. The penny caught his eye on the sidewalk and he picked that up and let it drop before her eyes into the purse. Then he stood up and leaned over and held his hands out to pull her up. She remained immobile. He sighed. Rising above them on either side were black apartment buildings, marked with irregular rectangles of light. At the end of the block a man came out of a door and walked off in the opposite direction. "All right," he said, "suppose somebody happens by and wants to know why you're sitting on the sidewalk?"

She took the hand and, breathing hard, pulled heavily up on it and then stood for a moment, swaying slightly as if the spots of light in the darkness were circling around her. Her eyes, shadowed and confused, finally settled on his face. He did not try to conceal his irritation. "I hope this teaches you a lesson," he said. She leaned forward and her eyes raked his face. She seemed trying to determine his identity. Then, as if she found nothing familiar about him, she started off with a headlong movement in the wrong direction.

"Aren't you going on to the Y?" he asked.

"Home," she muttered.

"Well, are we walking?"

For answer she kept going. Julian followed along, his hands behind him. He saw no reason to let the lesson she had had go without backing it up with an explanation of its meaning. She might as well be made to understand what had happened to her. "Don't think that was just an uppity Negro woman," he said. "That was the whole colored race which will no longer take your condescending pennies. That was your black double. She can wear the same hat as you, and to be sure," he added gratuitously (because he thought it was funny), "it looked better on her than it did on you. What all this means," he said, "is that the old world is gone. The old manners are obsolete and your graciousness is not worth a damn." He thought bitterly of the house that had been lost for him. "You aren't who you think you are," he said.

She continued to plow ahead, paying no attention to him. Her hair had come undone on one side. She dropped her pocketbook and took no notice. He stooped and picked it up and handed it to her but she did not take it.

"You needn't act as if the world had come to an end," he said, "because it hasn't. From now on you've got to live in a new world and face a few realities for a change. Buck up," he said, "it won't kill you."

She was breathing fast.

"Let's wait on the bus," he said.

"Home," she said thickly.

"I hate to see you behave like this," he said. "Just like a child. I should be able to expect more of you." He decided to stop where he was and make her stop and wait for a bus. "I'm not going any farther," he said, stopping. "We're going on the bus."

She continued to go on as if she had not heard him. He took a few steps and caught her arm and stopped her. He looked into her face and caught his breath. He was looking into a face he had never seen before. "Tell Grandpa to come get me," she said.

He stared, stricken.

"Tell Caroline to come get me," she said.

Stunned, he let her go and she lurched forward again, walking as if one leg were shorter than the other. A tide of darkness seemed to be sweeping her from him. "Mother!" he cried. "Darling, sweetheart, wait!" Crumpling, she fell to the pavement. He dashed forward and fell at her side, crying, "Mamma, Mamma!"

He turned her over. Her face was fiercely distorted. One eye, large and staring, moved slightly to the left as if it had become unmoored. The other remained fixed on him, raked his face again, found nothing and closed.

"Wait here, wait here!" he cried and jumped up and began to run for help toward a cluster of lights he saw in the distance ahead of him. "Help, help!" he shouted, but his voice was thin, scarcely a thread of sound. The lights drifted farther away the faster he ran and his feet moved numbly as if they carried him nowhere. The tide of darkness seemed to sweep him back to her, postponing from moment to moment his entry into the world of guilt and sorrow.

(1961)

Malcolm X
(El-Hajj Malik El-Shabazz) (1925–1965)

orn on May 19, 1925, in Omaha, Nebraska, Malcolm Little lived with his seven siblings and his mother and father. His father, Earl, was a Baptist minister and a civil rights activist who was greatly influenced by Marcus Garvey. Due to Earl Little's beliefs and activism the family was repeatedly threatened by the Black Legion, a white supremacist organization. The threats against the family culminated with the burning of their home in Michigan and with Earl's murder, although both incidents were ruled by the police to be accidents. After Malcolm's mother, Louise Norton Little, suffered a nervous breakdown, the seven siblings were separated and sent to foster homes and orphanages. Growing up primarily in Michigan, Malcolm graduated from junior high school at the top of his class but was discouraged by a teacher who told him that becoming a lawyer was not a realistic goal for a black man.

Malcolm then worked various odd jobs in Boston and Harlem before being convicted of burglary in 1946. While incarcerated at Charlestown State Penitentiary he devoted his time to self-education and was particularly interested in the teachings of Elijah Muhammad, the Nation of Islam leader. When Malcolm was paroled in 1952 he converted to Islam and changed his surname from "Little," which he considered to be a slave name, to "X." Soon after Malcolm became a minister and the national spokesman for the Nation of Islam and began establishing mosques in cities and neighborhoods with large African American populations, such as Detroit and Harlem. He was responsible for an enormous number of conversions to Islam during this time period, and he consequently received much attention from the national media and government. At odds with other civil rights leaders working toward integration, Malcolm advocated black separatism, pride, and independence. Because of his position on these issues he became a role model for activists in the Black Power movement. Malcolm also founded the Organization of Afro-American Unity, an interfaith-based group for African Americans working for social justice.

In 1958 Malcolm married Betty Shabazz, with whom he had six daughters, and in 1964 Malcolm published *The Autobiography of Malcolm X* with Alex Haley. That same year, he delivered a famous speech, "The Ballot or the Bullet," at an event sponsored by the Congress of Racial Equality (CORE) in Cleveland, Ohio, where he critiqued the approach of nonviolent direct action and characterized the struggle for rights as both an American and international (not merely a southern) phenomenon. Not long after the speech, his growing disillusionment with Elijah Muhammad led to a break with the Nation of Islam. Malcolm then founded the Muslim Mosque and traveled to Mecca, Africa, and parts of the Middle East. After seeing the unity among Muslims across ethnic backgrounds, Malcolm returned to the States and retracted his former advocacy of separatism. He then converted to orthodox Islam and changed his name to El-Hajj Malik El-Shabazz. After his renunciation Malcolm's life was threatened several times by his former supporters in the Nation of Islam, and his family's home was bombed in 1965. On February 21, 1965, Malcolm was shot and killed during a rally in Harlem. Three men were convicted for the crime, all members of the Nation of Islam.

Malcolm was a powerful voice of conscience for the movement's revolutionary spirit, and his death, as many literary works note, marked an emotional low point in the struggle. His life and his words, however, continue to inspire those who came after him. The selection from his *Autobiography*, reprinted below, describes his political awakening through reading and, thus, a significant moment of transformation in his life.

Selection from *The Autobiography of Malcolm X*

Chapter 11, Saved

I did write to Elijah Muhammad. He lived in Chicago at that time, at 6116 South Michigan Avenue. At least twenty-five times I must have written that first one-page letter to him, over and over. I was trying to make it both legible and understandable. I practically couldn't read my handwriting myself; it shames even to remember it. My spelling and my grammar were as bad, if not worse. Anyway, as well as I could express it, I said I had been told about him by my brothers and sisters, and I apologized for my poor letter.

Mr. Muhammad sent me a typed reply. It had an all but electrical effect upon me to see the signature of the "Messenger of Allah." After he welcomed me into the "true knowledge," he gave me something to think about. The black prisoner, he said, symbolized white society's crime of keeping black men oppressed and deprived and ignorant, and unable to get decent jobs, turning them into criminals.

He told me to have courage. He even enclosed some money for me, a five-dollar bill. Mr. Muhammad sends money all over the country to prison inmates who write to him, probably to this day.

Regularly my family wrote to me, "Turn to Allah . . . — pray to the East."

The hardest test I ever faced in my life was praying. You understand. My comprehending, my believing the teachings of Mr. Muhammad had only required my mind's saying to me, "That's right!" or "I never thought of that."

But bending my knees to pray — that *act* — well, that took me a week.

You know what my life had been. Picking a lock to rob someone's house was the only way my knees had ever been bent before.

I had to force myself to bend my knees. And waves of shame and embarrassment would force me back up.

For evil to bend its knees, admitting its guilt, to implore the forgiveness of God, is the hardest thing in the world. It's easy for me to see and to say that now. But then, when I was the personification of evil, I was going through it. Again, again, I would force myself back down into the praying-to-Allah posture. When finally I was able to make myself stay down — I didn't know what to say to Allah.

For the next years, I was the nearest thing to a hermit in the Norfolk Prison Colony. I never have been more busy in my life. I still marvel at how swiftly my previous life's thinking pattern slid away from me, like snow off a roof. It is as though someone else I knew of had lived by hustling and crime. I would be startled to catch myself thinking in a remote way of my earlier self as another person.

The things I felt, I was pitifully unable to express in the one-page letter that went every day to Mr. Elijah Muhammad. And I wrote at least one more daily letter, replying to one of my brothers and sisters. Every letter I received from them added something to my knowledge of the teachings of Mr. Muhammad. I would sit for long periods and study his photographs.

I've never been one for inaction. Everything I've ever felt strongly about, I've done something about. I guess that's why, unable to do anything else, I soon began writing to people I had known in the hustling world, such as Sammy the Pimp, John Hughes, the gambling house owner, the thief Jumpsteady, and several dope peddlers. I wrote them all about Allah and Islam and Mr. Elijah Muhammad. I had no idea where most of them lived. I addressed their letters in care of the Harlem or Roxbury bars and clubs where I'd known them.

I never got a single reply. The average hustler and criminal was too uneducated to write a letter. I have known many slick, sharp-looking hustlers, who would have you think they had an interest in Wall Street; privately, they would get someone else to read a letter if they received one. Besides, neither would I have replied to anyone writing me something as wild as "the white man is the devil."

What certainly went on the Harlem and Roxbury wires was that Detroit Red was going crazy in stir, or else he was trying some hype to shake up the warden's office.

During the years that I stayed in the Norfolk Prison Colony, never did any official directly say anything to me about those letters, although, of course, they all passed through the prison censorship. I'm sure, however, they monitored what I wrote to add to the files which every state and federal prison keeps on the conversion of Negro inmates by the teachings of Mr. Elijah Muhammad.

But at that time, I felt that the real reason was that the white man knew that he was the devil.

Later on, I even wrote to the Mayor of Boston, to the Governor of Massachusetts, and to Harry S. Truman. They never answered; they probably never even saw my letters. I handscratched to them how the white man's society was responsible for the black man's condition in this wilderness of North America.

It was because of my letters that I happened to stumble upon starting to acquire some kind of a homemade education.

I became increasingly frustrated at not being able to express what I wanted to convey in letters that I wrote, especially those to Mr. Elijah Muhammad. In the street, I had been the most articulate hustler out there — I had commanded attention when I said something. But now, trying to write simple English, I not only wasn't articulate, I wasn't even functional. How would I sound writing in slang, the way I would *say* it, something such as, "Look, daddy, let me pull your coat about a cat, Elijah Muhammad — "

Many who today hear me somewhere in person, or on television, or those who read something I've said, will think I went to school far beyond the eighth grade. This impression is due entirely to my prison studies.

It had really begun back in the Charlestown Prison, when Bimbi first made me feel envy of his stock of knowledge. Bimbi had always taken charge of any conversation he was in, and I had tried to emulate him. But every book I picked up had few sentences which didn't contain anywhere from one to nearly all of the words that might as well have been in Chinese. When I just skipped those words, of course, I really ended up with little idea of what the book said. So I had come to the Norfolk Prison Colony still going through only book-reading motions. Pretty soon, I would have quit even these motions, unless I had received the motivation that I did.

I saw that the best thing I could do was get hold of a dictionary — to study, to learn some words. I was lucky enough to reason also that I should try to improve my penmanship. It was sad. I couldn't even write in a straight line. It was both ideas together that moved me to request a dictionary along with some tablets and pencils from the Norfolk Prison Colony school.

I spent two days just riffling uncertainly through the dictionary's pages. I never realized so many words existed! I didn't know *which* words I needed to learn. Finally, just to start some kind of action, I began copying.

In my slow, painstaking, ragged handwriting, I copied into my tablet everything printed on that first page, down to the punctuation marks.

I believe it took me a day. Then, aloud, I read back, to myself, everything I'd written on the table. Over and over, aloud, to myself, I read my own handwriting.

I woke up the next morning, thinking about those words — immensely proud to realize that not only had I written so much at one time, but I'd written words that I never knew were in the world. Moreover, with a little effort, I also could remember what many of these words meant. I reviewed the words whose meanings I didn't remember. Funny thing, from the dictionary first page right now, that "aardvark" springs to my mind. The dictionary had a picture of it, a long-tailed, long-eared burrowing African mammal, which lives off termites caught by sticking out its tongue as an anteater does for ants.

I was so fascinated that I went on — I copied the dictionary's next page. And the same experience came when I studied that. With every succeeding page, I also learned of people and places and events from history. Actually the dictionary's A section had filled a whole tablet — and I went into the B's. That was the way I started copying what eventually became the entire dictionary. It went a lot faster after so much practice helped me to pick up the handwriting speed. Between what I wrote in my tablet, and writing letters, during the rest of my time in prison I would guess I wrote a million words.

I suppose it was inevitable that as my word-base broadened, I could for the first time pick up a book and read and now begin to understand what the book was saying. Anyone who has read a great deal can imagine the new world that opened. Let me tell you something: from then until I left that prison, in every free moment I had, if I was not reading in the library, I was reading on my bunk. You couldn't have gotten me out of books with a wedge. Between Mr. Muhammad's teaching, my correspondence, my visitors — usually Ella and Reginald — and my reading of books, months passed without my even thinking about being imprisoned. In fact, up to then, I never had been so truly free in my life.

The Norfolk Prison Colony's library was in the school building. A variety of classes was taught there by instructors who came from such places as Harvard and Boston universities. The weekly debates between inmate teams were also held in the school building. You would be astonished to know how worked up convict debaters and audiences could get over subjects like "Should Babies Be Fed Milk?"

Available on the prison libraries shelves were books on just about every general subject. Much of the big private collection that Parkhurst had willed to the prison was still in crates and boxes in back of the library — thousands of old books.* Some of them looked ancient: covers faded, old-time parchment-looking binding. Parkhurst, I've mentioned, seemed to have been principally interested in history and religion. He had the money and the special interest to have a lot of books that you wouldn't have in general circulation. Any college library would have been lucky to get that collection.

As you can imagine, especially in a prison where there was a heavy emphasis on rehabilitation, an inmate was smiled upon if he demonstrated an unusually intense interest in books. There was a sizable number of well-read inmates, especially the popular debaters. Some were said by many to be practically walking encyclopedias. They were almost celebrities. No university would ask any student to devour literature as I did when this new world opened to me, of being able to read and *understand*.

I read more in my room than in the library itself. An inmate who was known to read a lot could check out more than the permitted maximum number of books. I preferred reading in the total isolation of my own room.

When I had progressed to really serious reading, every night at about ten p.m. I would be outraged with the "lights out." It always seemed to catch me right in the middle of something engrossing.

Fortunately, right outside my door was a corridor light that cast a glow into my room. The glow was enough to read by, once my eyes adjusted to it. So when "lights out" came, I would sit on the floor where I could continue reading in that glow.

At one-hour intervals the night guards paced past every room. Each time I heard the approaching footsteps, I jumped into bed and feigned sleep. And as soon as the guard passed, I got back out of bed onto the floor area of that light-glow, where I would read for another fifty-eight minutes — until the guard approached again. That went on until three or four every morning. Three or four hours of sleep a night was enough for me. Often in the years in the streets I had slept less than that.

THE TEACHINGS OF Mr. Muhammad stressed how history had been "whitened" — when white men had written history books, the black man simply had been left out. Mr. Muhammad couldn't have said anything that would have struck me much harder. I had never forgotten how when my class, me and all of those whites, had studied seventh-grade United States history back in Mason, the history of the Negro had been covered in one paragraph, and the teacher had

---

* Lewis Parkhurst (1856 – 1949): a state senator from Winchester, Massachusetts, who willed his substantial library to the Norfolk Penal Colony.

gotten a big laugh with his joke, "Negroes' feet are so big that when they walk, they leave a hole in the ground."

This is one reason why Mr. Muhammad's teachings spread so swiftly all over the United States, among all Negroes, whether or not they became followers of Mr. Muhammad. The teachings ring true — to every Negro. You can hardly show me a black adult in America — or a white one, for that matter — who knows from the history books anything like the truth about the black man's role. In my own case, once I heard of the "glorious history of the black man," I took special pains to hunt in the library for books that would inform me on details about black history.

I can remember accurately the very first set of books that really impressed me. I have since bought that set of books and have it at home for my children to read as they grow up. It's called *Wonders of the World*. It's full of pictures of archeological finds, statues that depict, usually, non-European people.

I found books like Will Durant's *Story of Civilization*. I read H. G. Wells' *Outline of History*. *Souls of Black Folk* by W. E. B. Du Bois gave me a glimpse into the black people's history before they came to this country. Carter O. Woodson's *Negro History* opened my eyes about black empires before the black slave was brought to the United States, and the early Negro struggles for freedom.

J. A. Rogers' three volumes of *Sex and Race* told about race-mixing before Christ's time; about Aesop being a black man who told fables; about Egypt's Pharaohs; about the great Coptic Christian Empires; about Ethiopia, the earth's oldest continuous black civilization, as China is the oldest continuous civilization.

Mr. Muhammad's teaching about how the white man had been created led me to *Findings in Genetics* by Gregor Mendel. (The dictionary's G section was where I had learned what "genetics" meant.) I really studied this book by the Austrian monk. Reading it over and over, especially certain sections, helped me to understand that if you started with a black man, a white man could be produced; but starting with a white man, you never could produce a black man — because the white chromosome is recessive. And since no one disputes that there was but one Original Man, the conclusion is clear.

During the last year or so, in the *New York Times*, Arnold Toynbee used the word "bleached" in describing the white man. (His words were: "White (i.e. bleached) human beings of North European origin. . . .") Toynbee also referred to the European geographic area as only a peninsula of Asia. He said there is no such thing as Europe. And if you look at the globe, you will see for yourself that America is only an extension of Asia. (But at the same time Toynbee is among those who have helped to bleach history. He has written that Africa was the only continent that produced no history. He won't write that again. Every day now, the truth is coming to light.)

I never will forget how shocked I was when I began reading about slavery's total horror. It made such an impact upon me that it later became one of my favorite subjects when I became a minister of Mr. Muhammad's. The world's most monstrous crime, the sin and the blood on the white man's hands, are almost impossible to believe. Books like the one by Frederick Olmstead opened my eyes to the horrors suffered when the slave was landed in the United States. The European woman, Fannie Kimball, who had married a Southern white slaveowner, described how human beings were degraded. Of course I read *Uncle Tom's Cabin*. In fact, I believe that's the only novel I have ever read since I started serious reading.

Parkhurst's collection also contained some bound pamphlets of the Abolitionist Anti-Slavery Society of New England. I read descriptions of atrocities, saw those illustrations of black slave women tied up and flogged with whips; of black mothers watching their babies being dragged off, never to be seen by their mothers again; of dogs after slaves, and of the fugitive slave catchers, evil white men with whips and clubs and chains and guns. I read about the slave preacher Nat Turner, who put the fear of God into the white slavemaster. Nat Turner wasn't going around preaching pie-in-the-sky and "nonviolent" freedom for the black man. There in Virginia one night in 1831, Nat and eleven other slaves started out at his master's home and through the night they went from one plantation "big house" to the next, killing, until by the next morning 57 white people were dead and Nat had about 70 slaves following him. White people, terrified for their lives, fled from their homes, locked themselves up in public buildings, hid in the woods, and some even left the state. A small army of soldiers took two months to catch and hang Nat Turner. Somewhere I have read where Nat Turner's example is said to have inspired John Brown to invade Virginia and attack Harper's Ferry nearly thirty years later, with thirteen white men and five Negroes.

I read Herodotus, "the father of History," or, rather, I read about him. And I read the histories of various nations, which opened my eyes gradually, then wider and wider, to how the whole world's white men had indeed acted like devils, pillaging and raping and bleeding and draining the whole world's non-white people. I remember, for instance, books such as Will Durant's story of Oriental civilization, and Mahatma Gandhi's accounts of the struggle to drive the British out of India.

Book after book showed me how the white man had brought upon the world's black, brown, red, and yellow peoples every variety of the sufferings of exploitation. I saw how since the sixteenth century, the so-called "Christian trader" white man began to ply the seas in his lust for Asian and African empires, and plunder, and power. I read, I saw, how the white man never has gone among the non-white peoples bearing the Cross in the true manner and spirit of Christ's teachings — meek, humble, and Christ-like.

I perceived, as I read, how the collective white man had been actually nothing but a piratical opportunist who used Faustian machinations to make his own Christianity his initial wedge in criminal conquests. First, always "religiously," he branded "heathen" and "pagan" labels upon ancient non-white cultures and civilizations. The stage thus set, he then turned upon his non-white victims his weapons of war.

I read how, entering India — half a *billion* deeply religious brown people — the British white man, by 1759, through promises, trickery and manipulations, controlled much of India through Great Britain's East India Company. The parasitical British administration kept tentacling out to half of the sub-continent. In 1857, some of the desperate people of India finally mutinied — and, excepting the African slave trade, nowhere has history recorded any more unnecessary bestial and ruthless human carnage than the British suppression of the non-white Indian people.

Over 115 million African blacks — close to the 1930s population of the United States — were murdered or enslaved during the slave trade. And I read how when the slave market was glutted, the cannibalistic white powers of Europe next carved up, as their colonies, the richest areas of the black continent. And Europe's chancelleries for the next century played a chess game of naked exploitation and power from Cape Horn to Cairo.

Ten guards and the warden couldn't have torn me out of those books. Not even Elijah Muhammad could have been more eloquent than those books were in providing indisputable proof that the collective white man had acted like a devil in virtually every contact he had with the world's collective non-white man. I listen today to the radio, and watch television, and read the headlines about the collective white man's fear and tension concerning China. When the white man professes ignorance about why the Chinese hate him so, my mind can't help flashing back to what I read, there in prison, about how the blood forebears of this same white man raped China at a time when China was trusting and helpless. Those original white "Christian traders" sent into China millions of pounds of opium. By 1839, so many of the Chinese were addicts that China's desperate government destroyed twenty thousand chests of opium. The first Opium War was promptly declared by the white man. Imagine! Declaring war upon someone who objects to being narcotized! The Chinese were severely beaten, with Chinese-invented gunpowder.

The Treaty of Nanking made China pay the British white man for the destroyed opium; forced open China's major ports to British trade; forced China to abandon Hong Kong; fixed China's import tariffs so low that cheap British articles soon flooded in, maiming China's industrial development.

After a second Opium War, the Tientsin Treaties legalized the ravaging opium trade, legalized a British-French-American control of China's customs. China tried delaying that Treaty's ratification; Peking was looted and burned.

"Kill the foreign white devils!" was the 1901 Chinese war cry in the Boxer

Rebellion. Losing again, this time the Chinese were driven from Peking's choicest areas. The vicious, arrogant white man put up the famous signs, "Chinese and dogs not allowed."

Red China after World War II closed its doors to the Western white world. Massive Chinese agricultural, scientific, and industrial efforts are described in a book that *Life* magazine recently published. Some observers inside Red China have reported that the world never has known such a hate-white campaign as is now going on in this non-white country where, present birth-rates continuing, in fifty more years Chinese will be half the earth's population. And it seems that some Chinese chickens will soon come home to roost, with China's recent successful nuclear tests.

Let us face reality. We can see in the United Nations a new world order being shaped, along color lines — an alliance among the non-white nations. America's U.N. Ambassador Adlai Stevenson complained not long ago that in the United Nations "a skin game" was being played. He was right. He was facing reality. A "skin game" is being played. But Ambassador Stevenson sounded like Jesse James accusing the marshal of carrying a gun. Because who in the world's history ever has played a worse "skin game" than the white man?

MR. MUHAMMAD, to whom I was writing daily, had no idea of what a new world had opened up to me through my efforts to document his teachings in books. When I discovered philosophy, I tried to touch all the landmarks of philosophical development. Gradually, I read most of the old philosophers, Occidental and Oriental. The Oriental philosophers were the ones I came to prefer; finally, my impression was that most Occidental philosophy had largely been borrowed from the Oriental thinkers. Socrates, for instance, traveled in Egypt. Some sources even say that Socrates was initiated into some of the Egyptian mysteries. Obviously Socrates got some of his wisdom among the East's wise men.

I have often reflected upon the new vistas that reading opened to me. I knew right there in prison that reading had changed forever the course of my life. As I see it today, the ability to read awoke inside me some long dormant craving to be mentally alive. I certainly wasn't seeking any degree, the way a college confers a status symbol upon its students. My homemade education gave me, with every additional book that I read, a little bit more sensitivity to the deafness, dumbness, and blindness that was afflicting the black race in America. Not long ago, an English writer telephoned me from London, asking questions. One was, "What's your alma mater?" I told him, "Books." You will never catch me with a free fifteen minutes in which I'm not studying something I feel might be able to help the black man.

Yesterday I spoke in London, and both ways on the plane across the Atlantic I was studying a document about how the United Nations proposes to ensure the human rights of the oppressed minorities of the world. The American black man is the world's most shameful case of minority oppression. What makes the black man think of himself as only an internal United States issue is just a catch-phrase, two words, "civil rights." How is the black man going to get "civil rights" before first he wins his *human* rights? If the American black man will start thinking about his human rights, and then start thinking of himself as part of one of the world's great peoples, he will see he has a case for the United Nations.

I can't think of a better case! Four hundred years of black blood and sweat invested here in America, and the white man still has the black man begging for what every immigrant fresh off the ship can take for granted the minute he walks down the gangplank.

But I'm digressing. I told the Englishman that my alma mater was books, a good library. Every time I catch a plane, I have with me a book that I want to read — and that's a lot of books these days. If I weren't out here every day battling the white man, I could spend the rest of my life reading, just satisfying my curiosity — because you can hardly mention anything I'm not curious about. I don't think anybody ever got more out of going to prison than I did. In fact, prison enabled me to study far more intensively than I would have if my life had gone differently and I had attended some college. I imagine that one of the biggest troubles with colleges is there are too many distractions, too much panty-raiding, fraternities, and boola-boola and all of that. Where else but in a prison could I have attacked my ignorance by being able to study intensely sometimes as much as fifteen hours a day?

Schopenhauer, Kant, Nietzsche, naturally, I read all of those. I don't respect them; I am just trying to remember some of those whose theories I soaked up in those years. These three, it's said, laid the groundwork on which the Facist and Nazi philosophy was built. I don't respect them because it seems to me that most of their time was spent arguing about things that are not really important. They remind me of so many of the Negro "intellectuals," so-called, with whom I have come in contact — they are always arguing about something useless.

Spinoza impressed me for a while when I found out that he was black. A black Spanish Jew. The Jews excommunicated him because he advocated a pantheistic doctrine, something like the "allness of God," or "God in everything." The Jews read their burial services for Spinoza, meaning that he was dead as far as they were concerned; his family was run out of Spain, they ended up in Holland, I think.

I'll tell you something. The whole stream of Western philosophy has now wound up in a cul-de-sac. The white man has perpetrated upon himself, as well as upon the black man, so gigantic a fraud that he has put himself into a crack. He did it through his elaborate, neurotic necessity to hide the black man's true role in history.

And today the white man is faced head on with what is happening on the

Black Continent, Africa. Look at the artifacts being discovered there, that are proving over and over again, how the black man had great, fine, sensitive civilizations before the white man was out of the caves. Below the Sahara, in the places where most of America's Negroes' foreparents were kidnapped, there is being unearthed some of the finest craftsmanship, sculpture and other objects, that has ever been seen by modern man. Some of these things now are on view in such places as New York City's Museum of Modern Art. Gold work of such fine tolerance and workmanship that it has no rival. Ancient objects produced by black hands . . . refined by those black hands with results that no human hand today can equal.

History has been so "whitened" by the white man that even the black professors have known little more than the most ignorant black man about the talents and rich civilizations and cultures of the black man of millenniums ago. I have lectured in Negro colleges and some of these brainwashed black Ph.D.s, with their suspenders dragging the ground with degrees, have run to the white man's newspapers calling me a "black fanatic." Why, a lot of them are fifty years behind the times. If I were president of one of these black colleges, I'd hock the campus if I had to, to send a bunch of black students off digging in Africa for more, more and more proof of the black race's historical greatness. The white man now is in Africa digging and searching. An African elephant can't stumble without falling on some white man with a shovel. Practically every week, we read about some great new find from Africa's lost civilizations. All that's new is white science's attitude. The ancient civilizations of the black man have been buried on the Black Continent all the time.

Here is an example: a British anthropologist named Dr. Louis S. B. Leakey is displaying some fossil bones — a foot, part of a hand, some jaws, and skull fragments. On the basis of these, Dr. Leakey has said it's time to rewrite completely the history of man's origin.

This species of man lived 1,818,036 years before Christ. And these bones were found in Tanganyika. In the Black Continent.

It's a crime, the lie that has been told to generations of black men and white men both. Little innocent black children, born of parents who believed that their race had no history. Little black children seeing, before they could talk, that their parents considered themselves inferior. Innocent black children growing up, living out their lives, dying of old age — and all of their lives ashamed of being black. But the truth is pouring out of the bag now.

(1964)

Martin Luther King Jr. (1929–1968)

Martin Luther King Jr. was born on January 15, 1929, in Atlanta, Georgia, to Rev. Martin Luther King Sr. and Alberta Williams King. At age fifteen King began attending Morehouse College, a historically black institution in Atlanta, and graduated in 1948 with a bachelor's degree in sociology. The same year he was ordained at a Baptist church in Atlanta, where both his grandfather and father preached as he himself would later. King then attended Crozer Theological Seminary, in Chester, Pennsylvania, earning a bachelor's degree in divinity in 1951. In 1953 King met and married Coretta Scott, with whom he had four children. King then attended Boston University, earning a doctorate in systematic theology in 1955. King also received honorary degrees from numerous other institutions throughout the 1950s and 1960s.

After graduating from Boston University, King pastored a Baptist church in Montgomery, Alabama, where he helped organize the Montgomery Bus Boycott several days after Rosa Parks's arrest. The boycott successfully ended segregation in the city's public transit system. He also led the Montgomery Improvement Association and began serving on the executive committee of the National Association for the Advancement of Colored People (NAACP). In 1957 King founded the Southern Christian Leadership Conference (SCLC) in Atlanta, and he remained president of the conference until his death in 1968.

King was prolific in the civil rights movement, organizing marches and boycotts and teaching the strategy of nonviolent direct action, which he took from Gandhi and other sources, to end segregation and discrimination. Because of his stature in the movement King and his family were harassed and threatened during this time period, and King himself was assaulted and arrested numerous times. King was instrumental in the passage of civil rights laws, such as the Voting Rights Act of 1965. His leadership in the movement earned him many distinctions and awards, including becoming the youngest man to receive the Nobel Peace Prize (in 1964). King's speeches during movement events distinguish him as one of the most effective orators in American history. His 1963 "I Have a Dream" speech, which he gave during a march in Washington; his acceptance speech for the Nobel Peace Prize in 1964; and his last speech, given in Memphis, Tennessee, are among his most famous.

While traveling and speaking, King also wrote several books and numerous articles. After he was arrested in Birmingham, Alabama, for marching in protest without a permit, he wrote his "Letter from a Birmingham Jail," which remains an eloquent argument for racial equality and for using nonviolent protest as a means to achieve it. The "Letter" critiques segregation and other social practices as un-Christian and calls the nation to action.

In 1968 King was in Memphis to support sanitation workers who were pro-testing unacceptable conditions and demanding economic justice. On April 4, during the visit, King was assassinated by James Earl Ray while standing on the balcony of his room at the Lorraine Motel. Many see the death of this key leader as the terminal point of the civil rights movement. As civil rights literature about King suggests, he was a guiding spirit who encouraged the nation to live up to its ideals. For many writers, and for movement activists more generally, mourning the passing of Martin Luther King Jr. also means remembering that the struggle continues to keep freedom a reality for everyone.

Letter from a Birmingham Jail

April 16, 1963

MY DEAR FELLOW CLERGYMEN:

While confined here in the Birmingham city jail, I came across your recent statement calling my present activities "unwise and untimely." Seldom do I pause to answer criticism of my work and ideas. If I sought to answer all the criticisms that cross my desk, my secretaries would have little time for anything other than such correspondence in the course of the day, and I would have no time for constructive work. But since I feel that you are men of genuine good will and that your criticisms are sincerely set forth, I want to try to answer your statement in what I hope will be patient and reasonable terms.

I think I should indicate why I am here in Birmingham, since you have been influenced by the view which argues against "outsiders coming in." I have the honor of serving as president of the Southern Christian Leadership Confer-ence, an organization operating in every southern state, with headquarters in Atlanta, Georgia. We have some eighty-five affiliated organizations across the South, and one of them is the Alabama Christian Movement for Human Rights. Frequently we share staff, educational and financial resources with our affili-ates. Several months ago the affiliate here in Birmingham asked us to be on call to engage in a nonviolent direct-action program if such were deemed necessary. We readily consented, and when the hour came we lived up to our promise. So I, along with several members of my staff, am here because I was invited here. I am here because I have organizational ties here.

But more basically, I am in Birmingham because injustice is here. Just as the prophets of the eighth century B.C. left their villages and carried their "thus saith the Lord" far beyond the boundaries of their home towns, and just as the Apostle Paul left his village of Tarsus and carried the gospel of Jesus Christ to the far corners of the Greco-Roman world, so am I compelled to carry the gospel of freedom beyond my own home town. Like Paul, I must constantly respond to the Macedonian call for aid.

Moreover, I am cognizant of the interrelatedness of all communities and states. I cannot sit idly by in Atlanta and not be concerned about what happens in Birmingham. Injustice anywhere is a threat to justice everywhere. We are caught in an inescapable network of mutuality, tied in a single garment of destiny. Whatever affects one directly, affects all indirectly. Never again can we afford to live with the narrow, provincial "outside agitator" idea. Anyone who lives inside the United States can never be considered an outsider anywhere within its bounds.

You deplore the demonstrations taking place in Birmingham. But your statement, I am sorry to say, fails to express a similar concern for the conditions that brought about the demonstrations. I am sure that none of you would want to rest content with the superficial kind of social analysis that deals merely with effects and does not grapple with underlying causes. It is unfortunate that demonstrations are taking place in Birmingham, but it is even more unfortunate that the city's white power structure left the Negro community with no alternative.

In any nonviolent campaign there are four basic steps: collection of the facts to determine whether injustices exist; negotiation; self-purification; and direct action. We have gone through all these steps in Birmingham. There can be no gainsaying the fact that racial injustice engulfs this community. Birmingham is probably the most thoroughly segregated city in the United States. Its ugly record of brutality is widely known. Negroes have experienced grossly unjust treatment in the courts. There have been more unsolved bombings of Negro homes and churches in Birmingham than in any other city in the nation. These are the hard, brutal facts of the case. On the basis of these conditions, Negro leaders sought to negotiate with the city fathers. But the latter consistently refused to engage in good-faith negotiation.

Then, last September, came the opportunity to talk with leaders of Birmingham's economic community. In the course of the negotiations, certain promises were made by the merchants — for example, to remove the stores' humiliating racial signs. On the basis of these promises, the Reverend Fred Shuttlesworth and the leaders of the Alabama Christian Movement for Human Rights agreed to a moratorium on all demonstrations. As the weeks and months went by, we realized that we were the victims of a broken promise. A few signs, briefly removed, returned; the others remained.

As in so many past experiences, our hopes had been blasted, and the shadow of deep disappointment settled upon us. We had no alternative except to prepare for direct action, whereby we would present our very bodies as a means of laying our case before the conscience of the local and the national community. Mindful of the difficulties involved, we decided to undertake a process of self-purification. We began a series of workshops on nonviolence, and we repeatedly asked ourselves: "Are you able to accept blows without retaliating?" "Are you able to endure the ordeal of jail?" We decided to schedule our direct-action program for the Easter season, realizing that except for Christmas, this is the main shopping period of the year. Knowing that a strong economic-withdrawal program would be the by-product of direct action, we felt that this would be the best time to bring pressure to bear on the merchants for the needed change.

Then it occurred to us that Birmingham's mayoral election was coming up in March, and we speedily decided to postpone action until after election day. When we discovered that the Commissioner of Public Safety, Eugene "Bull" Connor, had piled up enough votes to be in the run-off, we decided again to postpone action until the day after the run-off so that the demonstrations could not be used to cloud the issues. Like many others, we waited to see Mr. Connor defeated, and to this end we endured postponement after postponement. Having aided in this community need, we felt that our direct-action program could be delayed no longer.

You may well ask: "Why direct action? Why sit-ins, marches and so forth? Isn't negotiation a better path?" You are quite right in calling for negotiation. Indeed, this is the very purpose of direct action. Nonviolent direct action seeks to create such a crisis and foster such a tension that a community which has constantly refused to negotiate is forced to confront the issue. It seeks so to dramatize the issue that it can no longer be ignored. My citing the creation of tension as part of the work of the nonviolent-resister may sound rather shocking. But I must confess that I am not afraid of the word "tension." I have earnestly opposed violent tension, but there is a type of constructive, nonviolent tension which is necessary for growth. Just as Socrates felt that it was necessary to create a tension in the mind so that individuals could rise from the bondage of myths and half-truths to the unfettered realm of creative analysis and objective appraisal, so must we see the need for nonviolent gadflies to create the kind of tension in society that will help men rise from the dark depths of prejudice and racism to the majestic heights of understanding and brotherhood.

The purpose of our direct-action program is to create a situation so crisis-packed that it will inevitably open the door to negotiation. I therefore concur with you in your call for negotiation. Too long has our beloved Southland been bogged down in a tragic effort to live in monologue rather than dialogue.

One of the basic points in your statement is that the action that I and my associates have taken in Birmingham is untimely. Some have asked: "Why didn't you give the new city administration time to act?" The only answer that I can give to this query is that the new Birmingham administration must be prodded about as much as the outgoing one, before it will act. We are sadly mistaken if we feel that the election of Albert Boutwell as mayor will bring the millennium to Birmingham. While Mr. Boutwell is a much more gentle person than Mr. Connor, they are both segregationists, dedicated to maintenance of the status quo. I have hope that Mr. Boutwell will be reasonable enough to see the futility of massive resistance to desegregation. But he will not see this without pressure from devotees of civil rights. My friends, I must say to you that we have not made a single gain in civil rights without determined legal and nonviolent pressure. Lamentably, it is an historical fact that privileged groups seldom give up their privileges voluntarily. Individuals may see the moral light and voluntarily give up their unjust posture; but, as Reinhold Niebuhr has reminded us, groups tend to be more immoral than individuals.

We know through painful experience that freedom is never voluntarily given by the oppressor; it must be demanded by the oppressed. Frankly, I have yet to engage in a direct-action campaign that was "well timed" in the view of those who have not suffered unduly from the disease of segregation. For years now I have heard the word "Wait!" It rings in the ear of every Negro with piercing familiarity. This "Wait" has almost always meant "Never." We must come to see, with one of our distinguished jurists, that "justice too long delayed is justice denied."

We have waited for more than 340 years for our constitutional and God-given rights. The nations of Asia and Africa are moving with jetlike speed toward gaining political independence, but we still creep at horse-and-buggy pace toward gaining a cup of coffee at a lunch counter. Perhaps it is easy for those who have never felt the stinging darts of segregation to say, "Wait." But when you have seen vicious mobs lynch your mothers and fathers at will and drown your sisters and brothers at whim; when you have seen hate-filled policemen curse, kick and even kill your black brothers and sisters; when you see the vast majority of your twenty million Negro brothers smothering in an airtight cage of poverty in the midst of an affluent society; when you suddenly find your tongue twisted and your speech stammering as you seek to explain to your six-year-old daughter why she can't go to the public amusement park that has just been advertised on television, and see tears welling up in her eyes when she is told that Funtown is closed to colored children, and see ominous clouds of inferiority beginning to form in her little mental sky, and see her beginning to distort her personality by developing an unconscious bitterness toward white people; when you have to concoct an answer for a five-year-old son who is asking: "Daddy, why do white people treat colored people so mean?"; when you take a cross-county drive and find it necessary to sleep night after night in the uncomfortable corners of your automobile because no motel will accept you; when you are humiliated day in and day out by nagging signs reading "white" and "colored"; when your first name becomes "nigger," your middle name becomes "boy" (however old you are) and your last name becomes "John," and your wife and mother are never given the respected title "Mrs."; when you are harried by day and haunted by night by the fact that you are a Negro, living constantly at tiptoe stance, never quite knowing what to expect next, and are plagued with inner fears and outer resentments; when you are forever fighting a degenerating sense of "nobodiness" — then you will understand why we find it difficult to wait. There comes a time when the cup of endurance runs over, and men are no longer willing to be plunged into the abyss of despair. I hope, sirs, you can understand our legitimate and unavoidable impatience.

You express a great deal of anxiety over our willingness to break laws. This is certainly a legitimate concern. Since we so diligently urge people to obey the Supreme Court's decision of 1954 outlawing segregation in the public schools, at first glance it may seem rather paradoxical for us consciously to break laws. One may well ask: "How can you advocate breaking some laws and obeying others?" The answer lies in the fact that there are two types of laws: just and unjust. I would be the first to advocate obeying just laws. One has not only a legal but a moral responsibility to obey just laws. Conversely, one has a moral responsibility to disobey unjust laws. I would agree with St. Augustine that "an unjust law is no law at all."

Now, what is the difference between the two? How does one determine whether a law is just or unjust? A just law is a man-made code that squares with the moral law or the law of God. An unjust law is a code that is out of harmony with the moral law. To put it in the terms of St. Thomas Aquinas: An unjust law is a human law that is not rooted in eternal law and natural law. Any law that uplifts human personality is just. Any law that degrades human personality is unjust. All segregation statutes are unjust because segregation distorts the soul and damages the personality. It gives the segregator a false sense of superiority and the segregated a false sense of inferiority. Segregation, to use the terminology of the Jewish philosopher Martin Buber, substitutes an "I-it" relationship for an "I-thou" relationship and ends up relegating persons to the status of things. Hence segregation is not only politically, economically and sociologically unsound, it is morally wrong and sinful. Paul Tillich has said that sin is separation. Is not segregation an existential expression of man's tragic separation, his awful estrangement, his terrible sinfulness? Thus it is that I can urge men to obey the 1954 decision of the Supreme Court, for it is morally right; and I can urge them to disobey segregation ordinances, for they are morally wrong.

Let us consider a more concrete example of just and unjust laws. An unjust law is a code that a numerical or power majority group compels a minority group to obey but does not make binding on itself. This is *difference* made legal. By the same token, a just law is a code that a majority compels a minority to follow and that it is willing to follow itself. This is *sameness* made legal.

Let me give another explanation. A law is unjust if it is inflicted on a minority that, as a result of being denied the right to vote, had no part in enacting or devising the law. Who can say that the legislature of Alabama which set up that state's segregation laws was democratically elected? Throughout Alabama all sorts of devious methods are used to prevent Negroes from becoming registered voters, and there are some counties in which, even though Negroes constitute a majority of the population, not a single Negro is registered. Can any law enacted under such circumstances be considered democratically structured?

Sometimes a law is just on its face and unjust in its application. For instance, I have been arrested on a charge of parading without a permit. Now, there is nothing wrong in having an ordinance which requires a permit for a parade. But such an ordinance becomes unjust when it is used to maintain segregation and to deny citizens the First-Amendment privilege of peaceful assembly and protest.

I hope you are able to see the distinction I am trying to point out. In no sense do I advocate evading or defying the law, as would the rabid segregationist. That would lead to anarchy. One who breaks an unjust law must do so openly, lovingly, and with a willingness to accept the penalty. I submit that an individual who breaks a law that conscience tells him is unjust, and who willingly accepts the penalty of imprisonment in order to arouse the conscience of the community over its injustice, is in reality expressing the highest respect for law.

Of course, there is nothing new about this kind of civil disobedience. It was evidenced sublimely in the refusal of Shadrach, Meshach and Abednego to obey the laws of Nebuchadnezzar, on the ground that a higher moral law was at stake. It was practiced superbly by the early Christians, who were willing to face hungry lions and the excruciating pain of chopping blocks rather than submit to certain unjust laws of the Roman Empire. To a degree, academic freedom is a reality today because Socrates practiced civil disobedience. In our own nation, the Boston Tea Party represented a massive act of civil disobedience.

We should never forget that everything Adolf Hitler did in Germany was "legal" and everything the Hungarian freedom fighters did in Hungary was "illegal." It was "illegal" to aid and comfort a Jew in Hitler's Germany. Even so, I am sure that, had I lived in Germany at the time, I would have aided and comforted my Jewish brothers. If today I lived in a Communist country where certain principles dear to the Christian faith are suppressed, I would openly advocate disobeying that country's antireligious laws.

I must make two honest confessions to you, my Christian and Jewish brothers. First, I must confess that over the past few years I have been gravely disappointed with the white moderate. I have almost reached the regrettable conclusion that the Negro's great stumbling block in his stride toward freedom is not the White Citizen's Counciler or the Ku Klux Klanner, but the white moderate, who is more devoted to "order" than to justice; who prefers a negative peace which is the absence of tension to a positive peace which is the presence of justice; who constantly says: "I agree with you in the goal you seek, but I cannot agree with your methods of direct action"; who paternalistically believes he can set the timetable for another man's freedom; who lives by a mythical concept of time and who constantly advises the Negro to wait for a "more convenient season." Shallow understanding from people of good will is more frustrating than absolute misunderstanding from people of ill will. Lukewarm acceptance is much more bewildering than outright rejection.

I had hoped that the white moderate would understand that law and order exist for the purpose of establishing justice and that when they fail in this purpose they become the dangerously structured dams that block the flow of social progress. I had hoped that the white moderate would understand that the present tension in the South is a necessary phase of the transition from an obnoxious negative peace, in which the Negro passively accepted his unjust plight, to a substantive and positive peace, in which all men will respect the dignity and worth of human personality. Actually, we who engage in nonviolent direct action are not the creators of tension. We merely bring to the surface the hidden tension that is already alive. We bring it out in the open, where it can be seen and dealt with. Like a boil that can never be cured so long as it is covered up but must be opened with all its ugliness to the natural medicines of air and light, injustice must be exposed, with all the tension its exposure creates, to the light of human conscience and the air of national opinion before it can be cured.

In your statement you assert that our actions, even though peaceful, must be condemned because they precipitate violence. But is this a logical assertion? Isn't this like condemning a robbed man because his possession of money precipitated the evil act of robbery? Isn't this like condemning Socrates because his unswerving commitment to truth and his philosophical inquiries precipitated the act by the misguided populace in which they made him drink hemlock? Isn't this like condemning Jesus because his unique God-consciousness and never-ceasing devotion to God's will precipitated the evil act of crucifixion? We must come to see that, as the federal courts have consistently affirmed, it is wrong to urge an individual to cease his efforts to gain his basic constitutional rights because the quest may precipitate violence. Society must protect the robbed and punish the robber.

I had also hoped that the white moderate would reject the myth concerning time in relation to the struggle for freedom. I have just received a letter from a white brother in Texas. He writes: "All Christians know that the colored people will receive equal rights eventually, but it is possible that you are in too great a religious hurry. It has taken Christianity almost two thousand years to accomplish what it has. The teachings of Christ take time to come to earth." Such an attitude stems from a tragic misconception of time, from the strangely irrational notion that there is something in the very flow of time that will inevitably cure all ills. Actually, time itself is neutral; it can be used either destructively or constructively. More and more I feel that the people of ill will have used time much more effectively than have the people of good will. We will have to repent in this generation not merely for the hateful words and actions of the bad people but for the appalling silence of the good people. Human progress never rolls in on wheels of inevitability; it comes through the tireless efforts of men willing to be co-workers with God, and without this hard work, time itself becomes an ally of the forces of social stagnation. We must use time creatively, in the knowledge that the time is always ripe to do right. Now is the time to make real the promise of democracy and transform our pending national elegy into a creative psalm of brotherhood. Now is the time to lift our national policy from the quicksand of racial injustice to the solid rock of human dignity.

You speak of our activity in Birmingham as extreme. At first I was rather disappointed that fellow clergymen would see my nonviolent efforts as those of an extremist. I began thinking about the fact that I stand in the middle of two opposing forces in the Negro community. One is a force of complacency, made up in part of Negroes who, as a result of long years of oppression, are so drained of self-respect and a sense of "somebodiness" that they have adjusted to segregation; and in part of a few middle-class Negroes who, because of a degree of academic and economic security and because in some ways they profit by segregation, have become insensitive to the problems of the masses. The other force is one of bitterness and hatred, and it comes perilously close to advocating violence. It is expressed in the various black nationalist groups that are springing up across the nation, the largest and best-known being Elijah Muhammad's Muslim movement. Nourished by the Negro's frustration over the continued existence of racial discrimination, this movement is made up of people who have lost faith in America, who have absolutely repudiated Christianity, and who have concluded that the white man is an incorrigible "devil."

I have tried to stand between these two forces, saying that we need emulate neither the "do-nothingism" of the complacent nor the hatred and despair of the black nationalist. For there is the more excellent way of love and nonviolent protest. I am grateful to God that, through the influence of the Negro church, the way of nonviolence became an integral part of our struggle.

If this philosophy had not emerged, by now many streets of the South would, I am convinced, be flowing with blood. And I am further convinced that if our white brothers dismiss as "rabble-rousers" and "outside agitators" those of us who employ nonviolent direct action, and if they refuse to support our nonviolent efforts, millions of Negroes will, out of frustration and despair, seek solace and security in black-nationalist ideologies — a development that would inevitably lead to a frightening racial nightmare.

Oppressed people cannot remain oppressed forever. The yearning for freedom eventually manifests itself, and that is what has happened to the American Negro. Something within has reminded him of his birthright of freedom, and something without has reminded him that it can be gained. Consciously or unconsciously, he has been caught up by the *Zeitgeist*, and with his black brothers of Africa and his brown and yellow brothers of Asia, South America and the Caribbean, the United States Negro is moving with a sense of great urgency toward the promised land of racial justice. If one recognizes this vital urge that has engulfed the Negro community, one should readily understand why public demonstrations are taking place. The Negro has many pent-up resentments and latent frustrations, and he must release them. So let him march; let him make prayer pilgrimages to the city hall; let him go on freedom rides — and try to understand why he must do so. If his repressed emotions are not released in nonviolent ways, they will seek expression through violence; this is not a threat but a fact of history. So I have not said to my people: "Get rid of your discontent." Rather, I have tried to say that this normal and healthy discontent can be channeled into the creative outlet of nonviolent direct action. And now this approach is being termed extremist.

But though I was initially disappointed at being categorized as an extremist, as I continued to think about the matter I gradually gained a measure of satisfaction from the label. Was not Jesus an extremist for love: "Love your enemies, bless them that curse you, do good to them that hate you, and pray for them which despitefully use you, and persecute you." Was not Amos an extremist for justice: "Let justice roll down like waters and righteousness like an ever-flowing stream." Was not Paul an extremist for the Christian gospel: "I bear in my body the marks of the Lord Jesus." Was not Martin Luther an extremist: "Here I stand; I cannot do otherwise, so help me God." And John Bunyan: "I will stay in jail to the end of my days before I make a butchery of my conscience." And Abraham Lincoln: "This nation cannot survive half slave and half free." And Thomas Jefferson: "We hold these truths to be self-evident, that all men are created equal . . ." So the question is not whether we will be extremists, but what kind of extremists we will be. Will we be extremists for hate or for love? Will we be extremists for the preservation of injustice or for the extension of justice? In that dramatic scene on Calvary's hill three men were crucified. We must never forget that all three were crucified for the same crime — the crime of extremism. Two were extremists for immorality, and thus fell below their environment. The other, Jesus Christ, was an extremist for love, truth and goodness, and thereby rose above his environment. Perhaps the South, the nation and the world are in dire need of creative extremists.

I had hoped that the white moderate would see this need. Perhaps I was too optimistic; perhaps I expected too much. I suppose I should have realized that few members of the oppressor race can understand the deep groans and passionate yearnings of the oppressed race, and still fewer have the vision to see that injustice must be rooted out by strong, persistent and determined action.

I am thankful, however, that some of our white brothers in the South have grasped the meaning of this social revolution and committed themselves to it. They are still all too few in quantity, but they are big in quality. Some — such as Ralph McGill, Lillian Smith, Harry Golden, James McBride Dabbs, Ann Braden and Sarah Patton Boyle — have written about our struggle in eloquent and prophetic terms. Others have marched with us down nameless streets of the South. They have languished in filthy, roach-infested jails, suffering the abuse and brutality of policemen who view them as "dirty nigger-lovers." Unlike so many of their moderate brothers and sisters, they have recognized the urgency of the moment and sensed the need for powerful "action" antidotes to combat the disease of segregation.

Let me take note of my other major disappointment. I have been so greatly disappointed with the white church and its leadership. Of course, there are some notable exceptions. I am not unmindful of the fact that each of you has taken some significant stands on this issue. I commend you, Reverend Stallings, for your Christian stand on this past Sunday, in welcoming Negroes to your worship service on a nonsegregated basis. I commend the Catholic leaders of this state for integrating Spring Hill College several years ago.

But despite these notable exceptions, I must honestly reiterate that I have been disappointed with the church. I do not say this as one of those negative critics who can always find something wrong with the church. I say this as a minister of the gospel, who loves the church; who was nurtured in its bosom; who has been sustained by its spiritual blessings and who will remain true to it as long as the cord of life shall lengthen.

When I was suddenly catapulted into the leadership of the bus protest in Montgomery, Alabama, a few years ago, I felt we would be supported by the white church. I felt that the white ministers, priests and rabbis of the South would be among our strongest allies. Instead, some have been outright opponents, refusing to understand the freedom movement and misrepresenting its leaders; all too many others have been more cautious than courageous and have remained silent behind the anesthetizing security of stained-glass windows.

In spite of my shattered dreams, I came to Birmingham with the hope that the white religious leadership of this community would see the justice of our cause and, with deep moral concern, would serve as the channel through which our just grievances could reach the power structure. I had hoped that each of you would understand. But again I have been disappointed.

I have heard numerous southern religious leaders admonish their worshipers to comply with a desegregation decision because it is the law, but I have longed to hear white ministers declare: "Follow this decree because integration is morally right and because the Negro is your brother." In the midst of blatant injustices inflicted upon the Negro, I have watched white churchmen stand on the sideline and mouth pious irrelevancies and sanctimonious trivialities. In the midst of a mighty struggle to rid our nation of racial and economic injustice, I have heard many ministers say: "Those are social issues, with which the gospel has no real concern." And I have watched many churches commit themselves to a completely other-worldly religion which makes a strange, un-Biblical distinction between body and soul, between the sacred and the secular.

I have traveled the length and breadth of Alabama, Mississippi and all the other southern states. On sweltering summer days and crisp autumn mornings I have looked at the South's beautiful churches with their lofty spires pointing heavenward. I have beheld the impressive outlines of her massive religious-education buildings. Over and over I have found myself asking: "What kind of people worship here? Who is their God? Where were their voices when the lips of Governor Barnett dripped with words of interposition and nullification? Where were they when Governor Wallace gave a clarion call for defiance and hatred? Where were their voices of support when bruised and weary Negro men and women decided to rise from the dark dungeons of complacency to the bright hills of creative protest?"

Yes, these questions are still in my mind. In deep disappointment I have wept over the laxity of the church. But be assured that my tears have been tears of love. There can be no deep disappointment where there is not deep love. Yes, I love the church. How could I do otherwise? I am in the rather unique position of being the son, the grandson and the great-grandson of preachers. Yes, I see the church as the body of Christ. But, oh! How we have blemished and scarred that body through social neglect and through fear of being nonconformists.

There was a time when the church was very powerful — in the time when the early Christians rejoiced at being deemed worthy to suffer for what they believed. In those days the church was not merely a thermometer that recorded the ideas and principles of popular opinion; it was a thermostat that transformed the mores of society. Whenever the early Christians entered a town, the people in power became disturbed and immediately sought to convict the Christians for being "disturbers of the peace" and "outside agitators." But the Christians pressed on, in the conviction that they were "a colony of heaven," called to obey God rather than man. Small in number, they were big in commitment. They were too God-intoxicated to be "astronomically intimidated." By their effort and example they brought an end to such ancient evils as infanticide and gladiatorial contests.

Things are different now. So often the contemporary church is a weak, ineffectual voice with an uncertain sound. So often it is an archdefender of the status quo. Far from being disturbed by the presence of the church, the power structure of the average community is consoled by the church's silent — and often even vocal — sanction of things as they are.

But the judgment of God is upon the church as never before. If today's church does not recapture the sacrificial spirit of the early church, it will lose its authenticity, forfeit the loyalty of millions, and be dismissed as an irrelevant social club with no meaning for the twentieth century. Every day I meet young people whose disappointment with the church has turned into outright disgust.

Perhaps I have once again been too optimistic. Is organized religion too inextricably bound to the status quo to save our nation and the world? Perhaps I must turn my faith to the inner spiritual church, the church within the church, as the true ekklesia and the hope of the world. But again I am thankful to God that some noble souls from the ranks of organized religion have broken loose from the paralyzing chains of conformity and joined us as active partners in the struggle for freedom. They have left their secure congregations and walked the streets of Albany, Georgia, with us. They have gone down the highways of the South on tortuous rides for freedom. Yes, they have gone to jail with us. Some have been dismissed from their churches, have lost the support of their bishops and fellow ministers. But they have acted in the faith that right defeated is stronger than evil triumphant. Their witness has been the spiritual salt that has preserved the true meaning of the gospel in these troubled times. They have carved a tunnel of hope through the dark mountain of disappointment.

I hope the church as a whole will meet the challenge of this decisive hour. But even if the church does not come to the aid of justice, I have no despair about the future. I have no fear about the outcome of our struggle in Birmingham, even if our motives are at present misunderstood. We will reach the goal of freedom in Birmingham and all over the nation, because the goal of America is freedom. Abused and scorned though we may be, our destiny is tied up with America's destiny. Before the pilgrims landed at Plymouth, we were here. Before the pen of Jefferson etched the majestic words of the Declaration of Independence across the pages of history, we were here. For more than two centuries our forebears labored in this country without wages; they made cotton king; they built the homes of their masters while suffering gross injustice and shameful humiliation — and yet out of a bottomless vitality they continued to thrive and develop. If the inexpressible cruelties of slavery could not stop us, the opposition we now face will surely fail. We will win our freedom because the sacred heritage of our nation and the eternal will of God are embodied in our echoing demands.

Before closing I feel impelled to mention one other point in your statement that has troubled me profoundly. You warmly commended the Birmingham police force for keeping "order" and "preventing violence." I doubt that you would have so warmly commended the police force if you had seen its dogs sinking their teeth into unarmed, nonviolent Negroes. I doubt that you would so quickly commend the policemen if you were to observe their ugly and inhumane treatment of Negroes here in the city jail; if you were to watch them push and curse old Negro women and young Negro girls; if you were to see them slap and kick old Negro men and young boys; if you were to observe them, as they did on two occasions, refuse to give us food because we wanted to sing our grace together. I cannot join you in your praise of the Birmingham police department.

It is true that the police have exercised a degree of discipline in handling the demonstrators. In this sense they have conducted themselves rather "nonviolently" in public. But for what purpose? To preserve the evil system of segregation. Over the past few years I have consistently preached that nonviolence demands that the means we use must be as pure as the ends we seek. I have tried to make clear that it is wrong to use immoral means to attain moral ends. But now I must affirm that it is just as wrong, or perhaps even more so, to use moral means to preserve immoral ends. Perhaps Mr. Connor and his policemen have been rather nonviolent in public, as was Chief Pritchett in Albany, Georgia, but they have used the moral means of nonviolence to maintain the immoral end of racial injustice. As T. S. Eliot has said: "The last temptation is the greatest treason: To do the right deed for the wrong reason."

I wish you had commended the Negro sit-inners and demonstrators of Birmingham for their sublime courage, their willingness to suffer and their amazing discipline in the midst of great provocation. One day the South will recognize its real heroes. They will be the James Merediths, with the noble sense of purpose that enables them to face jeering and hostile mobs, and with the agonizing loneliness that characterizes the life of the pioneer. They will be old, oppressed, battered Negro women, symbolized in a seventy-two-year-old woman in Montgomery, Alabama, who rose up with a sense of dignity and with her people decided not to ride segregated buses, and who responded with ungrammatical profundity to one who inquired about her weariness: "My feets is tired, but my soul is at rest." They will be the young high school and college students, the young ministers of the gospel and a host of their elders, courageously and nonviolently sitting in at lunch counters and willingly going to jail for conscience' sake. One day the South will know that when these disinherited children of God sat down at lunch counters, they were in reality standing up for what is best in the American dream and for the most sacred values in our Judaeo-Christian heritage, thereby bringing our nation back to those great wells of democracy which were dug deep by the founding fathers in their formulation of the Constitution and the Declaration of Independence.

Never before have I written so long a letter. I'm afraid it is much too long to take your precious time. I can assure you that it would have been much shorter if I had been writing from a comfortable desk, but what else can one do when he is alone in a narrow jail cell, other than write long letters, think long thoughts and pray long prayers?

If I have said anything in this letter that overstates the truth and indicates an unreasonable impatience, I beg you to forgive me. If I have said anything that understates the truth and indicates my having a patience that allows me to settle for anything less than brotherhood, I beg God to forgive me.

I hope this letter finds you strong in the faith. I also hope that circumstances will soon make it possible for me to meet each of you, not as an integrationist or a civil rights leader but as a fellow clergyman and a Christian brother. Let us all hope that the dark clouds of racial prejudice will soon pass away and the deep fog of misunderstanding will be lifted from our fear-drenched communities, and in some not too distant tomorrow the radiant stars of love and brotherhood will shine over our great nation with all their scintillating beauty.

Yours for the cause of Peace and Brotherhood,
Martin Luther King, Jr.

(1963)

Howard Sackler   (1929–1982)

oward Sackler achieved lasting fame when his play *The Great White Hope* (1968) won the Pulitzer Prize, the New York Drama Critics Circle Award, and a Tony Award. Although he is most often remembered for *The Great White Hope,* he had a varied career as a playwright, poet, screenwriter, and director. Born in New York City in 1929 Sackler graduated from Brooklyn College in 1950, and divided his adult life between homes in London, Ibiza, Hollywood, and New York. His published works include a volume of poetry, *Want My Shepherd* (1954), and several theater pieces collected under the title *A Few Enquiries* (1970). In addition to the screenplay for the film version of *The Great White Hope,* Sackler's screenwriting credits range from *Jaws 2* (1978) and an uncredited segment of the first *Jaws* (1975) to early Stanley Kubrick films *Fear and Desire* (1953) and *Killer's Kiss* (1955). By far, his largest body of work emerged through Caedmon Records, a company that he founded in 1953, which produced audio versions of more than two hundred theater productions, including multiple Shakespeare plays. Sackler's life was unfortunately cut short when he died unexpectedly of natural causes on October 12, 1982, leaving behind a wife and two children.

The Great White Hope, originally produced at Washington, D.C.'s Arena Stage in 1967, starred James Earl Jones and Jane Alexander, who went on to earn Academy Award nominations for their work in the 1970 film version. The play is based upon the life of the controversial early twentieth-century boxer Jack Johnson and charts the rise and fall of a heavyweight boxing champion named Jack Jefferson. After Jefferson defeats a white contender (the "great white hope" of the play's title) and flaunts his white mistress, Chicago authorities arrange to have him arrested for violating the newly passed Mann Act, which outlawed "white slavery," the transportation of women across state lines for "immoral purposes." A black baseball team helps Jefferson escape the country, and acts 2 and 3 follow his declining fortunes as exile takes its toll upon both his relationship and his career. In the scenes from act 1 reprinted here, Jefferson — like Johnson — militantly refuses to live within the social, economic, and physical boundaries that white society would place around him. His actions remind readers that the fight for civil rights has been waged in multiple arenas outside traditionally known venues of the courts and the streets.

The Great White Hope

Selections from Act 1

CHARACTERS (APPEARING IN THESE SELECTIONS)

Jack Jefferson	Mrs. Jefferson (Jack's mother)
Tick (Jack's trainer)	Clara (His former girlfriend)
Goldie (Jack's manager)	A Pastor
Ellie Bachman (Jack's girlfriend)	Seven to Eight Brothers and Sisters
Smitty (A famous sportswriter)	(Brothers One and Two and Sisters
Press One, Two, and Three	One and Two have speaking parts)
Dixon (A federal agent)	Rudy (A baseball player)
Six Men (Dixon's assistants)	

Act 1, Scene 2

San Francisco: A small gym. On the L. wagon, there is a wooden folding chair and a clothes rack with a maroon robe and towel. D. of the rack is a stool with Jack's training gloves; to the R. of the rack is Jack's bag. The body bag hangs a few feet L. of C.

JACK JEFFERSON, *shadow boxing.* TICK, *his Negro trainer.* ELEANOR BACHMAN, *a white girl, sits on a stool R., watching.* TICK *rides in on No. 3 wagon.* JACK *walks in D. of No. 3 wagon.* ELLIE *enters D.R. and sits.*

Tick: Mix it up, Jack honey, pace him, pace him out, hands up higher now, move, he's jabbin — don't follow them head fakes, you watch his body, there you go, jab! jab! Beauty — fake with the body, not just the head, baby — feint! jab! hook in behind it — send him the right now — no! What you at?

Jack: *(Continuing his movements.)* Givin him a right —

Tick: An where you givin it?

Jack: Chin-bone —

Tick: Sucker-bone! Boy, you a worry! He groggy now, right, you jabbin his liver till he runnin outa gas an his eyes goin fishy — Why you knock that chin! Could be you done what?

Jack: Wake him up, wake him up —

Tick: Watch him! He's bobbin, he's comin to you, block it — where you gonna take that right now?

Jack: Temple —

Tick: How!

Jack: Hook it, hook to the temple —

Tick: Why!

Jack: Softes place on his head —

Tick: Yeah! now you listenin to me, sugar! hook him again, a beauty, three now — (JACK *stops, makes sound, goes to clothes rack for towel.)* Hey, what you doin —

Jack: *(Crosses to* ELEANOR.*)* Now, honey, you just know you tired of sittin here, whyn't you go buy yourself a pretty or something —

Ellie: *(Rises.)* No, let me stay. Unless you mind me here, Jack.

Jack: You my Lady Luck! I don mind you nowhere —

Tick: *Oh long as you lookin at him, he don mind —*

Jack: But ain't this too much rough-house for you, honey?

Ellie: Well — I try not to listen.

Tick: Much obliged!

Ellie: Oh, Tick, I'm sorry —

Jack: *(Goes to* TICK, *then returns to* ELLIE.*)* She something, ain't she!

Tick: Darlin, you keep sittin there any way you like it, cause he sure workin happy. OK?

Ellie: OK! (JACK *kisses her.)*

Tick: Now we gonna mooch or we gonna move?

Jack: *(Moves L. and D.)* Reach me them gloves! (TICK *goes to the stool, L., and gets the training gloves.)* Gonna bust that bag wide open, then we all go out and have a champagne lunch!

Goldie: *(Entering D.R.)* Four soft-boiled eggs, that's what you're gonna have — *(He does not notice Ellie.)*

Jack: Hey, Goldie!

Tick: How you doin, boss — *(Puts gloves back on L. stool and takes the folding chair R. for* GOLDIE.*)*

Goldie: Oy, those stairs.

Jack: Figured you stayin in Reno till tomorrow — *(*TICK *goes to the clothes rack for* JACK'S *robe.* JACK *puts towel over his head.)*

Goldie: What, we got it settled there — how do you feel?

Tick: *(Puts robe on* JACK.*)* He feel like he look, boss!

Goldie: Not eating too quick?

Tick: No, sir, chewin good!

Jack: I'm chewin till it hurts —

Goldie: *Laugh, laugh!*

Jack: Come on, Goldie, when it gonna be?

Goldie: The Fourth of July. Now the newspaper guys —

Jack: *(Going L.)* The Fourth of July? *(*TICK *is R. of body bag.)*

Goldie: So, it makes a difference?

Jack: *(Prancing D.L.)* No, it just tickle my funny-bone, that's all —

Tick: *The Fourth of July and Lord you knows why!*

Goldie: We should worry, listen, will we have a gate there, 15,000! Jack, you know what they're callin it? Already by them it's the Fight of the Century — twenty years I never seen such a hooplah! Trains from St. Louis and Chicago, direct yet, tents they have to put up, it's a regular madhouse.

Tick: Lively times. I can hear you comin! Boy, you 'bout to win the Fight of the Century.

Jack: Yeah, or else lose and be the nigger of the minute. *(*TICK *goes U.R.)*

Goldie: *(Noticing* ELLIE — *goes to* JACK.*)* Listen, come here, Jack.

Jack: What kina odds goin?

Goldie: Brady 8 to 5. What's the girl doin here?

Jack: Oh, she lookin roun. She don't bother us none.

Goldie: Looking around for what?

Jack: *(Goes R. to* ELLIE.*)* You be nice now, Goldie — come on over, Ellie, don't be shy now, hon — *(Brings her C.)* she a friend of mine, you know?

Ellie: How do you do?

Jack: Goldie, shake hands with Miss Ellie Bachman.

Goldie: *(They shake hands.)* Please to meetcha, Miss Bachman. I apologize I didn't notice you before, such a tumult we got here.

Ellie: Oh, sure, I understand.

Goldie: You're a fan of Jack's, huh?

Jack: Ellie was on the same boat from Australia, she was visitin down there.

Goldie: Well it's great to be home again, I bet. You can't beat Frisco!

Ellie: Yes, I like it fine. My home is in Tacoma though.

Goldie: Oh . . . it's awful damp up there, ain't it?

Jack: Mm-hmm! You know it!

Ellie: Yes, I can't say I miss it much. *(Pause.)*

Tick: *(Comes D.)* Uncle of mine work up there in a laundry once, he didn't like it neither.

Jack: Drizzle on you all the time there!

Tick: Right!

Goldie: *(Goes to* ELLIE, *D. of* JACK. JACK *clears L.)* Yeah, well, Miss Bachman, the guys from the papers are comin any minute, you know what I mean, so if maybe you excuse us —

Jack: She stay where she is,

Tick: *(Goes U.)* Uh oh.

Goldie: Jackie, look what's the matter with you!

Jack: She stay where she is.

Goldie: I'm gonna pass out here

Ellie: *(Starts exiting D.R. Stops.)* I'll wait in the room, Jack.

Goldie: In the room! Jesus Christ!

Jack: You be nice now, hear?

Goldie: *(Moves D.)* I knew it! *Last night on the train it's like a voice—"Dumbbell, go home quick, somethin's goin on with him!"*

Jack: Ain't nobody's business!

Goldie: *(To* JACK.*)* Grow up, for God's sake —

Ellie: Let me go, it doesn't matter —

Goldie: No — please, one second — Tick, go lock the door. *(*TICK *goes off D.R. Returns.* GOLDIE *goes L. to* JACK.*)* So you don't know the score, huh? Well, I'll tell you the score, right now I'll tell you. And you should listen too, miss — *(Takes* ELLIE *to chair. She sits.)* I can see you're a fine serious girl, not a bum, better you should know, so there's no hard feelings here. *(Goes to* JACK.*)* First, Jack, they hate your guts a little bit — OK! You don't put on gloves everybody should like you. Then they hate your guts some more — still OK! That makes you wanna fight, some kinda pep it gives you. And then they hate you so much they're payin through the nose to see a white boy maybe knock you on your can — well, that's more than OK, cash in, after all, it's so nice to be colored you shouldn't have a bonus? But, Sonny, when they start in to hate you more than that, you gotta watch out. And that means now — oh I got ears, I get told things — guys who want to put dope in your food there, a guy who wants to watch the fight behind a rifle. OK, cops we'll get, dogs, that we can handle. *(Goes R. to her.)* But this on top of it, a white girl, Jack? What, do I have to spell it on the wall for you, you wanna drive them crazy, you don't hear what happens —

Jack: What I suppose to do! Stash her in a iddy biddy hole someplace in niggertown an go sneakin over there 12 clock at night, carry her roun with me inside a box like a pet bunny-rabbit or something —

Ellie: *(Rises, goes C.)* Jack —

Jack: Or maybe she just put black on her face, an puff her mouth up, so's nobody notice I took nothin from 'em — *(Knock at door.)* Let 'em wait! You
know I done fool roun plenty, Goldie, *(Crosses to* ELLIE. GOLDIE *breaks
D.)* she know it too, she know it all, but I ain't foolin roun now, unner-
stand — *(Points to* TICK*)* an if he say "that what you said lass time" I bust
his nappy head —

Tick: I ain't sayin nothin! *(Knocking.)*

Goldie: Hold on, I'm comin — Jack. I swear, I'll help you, just you shouldn't
throw it in their face, Jack, I'm beggin you.

Jack: See? This what you fell into, darlin.

Ellie: Do what he says.

Jack: You go long with him?

Ellie: Along with you.

Goldie: *(Motions to R. stool.)* Go, sit over there — let 'em in, for Chrissake —

(TICK admits the PRESSMEN. SMITTY leads, ELLIE sits on stool.)

Tick: Mornin, gents —

Jack: Hiya, fellers. Hey there, Smitty — *(Handshaking and greeting. TICK goes
C., U. of JACK.)*

Goldie: Just a few minutes, fellers, OK?

Press One: Well, you're sure looking good, Jack.

Jack: Thanks, boss!

Press Two: Guess you know about the Fourth —

Press One: You starting to get jumpy?

Jack: Yeah, I scared Brady gonna change his mind! *(TICK rubbing JACK's
shoulders.)*

Smitty: Still think you can take him, Jack?

Jack: Well, I ain't sayin I can take him straight off — an anyway, dat be kina
mean, you know, all them people, big holiday fight — how they gonna feel I
send em home early?

Smitty: So your only worry is deciding which round.

Jack: Yeah, an that take some thinkin, man! If I lets it go too long in there,
just sorta blocking, an keeping him offa me then evvybody say, "Now ain't
that one shif'less nigger, why they always so lazy?" An if I chop him down
quick 3rd or 4th roun, all at once then they holler "No tain't fair, that poor
man up there fightin a gorilla!" *But I gonna work it out.*

Press Two: What about that yellow streak Brady talks about?

Jack: *(Turns U. and flips up his robe.)* Yeah, you wanna see it?

Goldie: Don't clown aroun, Jackie —

Press Three: Any idea, Jack, why you smile when you're fighting?

Jack: Well, you know, I am a happy person. I always feel good, huh? An when
I'm fightin I feels double good. So what I wanna put a face on for? An you

know, it's a sport, right, like a game, so I like whoever I'm hittin' to see I'm still his friend.

Press Two: Going back to Chicago after the fight?

Jack: Yeah, I wanna see my little ole mamma —

Press One: *(R.)* Fried chicken, Jack?

Jack: Mmm-mmh! Can't wait!

Smitty: *(Goes to* ELLIE. GOLDIE *and* PRESS *follow.)* I believe that's Miss Bachman there, isn't it, Jack? You first met on the boat? *(*JACK *and* TICK *stay C.)*

Ellie: No, not exactly —

Goldie: Miss Bachman is my secretary, we hired her in Australia, she's from here, but she was over there and we, you know, we hired her, and she came over with the boys.

Smitty: I see —

Tick: Boss, if they finish I wanna rub him down —

*(*JACK *takes off robe and towel and puts them on rack.)*

Press One: We got plenty for now, Jack — (ELLIE *wanders U.R.C.)*

Press Three: Thanks —

Jack: Come again! *(*TICK *takes robe — hangs it up.)*

Press Two: *(Goes L., to* JACK.*)* Jack, one more question?

Jack: Yeah go 'head. (GOLDIE *puts chair back on platform.)*

Press Two: You're the first black man in the history of the ring to get a crack at the heavyweight title. Now the white folks of course are behind the White Hope, Brady's the redeemer of the race, and so on. But you Jack Jefferson, are you the Black Hope?

Jack: Well. I'm black and I'm hopin.

Smitty: *(Comes down to* PRESS TWO *L.)* Try and answer him straight, Jack.

Jack: Oh, I guess my cousins mostly want me to win.

Smitty: You imply that some don't?

Jack: Maybe some of them reckon they gonna pay a little high for that belt, if I take it.

Smitty: Won't you try and change their minds, Jack, get them all behind you?

Jack: Man, I ain't runnin for Congress! I ain't fightin for no race, ain't redeemin nobody. My mamma tole me Mr. Lincoln done that — ain't that why you shot him?

Act 1, Scene 6

Beau Rivage, Wisconsin. A cabin.

ELLIE *sitting up in bed, a sheet around her.* JACK, *wrapped in a towel, enters D.R. Crickets. Kerosene lamp on table beside bed. A woodbox with firewood is U.C. R. is a straight chair with* JACK's *sweater and* ELLIE's *dress.* JACK's *shoes are on floor — foot of bed.*

Jack: Shucks, honey, it ain't cold, this the finest time for swimmin —
Ellie: We have come to a parting of the ways.
Jack: Aw . . . big silvery moon, pine trees —
Ellie: Snapping turtles, moccasins —
Jack: *(At foot of bed.) Lawd, what to do when the romance done gone?*
Ellie: Oh, Jack, I couldn't make it to the door.
Jack: *(On bed, tries to pick her up.)* That right? Sposin I carry you down there
    then an sorta —
Ellie: No —
Jack: Ease you in —
Ellie: *(Sits up.)* No! No fair — Jack! — don't tickle me — *(Pulls away.)*
    Please — no! Ow! Jack, that hurts —
Jack: Hey, baby, I didn —
Ellie: I know, this damn sunburn.
Jack: *(Kneeling on bed.)* Aw, I'm sorry — here, lemme pat somethin on it —
    (Takes up a champagne bottle from table, applies some on her back.) Yeah . . .
Ellie: Oh, thanks . . . ooh . . . oh, yes, it's — Jack — ?
Jack: Don that feel good now — ?
Ellie: What are — ?
Jack: Cool — ?
Ellie: Not champagne, Jack.
Jack: Well, thass alright, baby, you worth the bess.
Ellie: All over me . . .
Jack: Get some lake on you, huh?
Ellie: No, I — *(Peering at him.)* Jack, turn around a little. . . more, this way. . . .
    Are you feeling alright?
Jack: I ain't feelin no diffrunt.
Ellie: Are you sure?
Jack: Yeah!
Ellie: You ate all those clams, maybe you — *(Feels his head.)*
Jack: What you doin that for? Ain't got no fever —
Ellie: Well, you look — a little peculiar, Jack.
Jack: *(Stands above bed.)* Oh . . . ? Kinda ashy, you mean?
Ellie: Yes, a sort of funny —
Jack: Honey, that ain't sick, that how I gets a sunburn. (ELLIE *tries not to*
    laugh.) Now, what you laughin at — ?
Ellie: *(Bursts out.)* I thought — I mean — oh! Oh, Jack —
Jack: Huh?
Ellie: I can't help it, I'm sorry — How you — Oh —
Jack: Yeah — come on, that ain't nice — *(Starts to laugh.)* You thought what,
    honey?
Ellie: I — thought it just — bounces off, that's all — *(Both laugh uproariously.)*
Jack: *(Kneels on bed.)* Bounces off —

Ellie: Yes — I

Jack: *(Shakes hands with* ELLIE.*)* Well, Miss Medium Rare, meet Mr. Well
    Done . . . ! *(Gales of laughter.) Oughta seen my cousin, Chester. He turned
    purple.*

Ellie: Oh . . . do we have to leave tomorrow?

Jack: *(Lying down.)* Shouldn't leave the place alone too long, honey.

Ellie: I know. All right.

Jack: *(Puts arm around her.)* Case there's any fussin or —

Ellie: Ssh. I know.

Jack: My, you do smell good though.

Ellie: Yes?

Jack: Mm-hmmm.

Ellie: You're not tired of being alone with me, are you?

Jack: Hey. You kiddin?

Ellie: Or tired of me asking questions like that?

Jack: Oh . . . I'm getting tired of plenny . . . but you ain't in there at all.

Ellie: It's lovely to hear you say that. . . . Have a swim if you want to.

Jack: No, I'm cozy here . . . I cozy, an you rosy . . . (ELLIE *chuckles.* JACK *turns
    down the lamp low. Sings softly.)*

    Woke up this mornin,

    Blues all round my head.

    Woke up this mornin,

    Blues all in my bread. . . .

    For how long, how long,

    I saying how long.

Ellie: Lying in the sun I was, you know, daydreaming . . . how maybe I'd stay
    there . . . and it would keep on burning me . . . day after day — oh, right
    through September. . . . And I'd get darker and darker. . . . I really get dark,
    you know, and then I'd dye my hair . . . and I'd change my name . . . and
    I'd come to you in Chicago . . . like somebody new . . . a colored woman, or
    a Creole maybe . . . and nobody but you would ever guess . . .

Jack: Won't work, honey.

Ellie: Hm.

Jack: Evvybody know I gone off cullud women.

Ellie: *(Hits him.)* Oh. Jack, don't tease.

Jack: *I has too, 'cept for my mamma.*

Ellie: Maybe if I . . .

Jack: Ssh.

Ellie:. What will we do . . .

Jack: Ssh . . . try an sleep, honey. . . . — *(Kisses her. Then turning the lamp down
    further.)* Creepin up on me a little too — *(Darkness. Sings.)*

    For how long, how long, I sayin.

    Always callin you honey . . ain't I?

Ellie: Mm.

Jack: Don remember I call no woman by that. Call em by their name . . . or jus baby, you know. . . . Don ever call you by you name.

Ellie: Oh . . . I don't care about my name. . . .

Jack: Honey . . . honey from the bees . . .

Ellie: Yes.

Jack: Nothin' like that stuff. . . . Used to sit . . . Oh, long time ago, in Texas . . . we'all ud have a lil honey-treat sometime . . . whole yellah mugful . . . used to set there with it . . . foolin with it, you know . . . liff up a spoonful . . . tip it a lil bit . . . watchin it curve up . . . start in to sli-i-i-de ovuh . . . oh, takin its time . . . slow . . . slow . . . hundred years up there . . . then down . . . stringing down . . . and then . . . *(Suddenly embracing her.)* Oh, my sweet sweet baby, I want to have it all—

Ellie: Yes—

(SOUND of SIX MEN *with a lantern—bursting in. Confusion of light and bodies.)*

Man One: On your feet, Jefferson—

Ellie: Jack—

*(*JACK *leaps over foot of bed.)*

Man Two: Get the window, Charlie—

Man Three: Hey—

Man One: Look out—

Man Four: Oh!

Man Five: Grab him—

Man Four: He's—choking me—

Man One: Here, you—*(THUD.* ELLIE *screams.)* Let go or I'll put a hole in you—

Man Two: Where is he—?

Man One: I said—

(THUD.)

Ellie: Stop it—

Man Four: Jesus—

Man Six: Light that goddamn lamp—

Ellie: Please—

Man Five: Sir there, lady—

Man One: We're the law.

(Kerosene lamp on. ELLIE *huddled at the head of the bed,* JACK *at the foot of bed, grasping a chunk of firewood, the others facing* JACK, *immobile.* DIXON *is among them. All are breathing heavily.* DIXON *moves forward.)*

Dixon: I'm a Federal marshal, Jefferson. *(Shows his badge.)* Put that down,
please. *(Pause.)* Come on. We don't want to make this any worse. *(Pause.
JACK drops it.)* At 10:00 A.M. this morning you drove Miss Eleanor Bachman across the Illinois-Wisconsin state line. Having done so you proceeded to have relations with her. Under the Mann Act this makes you
liable and I'm therefore placing you under arrest.

Ellie: No . . . no . . .

Dixon: Get dressed, please, Miss Bachman. We'll take you into town.

Ellie: Jack —

Jack: Don't worry — get dress — *(Handing her her clothes.)*

Man Two: Here.

Dixon: Hold a blanket up or something.

Ellie: Jack . . .

Jack: Don't you fret now . . . (MAN TWO *and* MAN THREE *screen her with a
blanket. To* DIXON.) Thanks, mistah.

Dixon: Sure.

Jack: How much this carry?

Dixon: 1 – 3.

Jack: She clear?

Dixon: Just you.

Jack: Yeah. Thanks.

Man One: *(Showing handcuffs.)* We need these, Jim?

Dixon: No. Find him his pants and let's get out of here. . . .

Act 1, Scene 7

Chicago: Mrs. Jefferson's House.

   Surrounding MRS. JEFFERSON *in her rocking choir on the C. wagon are the* PAS-
TOR *and 7 or 8* BROTHERS *and* SISTERS, *who still continue singing as the* PASTOR
speaks. U.R. is a Victorian table with a matching chair on each side. Other BROTH-
ERS *and* SISTERS *bring chairs on stage. At one side is* CLARA, *now dressed rather
plainly.* MRS. JEFFERSON *wears a dress, with a shawl over her shoulders.*

Pastor: Lawd, we prayin longside this sick unhappy mother here. She lookin
to You. Lawd, she know her boy been sinful, an she sorry bout that but
she do love him, Lawd. You give him another chance she nevah ask yo fo
anythin! She living by You Book all her days, Lawd, you seen it! We prayin
you touch them judges' eyes with mercy. Let em chastise him today, Lawd,
let em fine him so steep he leff withouta dime, let em scare him so hard he
nevah forget it but, Lawd, don let em lock this woman's boy away.

(End of singing.)

Brothers: Amen.

Mrs. Jefferson: An if they does, oh, please, Lawd, let it juss be fo a little.

Brothers: Amen.

Pastor: We callin with you, Sister.

Mrs. Jefferson: I thank ya, Pastor. Wish I could offuh ya some lil hospitality but honess —

Pastor: Don fret now, Sister.

Mrs. Jefferson: I mean I kin hardly —

Sister One: Nevah you mine, Tiny.

Clara: *(Goes R. to* MRS. JEFFERSON.*)* Ah can put on a potta fresh cawfee, Mrs. Jefferson.

Mrs. Jefferson: *(As* CLARA *goes.)* See if Tick or somebody comin down the street firss. *(*CLARA *goes to the window by D.R. chair.)*

Sister Two: Early yet, Sister.

Clara: Nobody. Mrs. Jefferson. Juss a buncha fellers there gawnta play baseball.

Mrs. Jefferson: *(Sighs.)* Awright. Clara. Thank ya.

Pastor: *(As* CLARA *goes to kitchen — D.R.)* Got a guardjin angel there!

Sister One: She been round evvy day. Heard Tiny was ailin, an —

Mrs. Jefferson: Should've brung word by this. Caint've took this long.

Pastor: We in de Lawd's hans. Sister.

Brothers: Amen.

Mrs. Jefferson: Fum when he was chile I knowed this day comin. Looka that, Momma, why cain't I, Momma, lemme lone, Momma. Nevah stop. Fidgety feet en oh, them great big eyes, roamin an reachin, all ovuh. Tried to learn him like you gotta learn a cullud boy. Dassnt, dassnt, dassnt, that aint for you! Roll right off him. Tried to learn it to him meaner — *Mo chile you got the meaner you go to if you lovin you chile. That plain cullud sense.* Hit him with my han, he say, "So what." Hit him with my shoe, he look up an smile. Took a razor-strop to him, that make him squint but then he do a funny dance an ask me fo a nickel. I prayed to de Lawd put mo strenf in my arm, the worse I was whippin the bigger he growed, leven years old an still wouden hear nothin. Hit him with a stick till I couden hit no mo, he pull it away fum me, an bust it in two, an then he run off —

Pastor: Sister —

Mrs. Jefferson: Lawd, forgive me treatin him so mean! Lawd, forgive me not beatin on him young enough or hurtin him bad enough to learn him cause I seen this day comin —

(Knock downstairs — off D.L.)

Sister One: I let em in. Tiny. *(Goes D.L.)*

Pastor: We hopin with you, Sister. Hole onter my han now.

Mrs. Jefferson: No, thass awright.

Sister One: But you all muss aint got de right house —
Rudy: *(Enters D. L.)* 231?
Teammate: Mis Jeffson's house, ain't it?
Sister One: Yeah but — hang on, whole lotta you caint fit here —
Rudy: OK, set on de stairway, de ress of you —

(SISTER ONE *backs into the room followed by three large young* NEGROES *wearing blue jackets and matching baseball caps; They carry valises from which bats and other gear protrude. Their leader, and the largest,* RUDY, *takes off his cap and the others follow suit.* CLARA *re-enters D.R. from the kitchen.)*

Rudy: Aftuhnoon, evvybody.
Mrs. Jefferson: You all comin fum de courthouse?
Rudy: No, ma'am. Us jus get a message — uh — askin we pay a call here. We
    de Blue Jays.
Mrs. Jefferson: You de which?
Rudy: De-troit Blue Jays. You know, de cullud baseball club? *Pulvrise de Afro
    Giants here Saddy?*
Brother Two: Oh yeah, my nephew tend dat game.
Rudy: *(Crosses to* MRS. JEFFERSON.) My name Rudy Sims, ma'm.
Mrs. Jefferson: Pleased to meet you, Mistah Sims —
Clara: *(Goes to C.)* Who say you sposeta call in here?
Rudy: Well, we sorta frens with Jack —
Clara: This here no celebratin party, you know!
Mrs. Jefferson: Hush, Clara, if they frens with Jack —
Clara: Why somebody sen us a baseball team here!
Rudy: Mebbe we bess wait outside in de hall, ma'm —
Mrs. Jefferson: Nothin of the kine! Clara —
Clara: Ah aint never seed Jack wif no baseball frens!

(TICK *enters D.L.)*

Rudy: Well, ah nevuh seed him wif you, so we even.
Tick: Don let her rile you Rudy. Thanks for comin.
Rudy: Any time, man. (TICK *goes D.R. Looks out window.)* Got here fas as I
    could Miz Jefferson.
Mrs. Jefferson: Well. You here. . . . come on. Talk.
Tick: *(Looking out window.)* It ain't good.
Sister One: Lawd have mercy.
Mrs. Jefferson: Come on. Finish up.
Tick: *(Comes C.) 20,000 fine and 3 years in Joliet.*
Sister Two: Jesus above.
Brother One: Three years.

Clara: *(Goes toward* TICK.*)* Why caint all dem Jew lawyers do nothing! Why
     caint —
Tick: Dey got de week ta try appealin on it —
Brother One: Three years.
Mrs. Jefferson: *I die they lock him up!* (CLARA *kneels R. of* MRS. JEFFERSON.
     SISTER ONE *to her L.)*
Sister Two: Don take on, Sister —
Pastor: Bring me them smellin salts —
Sister One: Tiny —
Mrs. Jefferson: No, I don want nothing —
Tick: He do have the week out on bail. Miz Jeffson — dey set it kina heavy but
     we figgered dey might and we gonna make it.
Mrs. Jefferson: A week. Drive him crazy.
Tick: Well, we gotta try an see it don't.
Clara: *(Rises and goes to* TICK.*)* That snaky lil wax-face bitch! Where she at
     now! Where she bloodsuckin! Oh, ah'll smoke her out, an, man —
Pastor: Sister —
Clara: *What I gonna do be worth a hunnerd three yearses!*
Mrs. Jefferson: Aint her fault, Clara.
Clara: She knowd this end-up comin, ain a deaf dumb bline pinhead living
     din know it, but oh, Daddy, she joyin herself so (Crosses D. of everyone
     to L.) it so good when it goin! *(Goes R. to* TICK.*)* Leave it alone? Oh but,
     Daddy, ah loves you!
Mrs. Jefferson: He brung her down once. She din seem too bad.
Tick: Nice an quiet too. *(Goes R. to window.)*
Clara: Ah ain talkin to you! Could be she love him! Why she scat off den, wid
     her man in trouble? Why she —
Pastor: Bess unwine dat serpint from you heart, Sister —
Clara: *Love him, my black ass!*
Pastor: Sister!
Mrs. Jefferson: *(As* CLARA *goes R. to kitchen.)* Poor gal been frettin so —

*(*JACK *and* GOLDIE *enter D.L.* JACK *greets everyone.* GOLDIE *goes to the L. of* MRS.
JEFFERSON.*)*

Pastor: Praise de Lawd an welcome.
Jack: Pastor . . . evvybody . . . good boy, Rudy.
Rudy: Ready for ya, Jack.
Jack: *(Kneels R. of* MRS. JEFFERSON.*)* Fine, no rush. . . . hiya, Momma Tiny.
Mrs. Jefferson: They din hurt you, Jack? You git nuff to eat?
Jack: *(L. of* MRS. JEFFERSON.*)* Sure. Momma. I'm perky as a turkey.
Goldie: *I should feel as good as he does.*

Jack: How are you, Momma?

Mrs. Jefferson: Oh . . .

Jack: Still kina poorly.

Mrs. Jefferson: It drain me out some, I guess.

Jack: (Kisses his mother.) Oh, Momma.

Brother Two: Hard luck, Jack.

Mrs. Jefferson: We been prayin an prayin here, son.

Jack: Well . . . de Lawd hear anyone he gonna hear you.

Mrs. Jefferson: Look like he aint this time — but he gonna put me on my feet.
I can feel it! An I gonna help him, gonna ress up an eat good, and I comin
down there soon, Jack —

Jack: *(Rises. Bends over and takes her hands.)* Momma —

*(*CLARA *enters D.R.)*

Mrs. Jefferson: Often as they 'low ya to, you wait an see, bring a big ole picnic
basket on my arm —

Jack: No, Momma, listen —

Clara: (Flinging herself upon him.) Oh, baby, baby, ah caint let em clap you in
there.

Jack: *What she doin here!*

Goldie: That all we need.

Jack: Git offa me, you! *(Goes L.)* Momma, what de hell —

Mrs. Jefferson: Clara come roun when she hear I was ailin —

Clara: I been doin fo you momma, Jack —

Mrs. Jefferson: She tryna menn her ways —

Tick: *(Stealing a look out of window.)* Jack. *(*JACK *looks at him. He nods. Pause.)*

Jack: *(To* CLARA.*)* I count ten fo you to beat it. One —

Clara: No!

Mrs. Jefferson: She been my helpmeet, Jack!

Jack: Sister find you a housekeeper!

Clara: I keepin house, baby!

Jack: I up to five, girl —

Tick: *(Tense. At the window.)* Let her be for now, Jack. She in here she caint
spoil it, screamin in the street or somethin.

Goldie: *(Mopping his face.)* That's all we need.

Rudy: Soun like sense, Jack.

Mrs. Jefferson: Spoil what? Mistah, what these boys up to?

Brother One: Yeah, what goin on here?

Clara: *(To* TICK *at window.)* Whuffo you playin peekaboo wif dat dere
automobile?

Pastor: *(R. end of platform.)* You aint about to make things worse, son, are you?

Mrs. Jefferson: Jack—

Jack: Awright. I gotta truss all you folks now—

Pastor: Son, however rough it 'pears today—

Tick: Oughta stan by the winder now, Jack. They lookin.

Mrs. Jefferson: Who? Who lookin?

Jack: *(Crosses D.R. to window.)* 'Tectives in that car, Momma.

Mrs. Jefferson: Jack— (CLARA *goes to U. of* MRS. JEFFERSON. TICK *watches from U.C.— U. of everyone.)*

Jack: Momma, listen—

Mrs. Jefferson: What they waitin out there for, Mistah Goldie?

Goldie: Well, even though Jack is out on bond, you see—

Jack: They worried I gonna try an jump my bail, Momma.

Goldie: *They're worried. I'm in hock up to here with this.*

Mrs. Jefferson: Jack . . . you just got let out.

Jack: Bess time, Momma. They don know I's ready.

Mrs. Jefferson: They follerin you, but!

Jack: Thinks they is.

Mrs. Jefferson: Jack, what if they catches you—

Jack: Wont never get near me! Now, firss thin what I do is take my coat off— *(Does so, revealing a raspberry colored shirt.* GIRL, *sitting in chair by window, takes his coat.)* then I stan here sorta talking—"Why heaven sake no foolin!"—now let em see my face— *(Looks out.)* "Oh my, it look like rain . . ." —an I know they seen my shirt—Mm-mm! *Don't you wish you had one!* Well, I goes on talking, right? Now over there is Rudy— (RUDY *looks at his watch.)* Uh-oh, he checkin his turnip again!

Tick: Hole her—

Clara: *(Shaking.)* Jack gonna— *(Struggles.)*

Sister One: Stop her mouf up—

(JACK goes R.)

Clara: He runnin ffff—

(They drag her to the floor near the window, kicking.)

Goldie: Oh, boy—

Brother One: Make some noise—

Sister Two: Sit on her—"Look ovuh, Beulah—"

Brother Two: Which—?

Pastor: Ready—

Mrs. Jefferson: No "Beulah" now, sen up a glad one—

Sister One: Quick, she bitin me—

Mrs. Jefferson: Sing, chillum—

All: *(But* CLARA *on whom the three largest* SISTERS *are sitting.)*
> Just to talk to Jesus
> Oh what a joy de-vine.
> I kin feel de lectric
> Movin on de line.
> All wired up by God de Father
> For his lovin own,
> Put a call to Jesus
> On the Royal Telephone —

Jack: *(Over the singing.)* Here, where that Jew's harp — *(Finds it.)* Plung on it, Rudy, it cover your face up — *(Tosses it to him.* RUDY *plays.* JACK *moves among them.)* Good luck — thank you — thank you — see you soon — you too — dont worry — Thank you, Momma Tiny — Get well, darlin, try, please try — Say you come an see me — Goodbye, my momma, Goodbye, my sweetheart —

*(*MRS. JEFFERSON *nods and sings right on, clapping to the beat, and with* GOLDIE *mopping his face,* CLARA *kicking and crying,* RUDY *twanging and all the rest in full chorus,* JACK *puts on his cap and disappears with the* JAYS.*)*

All:
> Angel operators
> Waitin for you call.
> Central up in heaven,
> Take no time at all.
> Ring, and God will answer
> In his happy tone.
> Put a call to Jesus
> On the Royal Telephone.

(BLACKOUT)

(1968)

Amiri Baraka
(LeRoi Jones)

Amiri Baraka was a defining voice of the Black Arts movement. Born in 1934 in Newark, New Jersey, as Everett LeRoi Jones, he began writing short stories and comic strips at a young age. At fifteen he graduated from high school and enrolled at Rutgers University. After spending some time on the predominately white campus, he transferred to Howard University in Washington, D.C., in 1952. While there, he studied under several famous black scholars, including Sterling A. Brown, who taught him about African American music. Jones, however, found the atmosphere of Howard to be too claustrophobic, and in 1954 he flunked out. He then joined the Air Force and spent three years in Puerto Rico, during which time he read widely and began writing poetry before being dishonorably discharged on the suspicion that he had Communist sympathies. Jones then moved to Greenwich Village, becoming part of the Beat scene and establishing himself as a jazz critic. In 1958 he married Hettie Cohen, who was the editor of *Partisan Review*. The couple had two daughters and founded the art magazine *Yugen*, which regularly featured Beat poets.

In 1960 Jones went to Cuba where he encountered third world politics, which challenged him artistically and politically. Upon his return, Jones began to embrace black nationalism. In 1961 he cofounded and edited an underground newspaper, *The Floating Bear*, and helped establish the American Theatre for Poets. In 1964 his play *Dutchman* won the Obie Award for the Best Off-Broadway Production, and in 1966 it was made into a film directed by Anthony Harvey. *Dutchman*, included below, is a modern parable about the interaction between stereotypes of black males and of white females, as well as an example of what Jones called "Black Revolutionary Theatre" in an essay by that title. Revolutionary Theatre, like the author's work more generally, intends to provoke the audience into critical thinking.

The year 1965 marked significant change. Jones greatly admired Malcolm X, and after Malcolm was assassinated, the author moved to Harlem, cut his ties with the East Village community, changed his name — to Imamu Amiri Baraka — and even divorced his wife, Hettie. His composition, "A Poem for Black Hearts," published in *Negro Digest*, was one of the first to memorialize the slain leader. A later play, *The Death of Malcolm X* (1969), also honors the man. While in Harlem, Baraka established the Black Arts Repertory Theatre and School, and in 1966 he moved to Newark where he established Spirit House, an arts institution. He also became politically active and contributed to the election of the city's first black mayor. In Newark, Baraka met and married Sylvia

Robinson, who later adopted the name Amina Baraka and with whom he had five children.

Baraka has received several awards for his work: an American Book Award, a lifetime achievement award from the Before Columbus Foundation, and the Langston Hughes Medal for Outstanding Contribution to African American Literature. In 2002 he was named New Jersey's poet laureate and served as such until a controversy arose over one of his poems, "Somebody Blew Up America," about the September 11, 2001, attacks on New York City's World Trade Center. He has held teaching positions at the State University of New York at Stony Brook, Yale, Rutgers University, and George Mason University. Baraka is also a cofounder of the Black Community Development and Defense Organization, the Congress of African Peoples, and the National Black Political Convention.

Baraka's most celebrated books include *Preface to a Twenty-Volume Suicide Note* (1961), *Cuba Libre* (1961), *Black Magic: Poetry 1961–1967* (1967), *It's Nation Time* (1970, the title poem of which is included below), *Transbluesency: The Selected Poems of Amiri Baraka/LeRoi Jones, 1961–1995* (1995), *Selected Poetry of Amiri Baraka/LeRoi Jones* (1979), and *Selected Plays and Prose of Amiri Baraka/LeRoi Jones* (1979). He also coedited *Black Fire: An Anthology of Afro-American Writing* (1968). Baraka's works interrogate American myths about race and gender stereotypes, frequently invoking African and African American history, such as references to the Dutch slave trade or the Underground Railroad. Baraka often deals with relationships between blacks and whites, and some of his plays, dedicated to black nationalism and a new black aesthetic, expose white racism in controversial ways. In the mid-1970s, Baraka shifted his focus from black nationalism to third world Marxism, bridging African American revisionary movements with other cultural and political movements.

Dutchman

CHARACTERS
Clay, twenty-year-old Negro
Lula, thirty-year-old white woman
Riders of Coach, white and black
Young Negro
Conductor

In the flying underbelly of the city. Steaming hot, and summer on top, outside. Underground. The subway heaped in modern myth.

Opening scene is a man sitting in a subway seat, holding a magazine but looking vacantly just above its wilting pages. Occasionally he looks blankly toward the window on his right. Dim lights and darkness whistling by against the glass.

(Or paste the lights, as admitted props, right on the subway windows. Have them move, even dim and flicker. But give the sense of speed. Also stations, whether the train is stopped or the glitter and activity of these stations merely flashes by the windows.)

The man is sitting alone. That is, only his seat is visible, though the rest of the car is outfitted as a complete subway car. But only his seat is shown. There might be, for a time, as the play begins, a loud scream of the actual train. And it can recur throughout the play, or continue on a lower key once the dialogue starts.

The train slows after a time, pulling to a brief stop at one of the stations. The man looks idly up, until he sees a woman's face staring at him through the window; when it realizes that the man has noticed the face, it begins very premeditatedly to smile. The man smiles too, for a moment, without a trace of self-consciousness. Almost an instinctive though undesirable response. Then a kind of awkwardness or embarrassment sets in, and the man makes to look away, is further embarrassed, so he brings back his eyes to where the face was, but by now the train is moving again, and the face would seem to be left behind by the way the man turns his head to look back through the other windows at the slowly fading platform, he smiles then, more comfortably confident, hoping perhaps that his memory of this brief encounter will be pleasant. And then he is idle again.

Scene 1

Train roars. Lights flash outside the windows.

LULA *enters from the rear of the car in bright, skimpy summer clothes and sandals. She carries a net bag full of paper books, fruit, and other anonymous articles. She is wearing sunglasses, which she pushes up on her forehead from time to time.* LULA *is a tall, slender, beautiful woman with long red hair hanging straight down her back, wearing only loud lipstick in somebody's good taste. She is eating an apple, very daintily. Coming down the car toward* CLAY.

She stops beside CLAY's *seat and hangs languidly from the strap, still managing to eat the apple. It is apparent that she is going to sit in the seat next to* CLAY, *and that she is only waiting for him to notice her before she sits.*

CLAY *sits as before, looking just beyond his magazine, now and again pulling the magazine slowly back and forth in front of his face in a hopeless effort to fan himself. Then he sees the woman hanging there beside him and he looks up into her face, smiling quizzically.*

Lula: Hello.
Clay: Uh, hi're you?
Lula: I'm going to sit down O.K.?
Clay: Sure.
Lula: *(Swings down onto the seat, pushing her legs straight out as if she is very weary)* Oooof! Too much weight.

Clay: Ha. doesn't look like much to me. *(Leaning back against the window, a little surprised and maybe stiff)*

Lula: It's so anyway. *(And she moves her toes in the sandals, then pulls her right leg up on the left knee, better to inspect the bottoms of the sandals and the back of her heel. She appears for a second not to notice that* CLAY *is sitting next to her or that she has spoken to him just a second before.* CLAY *looks at the magazine, then out the black window. As he does this, she turns very quickly toward him)* Weren't you staring at me through the window?

Clay: *(Wheeling around and very much stiffened)* What?

Lula: Weren't you staring at me through the window? At the last stop?

Clay: Staring at you? What do you mean?

Lula: Don't you know what staring means?

Clay: I saw you through the window . . . if that's what it means. I don't know if I was staring. Seems to me you were staring through the window at me.

Lula: I was. But only after I'd turned around and saw you staring through that window down in the vicinity of my ass and legs.

Clay: Really?

Lula: Really. I guess you were just taking those idle potshots. Nothing else to do. Run your mind over people's flesh.

Clay: Oh boy. Wow, now I admit I was looking in your direction. But the rest of that weight is yours.

Lula: I suppose.

Clay: Staring through train windows is weird business. Much weirder than staring very sedately at abstract asses.

Lula: That's why I came looking through the window . . . so you'd have more than that to go on. I even smiled at you.

Clay: That's right.

Lula: I even got into this train, going some other way than mine. Walked down the aisle . . . searching you out.

Clay: Really? That's pretty funny.

Lula: That's pretty funny. . . . God, you're dull.

Clay: Well, I'm sorry, lady, but I really wasn't prepared for party talk.

Lula: No, you're not. What are you prepared for? *(Wrapping the apple core in a Kleenex and dropping it on the floor)*

Clay: *(Takes her conversation as pure sex talk. He turns to confront her squarely with this idea)* I'm prepared for anything. How about you?

Lula: *(Laughing loudly and cutting it off abruptly)* What do you think you're doing?

Clay: What?

Lula: You think I want to pick you up, get you to take me somewhere and screw me, huh?

Clay: Is that the way I look?

Lula: You look like you been trying to grow a beard. That's exactly what you look like. You look like you live in New Jersey with your parents and are trying to grow a beard. That's what. You look like you've been reading Chinese poetry and drinking lukewarm sugarless tea. *(Laughs, uncrossing and recrossing her legs)* You look like death eating a soda cracker.

Clay: *(Cocking his head from one side to the other, embarrassed and trying to make some comeback, but also intrigued by what the woman is saying . . . even the sharp city coarseness of her voice, which is still a kind of gentle sidewalk throb)* Really? I look like all that?

Lula: Not all of it. *(She feigns a seriousness to cover an actual somber tone)* I lie a lot. *(Smiling)* It helps me control the world.

Clay: *(Relieved and laughing louder than the humor)* Yeah, I bet.

Lula: But it's true, most of it, right? Jersey? Your bumpy neck?

Clay: How'd you know all that? Huh? Really. I mean about Jersey . . . and even the beard. I met you before? You know Warren Enright?

Lula: You tried to make it with your sister when you were ten.

> (CLAY *leans back hard against the back of the seat, his eyes opening now, still trying to look amused)* But I succeeded a few weeks ago.
> *(She starts to laugh again)*

Clay: What're you talking about? Warren tell you that? You're a friend of Georgia's?

Lula: I told you a lie. I don't know your sister. I don't know Warren Enright.

Clay: You mean you're just picking these things out of the air?

Lula: Is Warren Enright a tall skinny black black boy with a phony English accent?

Clay: I figured you knew him.

Lula: But I don't. I just figured you would know somebody like that. *(Laughs)*

Clay: Yeah, yeah.

Lula: You're probably on your way to his house now.

Clay: That's right.

Lula: *(Putting her hand on Clay's closer knee, drawing it from the knee up to the thigh's hinge, then removing it, watching his face very closely, and continuing to laugh, perhaps more gently than before)* Dull, dull, dull. I bet you think I'm exciting.

Clay: You're O.K.

Lula: Am I exciting you now?

Clay: Right. That's not what's supposed to happen?

Lula: How do I know? *(She returns her hand, without moving it, then takes it away and plunges it in her bag to draw out an apple)* You want this?

Clay: Sure.

Lula: *(She gets one out of the bag for herself)* Eating apples together is always the first step. Or walking up uninhabited Seventh Avenue in the twenties on weekends. *(Bites and giggles, glancing at Clay and speaking in loose singsong)* Can get you involved . . . boy! Get us involved. Um-huh. *(Mock seriousness)* Would you like to get involved with me, Mister Man?

Clay: *(Trying to be as flippant as* LULA, *whacking happily at the apple)* Sure. Why not? A beautiful woman like you. Huh, I'd be a fool not to.

Lula: And I bet you're sure you know what you're talking about. *(Taking him a little roughly by the wrist, so he cannot eat the apple, then shaking the wrist)* I bet you're sure of almost everything anybody ever asked you about . . . right? Right? *(Shakes his wrist harder)*

Clay: Yeah, right. . . . Wow, you're pretty strong, you know? Whatta you, a lady wrestler or something?

Lula: What's wrong with lady wrestlers? And don't answer because you never knew any. Huh. *(Cynically)* That's for sure. They don't have any lady wrestlers in that part of Jersey. That's for sure.

Clay: Hey, you still haven't tole me how you know so much about me.

Lula: I told you I didn't know anything about you . . . you're a well-known type.

Clay: Really?

Lula: Or at least I know the type very well. And your skinny English friend too.

Clay: Anonymously?

Lula: What? *(Settles back in seat, single-mindedly finishing her apple and humming snatches of rhythm and blues song)*

Clay: Without knowing us specifically?

Lula: Oh boy. *(Looking quickly at* CLAY) What a face. You know, you could be a handsome man.

Clay: I can't argue with you.

Lula: *(Vague, off-center response)* What?

Clay: *(Raising his voice, thinking the train noise has drowned part of his sentence)* I can't argue with you.

Lula: My hair is turning gray. A gray hair for each year and type I've come through.

Clay: Why do you want to sound so old?

Lula: But it's always gentle when it starts. *(Attention drifting)* Hugged against tenements, day or night.

Clay: What?

Lula: *(Refocusing)* Hey, why don't you take me to that party you're going to?

Clay: You must be a friend of Warren's to know about the party.

Lula: Wouldn't you like to take me to the party? *(Imitates clinging vine)* Oh, come on, ask me to your party.

Clay: Of course I'll ask you to come with me to the party. And I'll bet you're a friend of Warren's.

Lula: Why not be a friend of Warren's? Why not? *(Taking his arm)* Have you asked me yet?

Clay: How can I ask you when I don't know your name?

Lula: Are you talking to my name?

Clay: What is it, a secret?

Lula: I'm Lena the Hyena.

Clay: The famous woman poet?

Lula: Poetess! The same!

Clay: Well, you know so much about me . . . what's my name?

Lula: Morris the Hyena.

Clay: The famous woman poet?

Lula: The same. *(Laughing and going into her bag)* You want another apple?

Clay: Can't make it, lady. I only have to keep one doctor away a day.

Lula: I bet your name is . . . something like . . . uh, Gerald or Walter. Huh?

Clay: God, no.

Lula: Lloyd, Norman? One of those hopeless colored names creeping out of New Jersey. Leonard? Gag . . .

Clay: Like Warren?

Lula: Definitely, Just exactly like Warren. Or Everett.

Clay: Gag.

Lula: Well, for sure, it's not Willie.

Clay: It's Clay.

Lula: Clay? Really? Clay what?

Clay: Take your pick. Jackson, Johnson, or Williams.

Lula: Oh. really? Good for you. But it's got to be Williams. You're too pretentious to be a Jackson or Johnson.

Clay: Thass right.

Lula: But Clay's O.K.

Clay: So's Lena.

Lula: It's Lula.

Clay: Oh?

Lula: Lula the Hyena.

Clay: Very good.

Lula: *(Starts laughing again)* Now you say to me, "Lula, Lula, why don't you go to this party with me tonight?" It's your turn, and let those be your lines.

Clay: Lula, why don't you go to this party with me tonight, Huh?

Lula: Say my name twice before you ask, and no huh's.

Clay: Lula, Lula, why don't you go to this party with me tonight?

Lula: I'd like to go, Clay, but how can you ask me to go when you barely know me?

Clay: That is strange, isn't it?

Lula: What kind of reaction is that? You're supposed to say, "Aw, come on, we'll get to know each other better at the party."

Clay: That's pretty corny.

Lula: What are you into anyway? *(Looking at him half sullenly but still amused)* What thing are you playing at, Mister? Mister Clay Williams? *(Grabs his thigh, up near the crotch)* What are you thinking about?

Clay: Watch it now, you're gonna excite me for real.

Lula: *(Taking her hand away and throwing her apple core through the window)* I bet. *(She slumps in the seat and is heavily silent)*

Clay: I thought you knew everything about me? What happened? *(LULA looks at him, then looks slowly away, then over where the other aisle would be. Noise of the train. She reaches in her bag and pulls out one of the paper books. She puts it on her leg and thumbs the pages listlessly. CLAY cocks his head to see the title of the book. Noise of the train. LULA flips pages and her eyes drift. Both remain silent)* Are you going to the party with me, Lula?

Lula: *(Bored and not even looking)* I don't even know you.

Clay: You said you know my type. *(Strangely irritated)*

Lula: Don't get smart with me, Buster. I know you like the palm of my hand.

Clay: The one you eat the apples with?

Lula: Yeh. And the one I open doors late Saturday evening with. That's my door. Up at the top of the stairs. Five flights. Above a lot of Italians and lying Americans. And scrape carrots with. Also *(looks at him)* the same hand I unbutton my dress with, or let my skirt fall down. Same hand. Lover.

Clay: Are you angry about anything? Did I say something wrong?

Lula: Everything you say is wrong. *(Mock smile)* That's what makes you so attractive. Ha. In that funnybook jacket with all the buttons. *(More animate, taking hold of his jacket)* What've you got the jacket and tie on in all this heat for? And why're you wearing a jacket and tie like that? Did your people ever burn witches or start revolutions over the price of tea? Boy, those narrow-shoulder clothes come from a tradition you ought to feel oppressed by. A three-button suit. What right do you have to be wearing a three-button suit and striped tie? Your grandfather was a slave, he didn't go to Harvard.

Clay: My grandfather was a night watchman.

Lula: And you went to a colored college where everybody thought they were Averell Harriman.*

Clay: All except me.

* William Averell Harriman (1891–1986) was a wealthy white businessman who served in various diplomatic positions and political appointments under Presidents John F. Kennedy and Lyndon B. Johnson.

Lula: And who did you think you were? Who do you think you are now?

Clay: *(Laughs as if to make light of the whole trend of the conversation)* Well, in college I thought I was Baudelaire. But I've slowed down since.

Lula: I bet you never once thought you were a black nigger. *(Mock serious, then she howls with laughter. CLAY is stunned but after initial reaction, he quickly tries to appreciate the humor. LULA almost shrieks)* A black Baudelaire.

Clay: That's right.

Lula: Boy, are you corny. I take back what I said before. Everything you say is not wrong. It's perfect. You should be on television.

Clay: You act like you're on television already.

Lula: That's because I'm an actress.

Clay: I thought so.

Lula: Well, you're wrong. I'm no actress. I told you I always lie. I'm nothing, honey, and don't you ever forget it. *(Lighter)* Although my mother was a Communist. The only person in my family ever to amount to anything.

Clay: My mother was a Republican.

Lula: And your father voted for the man rather than the party.

Clay: Right!

Lula: Yea for him. Yea, yea for him.

Clay: Yea!

Lula: And yea for America where he is free to vote for the mediocrity of his choice! Yea!

Clay: Yea!

Lula: And yea for both your parents who even though they differ about so crucial a matter as the body politic still forged a union of love and sacrifice that was destined to flower at the birth of the noble Clay . . . what's your middle name?

Clay: Clay.

Lula: A union of love and sacrifice that was destined to flower at the birth of the noble Clay Clay Williams. Yea! And most of all yea yea for you. Clay Clay. The Black Baudelaire! Yes! *(And with knifelike cynicism)* My Christ. My Christ.

Clay: Thank you, ma'am.

Lula: May the people accept you as a ghost of the future. And love you, that you might not kill them when you can.

Clay: What?

Lula: You're a murderer, Clay, and you know it. *(Her voice darkening with significance)* You know goddamn well what I mean.

Clay: I do?

Lula: So we'll pretend the air is light and full of perfume.

Clay: *(Sniffing at her blouse)* It is.

Lula: And we'll pretend the people cannot see you. That is, the citizens. And that you are free of your own history. And I am free of my history. We'll pretend that we are both anonymous beauties smashing along through the city's entrails. *(She yells as loud as she can)* GROOVE!

Black

Scene 2

Scene is the same as before, though now there are other seats visible in the car. And throughout the scene other people get on the subway. There are maybe one or two seated in the car as the scene opens, though neither CLAY *nor* LULA *notices them.* CLAY's *tie is open.* LULA *is hugging his arm.*

Clay: The party!
Lula: I know it'll be something good. You can come in with me, looking casual and significant. I'll be strange, haughty, and silent, and walk with long slow strides.
Clay: Right.
Lula: When you get drunk, pat me once, very lovingly on the flanks, and I'll look at you cryptically, licking my lips.
Clay: It sounds like something we can do.
Lula: You'll go around talking to young men about your mind, and to old men about your plans. If you meet a very close friend who is also with someone like me, we can stand together, sipping our drinks and exchanging codes of lust. The atmosphere will be slithering in love and half-love and very open moral decision.
Clay: Great. Great.
Lula: And everyone will pretend they don't know your name, and then . . . *(She pauses heavily)* later, when they have to, they'll claim a friendship that denies your sterling character.
Clay: *(Kissing her neck and fingers)* And then what?
Lula: Then? Well, then we'll go down the street, late night, eating apples and winding very deliberately toward my house.
Clay: Deliberately?
Lula: I mean, we'll look in all the shopwindows, and make fun of the queers. Maybe we'll meet a Jewish Buddhist and flatten his conceits over some pretentious coffee.
Clay: In honor of whose God?
Lula: Mine.
Clay: Who is . .
Lula: Me . . . and you?
Clay: A corporate Godhead.

Lula: Exactly. Exactly. *(Notices one of the other people entering)*

Clay: Go on with the chronicle. Then what happens to us?

Lula: *(A mild depression, but she still makes her description triumphant and increasingly direct)* To my house, of course.

Clay: Of course.

Lula: And up the narrow steps of the tenement.

Clay: You live in a tenement?

Lula: Wouldn't live anywhere else. Reminds me specifically of my novel form of insanity.

Clay: Up the tenement stairs.

Lula: And with my apple-eating hand I push open the door and lead you, my tender big-eyed prey, into my . . . God, what can I call it . . . into my hovel.

Clay: Then what happens?

Lula: After the dancing and games, after the long drinks and long walks, the real fun begins.

Clay: Ah, the real fun. *(Embarrassed, in spite of himself)* Which is . . . ?

Lula: *(Laughs at him)* Real fun in the dark house. Hah! Real fun in the dark house, high up above the street and the ignorant cowboys. I lead you in, holding your wet hand gently in my hand . . .

Clay: Which is not wet?

Lula: Which is dry as ashes.

Clay: And cold?

Lula: Don't think you'll get out of your responsibility that way. It's not cold at all. You Fascist! Into my dark living room. Where we'll sit and talk end-lessly, endlessly.

Clay: About what?

Lula: About what? About your manhood, what do you think? What do you think we've been talking about all this time?

Clay: Well, I didn't know it was that. That's for sure. Every other thing in the world but that. *(Notices another person entering, looks quickly, almost in-voluntarily, up and down the car, seeing the other people in the car)* Hey, I didn't even notice when those people got on.

Lula: Yeah, I know.

Clay: Man, this subway is slow.

Lula: Yeah, I know.

Clay: Well, go on. We were talking about my manhood.

Lula: We still are. All the time.

Clay: We were in your living room.

Lula: My dark living room. Talking endlessly.

Clay: About my manhood.

Lula: I'll make you a map of it. Just as soon as we get to my house.

Clay: Well, that's great.

Lula: One of the things we do while we talk. And screw.

Clay: *(Trying to make his smile broader and less shaky)* We finally got there.

Lula: And you'll call my rooms black as a grave. You'll say, "This place is like Juliet's tomb."

Clay: *(Laughs)* I might.

Lula: I know. You've probably said it before.

Clay: And is that all? The whole grand tour?

Lula: Not all. You'll say to me very close to my face, many, many times, you'll say, even whisper, that you love me.

Clay: Maybe I will.

Lula: And you'll be lying.

Clay: I wouldn't lie about something like that.

Lula: Hah. It's the only kind of thing you will lie about. Especially if you think it'll keep me alive.

Clay: Keep you alive? I don't understand.

Lula: *(Bursting out laughing, but too shrilly)* Don't understand? Well, don't look at me. It's the path I take, that's all. Where both feet take me when I set them down. One in front of the other.

Clay: Morbid. Morbid. You sure you're not an actress? All that self-aggrandizement.

Lula: Well, I told you I wasn't an actress . . . but I also told you I lie all the time. Draw your own conclusions.

Clay: And is that all of our lives together you've described? There's no more?

Lula: I've told you all I know. Or almost all.

Clay: There's no funny parts?

Lula: I thought it was all funny.

Clay: But you mean peculiar, not ha-ha.

Lula: You don't know what I mean.

Clay: Well, tell me the almost part then. You said almost all. What else? I want the whole story.

Lula: *(Searching aimlessly through her bag. She begins to talk breathlessly, with a light and silly tone)* All stories are whole stories. All of 'em. Our whole story . . . nothing but change. How could things go on like that forever? Huh? *(Slaps him on the shoulder, begins finding things in her bag, taking them out and throwing them over her shoulder into the aisle)* Except I go on as I do. Apples and long walks with deathless intelligent lovers. But you mix it up. Look out the window, all the time. Turning pages. Change change change. Till, shit, I don't know you. Wouldn't, for that matter. You're too serious. I bet you're even too serious to be psychoanalyzed. Like all those Jewish poets from Yonkers, who leave their mothers looking for other mothers, or others' mothers, on whose baggy tits they lay their fumbling heads. Their poems are always funny, and all about sex.

Clay: They sound great. Like movies.

Lula: But you change. *(Blankly)* And things work on you till you hate them. *(More people come into the train. They come closer to the couple, some of them not sitting, but swinging drearily on the straps, staring at the two with uncertain interest)*

Clay: Wow. All these people, so suddenly. They must all come from the same place.

Lula: Right. That they do.

Clay: Oh? You know about them too?

Lula: Oh yeah. About them more than I know about you. Do they frighten you?

Clay: Frighten me? Why should they frighten me?

Lula: 'Cause you're an escaped nigger.

Clay: Yeah?

Lula: 'Cause you crawled through the wire and made tracks to my side.

Clay: Wire?

Lula: Don't they have wire around plantations?

Clay: You must be Jewish. All you can think about is wire. Plantations didn't have any wire. Plantations were big open whitewashed places like heaven, and everybody on 'em was grooved to be there. Just strummin' and hummin' all day.

Lula: Yes, yes.

Clay: And that's how the blues was born.

Lula: Yes, yes. And that's how the blues was born. *(Begins to make up a song that becomes quickly hysterical. As she sings she rises from her seat, still throwing things out of her bag into the aisle, beginning a rhythmical shudder and twistlike wiggle, which she continues up and down the aisle, bumping into many of the standing people and tripping over the feet of those sitting. Each time she runs into a person she lets out a very vicious piece of profanity, wiggling and stepping all the time)* And that's how the blues was born. Yes. Yes. Son of a bitch, get out of the way. Yes. Quack. Yes. Yes. And that's how the blues was born, Ten little niggers sitting on a limb, but none of them ever looked like him. *(Points to* CLAY, *returns toward the seat, with her hands extended for him to rise and dance with her)*

And that's how blues was born. Yes. Come on, Clay. Let's do the nasty. Rub bellies. Rub bellies.

Clay: *(Waves his hands to refuse. He is embarrassed, but determined to get a kick out of the proceedings)* Hey, what was in those apples? Mirror, mirror on the wall, who's the fairest one of all? Snow White, baby, and don't you forget it.

Lula: *(Grabbing for his hands, which he draws away)*

Come on, Clay. Let's rub bellies on the train. The nasty. The nasty. Do the gritty grind, like your ol' rag-head mammy. Grind till you lose your mind. Shake it, shake it, shake it, shake it! OOOOweeee! Come on, Clay. Let's do the choo-choo train shuffle, the navel scratcher.

Clay: Hey, you coming on like the lady who smoked up her grass skirt.

Lula: *(Becoming annoyed that he will not dance, and becoming more animated as if to embarrass him still further)* Come on, Clay . . . let's do the thing. Uhh! Uhh! Clay! Clay! You middle-class black bastard. Forget your social-working mother for a few seconds and let's knock stomachs. Clay, you liver-lipped white man. You would-be Christian. You ain't no nigger, you're just a dirty white man. Get up, Clay. Dance with me, Clay.

Clay: Lula! Sit down, now. Be cool.

Lula: *(Mocking him, in wild dance)* Be cool. Be cool. That's all you know . . . shaking that wildroot cream-oil on your knotty head, jackets buttoning up to your chin, so full of white man's words. Christ! God! Get up and scream at these people. Like scream meaningless shit in these hopeless faces. *(She screams at people in train, still dancing)* Red trains cough Jewish underwear for keeps! Expanding smells of silence. Gravy snot whistling like sea birds. Clay. Clay, you got to break out. Don't sit there dying the way they want you to die. Get up.

Clay: Oh, sit the fuck down. *(He moves to restrain her)* Sit down, goddamn it.

Lula: *(Twisting out of his reach)* Screw yourself, Uncle Tom. Thomas Woolly-Head. *(Begins to dance a kind of jig, mocking Clay with loud forced humor)* There is Uncle Tom . . . I mean, Uncle Thomas Woolly-Head. With old white matted mane. He hobbles on his wooden cane. Old Tom. Old Tom. Let the white man hump his ol' mama, and he jes' shuffle off in the woods and hide his gentle gray head. Ol' Thomas Woolly-Head. *(Some of the other riders are laughing now. A drunk gets up and joins* LULA *in her dance, singing, as best he can, her "song."* CLAY *gets up out of his seat and visibly scans the faces of the other riders)*

Clay: Lula! Lula! *(She is dancing and turning, still shouting as loud as she can. The drunk too is shouting, and waving his hands wildly)* Lula . . . you dumb bitch. Why don't you stop it? *(He rushes half stumbling from his seat, and grabs one of her flailing arms)*

Lula: Let me go! You black son of a bitch. *(She struggles against him)* Let me go! Help! *(*CLAY *is dragging her towards her seat, and the drunk seeks to interfere. He grabs* CLAY *around the shoulders and begins wrestling with him.* CLAY *clubs the drunk to the floor without releasing* LULA, *who is still screaming.* CLAY *finally gets her to the seat and throws her into it)*

Clay: Now you shut the hell up. *(Grabbing her shoulders)* Just shut up. You don't know what you're talking about. You don't know anything. So just keep your stupid mouth closed.

Lula: You're afraid of white people. And your father was. Uncle Tom Big Lip!

Clay: *(Slaps her as hard as he can, across the mouth.* LULA's *head bangs against the back of the seat. When she raises it again,* CLAY *slaps her again)* Now shut up and let me talk. *(He turns toward the other riders, some of whom are sitting on the edge of their seats. The drunk is on one knee, rubbing his head, and singing softly the same song. He shuts up too when he sees* CLAY *watching him. The others go back to newspapers or stare out the windows)* Shit, you don't have any sense, Lula, nor feelings either. I could murder you now. Such a tiny ugly throat. I could squeeze it flat, and watch you turn blue, on a humble. For dull kicks. And all these weak-faced ofays squatting around here, staring over their papers at me. Murder them too. Even if they expected it. That man there *(Points to well-dressed man)* I could rip that *Times* right out of his hand, as skinny and middle-classed as I am, I could rip that paper out of his hand and just as easily rip out his throat. It takes no great effort. For what? To kill you soft idiots? You don't understand anything but luxury.

Lula: You fool!

Clay: *(Pushing her against the seat)* I'm not telling you again, Tallulah Bankhead! Luxury. In your face and your fingers. You telling me what I ought to do. *(Sudden scream frightening the whole coach)*

Well, don't! Don't you tell me anything! If I'm a middle-class fake white man let me be. And let me be in the way I want. *(Through his teeth)* I'll rip your lousy breasts off! Let me be who I feel like being. Uncle Tom, Thomas. Whoever. It's none of your business. You don't know anything except what's there for you to see. An act. Lies. Device. Not the pure heart, the pumping black heart. You don't ever know that. And I sit here, in this buttoned-up suit, to keep myself from cutting all your throats. I mean wantonly. You great liberated whore! You fuck some black man, and right away you're an expert on black people. What a lotta shit that is. The only thing you know is that you come if he bangs you hard enough. And that's all. The belly rub? You wanted to do the belly rub? Shit, you don't even know how. You don't know how. That ol' dipty-dip shit you do, rolling your ass like an elephant. That's not my kind of belly rub. Belly rub is not Queens. Belly rub is dark places, with big hats and overcoats held up with one arm. Belly rub hates you. Old bald-headed four-eyed ofays popping their fingers . . . and don't know yet what they're doing. They say, "I love Bessie Smith." And don't even understand that Bessie Smith is saying, "Kiss my ass, kiss my black unruly ass." Before love, suffering, desire, anything you can explain, she's saying, and very plainly, "Kiss my black ass." And if you don't know that, it's you that's doing the kissing.

Charlie Parker? Charlie Parker. All the hip white boys scream for Bird. And Bird saying, "Up your ass, feebleminded ofay! Up your ass." And they sit there talking about the tortured genius of Charlie Parker. Bird would've played not a note of music if he just walked up to East Sixty-seventh Street and killed the first ten white people he saw. Not a note! And I'm the great would-be poet. Yes. That's right! Poet. Some kind of bastard literature . . . all it needs is a simple knife thrust. Just let me bleed you, you loud whore, and one poem vanished. A whole people of neurotics, struggling to keep from being sane. And the only thing that would cure the neurosis would be your murder. Simple as that. I mean if I murdered you, then other white people would begin to understand me. You understand? No. I guess not. If Bessie Smith had killed some white people she wouldn't have needed that music. She could have talked very straight and plain about the world. No metaphors. No grunts. No wiggles in the dark of her soul. Just straight two and two are four. Money. Power. Luxury. Like that. All of them. Crazy niggers turning their backs on sanity. When all it needs is that simple act. Murder. Just murder! Would make us all sane.

(Suddenly weary)

Ahhh. Shit. But who needs it? I'd rather be a fool. Insane. Safe with my words, and no deaths, and clean, hard thoughts, urging me to new conquests. My people's madness. Hah! That's a laugh. My people. They don't need me to claim them. They got legs and arms of their own. Personal insanities. Mirrors. They don't need all those words. They don't need any defense. But listen, though, one more thing. And you tell this to your father, who's probably the kind of man who needs to know at once. So he can plan ahead. Tell him not to preach so much rationalism and cold logic to these niggers. Let them alone. Let them sing curses at you in code and see your filth as simple lack of style. Don't make the mistake, through some irresponsible surge of Christian charity, of talking too much about the advantages of Western rationalism, or the great intellectual legacy of the white man, or maybe they'll begin to listen. And then, maybe one day, you'll find they actually do understand exactly what you are talking about, all these fantasy people. All these blues people. And on that day, as sure as shit, when you really believe you can "accept" them into your fold, as half-white trusties late of the subject peoples. With no more blues, except the very old ones, and not a watermelon in sight, the great missionary heart will have triumphed, and all of those ex-coons will be stand-up Western men, with eyes for clean hard useful lives, sober, pious and sane, and they'll murder you. They'll murder you, and have very rational explanations. Very much like your own. They'll cut your throats, and drag you out to the edge of your cities so the flesh can fall away from your bones, in sanitary isolation.

Lula: *(Her voice takes on a different, more businesslike quality)* I've heard enough.

Clay: *(Reaching for his books)* I bet you have. I guess I better collect my stuff and get off this train. Looks like we won't be acting out that little pageant you outlined before.

Lula: No. We won't. You're right about that, at least. *(She turns to look quickly around the rest of the car)* All right! *(The others respond)*

Clay: *(Bending across the girl to retrieve his belongings)* Sorry, baby, I don't think we could make it. *(As he is bending over her, the girl brings up a small knife and plunges it into* CLAY's *chest. Twice. He slumps across her knees, his mouth working stupidly)*

Lula: Sorry is right. *(Turning to the others in the car who have already gotten up from their seats)* Sorry is the rightest thing you've said. Get this man off me! Hurry, now! *(The others come and drag* CLAY's *body down the aisle)* Open the door and throw his body out. *(They throw him off)* And all of you get off at the next stop.

*(*LULA *busies herself straightening her things. Getting everything in order. She takes out a notebook and makes a quick scribbling note. Drops it in her bag. The train apparently stops and all the others get off, leaving her alone in the coach. Very soon a young Negro of about twenty comes into the coach, with a couple of books under his arm. He sits a few seats in back of* LULA. *When he is seated she turns and gives him a long slow look. He looks up from his book and drops the book on his lap. Then an old Negro conductor comes into the car, doing a sort of restrained soft shoe, and half mumbling the words of some song. He looks at the young man, briefly, with a quick greeting)*

Conductor: Hey, brother!

Young Man: Hey.

(The conductor continues down the aisle with his little dance and the mumbled song. LULA *turns to stare at him and follows his movements down the aisle. The conductor tips his hat when he reaches her seat, and continues out the car)*

(1964)

A Poem for Black Hearts

For Malcolm's eyes, when they broke
the face of some dumb white man, For
Malcolm's hands raised to bless us
all black and strong in his image
of ourselves, For Malcolm's words
fire darts, the victor's tireless
thrusts, words hung above the world
change as it may, he said it, and

for this he was killed, for saying,
and feeling, and being / change, all
collected hot in his heart, For Malcolm's
heart, raising us above our filthy cities,
for his stride, and his beat, and his address
to the gray monsters of the world, For Malcolm's
pleas for your dignity, black men, for your life,
black man, for the filling of your minds
with righteousness, For all of him dead and
gone and vanished from us, and all of him which
clings to our speech black god of our time.
For all of him, and all of yourself, look up;
black man, quit stuttering and shuffling, look up,
black man, quit whining and stooping, for all of him,
For Great Malcolm a prince of the earth, let nothing in us rest
until we avenge ourselves for his death, stupid animals
that killed him, let us never breathe a pure breath
if we fail and white men call us faggots till the end of
the earth.

(1965)

It's Nation Time

Time to get
together
time to be one strong fast black energy space
        one pulsating positive magnetism, rising
time to get up and
be
come
be
come, time to
     be come
     time to
     get up be come
     black genius rise in spirit muscle
     sun man get up rise heart of universes to be
future of the world
the black man is the future of the world
be come
rise up

future of the black genius spirit reality
    move
    from crushed roach back
    from dead snake head
    from wig funeral in slowmotion
    from dancing teeth and coward tip
    from jibberjabber patme boss patme smmich
when the brothers strike niggers come out
come out niggers
when the brothers take over the school
help niggers
come out niggers
all niggers negroes must change up
come together in unity unify
for nation time
it's nation time . . .

              Boom
              Booom
              BOOOM
              Boom
              Dadadadadadadadadadad
              Boom
              Boom
              Boom
              Boom
              Dadadadad adadadad
                     Hey aheee (soft)
                     Hey ahheee (loud)
              Boom
              Boom
              Boom
sing a get up time to nationfy
singaa miracle fire light
sing a airplane invisibility for the jesus niggers come from the
    grave
for the jesus niggers dead in the cave, rose up, passt jewjuice
on shadow world
raise up christ nigger
Christ was black
krishna was black shango was black
        black jesus nigger come out and strike

come out and strike boom boom
            Heyahheeee come out
strike close ford
        close prudential burn the policies
    tear glasses off dead statue puppets even those
            they imitate life
                Shango budda black
            hermes rasis black
            moses krishna
                            black
when the brothers wanna stop animals
come out niggers come out
come out niggers niggers niggers come out
help us stop the devil
help us build a new world

niggers come out, brothers are we
    with you and your sons your daughters are ours
    and we are the same, all the blackness from one black allah
        when the world is clear you'll be with us
            come out niggers come out
            come out niggers come out
It's nation time eye ime
            It's nation ti eye ime
                        chant with bells and drum
                        it's nation time

It's nation time, get up santa claus   (repeat)
it's nation time, build it
    get up muffet dragger
        get up rastus for real to be rasta farari
        rasjua
            get up got here bow
                    It's Nation
                    Time!

                                                             (1970)

Audre Lorde (1934–1992)

Audre Geraldine Lorde was born on February 18, 1934, in New York City to Frederic and Linda Lorde. When she was fifteen Lorde published her first poem in *Seventeen* magazine. After graduating from Hunter High School in 1951, Lorde enrolled at Hunter College and worked odd jobs to support herself. She traveled widely in the United States and Mexico, including a year spent studying at the National University of Mexico. Upon her return to New York, Lorde graduated from Hunter College with a bachelor's degree in 1959 before earning her master's in library science from Columbia University in 1961. She then worked at Mount Vernon Public Library and at Town School Library in New York City. In 1962 Lorde married Edwin Rollins, an attorney, and the couple had two children before they divorced in 1970. Shortly afterward, Lorde came out as a lesbian.

In 1968 this later self-defined "black feminist lesbian warrior poet" published her first collection, *The First Cities*, and received a grant from the National Endowment for the Arts. That same year she took the position of writer-in-residence at Tougaloo College in Jackson, Mississippi. Lorde also held teaching positions at City University of New York, John Jay College of Criminal Justice, and Hunter College, where she was named the Thomas Hunter Distinguished Professor in 1987. Her second collection, *Cables to Rage* (1970), was published by Dudley Randall's Broadside Press. Lorde's collection, *From a Land Where Other People Live* (1973), was nominated for a National Book Award, and in 1981 her first published prose, *The Cancer Journals* (1980), won the American Library Association's Gay Caucus Book of the Year Award. Additionally, her collection of essays and speeches, *A Burst of Light* (1988), won an American Book Award. In 1991 Lorde was awarded the Walt Whitman Citation of Merit. She was named poet laureate of New York in 1991 and served in that capacity until 1992, when she lost a fourteen-year battle with cancer.

Lorde is identified with the Black Arts movement of the late 1960s for her critiques of racism and other social injustices. Her work ruptures the boundaries of race and sexuality and contributes significantly to African American studies and to feminist theory. Lorde also writes about interpersonal relationships, African culture and mythology, and feminist and lesbian themes. One of her most frequent themes is the importance of speaking out, rather than remaining silent, about oppression and violence. For Lorde, asserting one's right to speak is an act of defiance against those who would try to deny one's right to existence.

Remembered as a leading figure in the renaissance of black women's writing of the 1970s and 1980s, Lorde's most important works include several collections of poetry — *Coal* (1976), *The Black Unicorn* (1978), and *Chosen Poems, Old and New* (1982) — as well as a collection of essays, *Sister Outsider* (1984), and a memoir, *Zami: A New Spelling of My Name* (1982). In addition to writing, Lorde cofounded and was a member of Sisters in Support of Sisters in Africa (SISA) and of Kitchen Table: Women of Color Press, a black feminist publishing house. In 1994 the Audre Lorde Project was established in Brooklyn to honor her legacy and to provide a base for communal support and political organizing.

In selections below, the poem "Suffer the Children" (from *First Cities*) memorializes four girls whose lives were cut short in a 1963 Birmingham, Alabama, church bombing, and "Rites of Passage" (from *Coal*) returns to the theme of childhood to honor Martin Luther King Jr.

Suffer the Children

To Addie Mae Collins, 8, and Cynthia Wesley, 10, two of four
children killed in a racial bombing of a Baptist church in
Birmingham, Alabama, Sunday, September 16, 1963.*

He is forever trapped
who suffers his own waste.
Rain leaching the earth   for lack
of roots to hold it
and children who are murdered
before their lives begin.

Who pays his crops to the sun
when his fields lie parched by drought
will mourn the lost water
waiting another rain.
But who shall disinter these girls
to love the women they were to become
or read the legends written beneath their skin?

We who love them remember their child's laughter.
But he whose hate robs him of their gold
has yet to weep at night above their graves.

A year rolls out.   Rains come again.
But however many girls be brought to sun
someday a man will thirst for sleep
in a southern night

* Lorde received incorrect information at the time that she wrote the poem. Both Collins and Wesley were actually born in 1949, making them 14 at the time of their deaths.

seeking his peace where no peace is
and come to mourn these children
given to the dust.

(1964)

Rites of Passage

To MLK Jr.

Rock the boat to a fare-thee-well.
Once we suffered   dreaming
into the place where the children are playing
their child's games
where the children are hoping
knowledge survives if
unknowing
they follow the game
without winning.

Their fathers are dying
back to the freedom of wise children
playing
at knowing
their fathers are dying
whose deaths will not free them
from growing
from knowing
when the game becomes foolish
a dangerous pleading
for a time out of power.

Quick   children
kiss us
we are growing
through dream.

(1968)

Eldridge Cleaver (1935–1998)

Born August 31, 1935, in Wabbeseka, Arkansas, to Thelma and Leroy Cleaver, Eldridge Cleaver spent most of his childhood in Phoenix, Arizona, and then in Los Angeles, California. In 1957 he was convicted of assault with intent to murder and spent the better part of twelve years in California's Folsom and San Quentin prisons. While incarcerated, Cleaver converted to the Muslim faith, devoted his time to self-education, and produced a set of essays, published in 1968 as *Soul on Ice*. The essays express his views on racism and on strategies of resistance against it. The collection inspired a number of young activists and writers, particularly those involved in the Black Arts and the Black Power movements. "On Becoming," the first chapter of *Soul on Ice*, describes Cleaver's political awakening after the 1955 murder of Emmett Till in Money, Mississippi, and the subsequent, and controversial, course of action he decided to take as a result.

After serving his prison sentence, which ended in 1966, Cleaver wrote for *Ramparts* magazine and cofounded (with Huey Newton, Bobby Seale, and others) the Black Panther Party for Self-Defense, based in Oakland, California. In 1967 Cleaver began serving as minister of information for the Black Nationalist Party, which provided services and social programs for African Americans. He declared his candidacy for president of the United States in 1968, running on the Peace and Freedom Party ticket, and the following year, his autobiographical novella, *Black Moochie*, was published.

Fleeing criminal charges, Cleaver spent most of the 1970s abroad, living in Cuba, Europe, and Algeria. In 1979 he published *Soul on Fire*, which details the years he spent in exile. After returning to the States in 1975, Cleaver converted to fundamentalist Christian doctrine and ran for the Republican nomination for the U.S. Senate in California. From 1967 to 1987 Cleaver was married to fellow Black Panther Kathleen Neal, with whom he had two children. Cleaver passed away on May 1, 1998, in Pomona, California, while working for the University of La Verne as a diversity consultant.

Soul on Ice

Selection from Chapter 1, On Becoming

From our discussion, which began that evening and has never yet ended, we went on to notice how thoroughly, as a matter of course, a black growing up in America is indoctrinated with the white race's standard of beauty. Not that the whites made a conscious, calculated effort to do this, we thought, but since they constituted the majority the whites brainwashed the blacks by the very processes the whites employed to indoctrinate themselves with their own group standards. It intensified my frustrations to know that I was indoctrinated to see the white woman as more beautiful and desirable than my own black woman. It drove me into books seeking light on the subject. In Richard Wright's *Native Son*, I found Bigger Thomas and a keen insight into the problem.

My interest in this area persisted undiminished and then, in 1955, an event took place in Mississippi which turned me inside out: Emmett Till, a young Negro down from Chicago on a visit, was murdered, allegedly for flirting with a white woman. He had been shot, his head crushed from repeated blows with a blunt instrument, and his badly decomposed body was recovered from the river with a heavy weight on it. I was, of course, angry over the whole bit, but one day I saw in a magazine a picture of the white woman with whom Emmett Till was said to have flirted. While looking at the picture, I felt that little tension in the center of my chest I experience when a woman appeals to me. I was disgusted and angry with myself. Here was a woman who had caused the death of a black, possibly because, when he looked at her, he also felt the same tensions of lust and desire in his chest — and probably for the same general reasons that I felt them. It was all unacceptable to me. I looked at the picture again and again, and in spite of everything and against my will and the hate I felt for the woman and all that she represented, she appealed to me. I flew into a rage at myself, at America, at white women, at the history that had placed those tensions of lust and desire in my chest.

Two days later, I had a "nervous breakdown." For several days I ranted and raved against the white race, against white women in particular, against white America in general. When I came to myself, I was locked in a padded cell with not even the vaguest memory of how I got there. All I could recall was an eternity of pacing back and forth in the cell, preaching to the unhearing walls.

I had several sessions with a psychiatrist. His conclusion was that I hated my mother. How he arrived at this conclusion I'll never know, because he knew nothing about my mother; and when he'd ask me questions I would answer him with absurd lies. What revolted me about him was that he had heard me denouncing the whites, yet each time he interviewed me he deliberately guided the conversation back to my family life, to my childhood. That in itself was all right, but he deliberately blocked all my attempts to bring out the racial question, and he made it clear that he was not interested in my attitude toward whites. This was a Pandora's box he did not care to open. After I ceased my diatribes against the whites, I was let out of the hospital, back into the general inmate population just as if nothing had happened. I continued to brood over these events and over the dynamics of race relations in America.

During this period I was concentrating my reading in the field of economics. Having previously dabbled in the theories and writings of Rousseau, Thomas Paine, and Voltaire, I had added a little polish to my iconoclastic stance, without, however, bothering too much to understand their affirmative positions. In economics, because everybody seemed to find it necessary to attack and condemn Karl Marx in their writings, I sought out his books, and although he kept me with a headache, I took him for my authority. I was not prepared to understand him, but I was able to see in him a thoroughgoing critique and condemnation of capitalism. It was like taking medicine for me to find that, indeed, American capitalism deserved all the hatred and contempt that I felt for it in my heart. This had a positive, stabilizing effect upon me — to an extent because I was not about to become stable — and it diverted me from my previous preoccupation: morbid broodings on the black man and the white woman. Pursuing my readings into the history of socialism, I read, with very little understanding, some of the passionate, exhortatory writings of Lenin; and I fell in love with Bakunin and Nechayev's *Catechism of the Revolutionist* — the principles of which, along with some of Machiavelli's advice, I sought to incorporate into my own behavior. I took the *Catechism* for my bible and, standing on a one-man platform that had nothing to do with the reconstruction of society, I began consciously incorporating these principles into my daily life, to employ tactics of ruthlessness in my dealings with everyone with whom I came into contact. And I began to look at white America through these new eyes.

Somehow I arrived at the conclusion that, as a matter of principle, it was of paramount importance for me to have an antagonistic, ruthless attitude toward white women. The term *outlaw* appealed to me and at the time my parole date was drawing near, I considered myself to be mentally free — I was an "outlaw." I had stepped outside of the white man's law, which I repudiated with scorn and self-satisfaction. I became a law unto myself — my own legislature, my own supreme court, my own executive. At the moment I walked out of the prison gate, my feelings toward white women in general could be summed up in the following lines:

To a White Girl

I love you
Because you're white,
Not because you're charming
Or bright.
Your whiteness
Is a silky thread
Snaking through my thoughts
In redhot patterns
Of lust and desire.

I hate you
Because you're white.

Your white meat
Is nightmare food.
White is
The skin of Evil.
You're my Moby Dick,
White Witch,
Symbol of the rope and hanging tree,
Of the burning cross.

Loving you thus
And hating you so,
My heart is torn in two.
Crucified.

I became a rapist. To refine my technique and *modus operandi*, I started out by practicing on black girls in the ghetto — in the black ghetto where dark and vicious deeds appear not as aberrations or deviations from the norm, but as part of the sufficiency of the Evil of a day — and when I considered myself smooth enough, I crossed the tracks and sought out white prey. I did this consciously, deliberately, willfully, methodically — though looking back I see that I was in a frantic, wild, and completely abandoned frame of mind.

Rape was an insurrectionary act. It delighted me that I was defying and trampling upon the white man's law, upon his system of values, and that I was defiling his women — and this point, I believe, was the most satisfying to me because I was very resentful over the historical fact of how the white man has used the black woman. I felt I was getting revenge. From the site of the act of rape, the consternation spreads outwardly in concentric circles. I wanted to send waves of consternation throughout the white race. Recently, I came upon a quotation from one of LeRoi Jones' poems, taken from his book *The Dead Lecturer*:

> A cult of death need of the simple striking arm under the street lamp. The cutters from under their rented earth. Come up, black dada nihilismus. Rape the white girls. Rape their fathers. Cut the mothers' throats.

I have lived those lines and I know that if I had not been apprehended I would have slit some white throats. There are, of course, many young blacks out there right now who are slitting white throats and raping the white girl. They are not doing this because they read LeRoi Jones' poetry, as some of his critics seem to believe. Rather, LeRoi is expressing the funky facts of life.

After I returned to prison, I took a long look at myself, and for the first time in my life, admitted that I was wrong, that I had gone astray — astray not so much from the white man's law as from being human — civilized — for I could not approve the act of rape. Even though I had some insight into my own motivations, I did not feel justified. I lost my self-respect. My pride as a man dissolved and my whole fragile moral structure seemed to collapse, completely shattered.

That is why I started to write. To save myself.

I realized that no one could save me but myself. The prison authorities were both uninterested and unable to help me. I had to see the truth and unravel the snarled web of my motivations. I had to find out who I am and what I want to be, what type of man I should be, and what I could do to become the best of which I was capable. I understood that what had happened to me had also happened to countless other blacks and it would happen to many, many more.

I learned that I had been taking the easy way out, running away from problems. I also learned that it is easier to do evil than it is to do good. And I have been terribly impressed by the youth of America, black and white. I am proud of them because they have reaffirmed my faith in humanity. I have come to feel what must be love for the young people of America and I want to be part of the good and greatness that they want for all people. From my prison cell, I have watched America slowly coming awake. It is not fully awake yet, but there is soul in the air and everywhere I see beauty. I have watched the sit-ins, the freedom raids, the Mississippi Blood Summers, demonstrations all over the country, the FSM movement, the teach-ins, and the mounting protest over Lyndon Strangelove's foreign policy — all of this, the thousands of little details, show me it is time to straighten up and fly right. That is why I decided to concentrate on my writings and efforts in this area. We are a very sick country — I, perhaps, am sicker than most. But I accept that. I told you in the beginning that I am extremist by nature — so it is only right that I should be extremely sick.

I was very familiar with the Eldridge who came to prison, but that Eldridge no longer exists. And the one I am now is in some ways a stranger to me. You may find this difficult to understand but it is very easy for one in prison to lose his sense of self. And if he has been undergoing all kinds of extreme, involved, and unregulated changes, then he ends up not knowing who he is. Take the point of being attractive to women. You can easily see how a man can lose his arrogance or certainty on that point while in prison! When he's in the free world, he gets constant feedback on how he looks from the number of female heads he turns when he walks down the street. In prison he gets only hate-stares and sour frowns. Years and years of bitter looks. Individuality is not nourished in prison, neither by the officials nor by the convicts. It is a deep hole out of which to climb.

What must be done, I believe, is that all these problems — particularly the sickness between the white woman and the black man — must be brought out into the open, dealt with and resolved. I know that the black man's sick attitude toward the white woman is a revolutionary sickness: it keeps him perpetually out of harmony with the system that is oppressing him. Many whites flatter themselves with the idea that the Negro male's lust and desire for the white dream girl is purely an esthetic attraction, but nothing could be farther from the truth. His motivation is often of such a bloody, hateful, bitter, and malignant nature that whites would really be hard pressed to find it flattering. I have discussed these points with prisoners who were convicted of rape, and their motivations are very plain. But they are very reluctant to discuss these things with white men who, by and large, make up the prison staffs. I believe that in the experience of these men lies the knowledge and wisdom that must be utilized to help other youngsters who are heading in the same direction. I think all of us, the entire nation, will be better off if we bring it all out front. A lot of people's feelings will be hurt, but that is the price that must be paid.

It may be that I can harm myself by speaking frankly and directly, but I do not care about that at all. Of course I want to get out of prison badly, but I shall get out some day. I am more concerned with what I am going to be after I get out. I know that by following the course which I have charted I will find my salvation. If I had followed the path laid down for me by the officials, I'd undoubtedly have long since been out of prison — but I'd be less of a man. I'd be weaker and less certain of where I want to go, what I want to do, and how to go about it.

The price of hating other human beings is loving oneself less.

(1968)

Lucille Clifton   (b. 1936)

amed for her great-great-grandmother — who was born in Africa, brought to America as a slave, and escaped as a young girl — Thelma Lucille Sayles was born on June 27, 1936, in Depew, New York, to Samuel L. and Thelma Moore Sayles, both of whom were avid readers. The family soon moved to Buffalo, New York, where Lucille spent most of her childhood. At age sixteen, Clifton went to Howard University on a full scholarship from her church and majored in drama. While there, she studied under Sterling Brown and became acquainted with Amiri Baraka and Toni Morrison. In 1955 she transferred to Fredonia State Teacher's College (now the State University of New York at Fredonia). She graduated and married Fred J. Clifton in 1958, with whom she has six children, and began working as a claims clerk for the state of New York. Her first collection of poems, *Good Times*, came out in 1969 and was cited by the *New York Times* as one of the best books of the year. Other significant works include

Good News about the Earth (1972), where the poems "apology (to the panthers),"
"eldridge," and "malcolm" appear; *An Ordinary Woman* (1974), which contains
the poem "jackie robinson"; *Generations: A Memoir* (1976); *Good Woman: Poems
and a Memoir* (1987); and *Quilting: Poems 1987–1990* (1991).

In 1970 Clifton won her first National Endowment for the Arts Award; she
was given her second in 1972. She has taught at Coppin State College in Baltimore, Maryland; the University of California at Santa Cruz; St. Mary's College
in Maryland; and Duke University in Durham, North Carolina. She has been
nominated for a Pulitzer Prize three times and has won the National Book
Award. Clifton has also received the Coretta Scott King Award from the American Library Association for one of her children's books. In 1974 she was named
poet laureate of Maryland.

Writing about overwhelming issues in accessible ways, Clifton stresses the
resilience and dignity of black families and emphasizes the black community
and its heroes. Her work also deals with religious themes and with the legacies
and traditions created by African American women. Clifton is particularly concerned with the relationships between individual and cultural identities, cultural
diversity, racial heritage, and family life. The poetry selections reprinted here
offer powerful portraits of some of the civil rights movement's leading figures.

apology

(to the panthers)

i became a woman
during the old prayers
among the ones who wore
bleaching cream to bed
and all my lessons stayed

i was obedient
but brothers i thank you
for these mannish days

i remember again the wise one
old and telling of suicides
refusing to be slaves

i had forgotten and
brothers i thank you
i praise you
i grieve my whiteful ways

(1972)

eldridge

the edge
of this
cleaver
this
straight
sharp
single-
handled
man
will not
rust
break, or
be broken

(1972)

malcolm

nobody mentioned war
but doors were closed
black women shaved their heads
black men rustled in the alleys like leaves
prophets were ambushed as they spoke
and from their holes black eagles flew
screaming from the streets

(1972)

jackie robinson

ran against walls
without breaking.
in night games
was not foul
but, brave as a hit
over whitestone fences,
entered the conquering dark

(1974)

orn July 9, 1936, in Harlem to Jamaican immigrants Granville Ivanhoe and Mildred Maude Jordan, June Jordan spent most of her childhood in Brooklyn. She cultivated literary interests early, with Paul Laurence Dunbar as one of her favorite authors. After completing one year of high school at Mildwood High School, where she was the only black student, Jordan attended the Northfield School for Girls in Massachusetts, where she was one of only a few African Americans. After graduating in 1953 Jordan enrolled at Barnard College in New York City, where she met Michael Meyer, who was then a student at Columbia. The couple was married in 1955 and stayed together for ten years. Jordan graduated from Barnard in 1957, and her and Meyer's son was born in 1958. In 1960 Jordan returned to Harlem and became interested in city planning. She met R. Buckminster Fuller, and they made plans to revitalize Harlem, for which they were awarded the Prix de Rome in environmental design.

In the early 1960s Jordan published poems and stories in literary magazines and journals, sometimes under the name June Meyer. She published her first volume of poetry in 1969, *Who Look at Me*, where "In Memoriam: Martin Luther King, Jr." and "I Celebrate the Sons of Malcolm" appeared. In 1971, Jordan published her first novel, a young adult book called *His Own Where*, which uses black dialect in unprecedented ways. The novel was nominated for a National Book Award and caused a controversy that ended up in the Michigan courts, because some parents were upset about their children reading books that did not use standard American English. Ultimately, the court decided that black English, or dialect, could not be banned from public schools. Jordan has published numerous other children's books, including a biography of Fannie Lou Hamer (1972). A later poem, "1977: Poem for Mrs. Fannie Lou Hamer," also memorializes the Mississippi civil rights activist.

Jordan taught literature at the City University of New York (1966) and at Connecticut College (1968–74) before receiving tenure at the State University of New York at Stony Brook. She has also taught at Yale, at Sarah Lawrence College, and at the University of California at Berkeley, where she taught African American and women's studies and initiated the program Power for the People in 1991 to teach poetry to disadvantaged youth. For her role as founder and director of the program, Jordan won the 2001 Barnes and Noble Writers for Writers Award.

Jordan believed that the function of poetry is to tell the truth and that the truth is often political or can be used for political ends to attain social justice. In her work, Jordan protests prejudice of any kind, particularly racism and sexism, and she emphasizes the roles of both individuals and communities to accomplish political and social change.

Jordan died on June 14, 2002, after a long struggle with breast cancer. Her literary legacy includes *Things That I Do in the Dark: Selected Poems* (1977), *Passion: New Poems, 1977–1980* (1980), *Living Room* (1985), *Naming Our Destiny: New and Selected Poems* (1989), *The Haruko: Love Poems* (1994), *Kissing God Goodbye: New Poems* (1997), *Affirmative Acts: New Political Essays* (1998), and *Directed by Desire: The Collected Poems of June Jordan* (2005).

In Memoriam: Martin Luther King, Jr.

I
honey people murder mercy U.S.A.
the milkland turn to monsters teach
to kill to violate pull down destroy
the weakly freedom growing fruit
from being born

America

tomorrow yesterday rip rape
exacerbate despoil disfigure
crazy running threat the
deadly thrall
appall belief dispel
the wildlife burn the breast
the onward tongue
the outward hand
deform the normal rainy
riot sunshine shelter wreck
of darkness derogate
delimit blank
explode deprive
assassinate and batten up
like bullets fatten up
the raving greed
reactivate a springtime
terrorizing

death by men by more
than you or I can

STOP

II
They sleep who know a regulated place
or pulse or tide or changing sky

according to some universal
stage direction obvious
like shorewashed shells

we share an afternoon of mourning
in between no next predictable
except for wild reversal hearse rehearsal
bleach the blacklong lunging
ritual of fright insanity and more
deplorable abortion
more and
more

(1968)

I Celebrate the Sons of Malcolm

I celebrate the sons of Malcolm
multiplying powerful
implicit
passionate and somber
          Celebrate
the sons of Malcolm gather
black unruly as alive and hard
against the papal skirts the palace
walls collapsing
          Celebrate
the sons of Malcolm hold my soul
alert to children building
temples on their feet to face the
suddenly phantom terrors
          Celebrate
the sons of Malcolm fathering the person
destinies arouse a royals yearning
culminate magnificent
and new

(1969)

1977: Poem for Mrs. Fannie Lou Hamer

You used to say, "June?
Honey when you come down here you
Supposed to stay with me. Where
else?"
Meanin home

against the beer the shotguns and the
point of view of whitemen don'
never see Black anybodies without
some violent itch start up.
                        The ones who
Said, "No Nigga's Votin in This Town . . .
lessen it be feet first to the booth"
then jailed you
beat you brutal
bloody/battered/beat
you blue beyond the feeling
of the terrible

And failed to stop you.
Only God could but He
wouldn't stop
you
fortress from self-
pity

Humble as a woman anywhere
I remember finding you inside the Laundromat
in Ruleville
        lion spine relaxed/hell
        what's the point to courage
        when you washin clothes?

But that took courage

        just to sit there/target
        to the killers lookin
        for your face
        perspirey through the rinse
        and spin

and later
you stood mighty in the door on James Street
loud callin:

        "BULLETS OR NO BULLETS!
        THE FOOD IS COOKED
        AN' GETTING COLD!"

We ate
A family tremulous but fortified

by turnips/okra/handpicked
like the lilies

filled to the very living
full
one solid gospel
             (sanctified)

one gospel
         (peace)

one full Black lily
luminescent
in a homemade field

of love

(1977)

Michael S. Harper (b. 1938)

ichael S. Harper was born in Brooklyn, New York, on March 18, 1938, to Walter Warren and Katherine Johnson Harper. In 1951 the family moved to Los Angeles, where Harper attended both high school and college. While there he was greatly affected by his experiences with racial stereotypes and by the threat of racial violence. After earning a bachelor's degree in 1961 Harper attended Iowa's Writers' Workshop and received his M.F.A. in 1963. Harper had to live in segregated housing at Iowa and was the only African American in his class. After leaving for a year to teach at Pasadena City College, he returned and earned his master's in English in 1963. Harper then taught creative writing and English at numerous West Coast colleges before receiving an appointment at Brown University.

Although his work was already published in journals, Harper did not publish his first collection until 1970. This volume, *Dear John, Dear Coltrane*, uses the medium of jazz to explore racial conflict in America. It was nominated for a National Book Award, as was *Images of Kin: New and Selected Poems* (1977). Harper has also received awards from the Black Academy of Arts and Letters and the National Institute of Arts and Letters. In 1988 he was named Rhode Island's first poet laureate, and in 2008 he received the Frost Medal from the Poetry Society of America for lifetime achievement in poetry. In addition to his collections of poetry, Harper has coedited and compiled several anthologies of African American literature.

In his poetry, Harper explores the dual consciousness of African Americans, exposes the myths behind white supremacy as well as the violence and oppression used to reify it, and honors African American heroes, such as Martin Luther King Jr. in "Martin's Blues." "American History" pays tribute to four girls killed in a 1963 Birmingham, Alabama, church bombing, linking their deaths to a broader history of racism in America. Both poems appeared in *Dear John, Dear Coltrane*. Harper's most celebrated collections also include *Healing Song for the Inner Ear* (1985), *Honorable Amendments: Poems* (1995), *Songlines in Michaeltree: New and Collected Poems* (2000), and *Selected Poems* (2002).

Martin's Blues

He came apart in the open,
the slow motion cameras
falling quickly
neither alive nor kicking;
stone blind dead
on the balcony
that old melody
etched his black lips
in a pruned echo:
We shall overcome
Some day—
Yes we did!
Yes we did!

(1970)

American History

Those four black girls blown up
in that Alabama church
remind me of five hundred
middle passage blacks,
in a net, under water
in Charleston harbor
so *redcoats* wouldn't find them.
can't find what you can't see
can you?

(1970)

Haki Madhubuti
(Don L. Lee) (b. 1942)

orn Donald Luther Lee on February 23, 1942, in Little Rock, Arkansas, to Jimmy and Maxine Lee, Haki Madhubuti spent most of his childhood in Detroit, Michigan. From age ten he worked to help support his family, and after his mother passed away when he was sixteen he moved to Chicago, Illinois, to live with his aunt. Madhubuti attended Dunbar Vocational College, Wilson Junior College, and Roosevelt University before enlisting in the army at age eighteen. After his discharge, he returned to Chicago to work a series of odd jobs.

Madhubuti self-published his first collection of poems, *Think Black!* (1967), and sold over six hundred copies of it at railway stations in Chicago. In 1967 he attended a poetry workshop, where he met Gwendolyn Brooks and Dudley Randall, founder of Broadside Press. Randall consequently published Madhubuti's next four volumes of poetry. That same year Madhubuti cofounded the Third World Press with Carolyn M. Rodgers and Johari Amini, who were also dedicated to building black institutions and to publishing black authors who had been rejected by mainstream white presses. Until 1973 he published under his given name, Don L. Lee, before adopting his Swahili name, Haki Madhubuti, which means, among other things, justice. *Book of Life* (1973) was the first collection of his poetry published by Third World Press as well as the first to be published under his adopted name. Madhubuti's most celebrated works include *Don't Cry, Scream* (1969), where the poem "Malcolm Spoke / who listened?" appeared, *We Walk the Way of the New World* (1970), *Directionscore: New and Selected Poems* (1971), and *Groundwork: New and Selected Poems by Don L. Lee/Haki R. Madhubuti, 1966–1996* (1996).

Along with Amiri Baraka and Sonia Sanchez, Madhubuti was a major figure in the Black Arts movement of the 1960s and 1970s. In 1971 he cofounded the *Black Books Review* with Larry Neal, another important Black Arts movement voice. During its eight-year life span, the *Review* was one of the only journals devoted exclusively to black authors. Madhubuti was also a proponent of black nationalism. In 1972 he founded the New Concept Development Center in order to create new frameworks for African American education. Madhubuti championed pan-African causes, including the first Pan-African Festival in Algiers in 1969 and the sixth Pan-African Congress in Tanzania in 1974. In 1976 he was invited by Senegal to participate in Encounter: African World Alternatives.

Madhubuti earned his master's degree from the Writers' Workshop at the University of Iowa in 1984, and he is currently a professor of English at Chicago State University, where he also serves as a director for CSU's Gwendolyn Brooks

Center. He continues to encourage the black community to support and build up black institutions. Advocating an aesthetic that is unique to African American literature, Madhubuti's work emphasizes the positive aspects of African and African American culture and seeks to empower African Americans to resist racism and other forms of systemic oppression.

Malcolm spoke / who listened?

(this poem is for my consciousness too)

he didn't say
wear yr / blackness in
outer garments
& blk / slogans fr / the top 10.

he was fr a long
line of super-cools,
    doo-rag lovers &
    revolutionary pimps.
u are playing that
high-yellow game in blackface
minus the straighthair.
now it's nappy-black
& air-conditioned Volkswagens
with undercover whi
te girls who studied faulkner at
smith
& are authorities on "militant"
knee / grows
selling u at jew town rates:
    niggers with wornout tongues
    three for a quarter / will consider a trade

the double-breasted hipster
has been replaced with a
dashiki wearing rip-off
who went to city college
majoring in physical education.

animals come in all colors.
dark meat will roast as fast as whi-te meat
especially in

the unitedstatesofamerica's
new self-cleaning ovens.

if we don't listen.   (1969)

Nikki Giovanni   (b. 1943)

oth a celebratory and a revolutionary poet, Yolande Cornelia ("Nikki")
Giovanni Jr. was born on June 7, 1943, in Knoxville, Tennessee, to Gus
and Yolande Giovanni. Although she spent most of her childhood in
Cincinnati, Ohio, she spent a good deal of time with members of her
family who remained in Knoxville. After graduating from high school in 1960
Giovanni enrolled at Fisk University in Nashville, Tennessee, but she was dismissed after her first semester following a dispute with the dean of women over
a woman's place in the intellectual life of the academy. Before being readmit-
ted to Fisk several years later, she continued her studies at the University of
Cincinnati. After her readmittance, she resurrected the Fisk chapter of Student
Nonviolent Coordinating Committee (SNCC), and she graduated in 1967 with a
bachelor's degree in history.

Since then, Giovanni has taught literature, creative writing, and African
American studies at Rutgers University in New Jersey, Ohio State University in
Columbus, and Virginia Polytechnic Institute and State University (Virginia
Tech) in Blacksburg, Virginia. For her writing, Giovanni has received the Lang-
ston Hughes Award, the Jeanine Rae Award for the Advancement of Women's
Culture, and several other grants and fellowships. She has been nominated for
a National Book Award, and in 1989 the National Association for the Advance-
ment of Colored People (NAACP) named her woman of the year.

Giovanni's writing not only deals with issues of racism and sexism, but also
with the themes of family and love. Some of her most popular work, however,
is her earlier, more revolutionary writing. Advocating militancy as the proper
black response to white oppression, Giovanni was one of the first Black Arts
movement poets to receive widespread notoriety and recognition. Her first
three collections of poems were immediate hits due to her bold, yet accessible
style. Aware of the Black Aesthetic claim that poetry cannot be separated from
music in the African American tradition, she has recorded several albums of her
poetry being read to musical accompaniment. Her literary legacy ranges from
multiple volumes of poetry to children's books and spoken word performances,
including works such as *Black Feeling, Black/Black Judgment* (1970), *Re:Creation*
(1970), *My House* (1972), *The Women and the Men* (1975), *The Selected Poems of*

Nikki Giovanni (1986), *Love Poems* (1997), and *Blues: For All the Changes* (1999). Like many Black Arts movement writers, Giovanni originally had her first two books—where the poems "Adulthood," "Black Power," and "The Funeral of Martin Luther King, Jr." appeared—privately published (they were later picked up as one volume by a commercial press). In its style, theme, and manner of circulation, Giovanni's civil rights literature reflects the spirit of the 1960s.

Adulthood

(For Claudia)

i usta wonder who i'd be
when i was a little girl in indianapolis
sitting on doctors' porches with post-dawn pre-debs
(wondering would my aunt drag me to church sunday)
i was meaningless
and i wondered if life
would give me a chance to mean

i found a new life in the withdrawal from all things
not like my image

when i was a teen-ager i usta sit
on front steps conversing
the gym teacher's son with embryonic eyes
about the essential essence of the universe
(and other bullshit stuff)
recognizing the basic powerlessness of me

but then i went to college where i learned
that just because everything i was was unreal
i could be real and not just real through withdrawal
into emotional crosshairs or colored bourgeois
intellectual pretensions
but from involvement with things approaching reality
i could possibly have a life

so catatonic emotions and time wasting sex games
were replaced with functioning commitments to logic
and
necessity and the gray area was slowly darkened into
a Black thing

for a while progress was being made along with a certain
degree

of happiness cause i wrote a book and found a love
and organized a theatre and even gave some lectures on
Black history
and began to believe all good people could get
together and win without bloodshed
then
hammerskjöld was killed
and lumumba was killed
and diem was killed
and kennedy was killed
and malcolm was killed
and evers was killed
and schwerner, chaney and goodman were killed
and liuzzo was killed
and stokely fled the country
and leroi was arrested
and rap was arrested
and pollard, thompson and cooper were killed*
and king was killed
and kennedy was killed
and i sometimes wonder why i didn't become a
debutante
sitting on porches, going to church all the time,
wondering
is my eye make-up on straight
or a withdrawn discoursing on the stars and moon
instead of a for real Black person who must now feel
and inflict
pain   (1968)

---

* Giovanni's poem cites many figures in addition to those otherwise mentioned in this volume. Dag Hammarskjöld (1905–61) served as secretary-general of the United Nations from 1953 to 1961, when he died in a mysterious plane crash while on a diplomatic mission to the newly liberated Congo. Patrice Lumumba (1925–61), the Republic of the Congo's first legally elected prime minister, was imprisoned and assassinated after a few weeks in office. Ngo Dinh Diem (1901–63), elected first president of the Republic of Vietnam (South Vietnam) after independence from France, was killed in a 1963 coup. Viola Liuzzo (1925–65) was killed by Ku Klux Klansmen while driving civil rights workers home from the 1965 Selma to Montgomery, Alabama, march for voting rights. H. Rap Brown (Jamil Abdullah Al-Amin, b. 1943), a former member of SNCC and the Black Panthers, was arrested several times on various charges during this period. Aubrey Pollard (1948–67), Fred Temple (1949–67), and Carl Cooper (1950–67) were among the forty-three people who died during the 1967 Detroit, Michigan, riots. The three were killed when city police officers and National Guardsmen stormed the Algiers Motel where they were staying.

Black Power

(For All the Beautiful Black Panthers East)

But the whole thing is a miracle — See?

We were just standing there
talking — not touching or smoking
Pot
When this cop told
Tyrone
Move along buddy — take your whores
outa here

And this tremendous growl
From out of nowhere
Pounced on him

Nobody to this very day
Can explain
How it happened

And none of the zoos or circuses
Within fifty miles
Had reported
A panther
Missing

(1968)

The Funeral of Martin Luther King, Jr.

His headstone said
FREE AT LAST, FREE AT LAST
But death is a slave's freedom
We seek the freedom of free men
And the construction of a world
Where Martin Luther King could have lived
and preached non-violence

(1968)

REFLECTIONS AND CONTINUING STRUGGLES

The title of this book, *The Civil Rights Reader: American Literature from Jim Crow to Reconciliation*, ends on a word of hope. While the editors acknowledge the difficulty and the ongoing nature of civil rights struggle, we also believe in the forces of positive change. That, perhaps, is an underlying theme of all the literature collected in this volume. If change is impossible, then why bother writing in the first place? The act of writing, conversely, is also an act of faith. At minimum, writing for an audience implies belief in an audience—that one's words will reach out, connect, move, and possibly even transform. Sections 1 and 2 illustrate how closely literature was linked to social change from the 1890s through the 1970s. Section 3 comments upon those momentous civil rights developments: reflecting upon key events from a historical perspective, considering their influence upon the present, and examining the work that remains to be done. The "problem of the color-line" that W. E. B. Du Bois identified in 1903 has yet to be solved. Racism is no longer as overt as it was in Du Bois's day, or even fifty years ago. But race still permeates our daily lives—our neighborhoods, work, relationships, even our consumer habits—in subtle ways. Although many Americans believe that a "color-blind" society is the answer, contemporary civil rights literature suggests the opposite. What we really need to do is pay attention to race. Racial reconciliation, minding the color-line, means healing old wounds rather than letting them fester. It means recognizing how the past, especially our racial history, informs the present in ways that are sometimes hard to perceive. It means acknowledging where and when racial barriers exist between individuals and groups, and then building the right bridge across them. Most of all, minding the color-line means engaging in three key activities: listening, learning, and then acting upon what one has learned. Action does not necessarily involve devoting one's life to social justice causes, as it did for section 1's Iola Leroy. Action can be as simple as recognizing another individual's basic human dignity or remembering, as section 2's Eldridge Cleaver came to realize, "The price of hating other human beings is loving oneself less."

Historical Overview

The historical pattern of gains and losses remains in place for the contemporary civil rights struggle. On the one hand, African Americans hold local, state, and national offices in ways unseen since Reconstruction and maintain powerful positions in fields from media to education to business. On the other hand, unresolved issues of the past continue to cloud progress in the present. Backlash against civil rights mandates of the 1950s and 1960s began almost immediately. The desegregation of public schools led to "white flight" and "urban blight" in many parts of the country, with many white parents choosing suburban lifestyles and private school educations for their children, leaving mostly black inner cities, especially school systems, lacking the tax base to support adequate infrastructure. Public systems today still must deal with the problem of keeping schools integrated when neighborhoods remain segregated, yet few people question the roots of neighborhood segregation. Another form of opposition to civil rights gains came through the courts. In 1978 the Supreme Court's ruling in *Regents of the University of California v. Bakke* began the process of weakening affirmative action policies that had been in place just a few years. Because affirmative action's opponents often misrepresent it as a quota system where unqualified candidates of color are selected over qualified white ones, it remains controversial in workplaces and colleges today. In the nation's criminal justice system, racial inequities have become acute. African Americans (males especially) are prosecuted, convicted, and incarcerated at noticeably higher rates than their white counterparts accused of similar crimes. White police officers using excessive force against citizens of color remains a particular difficulty in urban areas, reminiscent of early twentieth-century racial violence. The civil unrest in Los Angeles following the 1992 acquittal of white police officers for beating Rodney King is only one of many high-profile cases. In another recent incident that made many Americans wonder if the country had time-traveled backward, thousands of black Floridians were turned away from voting because their names had been purged mysteriously from the 2000-year election lists as "convicted criminals" even though they had never been accused of any crime. Economic issues, finally, continue to complicate the racial ones. Few instances have laid bare the color-line between the "haves" and "have-nots" like the devastation wrought by Hurricane Katrina in 2005.

Contemporary civil rights struggles recall a famous quotation from writer William Faulkner, "The past is never dead. It's not even past." Still, many Americans tend to think of the civil rights *movement* as something that happened long ago — as history, not current event. It has become a story with a clear beginning, middle, and end; heroes and villains; triumph and tragedy, but ultimately a happy resolution, just like a Hollywood movie. That story typically begins with successful efforts to overturn Jim Crow in the 1950s (the Supreme Court's *Brown v. the Board of Education* decision and the Montgomery Bus Boycott) and reaches a crucial turning point with the violence of the 1960s (Birmingham, 1963; Mississippi, 1964; Selma, 1965). Various heroes, heroines, and villains appear along the way (Martin Luther King Jr., Malcolm X, Rosa Parks, Bull Connor, George Wallace). The period comes to a heartrending close with Martin Luther King Jr.'s assassination in 1968. By then, however, the movement's goals had been accomplished, and the problems it set out to solve were buried along with Jim Crow. The familiar civil rights story is a very satisfying one, which may be why several successful mainstream movies have been made about it. But that story also leaves out many years, many people, and many issues, as sections 1 and 2 clearly show. Most important, however, thinking about civil rights as a historical, not contemporary, movement is safe. It allows Americans to place responsibility for civil rights transformation somewhere else, in the past, not in the here and now, where those of us in the present face the hard work of dealing with its complex questions about economics, justice, and equality. The task seems overwhelming, something only superheroes (Martin, Malcolm, Rosa) could do. The civil rights story as it gets celebrated on Martin Luther King Day, during Black History Month, through street signs, and via other commemorative events often forgets that real people have always done the work of social change, and even heroes were real people too. The civil rights story as celebration does not mention that the "movie" is not yet over and that we are its heroes and heroines.

Literary Developments and Themes

So where do we go from here? Our dilemma is that, in addition to being the heroes and heroines, we also have to write the script. Luckily, we have a new generation of civil rights literature to guide us. That literature is primarily about everyday people, whether real or imagined, past or present. It teaches contemporary audiences how to grieve, how to fight back, and how to celebrate. It gives voice to frustration, joy, anger, and hope. In short, the new civil rights literature sheds light into most, if not all, of the necessary inner resources for continuing the struggle. Constance Curry recalls the heady, and difficult, days of nonviolent direct action in the early 1960s, but the protagonist of Anthony Grooms's story, set during those times, weighs the pros and cons of getting involved. Poetry by David Hernandez and Rita Dove provides new perspectives on familiar heroes, while poetry by Marilyn Nelson and Cyrus Cassells changes the definition of heroism to make it more inclusive. A central character in Bebe Moore Campbell's *Your Blues Ain't Like Mine* argues that old ideas about race are no longer relevant today, yet Toi Derricotte's and Patricia J. Williams's personal essays show how old ideas about race still manifest themselves in new ways. If oppression still exists, so do acts of resistance large and small, as the personal experiences of Williams, the protagonist of Walter Mosley's "Equal Opportunity," and characters in Honorée Fanonne Jeffers's "Confederate Pride Day at Bama" clearly demonstrate.

   The selections from section 3, like those from sections 1 and 2, must be read in the context of their historical moment. For literature produced since the 1980s, that moment is postmodernism. Descended from the earlier twentieth-century movement from which its name derives, postmodernism extends to bold, new levels modernism's innovations in style and form; the breakdown of barriers between high and low art, different genres, reality and its representation; and reflections upon the very nature of art itself. As the similarity of names suggests, the two actually represent different stages of one larger movement. For modernists, the twentieth century's beginning seemed to mark a rupture with the past, and new forms of expression offered possibilities for reorienting oneself in the world when all previous markers (such as truth, faith, family, and community) seemed to have been lost. For postmodernists, those markers (especially ones like race and gender) represent social constructions rather than fixed entities. Contemporary art does not begin from the position of loss, but from one of acceptance that modes of expression are limited in their ability to convey meaning and capture truth. In the meantime, art still creates moments of sublimity and insight, challenges notions of what is beautiful and true, and even celebrates the provisional, the fractured, the lacunae of the unexpressed. Wanda Coleman's tribute to Emmett Till offers an example of postmodern fragmentary poetics. Her recovery of this traumatic story from the past, narrated between chanted river names, offers hope for redemption while also acknowledging the provisional nature of healing and, especially, of justice. Jeffers's "Giving Thanks to Water" expresses similar sentiments, while also deploying experimental poetic strategies, about the 1921 Tulsa riots. Another example of a postmodern author is Patricia J. Williams, who blends the genres of professional journal article and memoir, calling into question traditional distinctions between academic and creative writing, not to mention the social constructions of race and the politics of shopping.

Each of these texts was published since the 1980s, decades that have marked a new age of politicized writing. Questioning accepted truths and modes of thinking is a hallmark of postmodern art. Literature especially provides new stories and ways of telling stories to counter the "master narratives" of the past. As the transformations of the 1960s and 1970s, from civil rights to other social justice movements, took hold in the culture at large, and in particular on college campuses, the stories Americans told about the past began to change. This meant, quite literally, a revolution within history, literature, and other humanities-based disciplines. Universities saw the rise of African American, Latino American, and other ethnic studies departments, in addition to women's, gender, and sexuality studies. As accepted fields of study changed, so did canons, the lists of traditionally studied authors and texts. For instance, very few of the writers included in sections 1 and 2 of this volume would have been read in high school or college classrooms during the times in which they were writing. Just as all revolutions result in backlash, however, the canon changes that took place in the last two decades of the twentieth century encountered opposition. This clash, known as the "culture wars," divided traditionalists from postmodernists. The former accused the latter of moral relativism and lax educational standards, while the latter accused the former of being reactionary, patriarchal, elitist, and, often, racist. Although some see this time period as quite difficult, one lesson that the civil rights movement teaches is that social change usually meets much frustration and controversy as the forces of progress and stasis negotiate new ground.

Postmodernism and the culture wars actually opened up several opportunities for civil rights scholarship, including anthologies such as this one. First, postmodernist fragmentation of history's master narratives into more local, "ground-up" (rather than "top-down") counternarratives redirected attention to previously neglected or underrepresented stories — such as the struggle for civil rights. Second, expanded historical and literary canons, along with increased opportunities for interdisciplinary work, allowed scholars to see something called "civil rights literature" as a legitimate field of study. Finally, the postmodern movement's tendency toward self-reflection offers one significant lesson, showing how the civil rights struggle — and any story one tells about it — remains an ever-evolving discourse, always open to new narratives, new challenges, and new possibilities.

Constance Curry   (b. 1933)

onstance Curry has remained active in the struggle for civil rights for almost fifty years. Born in 1933 to Irish immigrant parents, Curry grew up in Greensboro, North Carolina, and graduated from Georgia's Agnes Scott College in 1955. In 1984 she went on to receive a juris doctorate from the Woodrow Wilson College of Law. A memoir excerpted here and published in *Deep in Our Hearts: Nine White Women in the Freedom Movement* (2000) recounts Curry's political awakening at Agnes Scott and the increasing activism that led her to become, in 1960, the first white woman appointed to the executive committee of the Student Nonviolent Coordinating Committee (SNCC). Curry's primary work during those years centered on the National Student Association's Southern Advisory Committee, which facilitated communication between various civil rights organizations and reported on direct action campaigns. After her NSA years, Curry served for nearly a decade as a southern field representative for the American Friends Service Committee (AFSC), where she worked to facilitate school desegregation, voter registration, and economic development. In 1975 Maynard Jackson (first black mayor of Atlanta) appointed her to direct the city's Office of Human Services, a position that she held until 1990, when she began writing full-time.

Curry's first major publication was *Silver Rights* (1995), the true story of Matthew and Mae Bertha Carter's thirteen children, who desegregated the all-white school system in Sunflower County, Mississippi, in 1965. Curry's account of the Carter family's determination to obtain the best education they could get earned her a Lillian Smith Book Award for Nonfiction and a reputation for writing powerful chronicles of race relations in the Mississippi Delta. Two later books, *Aaron Henry: The Fire Ever Burning* (2000) and *Mississippi Harmony* (2002), continued her collaboration with area activists to create inspiring profiles of their struggles. Curry's most recent work focuses on criminal justice reform. In 2004 she produced a documentary, *An Intolerable Burden*, which returns to Sunflower County (home of Mississippi's infamous Parchman Farm, the state penitentiary) to show how resegregation in the school system leads directly to an increasing number of black males in the prison system.

The selections from Curry's memoir, "Wild Geese to the Past," included below, focus primarily on the pivotal year of 1960, when the sit-in movement began in Greensboro, North Carolina, and SNCC was founded in Raleigh. Curry recounts organizational strategies that underlay nonviolent direct action, the backlash that participants faced, and the many ways that the freedom struggle touched individual lives on a personal level. Her story features activists such as Ella Baker, Julian Bond, James Lawson, Marion Barry, and Chuck McDew, whose names appear regularly in early 1960s civil rights history, as well as many people whose stories are not so well known.

Selections from "Wild Geese to the Past"

I have been acutely aware of my Irish roots as far back as memory allows. My sister Eileen and I knew early on that our mother and father had been born in Belfast, Northern Ireland, of Protestant heritage, had come to the United States in the 1920s, had married and settled in Paterson, New Jersey, where Daddy worked in the textile business as a silk dyer and where Eileen and I were born — though our family continued to move around until finally settling in Greensboro, North Carolina, in 1943. There were just the four of us — no relatives. I remember singing "Over the river and through the woods to grandmother's house we go," feeling sad and not knowing why. Every Christmas, Eileen and I received by mail either linen handkerchiefs or whimsical colored pictures of dogs or cats with small rectangular calendars attached at the bottom. These were gifts from our Grandmother Curry, Daddy's mother in Belfast. We heard Daddy speak of Uncle Bob, his older brother, or Aunt Winnie, his sister, also in Belfast, and I remember Daddy getting newsletters in the mail from Uncle George, his younger brother, a missionary in Africa. I also see Daddy in 1940, sitting at the dining room table, crying, letter in hand telling him his father had died. (Daddy had not been able to get back to Ireland since his departure in 1925, although he later visited several times before his own death.)

In the fourth grade I cut out shamrocks, colored them green, and pinned them all over my brown coat to wear to school on Saint Patrick's Day. Later in college I wrote a paper titled "Sinn Fein and the Easter Rebellion." The opening sentence tells of the Easter Rising of 1916 against England, "condemned as a bloodstained failure which came to be regarded as a signal success." The paper closes with the lines, "The sacrifice of the leaders of the rebellion had set Ireland's soul free again. They had said 'Our blood will rebaptize and revitalize our land' and the prophecy was fulfilled." I read William Butler Yeats and other Irish poets and embraced the words from "The Rebel" by Irish revolutionary Padraic Pearse:

And I say to my people's masters:
Beware, Beware of the thing that is coming.
Beware of the risen people,
Who shall take what ye would not give.

I have often thought that these lines could have come straight from the Freedom Movement of the 1960s. It is clear to me that the Irish struggle got planted deep in my heart and soul at an early age, and that its lessons and music and poetry were easily transferred to the southern freedom struggle. . . .

I AM OFTEN ASKED how I "got involved" in the civil rights movement, and it's a difficult question to answer. When it comes to 1960, however, I have a specific response: it was a matter of being in the right place at the right time. In December 1959 I found an apartment on Adair Avenue, and Donna McGinty, my college roommate, moved in with me and became the assistant at the project. With the help of the Southern Regional Council, one of the first agencies working for racial equality, I moved into a small office at 45 Exchange Place, S.E. The building housed other "human relations" agencies, a fact that often prompted us to joke about "one bomb destroying half the Atlanta support of the movement."

My first job was to convene the initial meeting of the extraordinary Southern Advisory Committee that I had inherited from previous years of NSA work in the South — comprising representatives from the National Council of Churches, the Anti-Defamation League, American Friends Service Committee, Southern Regional Council, Southeastern Regional NAACP, Community Church of Chapel Hill, University of Louisville, UNC Woman's College, Loyola University of New Orleans, Morehouse College, Atlanta University, and the editor of the Atlanta paper. The listing shows the quality of leadership and diversity of agencies working with NSA from 1956 on, to establish a different framework for students living in a segregated society. Don Hoffman, NSA president, and Curtis Gans, national affairs vice-president, were also at the meeting. Although new NSA officers were elected each year at the national congress, I received unswerving support from all of the administrations during my four years with the Southern Project. That first advisory group suggested that we continue with the annual summer seminars and organize smaller integrated workshops and conferences across the South, while establishing a network of like-minded students and faculty. Advisory Committee members put me in touch with all of their contacts from the past seminars' work. With broad goals and lots of encouragement, I was ready to go.

Everything changed within five weeks. On February 1, 1960, I was in Greensboro to visit my sister Eileen and pick up some furniture and clothes. The sit-in movement started — right as I was driving down one of the city's main streets. The news announcer on the car radio reported with some wonderment that four students from the Negro A&T College had just been arrested for refusing to leave lunch counter stools at the downtown Woolworth's store. I had never heard of such a thing — although my neighbor remained convinced until the day she died that I had started the sit-in. I was the only person she knew who was involved in "interracial things," I was in town, and, as she told me, "I can put two and two together."

The sit-in movement spread like wildfire during the spring of 1960, and my office, supported by the Southern Regional Council's network, began to report on what was happening. By March 1, we had put out a newsletter listing the places where demonstrations were occurring, how many arrests were being made, and what help was needed. NSA in Philadelphia quickly passed this information on to a national student network, and the chain reaction of northern student support and demonstrations led to many of our breakthroughs. Several variety-store chains desegregated their lunch counters partly because of national picket lines and demonstrations.

By Easter, more than seventy thousand mostly black southern college students were involved in demonstrations. Students in the United States seized the chance to participate in direct action to bring about social change. It was an exciting time, and the direction of my project soon changed drastically. I don't think I ever even wondered if the Field Foundation would mind this new approach as I set about actually witnessing demonstrations and sit-ins and marches and then reporting to groups who wanted to help or to the media. Maxwell Hahn, the director of the Field Foundation, never questioned me, not in the beginning months, or later when we were actually paying SNCC phone and other bills. Julian Bond, reminding me that he had a key to our small office, used to come in at all hours of the night to use my mimeograph machine to run off press releases, fund-raising letters, and SNCC's newsletter, "The Student Voice."

Ella Baker and I went together to the organizational meeting of the Student Nonviolent Coordinating Committee at Shaw University in Raleigh, North Carolina, during Easter weekend 1960. Details of the conference — where I stayed, where we ate — remain vague. What I see now is like a view through a kaleidoscope imaging young black college students setting up and speaking passionately and eloquently of what had taken place already in their towns or on their campuses and what they were planning to do in this new fight for freedom. And of course I remember Reverend James Lawson and his call for nonviolence to be the credo of the movement, seeing and hearing Dr. Martin Luther King Jr. for the first time, and being inspired by Ella Baker's now-famous speech about the fight and the struggle being for "more than a hamburger."

This meeting gave birth to the student group that was going to follow the call of James Lawson and the Nashville movement for nonviolence as "a way of life" — the SNCC. Marion Barry, from Nashville, was elected the first chair, but the Atlanta delegation won the contest over where the organization's office should be located. The Raleigh meeting was the first time that I stood in a circle, joined hands, and sang "We Shall Overcome." For me, that song always elicits tears, no matter the lapse of time or the occasion of the singing. Following the Raleigh conference, student representatives from the most active colleges met in Atlanta, and the SNCC executive committee chose Ella Baker and me as adult advisors. I was only a few years older than the students, certainly not well schooled in social revolutions, but I was out of college, had a job, and could use the Field grant money to help the fledgling movement. The majority of the campus representatives to the early executive committee meetings were black men, and I became close friends with many of them. Since we are asked so often about sexual relations between white women and black men, I need to say here that I was approached by two in those early days. I said no. One asked if it was because he was black, and I said no. That was the end of it — with no jeopardy to friendships that continue to this day.

Delegates to the May meeting and students at other black colleges began forming their response to the sit-ins and the burgeoning movement. In Atlanta, students from the six black universities and colleges there formed the Atlanta Committee on Appeal for Human Rights. Their first move was to publish a full-page ad in the *Atlanta Journal and Constitution*. The ad was an eloquent expression of the changes needed in Atlanta, which went far beyond the freedom to eat at a lunch counter. Georgia's governor, Ernest Vandiver, was sure that the piece had been written in Moscow, if not Peking. In fact, the money to pay for that ad came from Lillian Smith, a white southerner and author who lived in the north Georgia mountains and was a longtime believer in integration.

In early summer 1960 Ella Baker asked if Jane Stembridge could stay at the apartment on Adair Avenue with Donna and me. Jane, born in Georgia and the daughter of a Southern Baptist minister, was a white seminary student from Union Theological Seminary in New York. She had met Ella at the Raleigh Easter Conference, and Ella asked her to come to Atlanta as SNCC's first executive secretary. Jane, pixie and poet, was wide-eyed and full of Christian existentialism and faith in the movement. She, Ella, and I would sit in the tiny office that housed SNCC at 197 1/2 Auburn Avenue and, as I remember, laugh a lot. The first check that SNCC received that summer to support our work was for $100, from Eleanor Roosevelt. The second check was from Reverend Will Campbell, given in memory of country singer Patsy Cline, who had died that June. I did not realize until much later that it was three women — Ella, Jane, and I — albeit behind the scenes, who helped build SNCC in its early days.

A few months later another roommate moved into our apartment. Bonnie Kilstein was a student from New York University who had come to Atlanta for the summer to work for the Episcopal Society for Cultural and Racial Unity. On August 29, 1960, the *Augusta Courier*, a widely circulated segregationist weekly, reported the following under the headline "Bonnie Kilstein Leads the Attack on Segregation at Episcopal Cathedral": "Miss Kilstein is a 25-year-old-blonde . . . she has the habit of dating Negro men and she took communion at the Cathedral of St. Philip with one of her Negro boyfriends. This Bonnie Kilstein is reported to subscribe to the doctrine that the Negro is 'the Divine Image carved in ebony.'"

While the whirlwind of sit-ins and demonstrations and SNCC meetings absorbed our 1960 spring and early summer, Donna and I worked hard on the Third Southern Student Human Relations Seminars, to be held over three weeks in August at the University of Minnesota, just before the NSA National Congress. We recruited participants by sending letters to the small band of faithful on campuses in the South or by my making personal contacts while traveling. In March, with the violence of the Nashville sit-ins dogging my consciousness, I went to the University of Texas to meet Sandra Cason, nicknamed Casey. Casey, a member of the Christian Faith and Life Community and active in the YWCA, had been recommended as a seminar participant. We walked to the Night Hawk Cafe near campus, and I told her what I had witnessed as the sit-in movement swept the South. By that time, Casey had become involved herself in direct action. We soon found ourselves crying together into our hamburgers and milk shakes. She came to the seminar, has remained one of my best friends over these forty years, and has been the propelling force behind this book.

That spring of 1960, through SNCC, I had come to know Chuck McDew, a sit-in leader at South Carolina State, a black college in Orangeburg. He came to that first seminar, along with an outspoken, irreverent, brilliant young man, Bill Caldwell from Loyola University in New Orleans, and representatives from thirteen other southern campuses. Reverend Will Campbell, from my advisory committee, had agreed to be the consultant for the seminar and helped me select the group who came to Minnesota on August 3. I remember talking with Will about whether it was more important to have students who were just realizing the need for change in race relations or students like Chuck, who had actually demonstrated and been arrested. We never set a policy and ended up with a group of students at various stages of knowledge and commitment

The students at that first seminar were in an emotional maelstrom. Valerie, a white woman from Texas Christian University, fell in love with Chuck McDew. (This happened at all of the seminars, and for most students it was the first time to be part of or witness to an interracial relationship.) Henrietta, from black Fisk University, came from a privileged background and had spent some time abroad. While one seminar lecturer talked about the cruelty of the cotton sharecropping system and its perpetuation of racism, Henrietta burst into tears and began to frantically rub her hands together—"hands," she told us, "that had never even touched a cotton plant." One participant from North Carolina State, it seemed to me, spent much of his time warily wondering what he was doing there in the first place, and wild Bill Caldwell exhorted the group to "act" when they returned to their colleges.

The closing of the seminars was always hard. The intensity of the three weeks bound us all together and changed us irrevocably. On that last day in Minnesota, knowing that we were all going back to a separated life, Will Campbell told us good-bye with an offering that was later published in a magazine as

"The Display of a Feather." I wish I could print the whole piece here, because it is eloquent and speaks in a timeless manner of the relations among human beings. Essentially he tells of a primitive savage returning from battle who stooped over and picked something up. "It was red and brown and yellow and green. It was pretty—it wasn't worth a thing. He took it back to his cave and kept it because it spoke to his deepest feelings. But soon he knew that its beauty spoke forth only if he shared it with his fellows. With this feather, civilization began and human relations began." Will told us that human relations still relied on the display of a feather, the effort to say there is some other way; that things didn't have to be as they were; that the times were out of joint. It was a matter of aesthetics, having to do with that which is true, which is pure, lovely, gracious—and with justice and love. Will then said each participant would be playing a different role in the struggle, for there was no one way. "As to how you involve yourself in the crisis, I have no parting words of advice . . . that role you must now go forth and find. In this moment of farewell, I say that your heart will not rest till it finds rest in personal involvement. And so, good-bye."

That 1960 seminar is especially memorable, perhaps because it was my first one, but also because that year was so pivotal for the movement. During the national congress following the seminar, Casey was on a panel at a plenary session. The night before, representatives of the Student Nonviolent Coordinating Committee had told the congress the meaning of the sit-ins and civil disobedience and had asked for NSA's support. The panel had been hastily assembled to meet demands by white southern students to answer the SNCC presentation, and I, responding to NSA officers' request for advice, recommended that Casey be on it. The five hundred mostly white delegates from colleges and universities across the country were dumbstruck when Casey took the microphone. The headline of the *Minneapolis Tribune* article covering the event was "White Coed Backs Sit-ins, Gets Ovation." The opening paragraph read: "A beautiful University of Texas coed with honey blond hair and a southern voice so soft it would not startle a boll weevil made a statement of ethical principles on the Negro sit-in movement Thursday." Part of her speech was quoted:

> I cannot speak for the sit-ins or for white southerners. I consider this problem to be an ethical one for which there can be only a personal decision. On this question, I hope we do not lose its essential simplicity because of its complexities. The simplicity is this: when an individual human being has been denied by the attitudes of his community the exercise of his rights as a human being, has he the right to peaceably protest? The answer to this simple question can only be yes.

To this day, I can close my eyes and recall Casey, fresh from the South, where the jails had been packed with young demonstrators, saying to a packed auditorium, "When Thoreau was jailed for refusing to pay taxes to a government which supported slavery, Emerson went to visit him. 'Henry David,' said Emerson, 'what are you doing in there?' Thoreau looked at him and replied, 'Ralph Waldo, what are you doing out there?'" My scalp tingles as I hear again the thunder of the standing ovation and see all the eyes filled with tears. There is no question that this was a personal turning point for many of the white delegates and probably a decisive moment in the history of NSA's civil rights activism. Although I was not aware of it at the time, Casey and I, two southern women, through my suggestion of her and her participation on the panel, helped solidify NSA support for civil disobedience and the Freedom Movement.

The other three panelists, white southern men, spoke against the sit-ins as "being violations of the law, involving private property and legal rights of businessmen." Following the panel, the congress, by a great majority, passed a resolution endorsing the sit-ins and promising support for the movement on the national and local campus levels.

In December of that year, seminar participant Valerie Brown, then editor of a campus publication at Texas Christian University, sent me a copy of their fall issue. It carried a reprint of a letter from Chuck McDew written to Valerie in October, on brown paper towels, from the Orangeburg jail:

Hi Val, . . . Please excuse my stationery. I was arrested over an hour ago along with three other students. We sat down at the S. H. Kress & Co. lunch counter and asked to be served. . . . I can hear singing outside. They are singing "We Shall Overcome" and it sounds so wonderful that I kind of want to cry. Dot, the girl in the next cell, can see them and there are nearly four hundred students outside . . . all singing. Now they are singing the "Star Spangled Banner" and I feel a kind of bitter sick feeling deep inside. I know that singing as well as we who are in here believe that "we shall overcome and the truth will make us free" and I'm trying so very, very hard to believe too that this is the "home of the brave and the free." I keep asking myself just how brave are the people who put me here? . . . Oh, God why must it be this way? Why can't we be a world of blind men. Then we would all be free and equal. Or would a group of blind bigots start discriminating on the basis of tone quality. Would all people with high voices have to live in filthy ghettos and be second class citizens?

Would the children of high-voiced people have to fight mobs to get into school. Would their braille tablets say that they aren't as good as the low-voiced and that they smell bad, have V.D. and live from day to day with one dream in their dark world — to sleep with a low-voiced woman? Oh, sickness, oh hate. Go and leave the hearts of man. Let me be me, Charles Frederick McDew, man, student, lover of life. I don't want to be that nigger with no personality, no being, just a dark blob. I want to be me with my color that I love, with my eyes, my body, my dreams and aspirations. I'd better close now. It has been a very trying day and we have trial in the morning. Pray for us, Val; pray for us all.

Chuck, or as the fellows in this cell call me, 24771

When I came back from the seminar and NSA congress in late August, I found that my belongings had been moved, lock, stock, and barrel, to another apartment. Bonnie, it turned out, had invited Ed King, a black SNCC worker, to our upstairs apartment, and the landlady had seen them going in the door. She had then called immediately and given us notice to be "out by sunset" that same day. Donna and Jane found another apartment; Bonnie left Atlanta. It was a strange feeling to go from the airport to the totally different place where Jane and Donna were living. That same summer, my red and white Karmann Ghia, my first car and pride and joy, was spray-painted with blue KKK signs and circles, we received threatening phone calls, and a friend of Donna's told us that we were under surveillance by the Georgia Bureau of Investigation. In an issue of the *Augusta Courier*, the NSA Southern Project address and phone number were listed under "Atlanta Mixing Organizations," and Donna and I were specifically cited as two white women working for "mixing the races." I don't remember ever being afraid during this period — only angry at the stupidity of the harassment. In retrospect, I believe my lack of fear is indicative of the heartfelt faith among our small band that we were engaged in a right and just struggle. . . .

ONE OCCASION WHEN I was an observer/reporter remains especially clear in my memory. Paine College, in Augusta, Georgia, was established by the United Methodist Church and the Christian Methodist Episcopal Church in the early 1900s. In 1930 the college started an annual statewide Christian conference — one of the earliest attempts at an integrated meeting for students. Over the years, a few faithful white and black campus ministers silently and secretly took students to spend that weekend at Paine. By mid-April 1961, the students who came to the conference were seeing a new interpretation of their duty as Christians. Reverend James Lawson, still one of the strongest leaders in nonviolent training for direct action, was there, and by Saturday of the weekend conference an integrated group of students was ready to sit in at the H. L. Green store in downtown Augusta.

Silas Norman (later with SNCC) was chair and William Didley was vice-chair of the ongoing movement at Paine. They had been demonstrating since early April, using structured methods, with people designated as security (the larger men), monitors, and observers. They had been notifying the Augusta police thirty minutes before the demonstrations. On this Saturday afternoon, for some reason, the student security was not in place as the interracial group of sixty students from the conference walked toward the store. William Didley was one of the black leaders at the front of the group. Suddenly a man from Bennettsville, South Carolina, emerged from the gathering white mob, pulled a knife, and stabbed Didley close to the heart. Didley was quickly put into a car and taken back to campus and then to the hospital.

Inside the store, Silas Norman, who was in charge of the demonstration, told the white students to get out and head for a safe place. They dashed into a store nearby and, men and women alike, huddled in a dressing room in the women's ready-to-wear department.

As one of the designated observers, I had been walking on the sidewalk outside the store as the group of marchers quietly approached. The stabbing had taken place right in front of me, and I think I went into a brief state of shock. I remember wandering on down the street looking into store windows, trying to assimilate what I had just witnessed. The police finally arrived, after the violence.

Joan Browning, then a student at Georgia State College for Women, was also at the Paine conference and the Saturday demonstration. She and I drove to Augusta later to testify at the hearing. Although the students' lawyer tried to prove that William Didley had been targeted as one of the Paine leaders, his assailant was released. The charges pressed against William, for carrying a concealed weapon (not true) and inciting to riot, were dropped, and he was released on his own recognizance. . . .

GOING BACK TO Mississippi, reliving those earlier times with the Carters and Aaron Henry, and then telling my own story for this book have caused the floodgates to be lifted. The remembering has jelled into an awareness — viscerally deep my whole life — that I have no true "sense of place." That awareness took form when I went to a conference of southern writers a few years ago. All of the speakers talked about their sense of place and how their books are rooted in the call and recall of early years with parents and grandparents — a house, a farm, a school — and patterns. "Sense of place" is also strong in the chapters of my co-writers on this project, particularly the southern women. If this sense has to do with feeling at home, or secure, or belonging, then mine lies in the Beloved Community and Freedom Movement of the early sixties, with our vision of a truly integrated society. Can one have a "sense of place" in a vision or movement rather than in a special geographical spot on the earth? When I articulated this question to a friend, he said, "Hmm, there's something biblical about that. The early Christians were called the 'People of the Way.' They weren't rooted in a certain space, and 'way' referred to a way of living."

The other difference I have observed about my life is that, other than my mother, who died early on, I have had no real women role models. Thus, instead of being guided into the civil rights movement by a strong-willed woman, as some of my co-writers were, I just sort of barreled my way into a place where my heart felt right. On the other hand, I have been lucky in that my "way of living" has meant working for forty years in jobs and with people whose goals and values were close to those of the early Freedom Movement. I am grateful for the continuity that has provided for me. Today, in addition to writing, I devote my time to fighting for drastic change in the criminal justice system. With the staggering number of young black men already incarcerated and the increasing number of black women going to jail, the struggle is, for me, the cutting edge of the civil rights movement of our day.

My years have also been filled with an unfaltering circle of friends, including women from forty-odd years ago at Agnes Scott; a family that expanded with my father's two remarriages and added a half sister, three stepbrothers, in-laws, and nieces and nephews. I did not marry, and I have no children.

I was sustained through the whole of the sixties by a relationship with a man with whom I shared completely my passion for the movement. He had commitments elsewhere that left me free to conduct my life independently, as I preferred. Sadly, that affair had to end. Nowadays, they say women who choose unavailable men are afraid of intimacy. I don't know about that. There is an intimacy born of shared struggle, dedication, excitement, compassion, sorrow, and danger that is matched by no other. The fire of that love fueled my work for racial justice and gave me a safe place for all of my passions. It also gave me time to learn how to lead a life as a single woman, with freedom to follow my basic, unorthodox beliefs. I have stayed in Atlanta for thirty-nine years, saved enough money to buy a house fourteen years ago, and, following another passion, have traveled extensively, including visits to Russia, China, Cuba, Chile, and fifteen trips to Ireland.

I have had a long string of crushes, flings, and trysts and an even longer time of celibacy. I carry little sense of sacrifice or regret for the choices I have made freely along the way. Enhanced loneliness may come with growing older, but I am gratified to be around long enough to tell the stories — to shine the light on some heroes from the Freedom Movement. In writing about the Carter family and Aaron Henry, I came to realize that it is indeed the telling of the stories that is important — the passing on of the legacy. Perhaps lessons of hope and courage can make the future way a little brighter, a little clearer. As I continue to write about people and times that require memory to fly backward, lines from Thomas Kinsella, a contemporary Irish poet, inspire me:

Ended and done with never ceases,
Constantly the heart releases
Wild geese to the past.

(2000)

B orn Toi Webster on April 12, 1941, in Detroit, Michigan, to Antonia Baquet and Benjamin Sweeney Webster, Toi Derricotte began writing poetry and keeping a journal at a young age. In her journal she recorded feelings of isolation and of marginalization, which she attributed to others' reactions to her light skin. After graduating from a local girls' Catholic school in 1959, Derricotte enrolled in Wayne State College. Several years later, Derricotte's son was born, and in 1962 she married her son's father, Clarence Reese, although the couple divorced several years later. In 1965 Derricotte graduated with a bachelor's degree in special education and began teaching mentally impaired children at Detroit's Farland School. She moved to New York in 1967 and married Bruce Derricotte; two years later, she began teaching remedial reading at the Jefferson School in New Jersey.

In 1972 Derricotte published her first poem in the *New York Quarterly*, and her first collection of poetry, *Empress of the House of Death*, appeared in 1978. From 1974 to 1988 Derricotte served as a teacher and poet-in-residence for the New Jersey State Council on the Arts, and she began holding community workshops on creative writing. Derricotte published her second volume of poetry, *Natural Birth*, to critical acclaim in 1983, and the following year she earned a master's degree in English and creative writing from New York University. Many of Derricotte's poems reflect transitions in her personal life, and she connects those transitions to broader cultural forces, including racism, by illustrating how such forces affect individuals.

Derricotte's third collection of poetry, *Captivity*, appeared in 1989, and in 1997 her fourth volume, *Tender*, was published and won the Paterson Poetry Prize. That same year Derricotte's memoir, *The Black Notebooks: An Interior Journey*, was published. The memoir, excerpted here, collects her journal entries spanning twenty years. It received the 1998 Anisfield-Wolf Book Award and the Black Caucus of the American Library Association Nonfiction Award, and it was nominated for the PEN/Martha Albrand Award for the Art of the Memoir and named a *New York Times* Notable Book of the Year. Derricotte's other literary honors include the Lucille Medwick Memorial Award from the Poetry Society of America, two Pushcart Prizes, the Folger Shakespeare Library Poetry Book Award, the Distinguished Pioneering of the Arts Award from United Black Artists Inc., a Guggenheim fellowship, two fellowships from the National Endowment for the Arts, and one from the Rockefeller Foundation.

In 1996 Derricotte cofounded Cave Canem, a summer retreat and workshop that developed into a major resource for numerous prominent African American writers, such as Sonia Sanchez. She has taught creative writing and minority literature at several universities, including Old Dominion University, George Mason University, and the University of South Florida. In 1991 she began teaching at the University of Pittsburgh, where she currently serves as an associate professor of English.

The Black Notebooks

Selections from "The Club"

"Herein lie buried many things which if read with patience
may show the strange meaning of being black here in the
dawning of the Twentieth Century. This meaning is not
without interest to you, Gentle Reader; for the problem of
the Twentieth Century is the problem of the color-line."
— W. E. B. Du Bois

On Sunday afternoons Bruce and I would drive through the small bedroom communities close to New York, blocks and blocks of stately colonials and overpowering elms, and I would imagine a kind of life, a kind of happiness — a light on in an upstairs bedroom, a tricycle turned over in a drive, a swing on a front porch barely moving, as if it were just waiting for someone to come and sit down. I began to think that that was happiness. The happiness of expectancy. Everything that had to be prepared had been prepared, and now all that was needed was for the human heart to begin beating. I wanted to be in those houses, to be those people. I wanted to go all the way, as a pilot will make up his mind on a dangerous mission that there is no turning back. There were all kinds of practical reasons why we chose Upper Montclair, but, looking back, it was love that drove me through the streets of that unsuspecting city. Love.

September

Last month, seeing an advertisement in the newspaper for a contemporary in our price range, I called an agent. "I shouldn't be telling you about this on the phone," she said, "but there is a house I think you would be interested in. It's on an estate on Highland Avenue, and the people are very particular about who buys it."

My heart shriveled. Should I find out whom they are "particular" not to have? Should I let her think I'm white and go without Bruce to see it? When I take Bruce, we are shown entirely different neighborhoods, all-black or integrated.

I decided to act dumb. "Oh, really? That seems strange. Why isn't the house multiple-listed? What are they so careful about?"

"Well, you know, some people like to do it this way. Let me have your phone number; I'll call you back." But she never called back. So I wonder if our name is known —"That black couple looking for a house in town and the wife looks white."

This week I called another agent and played a game. "We'd like to look at the house you're describing, but we'd also like to see a house we heard about on an estate."

"Oh," she gargled, "you mean, ah, the one that came on the market this morning?"

"I don't know when it came on the market, but I do know it's on Highland Ave."

"I don't know if you'd be interested in that. The rooms are small, it's over-grown, overpriced, no view." She went on and on. I was still interested.

"Well," she finally agreed, "I'll see if I can get the owners on the phone and we can go and see it."

When Bruce and I got to her office, of course she hadn't gotten hold of them. "The man works at night. No one is at home."

"I'd still like to see it. Drive by on the way to the other house." She got lost! Imagine a real estate dealer getting lost in her own town!

"That's all right," I reassured her. "We can go past it on the way back."

The house she showed us, in the integrated part of town, was expensive and run-down. On the way to the "particular" house, once again she got lost. We had to direct her. Bruce said, "There it is! There it is!" It was all lit up. And she kept driving. Finally, a half mile down the road (I was waiting to see if she would ever stop), I said, "Why didn't you stop at the house?"

"Oh," she stammered, "did we pass it?"

"My husband pointed it out to you."

"It's so dark, I can't find it. It's too dark tonight. I think we should come back tomorrow."

"I don't mind the dark."

"You mean you want me to turn around and go back?" she gasped.

When we got to the house, we sat in the car while she "checked." We could see in the front window. Two old ladies were reading the paper. She came back and said they didn't want visitors.

I felt a hopelessness descend. No matter how clever and determined I am, they can always find a way to stop me. Perhaps I should call a lawyer, sue. . . . But it would probably take forever and I'd need a courage and commitment that I don't feel. I decide to look for a house in another community, one where we are not yet known, and this time I'll go to the real estate agent's alone.

October

It's the overriding reality I must get through. Each time I drive down the streets and see only whites, each time I notice no blacks in the local supermarket or walking on the streets, I think, I'm not supposed to be here. When I go into real estate agents' offices, I put on a mask. At first they hope you are in for a quick sell. They show you houses they want to get rid of. But if you stick around, and if you are the "right kind" they show you ones just newly listed, and sometimes not even on the market. There are neighborhoods that even most white people are not supposed to be in.

I make myself likable, optimistic. I am married, a woman who belongs to a man. Sometimes I reveal I am Catholic, if it might add a feeling of connection. It is not entirely that I am acting. I am myself but slightly strained, like you might strain slightly in order to hear something whispered.

Yesterday an agent took me into the most lily-white neighborhood imaginable, took me right into the spotless kitchen, the dishwasher rumbling, full of the children's dishes. I opened the closets as if I were a thief, as if I were filthying them, as if I believe about myself what they believe: that I'm "passing," that my silence is a crime.

The first woman I knew about who "passed" was the bronze-haired daughter of insurance money, one of the wealthiest black families in the United States. I remember my mother telling me stories of her white roadster, how she wrote plays and opened a theater. She had directed several of the plays in which my mother and father had acted. She went to New York to "make it" and was published in *The New York Times*. I was seven when my father went down to meet the midnight train that brought her home: people said she had confessed to her rich fiancé that she was black and he had jilted her. They dressed her in a long bronze dress, a darkened tone of her long auburn hair. She looked like Sleeping Beauty in a casket made especially for her with a glass top.

My mother told me how, when she was young, her mother used to get great pleasure when she would seat her daughter in the white part of the train and then depart, as if she were her servant. She said her mother would stand alongside the train and wave good-bye with a smile on her face, like a kid who has gotten away with the cookies. And my father told how, during the Detroit riots of 1943, when black men were being pulled off the buses and beaten to death, he used to walk down East Grand Boulevard as a dare.

Of course, we are never caught; it is absolutely inconceivable that we could go unrecognized, that we are that much like them. In fact, we are the same.

When Bruce and I first got married, I had been looking for an apartment for months. Finally, I found a building in a nice neighborhood with a playground nearby, and a school that was integrated. I rang the bell and was relieved when the supervisor who came to the door was black. I loved the apartment. Then I became terrified. Should I tell him we're black? Would that make my chances of getting the apartment greater? I wondered if he would be glad to have another black family in the building, or if maybe his job was dependent on his keeping us out. I decided to be silent, to take the chance that he liked me.

When I left, sailing over the George Washington Bridge, I had my first panic attack. I thought I might drive my car right over the edge. I felt so high up there, so disconnected, so completely at my own mercy. Some part of me doesn't give a fuck about boundaries — in fact, sees the boundaries and is determined to dance over them no matter what the consequences are. I am so precarious, strung out between two precipices, that even when I get to the other side, I am still not down, still not so low I can't harm myself.

I could hardly control my car, my heart pounding, my hands sweaty on the wheel. I had to pull off the West Side Highway as soon as I could, and I went into the first place I could find, a meat-packing house. The kind white man let me use the phone to call Bruce before he took me in a big meat truck to the nearest hospital. The doctor said it was anxiety, and I should just go home and rest. For days I was afraid to come out of my house, and even now, though I push myself to do it, every time I go over a high place, or am in a strange territory, I fear I will lose control, that something horrible and destructive will come out of me.

Each night Bruce and I don't talk about it, as if there were no cost to what I'm doing, or as if whatever the cost is I've got to pay.

March

I had told the real estate dealers that Bruce was away on a long trip — I had looked at over eighty houses! — and that I had to make the decision by myself. At night, under cover of darkness, we'd go back and circle the houses and I'd describe the insides.

In Maplewood, a nearby town in which I had looked, the real estate agent took us to the house I had seen alone the day before — a dark, sturdy Tudor — without seeming to bat an eye. However, when we got back to his office and were ready to close the deal, the head broker had intervened. "That house has been sold," he said.

Our agent looked shocked. "No it hasn't," he said stupidly. "I just checked the listing before we went out!"

"Yes it has," the other insisted.

We had called a lawyer who specializes in civil rights cases and he had not been encouraging. "These kinds of cases are hard to prove and your money will be tied up for months."

We finally decided on Upper Montclair. The houses in Essex County are comparatively cheaper than the houses in Bergen County, and even though the neighborhoods aren't integrated, the schools are, since busing is in effect. Many afternoons, instead of asking — not wanting to arouse the suspicions of the real estate agents — I would sit outside the neighborhood schools at lunch hour like a pederast, counting the number of black faces. Though sometimes

I'd be brave and ask. I didn't only want information; I wanted to commit a small revolutionary act — to leave the impression that the world is full of liberal white parents who want change.

When Bruce finally saw the house in Upper Montclair he said, "It's all right. I liked the Tudor much better." I was furious. Didn't he know how hard I had tried! "Next time you look at eighty houses," I had burst out on the way home. At each point, even as we accomplished our goals, we didn't feel proud of ourselves and confirmed in our powers, we felt divided, muted, and out of control.

The real estate dealer in Montclair had been flustered when Bruce showed up at her office. I had hoped that, maybe, since I had purposely let slip he is a vice president at the bank and has hundreds of people working for him (Bruce has the highest position of any black person at the bank), she would decide, as many whites have, that a person with his credentials, whose skin and hair is, in the least, indeterminate, must be something else, Spanish or Arab. But when we signed the contract, she had insisted she and her husband pick up the deposit at our apartment, though it was a half-hour drive. They want to check us out, I thought. I cleaned all day, fixed hors d'oeuvres. I opened a bottle of champagne and we toasted each other, as if we were friends.

During the months we waited for the closing, neither one of us went to the house. We didn't want to rock the boat. Several times minor problems arose, and I couldn't decide whether to get very involved, to bother people, or to stay out of the way.

The week before we moved in, I made a dozen trips with lamps, paintings, books. Emptied of the lady's furniture, the walls showed hand prints, rubs; the carpet was drab, muddied, there was a dinginess to the light. Had they gotten rid of a loser? A few days after, Bruce warned: "Be careful, they know more about us than you think!" A neighbor had come up to him while he was out shoveling snow. "I hear you're a V.P. at the bank and a Michigan man!" Bruce hadn't told *anybody* where he worked or went to school!

Last week the people across the street gave us a cocktail party. I felt grateful, but out of place. Would I break a glass or say something unforgivable? I couldn't get over the feeling that I had to prove myself different from what I was sure almost all of them took for granted — that Bruce and I didn't know anything about wine or art and had never seen an Oriental carpet in our lives — yet at the same time, I had to be absolutely "myself," that was the only way I could earn their respect. I told one woman she had the most beautiful violet eyes — I found out later she was the wife of the president of one of the largest New York brokerage houses — and she looked shocked. She avoided me the rest of the night. Was it wrong to confess love as well as hatred? Suddenly, right in the middle of my urgent desire to belong, came my hatred of them and everything they stood for.

Bruce and I went our separate ways, like those black people who have learned not to sit together in the lunchroom. Sometimes I looked at him from across the room and thought, he looks so uncomfortable. It comes out in the way he spills his drink or drops some dip on his tie and then calls attention to himself: "I spilled something," he says, looking down and dabbing it with his handkerchief.

I know that way we stumble, trying so hard, how something gets blocked so that we either become hard and inflexible or so muted we can't be heard, or maybe something gets out of control, so that no matter what we do, for how long, for countless years, finally we make some mistake, something that we can't make up for, and we don't know why, can't stop ourselves, and, in the end, we are more sorry for our mistake than the ones it hurt.

April

Montclair is divided into two parts, Upper and — though not referred to as such on maps — so-called Lower. A neighbor said that a hundred years ago Upper Montclair was where the rich people lived and Lower Montclair was where the people lived who worked for them. There are lots of mansions and estates on that side of town, but even so, in a way, an invisible map has grown into the nerves and bones of the people, a reference not only to geography but to the importance of the self, who you are in relation to the other. The map is pressed into the feet of the children. The dividing line is Watchung Avenue — you're on one side or the other.

The kids are mixed in the schools because of busing, but lots of white families, and some black, still try to stop it. Just because the kids are in school together doesn't mean things are better. Things seem to be worse. There is a great deal of pain when the dividing line is broken. It is like breaking the self in two. We have nothing to heal it, and no medicine to relieve the pain. We think, Break it and it will heal itself. We just don't know whether it will grow together in such a crooked way that it will never be able to be used.

We know so little — almost nothing about how the cells become part of the body — whether to root the sickness out with surgery, whether that will destroy too many healthy parts, or whether to take tiny pills, every day, for the rest of our lives, to admit we have a chronic disease that we must attend to.

I ran into a woman at the vet's today, a white woman married to a black man whose son is very, very dark. We got into a heavy conversation about Montclair, and when I told her I was black, she couldn't believe it. She wanted to know what color my parents were. I think she feels sad that her son is so dark. She said she and her husband had had a daughter but they "lost" her (a miscarriage?). She never saw her. I guess, looking at me, she wondered what color her daughter would have been.

This woman wanted her son to have the best education, so she put him in a private school in Montclair. But there was so much prejudice, she took him out. He's now in one of the lowest sections in public school. She says he's very bright, but he told her he liked being the smartest kid in the group. He told her, "Don't worry, Mom. I don't want to ever be anything really big. I just want to get by." He's in the sixth grade.

She told me they couldn't get an apartment in Upper Montclair because of her son. When they saw her, fine, but when they saw her son, no way. She said finally they bought a house and as soon as they moved in the neighbors called the law. They had to spend ten thousand dollars on repairs right away. She said she's not running. She's not going no place. If anyone runs, it will be them. She says she doesn't make friends with anyone. Since she's married a black man, she's realized the only real friends you have are your family. She says she's happy with her life. It's the other people who must be unhappy to do all these things. She's just fine.

July

This morning I put my car in the shop. The neighborhood shop. When I went to pick it up I had a conversation with the man who had worked on it. I told him I had been afraid to leave the car there at night with the keys in it. "Don't worry," he said. "You don't have to worry about stealing as long as the niggers don't move in." I couldn't believe it. I hoped I had heard him wrong. "What did you say?" I asked. He repeated the same thing without hesitation.

In the past, my anger would have swelled quickly. I would have blurted out something, hotly demanded he take my car down off the rack immediately, though he had not finished working on it, and taken off in a blaze. I love that reaction. The only feeling of power one can possibly have in a situation in which there is such a sudden feeling of powerlessness is to "do" something, handle the situation. When you "do" something, everything is clear. But this is the only repair shop in the city. Might I have to come back here someday in an emergency?

Blowing off steam is supposed to make you feel better. But in this situation it *doesn't*! After responding in anger, I often feel sad, guilty, frightened, and confused. Perhaps my anger isn't just about race. Perhaps it's like those rapid-fire responses to Bruce — a way of dulling the edge of feelings that lie even deeper.

I let the tension stay in my body. I go home and sit with myself for an hour, trying to grasp the feeling — the odor of self-hatred, the biting stench of shame.

July

Last week a young woman who lives down the street came over for dinner. She's thirty, the daughter of a doctor. She lived in New York for a few years on her own, lost her job, may have had a breakdown, and came home to "get herself together."

After dinner we got into a conversation about Tall Oaks Country Club, where she is the swimming instructor. I asked her hesitantly, but unwilling not to get this information, if blacks were allowed to join. (Everybody on our block belongs; all were told about "the club" and asked to join as soon as they moved in. We were never told or asked to join.)

"No," she said.

"You mean the people on this block who have had us over for dinner, who I have invited to my home for dinner, I can't swim in a pool with them?"

"That's the rule," she said, as if she were stating a mathematical fact. She told us about one girl, the daughter of the president of a bank, who worked on the desk at Tall Oaks. When they told her blacks couldn't join, she quit. I wondered why she told this — the swimming instructor — as if she wasn't ashamed of herself.

I remembered how once she had looked at pictures in our family album and seen my mother's house.

"This is like one of the houses on Upper Mountain Avenue," she had exclaimed. "I didn't know black people had homes like this!"

I have begun therapy — with a white therapist — and when I told him about how disturbed I was by this conversation, he said he didn't believe that people were like this anymore. He said I would have to try to join to be able to tell. He told me it had something to do with how I see myself as deprived by my family, my neurosis.

Four days ago Ann called, the woman down the street, asking if my son could baby-sit. I like this woman. I don't know why. She has that red hair and ruddy coloring out of a Rubens painting. Easy to talk to. She and her husband are members of the club, and I couldn't resist telling her the story.

She said, "Oh, Toi, John and I wanted to invite you and Bruce to be our guests at a dinner party. I was just picking up the phone to call when Holly [a woman who lives across the street] called and said, 'Do you think that's a good idea? You better check with the Stevens [old members of the club] first.' I called George and he called a meeting of the executive committee. We met for four hours. Several of us said we would turn in our resignations unless you could come. But the majority felt it wouldn't be a good idea because you would see all the good things and want to join, and since you couldn't join, it would just hurt you and be frustrating. John and I wanted to quit. I feel very ashamed of myself, but the next summer when I was stuck in the house with the kids and nothing to do, we started going again."

When I related this to my therapist, he said it sounded like my feelings about my mother. I see my mother as having something that she is keeping from me, some love that I can't get from her. He said that all this feeling of deprivation is really because I can't get to the sadness of living without her.

Yesterday the executive board of Poets & Writers of New Jersey met to read the poetry of a new applicant. I am a member. Right away I said to myself,

"The poetry is too loose. Not precise enough. She's not ready." But soon after I recognized certain colloquialisms, settings. She is probably black, I thought.

I know these people are very particular about who they let in. They vote no on just about everybody. I'm usually the one who believes that seriousness is the best criterion for entrance. I got terrified. Would I have to stand up for this woman's work against all these people? How could I do so when I didn't really believe in it? Was I judging her too harshly because she is black? Was I putting myself down by judging her harshly? Could I hear her voice inside these poems? Or am I too brainwashed by the sound of Yeats, Eliot, Lowell, Plath? What was I expecting? I went foggy. If I was going to have to fight for her, I'd do it. But I prayed I wouldn't have to. She had to get in. Her voice had to have a place.

Luckily, everyone in the group said she was good. I put her poems back on the table. I didn't say anything.

August

It's the loneliness I can't take, the way the house stuffs up with it like a head that can't breathe. The sun coming through the glass in the middle of the afternoon magnifies perfection. Everything's right. The floors shine with an underlife like the several colors in a woman's hair, the chandelier's sounding brilliance, the little islands of furniture placed like this and this, the red throw's splash of color. Everything wakes me as if my feet were electrified. My eyes are driven outward, out of my body. Such cleanliness hates me; it wants me to concede to its beauty. It asks, *Are you doing your part? Did you turn the burner off? Did you check the gas? Did you take the keys?* "Did you" has a life of its own, a furious life that could commit murder and put the blame on me! Oh boiler in the basement, red eye of some miserable housewife, or some child locked in the basement with spiders. Yesterday, taking the clothes down into the dark, I felt that emptiness at the top of a scream. I feel the atmosphere, like a woman in a huge tank walking underwater. The house is so large it never ends. Or else I am lying on my back like an upturned turtle. Am I dreaming they hate me? Am I dreaming the house, the block, the neighborhood? Is the whole world my evil dream?

My son comes home. I make all the right motions. I move the pots, my lips ask questions. I reassure. I'm not pretending! I can become the actual thing. It animates me, like a machine that knows its own duties. It's hardest when Bruce comes home, when part of me for an instant hopes, when I can almost touch the end of loneliness—like a smell you can almost name.

Each night we sit in the TV dark. He is calm, contained. Sometimes I tell him I don't feel love. One time I even went back to Detroit, to my mother's house. But he came and got me and just said, "Get in the car." Such love I don't deserve! The best thing I can do is keep my mouth shut. But he opens the door, puts his coat away, and speaks, and his actual weight enters me. When I come home late, I notice our bedroom windows mildly lit, just like the windows of the house next door.

It makes you have to bear it, like a cross, like the weight of a body that isn't there, like a blessing you go on and on expecting, until it burns you raw, sharpens, and turns to pain.

August

I haven't slept much at all for several weeks, and when I do I dream of shit, overflowing toilets, water and shit up to my ankles. A few weeks ago I was at the doctor's office and picked up an issue of *Time*. I see that a comet is coming toward the earth and a feeling came over me as if I were paralyzed, in a box without a key. I keep seeing the comet, like that dream I had when I was twelve when my mother and father were divorcing, the moon and sun rushing toward each other. I sit up in bed all night, or fall asleep and dream dreams I can't bear to remember.

My father called last night to say he was sending my half-brother this summer and I wanted to scream, "How dare you assume I'll take care of your son, your precious son, when you didn't do a goddamned thing for me!" But I didn't. I said OK so fast it was as if I didn't even need to think it over. I love my brother and am happy to see him. But I am depressed and I can hardly take care of myself and my own family.

I am reading a book by Arthur Janov called *The Primal Scream*. I heard John Lennon used this form of therapy. There was a pain locked up inside him since childhood about his mother abandoning him, and the only way he could express it was by letting himself go, screaming until the deepest part of his pain came to the surface. I'm terrified to do this, that I might start screaming and never stop, but I'm desperate to get better so tonight I creep downstairs to the basement when everyone is sleeping. It is two o'clock and I am so frightened of the darkness, the furnace's glowing eye, the thousand leggers and spiders, my whole body is cold. I go down on all fours like an animal, I put a pillow over my mouth so that I won't wake anybody, and I start to scream. At first it is a small scream, as if I know what I am doing, but the longer I scream, the more crazy I sound. I scream and I can't remember what the scream before sounded like. I hear myself call my grandmother's name, the one whose breast I sucked until I was seven and she died. The one who wasn't afraid of my father. "Re," I scream, "Re." I want her to come back and protect me.

Bruce comes down in his tee shirt and jockey shorts. There must be a moon out because I see his naked thighs and forearms lit up in a slash of silvery light as he comes down the stairs, slowly, as if he's sinking in water. He seems afraid to touch me. He speaks softly, "Are you all right?" I tell him to go back to bed. What can he do? He has to go to work tomorrow. He can't stay up all night and hold me. And he won't. Even when he tries, he falls asleep. I feel his body trying, it jerks a little, and then he falls off to that slow regular breathing, and I know I am alone.

I go back upstairs and sit at the dining room table in the dark. I sit there under the chandelier I've cleaned until the dark sets it to music. It makes a clear inhuman sound, as if it has no memory of touch.

I pick up a pencil and open my notebook. I can't think of anything to write, just little marks like chicken scratch. The only words that come are: "Like a tree in hostile soil."

(1997)

Wanda Coleman   (b. 1946)

anda Coleman was born on November 13, 1946, in Los Angeles, California, to George and Lewana Scott Evans. Growing up in the Watts section of Los Angeles, Coleman began writing poetry in high school and was published in several local newspapers. The Watts riots of 1965 not only greatly influenced Coleman but also fueled the civil rights debates by highlighting racial tensions and poor inner-city conditions. Coleman stayed in Los Angeles to attend college and then to serve as writer-in-residence at Studio Watts from 1968 to 1969. She also worked as a transcriber, clerk, waitress, editor, and recruiter, as well as a staff writer for the National Broadcasting Company's *Days of Our Lives* (1975–76), for which she won an Emmy in 1976 for the Best Writing in a Daytime Drama.

Ranging from drama to fiction and poetry, Coleman's works include *Art in the Court of the Blue Flag* (1977), *Mad Dog, Black Lady* (1979), *Imagoes* (1983), *War of Eyes and Other Stories* (1988), *African Sleeping Sickness: Stories and Poems* (1990), *Hand Dance* (1993), *Native in a Strange Land: Trials and Tremors* (1996), *Mambo Hips and Make Believe: A Novel* (1999), *Love-ins with Nietzsche* (2000), and *Mercurochrome: New Poems* (2001). Much of Coleman's writing examines exclusion in America with the goal of eliminating racism and sexism from social institutions, and it often highlights the struggles of the urban poor, especially those who are women. Because Coleman is not strictly an academic writer, she challenges some of the critical methods through which literature is often examined. Nonetheless, she has received numerous literary honors, including a National Endowment for the Arts Fellowship (1981) and a Guggenheim Fellowship (1984). In addition to being a finalist for the National Book Award, she won the Lenore Marshall Poetry Prize for *Bathwater Wine* (1998) and the Harriette Simpson Arnow Prize for Fiction for *African Sleeping Sickness* (1990).

Coleman's work has appeared in several literary magazines and journals, including *Partisan Review, Black American Literary Forum, Callaloo, Negro Digest*, and *Michigan Quarterly Review*. Coleman continues to give powerful spoken word performances, often accompanied by jazz or blues music. Her poem "Emmett Till," first published in the journal *Callaloo* in 1986, and later reprinted in *African Sleeping Sickness*, remembers the fourteen-year-old whose 1955 murder became a touchstone for civil rights activism.

Emmett Till

1
river jordan run red

rainfall panes the bottom acreage — rain
black earth blacker still

blackness seeps in seeps down
the mortal gravity of hate-inspired poverty
Jim Crow nidus

*the alabama the apalachicola the arkansas the arroostook
the altamaha*

killing of 14-year-old
stirs nation, there will be a public wake

works its way underground
scarred landscape veined by rage
sanctified waters flow
go forth

the bighorn the brazos

along roan valley walls blue rapids
wear away rock
flesh current quickly courses thru
the front page news amber fields purple mountains
muddies

*the chattahoochee the cheyenne the chipewa the cimarron
the colorado the columbia the connecticut the cumberland*

waftage

spirit uplifted eyes head heart
imitation of breath chest head heart
the grotesque swim up the styx
level as rainwater into its floodplain

the des moines

blood river born

2

ebony robe aflow
swathed hair of the black madonna
bereft of babe

the flint

that hazel eye sees
the woman
she fine mighty fine
she set the sun arising in his thighs

the hudson the humboldt the illinois

and he let go a whistle
a smooth long all-american hallelujah whistle
appreciation. a boy

the james the klamath

but she be a white woman. but he be
a black boy

*the maumee the minnesota the mississippi the missouri
the mohican*

raping her with that hazel eye

the ohio

make some peckerwood pass water mad
make a whole tributary of intolerance

*the pearl the pecos the pee dee the penobscot
the north platte the south platte the potomac*

vital fluid streaming forth in holy torrents

think about it. go mad go blind
go back to africa go civil rights go go

the red the white and the blue

run wine

3

silt shallows the slow sojourn seaward

they awakened him from sleep
that early fall morning
they made him dress
they hurried Emmett down to the water's edge

the roanoke

after the deed
they weighted him down

tossed him in
for his violation

the sacramento the salt the san juan the savannah
the smoke

from the deep dank murk of consciousness a birth
oh say do you see the men off
the bank dredging in that
strange jetsam

the tennessee the trinity

a lesson
he had to be taught — crucified (all a nigger
got on his mind) for rape by eye that
wafer-round hazel offender plucked out
they crown him

the wabash

cuz she was white woman virtue and he
be a black boy lust

the yazoo the yellowstone

oh say Emmett Till can you see Emmett Till
crossed over into campground

spill tears
nimbus threatening downpour
sweetwater culls into its soulplain

come forth to carry the dead child home

4
at my mouth forking

autumn 1955, lord
kidnapped from his family visit
lord!
money road shanty
lord!
his face smashed in
lord! lord!
His body beaten beyond cognition

river mother carries him

laid in state
sovereign at last

that all may witness true majesty
cast eyes upon

murder

the youth's body too light
was weighted down in barbed wire & steel

dumped into the river agape a ripple a wave
(once it was human)

aweigh. awade in water. bloated
baptized

and on that third day awaft
from the mulky arm of the tallahatchie
stretched cross cotton-rich flats
of delta

on that third day
he rose

and was carried forth to that promised land

(1986)

David Hernandez (b. 1946)

Born on May 1, 1946, in Cidra, Puerto Rico, David Hernandez immigrated to Chicago with his parents in 1955. In order to make poetry more accessible, particularly to people outside of the academy, Hernandez began performing his poetry in the late 1960s, first to street gangs in Chicago, then at local community centers, including Hull House. He was working in 1967 as a community activist with the Commission of Youth Welfare for the City of Chicago when he encountered one of the city's North Side gangs, which later reformed to become La Gente, or "the people" — an inclusive organization in Chicago's Lakeview neighborhood that provides community services, such as free breakfast programs. In addition to helping found La Gente, Hernandez served as the organization's minister of information and edited the group's newsletter, *The Roscoe Street Blues*. In 1971 Hernandez organized a band, Street Sounds, to play with him at poetry readings. After teaching poetry workshops at Chicago's public schools and community centers, he developed El Taller, or "the workshop," along with other artists from diverse cultural backgrounds, in order to conduct arts programs for local children and adults. The group also organized numerous local festivals and block parties.

Many label Hernandez as Chicago's "unofficial poet laureate," as the city commissioned him to write a poem for its 150th anniversary in 1987. His poetry has appeared in numerous literary magazines, journals, and newspapers, including *TriQuarterly*, *Overtures*, the *Chicago Sun-Times*, and the *Chicago Tribune*, as well as in several anthologies, such as *From the Belly of the Shark* (1973), *Stray Bullets* (1991), and *Unsettling America* (1994). Hernandez's published volumes of poetry include *Despertando/Waking Up* (1971), *Collected Words for a Dusty Shelf* (1973), *Satin City Lullaby* (1987), *Automaton Amok* (1989), *Rooftop Piper* (1991), and *Elvis Is Dead but at Least He's Not Gaining Any Weight* (1995). Additionally, he has served as editor for three anthologies, including the *Nosotros Anthology*, *Revista Chicano-Riquena* (1977) — one of the first collections of Chicano and Latino writers to receive national acclaim. Hernandez has also produced, along with Street Sounds, several audio recordings of his poetry, and for a time, he wrote a column for the independent literary magazine *U-Direct*.

Hernandez's poem "Martin and My Father" is included both in the anthology *Unsettling America* and in his volume *Elvis Is Dead but at Least He's Not Gaining Any Weight*. The poem addresses accepting nonviolent direct action as a viable means of protest and change and explores the relationship between art and political activism. Hernandez's poetry frequently reflects his belief that the arts can and should unite different communities for political struggles and his desire to break down the ethnic barriers that divide people in order to build coalitions. To that end, Hernandez often writes in English and Spanish, bridging communication between people who speak those languages. His poetry depicts how different forms of oppression, such as racism, economic exploitation, and sexism, are linked and examines the tensions between individual identities and larger communities.

Hernandez's honors include awards and fellowships from the Illinois Arts Council, the National Council of Christians and Jews, and the National Endowment for the Arts. Currently, he teaches poetry classes for Chicago's public schools and at several universities, including Malcolm X College in Chicago.

Martin and My Father

Martin was too peaceful for me.
He let those Deep-South dogs bite him
Police club his head
Suburbanites stone him
Cowards bomb his house
Firemen hose him down
and judges throw him in jail.

I used to pack a .357 Magnum
and if anybody messed with me,
I would aim, pull the trigger
and feel the kick of the gun
saturated in spic anger.
I wanted to kill all the
racist pigs in the world
and marching peacefully
like Martin did, wasn't
about to do it.

One time while arguing with my father
I pulled a knife on him.
That night he cried himself to sleep
and I felt like an assassin.
The next day I heard that Martin
was shot dead and my heart crumbled
for him and my father.

My anger turned ice-blue hot,
well-kept, on target,
proportionately forever
and it was on this anvil
that my pen was forged.

So I took my gun and knife,
threw them in the lake
and watched them drown.
Then I went home and while
my father took a nap on the couch
with the t.v. blaring about
Martin's death,
I kissed him with a poem.

And I'll tell you,
      That Martin,
            He was something else.

(1994)

Marilyn Nelson   (b. 1946)

arilyn Nelson was born on April 26, 1946, in Cleveland, Ohio, to Melvin M. Nelson, an air force officer, and Johnnie Mitchell Nelson, a teacher. After graduating in 1968 with a bachelor's degree from the University of California at Davis, Nelson attended the University of Pennsylvania, where she earned a master's degree in 1970. That same year, she married Erdmann F. Waniek, although the couple later divorced. In 1979 she graduated from the University of Minnesota with a doctorate and married Roger R. Wilkenfeld, with whom she has two children.

Nelson taught at several universities in the United States and Europe, including Nissum Seminarium in Denmark and Vanderbilt University in Nashville, Tennessee, before she began teaching creative writing and Aframerican and American Ethnic Literature at the University of Connecticut in 1978. Nelson's published volumes of poetry include *For the Body* (1978); *The Homeplace* (1990) — a finalist for the 1991 National Book Award and winner of the 1992 Anisfield-Wolf Book Award; *Magnificat* (1994); *The Fields of Praise: New and Selected Poems* (1997), which earned her a second nomination for the National Book Award; *Fortune's Bones: The Manumission Requiem* (2004); and *A Wreath for Emmett Till* (2005). Nelson's poetry often explores her ancestry and family history in addition to examining the issue of racial identity. Some of her poetry volumes include photographs as well. "Tuskegee Airfield," along with several other poems in *The Homeplace*, focuses on her father's experiences as one of the Tuskegee Airmen, an all-black squadron famous for its accomplishments during World War II. Collaborating with Pamela Espeland, Nelson also published two volumes of children's poetry, *Hundreds of Hens and Other Poems for Children* (1982) and *The Cat Walked through the Casserole and Other Poems for Children* (1984).

Nelson is the recipient of numerous fellowships, including a Fulbright (1995), a Guggenheim (2001), a Kent (1976), and two from the National Endowment for the Arts (1981 and 1990). Additionally, she won the Coretta Scott King Honor Book citation in 2002 for *Carver: A Life in Poems* (2001) — a lyrical biography of George Washington Carver — and in 2001 Nelson was named Connecticut's poet laureate.

Tuskegee Airfield

(For the Tuskegee Airmen)

These men,
these proud black men:
our first to touch
their fingers to the sky.

The Germans learned to call them
Die Schwarzen Vogelmenschen.
They called themselves
The Spookwaffe.

Laughing.
And marching to class under officers
whose thin-lipped ambition
was to *wash the niggers out.*

Sitting at attention
for lectures about ailerons, airspeed, altimeters
from boring lieutenants who believed
you monkeys ain't meant to fly.

Oh, there were parties,
cadet-dances, guest appearances
by the Count
and the lovely Lena.

There was the embarrassing
adulation of Negro civilians.
A woman approached my father in a bar
where he was drinking with his buddies.
Hello, Airman. She held out her palm.
Will you tell me my future?

There was that,
like a breath of pure oxygen.
But first
they had to earn wings.

There was this one instructor
who was pretty nice.
I mean, we just sat around
and *talked* when a flight had gone well.

But he was from Minnesota,
and he made us sing
the Minnesota Fight Song
before we took off.

If you didn't sing it,
your days were numbered.
"Minnesota, hats off to thee . . ."
That bastard!

One time I had a check-flight
with an instructor from Louisiana.
As we were about to head for base,
he chopped the power.

Force-landing, nigger.
There were trees everywhere I looked.
Except on that little island
I began my approach.

The instructor said, *Pull Up.*
That was an excellent approach.
Real surprised.
But where would you have taken off, wise guy?

I said, Sir,
I was ordered
to land the plane.
Not take off.

The instructor grinned.
Boy, if your ass
is as hard as your head,
you'll go far in this world.

(1990)

Bebe Moore Campbell (1950–2006)

Born Elizabeth Bebe Moore on February 18, 1950, Bebe Moore Campbell was the only child of George and Doris Moore. After the couple divorced, Campbell stayed in Philadelphia, Pennsylvania, where she attended school, to live with her mother and grandmother, but she spent summers in North Carolina with her father, who was rendered paraplegic in an automobile accident when Campbell was not yet a year old. Campbell's second book, *Sweet Summer: Growing Up with and without My Dad* (1989), recounts her childhood visits to North Carolina — visits that expanded her personal understanding of segregation from its veiled northern version to include its explicit southern manifestation. After graduating from Philadelphia's High School for Girls in 1968, Campbell attended the University of Pittsburgh, where she earned a bachelor's degree in elementary education in 1972. Campbell taught for five years and then stopped in order to pursue her writing and move to Washington, D.C., where she lived with her daughter and husband, whom she later divorced. Campbell then lived in Los Angeles with her second husband, Ellis Gordon, a banker with whom she had a son. In addition to writing, Campbell served as a regular commentator for National Public Radio's *Morning Edition*. She died on November 27, 2006, in Los Angeles, of brain cancer.

Campbell's fiction often depicts the detrimental effects of racism on individuals and their relationships. Her first, most critically acclaimed novel, *Your Blues Ain't Like Mine* (1992), was commended by the *New York Times* as one of the most notable books of 1992. Inspired by the 1955 murder of Emmett Till — called Armstrong Todd in the book — *Your Blues Ain't Like Mine* traces through several decades the impact of Till's death on families from Mississippi and Chicago. The excerpt below features a family based upon that of Till's killers, as they watch the 1987 civil rights documentary *Eyes on the Prize* and consider their role in historic events.

Campbell's second novel also had its basis in real life. *Brothers and Sisters* (1994) was inspired by the beating of Rodney King and the ensuing Los Angeles riots and was named a *New York Times* bestseller within two weeks of its release. Campbell also published two more bestsellers, *Singing in the Comeback Choir* (1998) and *What You Owe Me* (2001), which the *Los Angeles Times* named the best book of 2001. In addition to portraying the effects of racism, Campbell's writing depicts class discrimination, poverty, and sexual harassment, and her fiction focuses on black communities in both urban and rural settings.

Though she is known for her fiction, Campbell also wrote two radio plays, *Sugar on the Floor* and *Old Lady Shoes*; a stage play, *Even with the Madness*, which debuted in New York in 2003; and nonfiction, *Successful Women, Angry Men: Backlash in the Two-Career Marriage* (1986). Campbell published articles and essays as well in *Time, Essence, New York Times Magazine*, the *Washington Post*, the *Los Angeles Times*, and *Ebony*. Campbell's literary awards include the National Association of Negro Business and Professional Women's Literature Award (1978), the National Association for the Advancement of Colored People's Image Award for Literature (1994), a National Endowment for the Arts Literature Grant (1980), and the Distinguished Alumni Award from the University of Pittsburgh. Campbell was a member of the National Alliance for the Mentally Ill (NAMI) and a founding member of NAMI-Inglewood. Her children's book, *Sometimes My Mommy Gets Angry*, won the National Alliance for the Mentally Ill's Outstanding Literature Award in 2003.

Selection from *Your Blues Ain't Like Mine*

Chapter 44

At twenty-four, Doreen was the Delta beauty her mother had been, but already the loveliness that clung to her had a fleeting, fragile quality, like that of a ripe peach just before it begins to spoil. There was a hardness about the set of her mouth and in her eyes, and a vertical line was etched between her eyebrows. The line deepened as she drove up to her parents' house, the last notes of "Thriller" were playing on the radio. For a moment she smiled, thinking of how her three-year-old, Melanie, started dancing whenever she heard the Michael Jackson song; but when she saw her father rushing out the front door onto the porch, his eyes wild and hollow and red-rimmed from drinking, her smile faded. She thought of her mother's hysterical voice on the telephone and then recalled her own tears when her ex-husband, Crosby, used to hit her. Asshole, she thought, looking at her father.

Floyd shouted at his daughter. "That nigger mayor in Philadelphia bombed a whole house full of niggers." He started to laugh.* "They say we treat them bad." When Doreen didn't speak, when she kept walking, he ran and stood in front of the door and yelled, "Hey! Hey! You ain't got no business coming between a man and his wife. That's what's wrong with this country now."

"Mama!" Doreen yelled, and pushed right past Floyd, who stamped around on the porch and then sat down mumbling to himself.

"Lordhavemercy," Doreen said as she stepped over beer bottles, spilled food, and empty plates on the living room floor. Three of the four kitchen chairs were turned over, pillows from the tattered tweed sofa were thrown all over the tiny room, and the one good lamp they had was broken. The inside of the house looked as though King Kong had used it as a dance floor. Lily was balled up in

---

* In 1985, Philadelphia, Pennsylvania, police bombed a row house occupied by an African solidarity organization called MOVE, killing eleven people (including five children) and devastating a full city block. The city's mayor at the time was an African American named Wilson Goode.

a corner of the sofa, crying softly. "Mama — " Doreen gasped when she saw her mother's eye.

There was ice in the tiny freezer compartment of the refrigerator, and Doreen picked out three cubes and stuck them inside a sour-smelling dishcloth. She put the ice pack on her mother's eye, which was swollen and darkening rapidly, then fixed them both a cup of coffee, "Mama," she said to Lily, "you can't stay with him no more."

"Doreen . . ." Lily began, wiping her uncovered eye, struggling to stand up.

Doreen held up her hand. As she held the ice over her mother's eye, she said, "Mama, he's an alcoholic, and he won't get any better, with you taking this kinda shit offa him."

"Well, I just don't believe Floyd is no real alcoholic," Lily said, her words coming out fluttery and soft as magnolia petals. "He's just been a little down ever since he had that accident. And he took it kinda hard when Mamie passed."

"It's been eight years since he got hurt, and Grandma's been dead for three. Mama, he's addicted to alcohol, and your not owning up to it makes it easier for him to deny it. You're what they call a codependent. My girlfriend said they talked about that on Donahue." Doreen's voice was dull with fatigue. Lily pulled her daughter's hand away and placed the ice pack on the table next to her coffee; her black eye shimmered under the kitchen light.

Lily said quickly, "Now listen, sugar. Men are gon' always get drunk every now and then." She squeezed her daughter's knee with her palm and let out a little conspiratorial giggle. "Us women just have to put up with it as best we can and learn to stay out of their way."

"That's bullshit, Mama," Doreen said, and she instantly regretted the harshness in her voice; her mother looked as though she'd been slapped. She said gently, "Hasn't he made your life a living hell already? All that meanness he got inside of him, all that ugliness he can't control. What do you think he's gon' do with it? He will kill you. Just like he done that boy."

She could see her mother struggling with the twin fears: of being with her father and of being alone. Why couldn't she see that she'd be better off without him? Doreen reached across the table and picked up the dishcloth and dabbed at her forehead, then fanned herself, spreading the sour odor all through the room. Her mother's knuckles were scraped raw, probably from trying to crawl away from Floyd. The last time, he'd kicked her in her side and cracked a rib. Before that he broke her tooth.

"Floydjunior was by here yesterday," Lily said softly. "He looked good. He's talking about going up to Jackson or Memphis and getting a job."

Doreen pulled a pack of cigarettes out of her pocket and lit one. She stood up. "Yeah, he's always talking about working. How much did he hit you up for this time?"

Lily looked hurt. "Well, he's trying. Doreen, he's sticking with the program. He's gon' beat them drugs this time. You'll see."

"Mama. Mama. You done had faith in the wrong men your whole life." Doreen sighed.

"I'm not like you young girls. I was raised to trust men. All of them."

"Go get you some clothes. You're coming to live with me."

THE FLUORESCENT LIGHTS inside the Jitney Jungle were bright as a noonday sun; Lily had to step back and blink to adjust her eyes, but the chilled air felt good on her back. She wished that she could put that cool air in a bottle and carry it to the cramped, stuffy trailer that she and Doreen and her two granddaughters shared.

The store was pretty near empty. The only clerks, two young white girls with identical blond dye jobs, were gossiping with each other as though they were at home in their own bedrooms with the door shut, talking on the telephone. When Lily walked past, the smaller one was saying, "He ain't that good a kisser." Then Lily heard the taller of the two, her stage whisper rough as a Brillo pad: "There go Miss America, forty years later." Lily stood absolutely still. Forty years. She heard the two girls snicker, and she sucked in her stomach hard and held it for the minute or two it took to pass by them. By the time she reached the row of cookies and snacks, her belly was hanging out dispiritedly. Her rubber thongs slapped hard against the concrete floor, and she left a little trail of mud behind her as she walked through the aisles.

The meat was kept toward the back of the store. Lily didn't have any business even looking, and she knew it, but she stopped to examine the roasts and legs of lamb. The meat looked fresh and inviting. If she could have that roast, she would bake homemade biscuits and peach pie and make lemonade to wash it down. She'd smother her some cabbage and throw carrots and new potatoes in the pot. Then she and Doreen and the kids would sit down at the table and they'd light candlesticks and have music playing in the background. Her grandbabies deserved a nice dinner. Lily stared at the meat a long time before she reached into the freezer. She looked at the price: $14.89. Tears stung her eyes. Didn't make no sense. You could work like a goddamn slave and still not be able to have the kind of Sunday dinner you wanted for your grandbabies. Not even a little thing like Sunday dinner.

Lily stood at the short girl's register, behind a trim black woman wearing high heels and a business suit, who pulled three steaks out of her basket, a box of Rice-A-Roni, a head of lettuce, some tomatoes, and diet Thousand Island dressing. Seemed like everyplace she went there were dressed-up black people, looking like they were in a hurry. They even had them a couple of mayors in towns right in the Delta, and there was a black congressman, light-skinned, with sharp, white-man's features. Lily forced herself not to stare at the food; she didn't want to look at the checker, either, so her unfocused eyes wandered around the store. When the woman stepped back and bumped into her, Lily froze, not out of pain but from the sheer panic that the lady would turn around and look at her to apologize; she didn't want anyone's eyes on her. But the woman never said a word, which left Lily feeling outraged and relieved at the same time. While the checker was ringing up three packs of Winstons and a box of Pampers, Lily read the headlines on the *Star*. There were photos of Michael Jackson, showing the progressive changes that plastic surgery had made on his face. Lily stared at each face carefully, trying to discern exactly how the surgery had altered the singer. Melanie, the older girl, loved Michael Jackson. The checker rang up Lily's purchases and gave her eighty-three cents back. The giggles started up again as soon as she walked away, but Lily tried not to hear them.

She didn't miss Floyd, and it was shocking to think that she could live with a man for all those years, have his babies, go through all kinds of trials and tribulations, and then just walk away and not feel anything but relief. In the last two weeks she had had to ask herself just why in hell she had always been so afraid of being without him. She didn't even miss having sex, or what was left of their sex life, which was pretty much nothing but huffing and puffing and fumbling around, her looking off at the ceiling while he put his mouth on her.

And it was a relief not to have to listen to him talking about niggers. It got so that all he talked about was how much he hated niggers, like that was filling the space that a job would have occupied. Talking about how he'd like to kill Jesse Jackson. How Bill Cosby and Michael Jackson were part of a plot for blacks to take over the world. And then the next thing she knew, all those mean-looking men, mostly young, were coming to her house, drinking beer and talking about the niggers. Such an assortment of tattoos she'd never seen in all her life. Just trash. And she could hardly believe it when Floyd started bragging to them about killing Armstrong Todd. And those bums egging him on.

Hating niggers was one thing, but being crazy was another, and that crew Floyd had joined, well, they weren't dealing with a full deck half the time.

She didn't even miss cooking for him, or talking to him, or lying next to him in bed, not even that. Now she slept with Melanie and cuddled her warm little body all night long, and that sleep was sweeter than any she could remember.

The trailer was even hotter than when she'd left for the store. Doreen was sitting on the sofa with the baby sprawled across her lap, and she was fanning her with a magazine cover and had her other hand soaking in a pot of hot water and Epsom salts. Melanie was sitting on the floor, drinking purple Kool-Aid and watching television. "You get Crystal's diapers?" Doreen asked.

Lily nodded. "Your hands still bothering you?"

"They hurt something terrible, and I believe my fingers will smell like catfish for the rest of my natural life."

"I don't see why you just don't quit that job, Doreen," Lily said.

"And do what?"

"Well, you could —"

"I'm not getting back on the county, Mama," Doreen said sharply. "I don't want Melanie and Crystal to grow up seeing me standing in no welfare office with everybody looking down on us like we're some kind of sewer-rat trash. Cleaning catfish for the New Plantation may not be the easiest job in the world, but it beats welfare every day. No offense," she added, noticing her mother's lowered eyes.

"At least your hands wouldn't be hurting you."

Switching the pan of water, Doreen said, "Don't worry, Mama. There's gon' be some changes at the New Plantation. You'll see."

THE NEXT MORNING, while Doreen was at work, Lily cleaned the trailer until it was gleaming, and later she started a garden, planted string beans, squash, cucumbers, lettuce, and tomatoes in the plot near the trailer. She put the girls down for a nap after lunch, and then she watched her stories. And when the stories went off, she turned on *The Oprah Winfrey Show*. How she started watching that was by accident. One time she was changing the channel, and she saw a black woman holding a microphone and crying. Lily hadn't heard anything about her, but she was so startled and comforted by the sight of the plump, brown-skinned woman crying that she sat down and watched the whole thing. She was amazed when it turned out that what Oprah was weeping about was the fact that her cousin had molested her when she was a child, and that all the women on the stage had been abused when they were children. And of course Lily sobbed too, and thought about her uncle Charlie. An 800 number for victims of child abuse to call came across the screen, and she wrote it down, but she never did use it.

BY LATE AUGUST they were eating the vegetables from the garden. At the dinner table, Melanie sat close to her grandmother and Doreen put the baby in a high chair next to her. "I feel good for the first time in a long time," Lily told her daughter after dinner was finished and they were sipping coffee. "I mean, I feel peaceful." She lit a cigarette.

"You deserve peace, Mama."

Stinging tears sprang to Lily's eyes. "Do I? Sometimes I wake up in the middle of the night and I just feel so sorry, so sorry for everything."

The heat didn't let up until late in October, and some nights Lily would get in Doreen's Pinto and roll down all the windows and drive along the road as fast as she could, just so she could get a breeze. That was what she thought she wanted, but when she discovered that along with the breeze she got a heady sensation of freedom, she realized that she craved that even more.

Right before Thanksgiving, Doreen came home crying that her hands felt as if they were on fire. Lily had her soak them in Epsom salts, and rubbed them with salve, but nothing gave her relief. "You think you need to see a doctor?" Lily asked.

"I ain't got no money for no doctor," Doreen said. "I get so mad sometimes. Here I am aching like a mule and ain't even got no medical insurance. If one of the kids gets sick, what am I supposed to do? Them same people that own the New Plantation, they worked the niggers to death picking cotton. Now they're trying to pull the same shit. They work us all like dogs. That goddamn Reagan don't give a good goddamn if you ain't rich. I'da been better off with Jesse Jackson for President."

"Lordhavemercy!" Lily said.

"You figure it out, Mama."

"I told you not to work with them," Lily whispered. "They're making you crazy."

Doreen's eyes were red and tired-looking as she spoke. "Mama, either I work with them or I get in the welfare line with them, and you know how I feel about that. I was raised around here, and even though I went to school with them, I always felt like they was different from white people, like I was better than they were. Hell, I was raised on that feeling, and I'll probably take it to my grave, but Mama, you know one thing: It's getting to where I just can't afford thinking like that no more. Them feelings just ain't practical when you work at the New Plantation."

THEY WERE ALL ASLEEP, Doreen and the baby in the bedroom, Lily and Melanie on the daybed, when the phone rang late in January. Lily looked at the clock before she picked it up. It was after midnight.

"Lily," the voice on the other end of the receiver said. "Lily, it's me."

"Who is this?"

"Louetta."

She hadn't heard from her sister-in-law in several years. "Is something wrong, Louetta?"

"You know, I been born again, Lily. I wanted you to know that life has more meaning for me, knowing that Jesus Christ is my personal savior. Praise his name."

The way Louetta said "my personal savior" made Lily think of the Lord dressed in a butler's uniform, walking around picking up her dirty drawers and the banana peels that she'd thrown on the floor. She stifled a giggle and propped herself up on her elbow. "I'm happy for you," Lily said. There was silence on the other end of the line. "Louetta? You still there?"

"Amen," Louetta said. "Lily, I didn't know if you knew about the television program that comes on in February."

"What program?"

"You know how they done give the month of February to the niggers. All over the radio and television, everything is black this and black that. Black History Month. It's like niggers done got to be real people. You know about that?" she said, her Christian voice suddenly full of nails and vinegar.

"I think I heard something about it."

"In February they have right many of them programs about niggers. Anyway, next Monday at nine o'clock they're gon' have a series on, and it's about when they integrated and all. And there's a part about Armstrong Todd. You're in that. I seen it in an ad." Her voice trailed off, spiraling down like a balloon that had been popped. When she spoke again she sounded old. She mumbled, "I don't know. Maybe you can sue them."

"Sue who?"

"The people who put on the television program. Maybe we can make some money offen it."

Lily tasted the words for a little bit, not just the part about the lawsuit or even the "we," but the fact that the whole confusion was going to start up again. Lily spoke slowly, so that Louetta wouldn't miss her meaning. "Somebody told me once that you can't sue if it's history. That makes it what they call public domain. What Floyd and John Earl done is history."

"Oh." Louetta paused for a moment, then sighed. "Well, anyway," she said softly, her voice turning girlish, "it's a five-part series, and it starts Monday." She got quiet, and Lily was afraid she was praying again. Then she said, "I didn't know that you and Floyd was separated. You know, I called over to his house. He didn't want to give me your new number. He must still be mad."

"Floyd stays mad, Louetta. That's what he does for a living."

Louetta started giggling and then got louder and louder, until Lily had to either put the phone down or join in. She laughed.

"Don't it feel good, getting away from them mean ole men?" Louetta said. "Damn! It's like being let out of jail, ain't it? Lily" — her voice cut right through the last vestiges of her laughter so quickly that she sounded hysterical — "Lily, John Earl died last week."

Lily was surprised that she felt nothing. "How?"

"Cancer. He was at the charity hospital in Birmingham. They say he was bad off before he died." Her voice trailed away. "I just thought you'd like to know."

"I reckon I need to know it."

"Sometimes I sit and think about things that have happened. That night, Lily, that night when Floyd and John Earl went after that boy, we couldn't have stopped neither one of them if we . . . I was wrong, Lily. Loving us didn't have nothing to do with it."

"Louetta, I been figured that out."

THE TELEVISION PROGRAM had bouncy theme music. She had watched Cosby and was just having the last laugh with Melanie and Doreen.* She shooed her granddaughter to bed and turned the channel. She and Doreen sat in the dark, smoking Marlboros. Doreen placed her rough, fishy hands in her mother's, and Lily started rubbing them. "Mama, you sure you want to watch this?"

"I'm sure."

And then, halfway through the program, there she was, a pretty girl again, with a waist small enough for a man to put two hands around, a full, firm bustline, hair so shiny a boy could see his face in it.

She couldn't bear looking at herself. She could watch fat Judge Chisolm bellowing for the room to get quiet, and Phineas Newsome and Waldo Anderson admonishing the twelve stern-faced men. She could look at all of them, but when it came to seeing herself, she felt as if she was looking at somebody who didn't know she was about to be ambushed.

All that beauty she had had. Just squandered.

And then she was standing next to Floyd, holding Floydjunior, and the two of them were kissing and the child was squeezed between them.

They showed the niggers being interviewed. The men in suits at the table. The grandmother and mother, tearful and holding on to each other.

And Ida, looking like a young white girl in the black-and-white film. Ida saying, "He didn't deserve to die."

That was hard to watch too.

"Is that you, Grandma?"

Lily turned around, and there was Melanie, standing behind the sofa, her finger in her mouth.

"You get in the bed, Melly," Doreen said, scooping her up and taking her into the bedroom with the baby.

When Doreen returned, Lily said, "Ain't nobody ever loved me the way Melanie does."

"She does love her grandma," Doreen said.

"I don't want her to know about me."

Doreen patted her mother's hand. "Mama, some things you just can't hide."

Lily sighed. "I don't know why I set through that," she said.

"The television made out like it was their story, like the whole thing belonged to them. Like they got all the heroes and all the victims."

The next day Lily was watching Oprah Winfrey interview women who were addicted to food, when she heard the sharp, sudden sound of banging on the

---

* The characters that Lily and Doreen watch in the civil right documentary *Eyes on the Prize* — Judge Chisolm, Phinease Newsome, Waldo Anderson, and Ida Long — appear earlier in the book.

front door. She peered out the window and saw Floyd. She crawled along the floor to the television and turned it down low. Her plan was to lie on her belly. That way she could still watch Oprah, until Floyd got tired and went away.

"I know you're in there, Lily," Floyd yelled. "You open this door. I ain't gon' hurt you none."

"Go away. I got sleeping babies here. You leave me alone."

The air around Lily was quiet for a moment, and then the knocking resumed. She ran to the door. "You go away," she yelled.

"Lily, open the door. I love you. I ain't never loved nobody but you. Things will be different. I won't hurt you no more. I love you, Lily."

She sat on the floor, holding her hands over her ears so she wouldn't hear Floyd's seductive pleading, but her arms started hurting, and after a while she took them down.

"Lily, I love you. Let me come in."

If he hadn't lost his job, he'd be sweet to her, like he used to be when he bought her perfume and lipstick. If only she didn't always make him so mad. "Please go away, Floyd. I want peace." There was a long, heavy silence, and then she heard his receding footsteps.

Doreen sucked her teeth when Lily told her that Floyd had come by. "Crosby tried that same bullshit after I put him out. I knowed that son of a bitch was lying. I told him if he kept bothering me I'd call the sheriff and have him lock his ass up. That's what I told him."

"Your daddy sounded right pitiful," Lily said.

Doreen gave her a sharp look and grabbed her wrist so hard Lily almost cried out. "Don't listen to him, Mama. You be strong."

THE PERVASIVE ODOR of fish was enough to make anyone swoon, but Doreen was used to the smell at the New Plantation. She stood in front of a long steel table that was covered with hundreds of catfish, ripping open their bellies — one every second; that was the requirement. Above the din of the electric head saws, she heard screams coming from the other end of the floor, where the women who chopped off fish heads were stationed. She looked around quickly to see if a supervisor was near, then put down her knife and ran toward the commotion.

By the time she got there, a crowd had formed. Pushing her way to the front, Doreen saw a huge black woman, Fannie, her hand slit from the wrist to the tip of her middle finger. Blood was dripping down her gray uniform onto the floor.

"All right. All right. Everybody back to your stations. The ambulance is coming. Get back to work," called Joe, the supervisor, a short, stocky white man.

"Yeah, but is she gon' have a job when she gets back?" a voice next to Doreen said. She looked up and saw Ida Long and smiled at her. Ida was always talking back to the supervisors and asking questions nobody else had the guts to ask. Now Joe, whose face was turning red from yelling, barked at Ida. "Get back to work. The excitement's over."

But the real excitement began two weeks later, when Fannie returned to work. This time the screams Doreen heard were filled with rage.

When she looked up, she saw Joe and his assistant grab Fannie, each white man taking hold of one of her tremendous arms and pulling her past the workers, who were watching the disturbance with growing agitation on their faces. Fannie broke loose just beyond the head-saw section and turned to face her adversaries, with sweat streaking her face. For a moment she didn't say anything but just stood silent before them, the flesh on her massive body quivering. The entire room was eerily silent, and then Fannie's voice broke over them all like a lightning bolt. "Y'all sons of bitches may think you done seen the last of me, but I'm getting me a lawyer and suing your asses if it's the last thing I do. I ain't taking this shit, you can believe that. You got us holed up in this stinking room working like goddamn slaves for bullshit money, walking around here feeling on our asses and trying to get some pussy, and then when one of us gets hurt on your goddamn machinery, you fire us. Shiiit! You can kiss my black ass. New Plantation can go to hell."

Doreen heard a sudden thunderous sound, like a herd of stampeding bulls, and when she looked around, to her amazement, the whole floor was applauding. The two white men, whose faces were like tomatoes, began turning purple. Someone shouted, "New Plantation can go to hell!" and suddenly the chant was taken up: "New Plantation can go to hell!" The women screamed the words over and over, until the helpless men walked away.

"A WHOLE BUNCH of us who work at New Plantation are meeting over to Ida's tomorrow night," Doreen told her mother at dinner that evening.

Lily opened her mouth, but nothing came out. She swallowed and tried again. "Ida who?"

"Ida Long." Doreen looked at her mother's eyes. "You know her, Mamma?"

"I used to." Lily got up and began clearing the table.

"Yeah, well, Ida's an all-right woman. She's kind of our leader. There's gon' be some changes made at New Plantation. The sisters are coming on strong," Doreen said. She started grinning, and then she let out a war whoop and leaned her head back and started laughing.

"I can't believe you come outta me," Lily said, shaking her head. "You got such gumption."

"Aww, Mama. You got it too."

"No. I don't know what fighting back feels like."

(1992)

Patricia J. Williams (b. 1951)

orn on August 28, 1951, in Boston, Massachusetts, to Isaiah and Ruth Williams, Patricia Joyce Williams began her education on the heels of the Supreme Court's 1954 *Brown v. Board of Education* decision, which drastically altered the dynamics in her predominantly white neighborhood. In 1972 Williams became one of the first African American women to graduate from Wellesley College. Then she attended Harvard Law School, graduating with a juris doctorate in 1975. Williams began teaching at numerous institutions of higher education, including the City University of New York in Queens, the University of Wisconsin Law School, and Columbia University Law School, her current position. Her lectures often focus on the ways that law can maintain or disrupt social hierarchies. Williams also worked as a consumer advocate in the office of the city attorney in Los Angeles and served on the advisory council for the Medgar Evers Center for Law and Social Justice of the City University of New York as well as on the board of directors for the National Organization for Women.

Williams's writing frequently illustrates how government policies affect real individuals, humanizing oppression and creating a new form of legal scholarship. Her essay style, blending the personal and the academic, also helped craft new limits for professional writing in her field. "The Death of the Profane" gives an example of the difficulties she faced as an experimental writer and as an African American woman trying to pass a New York City store's "buzzer test." In addition to a regular column for the *Nation*, Williams's publications include *The Alchemy of Race and Rights* (1991), which won the Bruce K. Gould Book Award; *The Rooster's Egg: On the Persistence of Prejudice* (1995); *Seeing a Colorblind Future: The Paradox of Race* (1998); and *Open House: Of Family, Food, Friends, Piano Lessons, and the Search for a Room of My Own* (2004). Williams won the National Conference of Black Lawyers' Pioneer of Civil and Human Rights Award in 1990; three years later she received the National Women's Political Caucus award for Exceptional Merit Media, and in 2000 she was awarded a MacArthur Fellowship.

Selection from *The Alchemy of Race and Rights*

The Death of the Profane

(a commentary on the genre of legal writing)

Buzzers are big in New York City. Favored particularly by smaller stores and boutiques, merchants throughout the city have installed them as screening devices to reduce the incidence of robbery: if the face at the door looks desirable, the buzzer is pressed and the door is unlocked. If the face is that of an undesirable, the door stays locked. Predictably, the issue of undesirability has revealed itself to be a racial determination. While controversial enough at first, even civil-rights organizations backed down eventually in the face of arguments that the buzzer system is a "necessary evil," that it is a "mere inconvenience" in comparison to the risks of being murdered, that suffering discrimination is not as bad as being assaulted, and that in any event it is not all blacks who are barred, just "17-year-old black males wearing running shoes and hooded sweatshirts."[1]

The installation of these buzzers happened swiftly in New York; stores that had always had their doors wide open suddenly became exclusive or received people by appointment only. I discovered them and their meaning one Saturday in 1986. I was shopping in Soho and saw in a store window a sweater that I wanted to buy for my mother. I pressed my round brown face to the window and my finger to the buzzer, seeking admittance. A narrow-eyed, white teenager wearing running shoes and feasting on bubble gum glared out, evaluating me for signs that would pit me against the limits of his social understanding. After about five seconds, he mouthed "We're closed," and blew pink rubber at me. It was two Saturdays before Christmas, at one o'clock in the afternoon; there were several white people in the store who appeared to be shopping for things for their mothers.

I was enraged. At that moment I literally wanted to break all the windows of the store and take lots of sweaters for my mother. In the flicker of his judgmental gray eyes, that saleschild had transformed my brightly sentimental, joy-to-the-world, pre-Christmas spree to a shambles. He snuffed my sense of humanitarian catholicity, and there was nothing I could do to snuff his, without making a spectacle of myself.

I am still struck by the structure of power that drove me into such a blizzard of rage. There was almost nothing I could do, short of physically intruding upon him, that would humiliate him the way he humiliated me. No words, no gestures, no prejudices of my own would make a bit of difference to him; his refusal to let me into the store — it was Benetton's, whose colorfully punnish ad campaign is premised on wrapping every one of the world's peoples in its cottons and woolens — was an outward manifestation of his never having let someone like me into the realm of his reality. He had no compassion, no remorse, no reference to me; and no desire to acknowledge me even at the estranged level of arm's-length transactor. He saw me only as one who would take his money and therefore could not conceive that I was there to give him money.

In this weird ontological imbalance, I realized that buying something in that store was like bestowing a gift, the gift of my commerce, the lucre of my patronage. In the wake of my outrage, I wanted to take back the gift of appreciation that my peering in the window must have appeared to be. I wanted to take it back in the form of unappreciation, disrespect, defilement. I wanted to work so hard at wishing he could feel what I felt that he would never again mistake my hatred for some sort of plaintive wish to be included. I was quite willing to disenfranchise myself, in the heat of my need to revoke the flattery of my purchasing power. I was willing to boycott Benetton's, random white-owned businesses, and anyone who ever blew bubble gum in my face again.

My rage was admittedly diffuse, even self-destructive, but it was symmetrical. The perhaps loose-ended but utter propriety of that rage is no doubt lost not just to the young man who actually barred me, but to those who would appreciate my being barred only as an abstract precaution, who approve of those who would bar even as they deny that they would bar me.

The violence of my desire to burst into Benetton's is probably quite apparent. I often wonder if the violence, the exclusionary hatred, is equally apparent in the repeated public urgings that blacks understand the buzzer system by putting themselves in the shoes of white storeowners — that, in effect, blacks look into the mirror of frightened white faces for the reality of their undesirability; and that then blacks would "just as surely conclude that [they] would not let [themselves] in under similar circumstances."[2] (That some blacks might agree merely shows that some of us have learned too well the lessons of privatized intimacies of self-hatred and rationalized away the fullness of our public, participatory selves.)

On the same day I was barred from Benetton's, I went home and wrote the above impassioned account in my journal. On the day after that, I found I was still brooding, so I turned to a form of catharsis I have always found healing. I typed up as much of the story as I have just told, made a big poster of it, put a nice colorful border around it, and, after Benetton's was truly closed, stuck it to their big sweater-filled window. I exercised my first-amendment right to place my business with them right out in the street.

So that was the first telling of this story. The second telling came a few months later, for a symposium on Excluded Voices sponsored by a law review. I wrote an essay summing up my feelings about being excluded from Benetton's and analyzing "how the rhetoric of increased privatization, in response to racial issues, functions as the rationalizing agent of public unaccountability and, ultimately, irresponsibility." Weeks later, I received the first edit. From the first page to the last, my fury had been carefully cut out. My rushing, run-on-rage had been reduced to simple declarative sentences. The active personal had been inverted in favor of the passive impersonal. My words were different; they spoke to me upside down. I was afraid to read too much of it at a time — meanings rose up at me oddly, stolen and strange.

A week and a half later, I received the second edit. All reference to Benetton's had been deleted because, according to the editors and the faculty adviser, it was defamatory; they feared harassment and liability; they said printing it would be irresponsible. I called them and offered to supply a footnote attesting to this as my personal experience at one particular location and of a buzzer system not limited to Benetton's; the editors told me that they were not in the habit of publishing things that were unverifiable. I could not but wonder, in this refusal even to let me file an affidavit, what it would take to make my experience verifiable. The testimony of an independent white bystander (a requirement in fact imposed in U.S. Supreme Court holdings through the first part of the century)?[3]

Two days *after* the piece was sent to press, I received copies of the final page proofs. All reference to my race had been eliminated because it was against "editorial policy" to permit descriptions of physiognomy. "I realize," wrote one editor, "that this was a very personal experience, but any reader will know what you must have looked like when standing at that window." In a telephone conversation to them, I ranted wildly about the significance of such an omission. "It's irrelevant," another editor explained in a voice gummy with soothing and patience. "It's nice and poetic," but it doesn't "advance the discussion of any principle . . . This is a law review, after all." Frustrated, I accused him of censorship; calmly he assured me it was not. "This is just a matter of style," he said with firmness and finality

Ultimately I did convince the editors that mention of my race was central to the whole sense of the subsequent text; that my story became one of extreme paranoia without the information that I am black; or that it became one in which the reader had to fill in the gap by assumption, presumption, prejudgment, or prejudice. What was most interesting to me in this experience was how the blind application of principles of neutrality, through the device of omission, acted either to make me look crazy or to make the reader participate in old habits of cultural bias.

That was the second telling of my story. The third telling came last April, when I was invited to participate in a law-school conference on Equality and Difference. I retold my sad tale of exclusion from Soho's most glitzy boutique, focusing in this version on the law-review editing process as a consequence of an ideology of style rooted in a social text of neutrality. I opined:

> Law and legal writing aspire to formalized, color-blind, liberal ideals. Neutrality is the standard for assuring these ideals; yet the adherence to it is often determined by reference to an aesthetic of uniformity, in which difference is simply omitted. For example, when segregation was eradicated from the American lexicon, its omission led many to actually believe that racism therefore no longer existed. Race-neutrality in law has become the presumed antidote for race bias in real life. With the entrenchment of the notion of race-neutrality came attacks on the concept of affirmative action and the rise of reverse discrimination suits. Blacks, for so many generations deprived of jobs based on the color of our skin, are now told that we ought to find it

demeaning to be hired, based on the color of our skin. Such is the silliness of simplistic either-or inversions as remedies to complex problems.

What is truly demeaning in this era of double-speak-no-evil is going on interviews and not getting hired because someone doesn't think we'll be comfortable. It is demeaning not to get promoted because we're judged "too weak," then putting in a lot of energy the next time and getting fired because we're "too strong." It is demeaning to be told what we find demeaning. It is very demeaning to stand on street corners unemployed and begging. It is downright demeaning to have to explain why we haven't been employed for months and then watch the job go to someone who is "more experienced." It is outrageously demeaning that none of this can be called racism, even if it happens only to, or to large numbers of, black people; as long as it's done with a smile, a handshake and a shrug; as long as the phantom-word "race" is never used.

The image of race as a phantom-word came to me after I moved into my late godmother's home. In an attempt to make it my own, I cleared the bedroom for painting. The following morning the room asserted itself, came rushing and raging at me through the emptiness, exactly as it had been for twenty-five years. One day filled with profuse and overwhelming complexity, the next day filled with persistently recurring memories. The shape of the past came to haunt me, the shape of the emptiness confronted me each time I was about to enter the room. The force of its spirit still drifts like an odor throughout the house.

The power of that room, I have thought since, is very like the power of racism as status quo: it is deep, angry, eradicated from view, but strong enough to make everyone who enters the room walk around the bed that isn't there, avoiding the phantom as they did the substance, for fear of bodily harm. They do not even know they are avoiding; they defer to the unseen shapes of things with subtle responsiveness, guided by an impulsive awareness of nothingness, and the deep knowledge and denial of witchcraft at work.

The phantom room is to me symbolic of the emptiness of formal equal opportunity, particularly as propounded by President Reagan, the Reagan Civil Rights Commission and the Reagan Supreme Court. Blindly formalized constructions of equal opportunity are the creation of a space that is filled in by a meandering stream of unguided hopes, dreams, fantasies, fears, recollections. They are the presence of the past in imaginary, imagistic form — the phantom-roomed exile of our longing. It is thus that I strongly believe in the efficacy of programs and paradigms like affirmative action. Blacks are the objects of a constitutional omission which has been incorporated into a theory of neutrality.

It is thus that omission is really a form of expression, as oxymoronic as that sounds: racial omission is a literal part of original intent; it is the fixed, reiterated prophecy of the Founding Fathers. It is thus that affirmative action is an affirmation; the affirmative act of hiring — or hearing — blacks is a recognition of individuality that re-places blacks as a social statistic, that is profoundly interconnective to the fate of blacks and whites either as subgroups or as one group. In this sense, affirmative action is as mystical and beyond-the-self as an initiation ceremony. It is an act of verification and of vision. It is an act of social as well as professional responsibility.

The following morning I opened the local newspaper, to find that the event of my speech had commanded two columns on the front page of the Metro section. I quote only the opening lines:

"Affirmative action promotes prejudice by denying the status of women and blacks, instead of affirming them as its name suggests. So said New York City attorney Patricia Williams to an audience Wednesday."[4]

I clipped out the article and put it in my journal. In the margin there is a note to myself: eventually, it says, I should try to pull all these threads together into yet another law-review article. The problem, of course, will be that in the hierarchy of law-review citation, the article in the newspaper will have more authoritative weight about me, as a so-called "primary resource," than I will have; it will take precedence over my own citation of the unverifiable testimony of my speech.

I HAVE USED THE Benetton's story a lot, in speaking engagements at various schools. I tell it whenever I am too tired to whip up an original speech from scratch. Here are some of the questions I have been asked in the wake of its telling:

Am I not privileging a racial perspective, by considering only the black point of view? Don't I have an obligation to include the "salesman's side" of the story?

Am I not putting the salesman on trial and finding him guilty of racism without giving him a chance to respond to or cross-examine me?

Am I not using the store window as a "metaphorical fence" against the potential of his explanation in order to represent my side as "authentic"?

How can I be sure I'm right?

What makes my experience the real black one anyway?

Isn't it possible that another black person would disagree with my experience? If so, doesn't that render my story too unempirical and subjective to pay any attention to?

Always a major objection is to my having put the poster on Benetton's window. As one law professor put it: "It's one thing to publish this in a law review, where no one can take it personally, but it's another thing altogether to put your own interpretation right out there, just like that, uncontested, I mean, with nothing to counter it?"[5]

Notes

1. "When 'By Appointment' Means Keep Out," *New York Times*, December 17, 1986, p. B1. Letter to the Editor from Michael Leven and Marguerita Levin, *New York Times*, January 11, 1987, p. E32.

2. *New York Times*, January 11, 1987, p. E32.

3. See generally *Blyew v. U.S.*, 80 U.S. 581 (1871), upholding a state's right to forbid blacks to testify against whites.

4. "Attorney Says Affirmative Action Denies Racism, Sexism," *Dominion Post* (Morgantown, W. Va.), April 8, 1988, B1.

5. These questions put me on trial — an imaginary trial where it is I who have the burden of proof — and proof being nothing less than the testimony of the salesman actually confessing yes yes I am a racist. These questions question my own ability to know, to assess, to be objective. And of course, since anything that happens to me is inherently subjective, they take away my power to know what happens to me in the world. Others, by this standard, will always know better than I. And my insistence on recounting stories from my own perspective will be treated as presumption, slander, paranoid hallucinations, or just plain lies.

Recently I got an urgent call from Thomas Grey of Stanford Law School. He had used this piece in his jurisprudence class, and a rumor got started that the Benetton's story wasn't true, that I had made it up, that it was a fantasy, a lie that was probably the product of a diseased mind trying to make all white people feel guilty. At this point I realized it almost didn't make any difference whether I was telling the truth or not — that the greater issue I had to face was the overwhelming weight of a disbelief that goes beyond mere disinclination to believe and becomes active suppression of anything I might have to say. The greater problem is a powerfully oppressive mechanism for denial of black self-knowledge and expression. And this denial cannot be separated from the simultaneously pathological willingness to believe certain things about blacks — not to believe them, but certain things about them.

When students in Grey's class believed and then claimed that I had made it all up, they put me in a position like that of Tawana Brawley.* I mean that specifically: the social consequence of concluding that we are liars operates as a kind of public absolution of racism — the conclusion is not merely that we are troubled or that I am eccentric, but that we, as liars, are the norm. Therefore, the nonbelievers can believe things of this sort really don't happen (even in the face of statistics to the contrary). Racism or rape is all a big fantasy concocted by troublesome minorities and women. It is interesting to recall the outcry in every national medium, from the *New York Post* to the *Times* to the major networks, in the wake of the Brawley case: who will ever again believe a black woman who cries rape by a white man? Now shift the time frame a bit, and imagine a white male facing a consensus that he lied. Would there be a difference? Consider Charles Stuart, for example, the white Bostonian who accused a black man of murdering his pregnant wife and whose brother later alleged that in fact the brothers had conspired to murder her. Most people and the media

---

* Tawana Brawley was a fifteen-year-old African American girl from New York who, in 1987, accused six white men of kidnapping her, raping her, and smearing her with dog feces. The Charles Stuart incident occurred in 1989.

not only did not claim but actively resisted believing that Stuart represented any kind of "white male" norm. Instead he was written off as a troubled weirdo, a deviant—again even in the face of spousal abuse statistics to the contrary. There was not a story I could find that carried on about "who will ever believe" the next white man who cries murder.

(1991)

Rita Dove   (b. 1952)

Rita Frances Dove was born on August 28, 1952, in Akron, Ohio, to Ray A. Dove, the first African American chemist for Goodyear Tire, and Elvira Elizabeth Hord. After graduating from high school in 1970 and receiving the distinction of Presidential Scholar, Dove attended Miami University in Oxford, Ohio, earning a bachelor's degree in English in 1973. Dove then studied literature at Tübingen University, in what was then West Germany, on a Fulbright Scholarship, before enrolling in the University of Iowa's Writers' Workshop, where she earned her master's of fine arts degree in 1977. In 1979 she married German writer, Fred Viebahn, and their daughter was born in 1983.

After publishing work in literary magazines and journals and producing two chapbooks of poetry, *Ten Poems* (1977) and *The Only Dark Spot in the Sky* (1980), Dove published her first major collection of poetry, *The Yellow House on the Corner*, in 1980. Her next collection, *Museum*, appeared in 1983 and garnered national attention and critical acclaim. Dove's 1986 collection, *Thomas and Beulah*, won both the Lavin Younger Poet Award, given by the Academy of American Poets, and the 1987 Pulitzer Prize for poetry—only the second awarded to an African American (the first was to Gwendolyn Brooks in 1950). The collection traces the lives of Dove's maternal grandparents from Georgia and Tennessee to Akron, Ohio.

In addition to serving as poet laureate for Virginia, Dove served two terms as poet laureate of the United States from 1993 to 1995, becoming the first African American to serve in the position since it was renamed as such in 1986. In 1999 Dove published *On the Bus with Rosa Parks*, a collection of poetry that honors civil rights workers and their struggle, in which the selections following appear (both were originally published in 1998 in the *Georgia Review*). The collection won the *New York Times* Notable Book of the Year Award. Dove's other published works include *The Other Side of the House* (1988), *Grace Notes* (1989), *Selected Poems* (1993), *Mother Love: Poems* (1995), and *American Smooth* (2004). Her poetry frequently explores southern history and its effects on African Americans, particularly her family, and addresses the issues of segregation, migration, poverty, and domestic work. In addition to her volumes of poetry,

Dove published a novel, *Through the Ivory Gate* (1992); a collection of short stories, *Fifth Sunday* (1985); and a play, *The Darker Face of the Earth* (1994).

Dove's literary honors include a Guggenheim Fellowship, grants from the National Endowments for the Arts and for the Humanities, a grant from the Ohio Arts Council, the National Association for the Advancement of Colored People's Great American Artist Award, and the 2001 Duke Ellington Lifetime Achievement Award in the Literary Arts. In addition to serving as the writer-in-residence at Tuskegee University, she has taught at Arizona State University and the University of Virginia in Charlottesville. She has also served as a member of the Commission for the Preservation of Black Culture at the New York Public Library's Schomburg Center.

The Enactment

"I'm just a girl who people were mean to on a bus. . . .
I could have been anybody."
— Mary Ware, Née Smith

Can't use no teenager, especially
no poor black trash,
no matter what her parents do
to keep up a living. Can't use
anyone without sense enough
to bite their tongue.

It's gotta be a woman,
someone of standing:
preferably shy, preferably married.
And she's got to know when the moment's right.
Stay polite, though her shoulder's
aching, bus driver
the same one threw her off
twelve years before.

Then all she's got to do is
sit there, quiet, till
the next moment finds her — and only then
can she open her mouth to ask
Why do you push us around?
and his answer: I don't know
*but the law is the law and you
are under arrest.*

She must sit there, and not smile
as they enter to carry her off;
she must know who to call
who will know whom else to call
to bail her out . . . and only then

can she stand up and exhale,
can she walk out the cell
and down the jail steps
into flashbulbs and
her employer's white
arms — and go home,
and sit down in the seat
we have prepared for her.   (1998)

Rosa

How she sat there,
the time right inside a place
so wrong it was ready.

That trim name with
its dream of a bench
to rest on. Her sensible coat.

Doing nothing was the doing:
the clean flame of her gaze
carved by a camera flash.

How she stood up
when they bent down to retrieve
her purse. That courtesy.   (1998)

Walter Mosley   (b. 1952)

orn on January 12, 1952, in the Watts section of Los Angeles, Walter Mosley was the only son of his African American father, LeRoy, who was from the Deep South, and his Jewish mother, Ella, whose family was from Eastern Europe. The dynamics of his biracial family inspired Mosley with a desire for social justice, which increased after he witnessed first-hand the Watts riots of 1965. Mosley attended Goddard College and Johnson State College in Vermont, where he earned a bachelor's degree in 1977. After graduating he worked a series of odd jobs, and in 1982 he moved to New York, where he continues to reside, with Joy Kellman, whom he married in 1987. After working as a computer programmer for several years, Mosley quit and began attending writing classes at the City College of New York.

Mosley's writing has appeared in the *New Yorker, GQ, Esquire, Los Angeles Times Magazine, Savoy, New York Times Magazine,* and the *Nation.* Mosley served as editor for *Black Genius* (2000) and for the 2003 edition of *The Best American Short Stories.* He is perhaps best known for his detective fiction as he uniquely employs the genre to chronicle African American social history. Many of his novels are set in post–World War II Los Angeles and depict characters living working-class urban lives. Several novels focus on the character of Easy Rawlins, including his first novel, *Devil in a Blue Dress* (1990), which was nominated for an Edgar Award by the Mystery Writers of America. Other novels in the series include *A Red Death* (1991); *White Butterfly* (1992); *Black Betty* (1994); *A Little Yellow Dog* (1996); *Gone Fishin'* (1997); *Bad Boy Brawly Brown* (2002); *Six Easy Pieces* (2003); *Little Scarlet* (2004); *Cinnamon Kiss* (2005), which was a *New York Times* best seller; and *Blonde Faith* (2007).

Mosley's other works of fiction similarly and consistently garner awards. *R.L.'s Dream* (1995) won the 1996 Black Caucus of the American Library Association's Literary Award. Mosley's *Always Outnumbered, Always Outgunned* (1997) received the Anisfield Book Award from the Cleveland Foundation and was made into a feature film starring Laurence Fishburne as the short story collection's main character, Socrates. "Equal Opportunity," from that volume, originally appeared in *Buzz* magazine. One of Mosley's science fiction novels, *Blue Light* (1998), was named a *New York Times* Notable Book of the Year, and Mosley was a finalist for the National Association for the Advancement of Colored People's Award in Fiction. Additionally, he has won the O. Henry Award and the Trans-Africa International Literary Prize. Mosley's other publications include *Walkin' the Dog* (1999), *Whispers in the Dark* (2000), *Futureland* (2001), *Fearless Jones* (2001), *Fear Itself* (2003), *47* (2005), *The Wave* (2006), *Fortunate Son* (2006), *Fear of the Dark* (2006), and *Killing Johnny Fry: A Sexistential Novel* (2007).

Although Mosley is best known for his fiction, he also writes nonfiction, which frequently addresses racism, economic exploitation, and other violations of civil and human rights. Mosley's nonfiction publications include *Workin' on the Chain Gang: Contemplating Our Chains at the End of the Millennium* (1999), a critique of American capitalism; *What Next: An African American Initiative toward World Peace* (2002), a reaction to the attacks on the World Trade Center on September 11, 2001; and *Life Out of Context* (2006), which urges African Americans to form a separate political party.

Equal Opportunity

1

Bounty Supermarket was on Venice Boulevard, miles and miles from Socrates' home. He gaped at the glittering palace as he strode across the hot asphalt parking lot. The front wall was made from immense glass panes with steel framing to hold them in place. Through the big windows he could see long lines of customers with baskets full of food. He imagined apples and T-bone steaks, fat hams and the extra-large boxes of cereal that they only sold in supermarkets.

The checkers were all young women, some of them girls. Most were black. Black women, black girls — taking money and talking back and forth between themselves as they worked; running the packages of food over the computer eye that rang in the price and added it to the total without them having to think a thing.

In between the checkout counters black boys and brown ones loaded up bags for the customers.

Socrates walked up to the double glass doors and they slid open moaning some deep machine blues. He came into the cool air and cocked his ear to that peculiar music of supermarkets; steel carts wheeling around, crashing together, resounding with the thuds of heavy packages. Children squealing and yelling. The footsteps and occasional conversation blended together until they made a murmuring sound that lulled the ex-convict.

There was a definite religious feel to being in the great store. The lofty ceilings, the abundance, the wealth.

Dozens of tens and twenties, in between credit cards and bank cards, went back and forth over the counters. Very few customers used coupons. The cash seemed to be endless. How much money passed over those counters every day?

And what would they think if they knew that the man watching them had spent twenty-seven years doing hard time in prison? Socrates barked out a single-syllable laugh. They didn't have to worry about him. He wasn't a thief. Or, if he was, the only thing he ever took was life.

"Sir, can I help you?" Anton Crier asked.

Socrates knew the name because it was right there, on a big badge on his chest. ANTON CRIER ASST. MGR. He wore tan pants and a blue blazer with the supermarket insignia over the badge.

"I came for an application," Socrates said. It was a line that he had spent a whole day thinking about; a week practicing. I came for an application. For a couple days he had practiced saying job application, but after a while he dropped the word job to make his request sound more sure. But when he went to Stony Wile and told him that he planned to say "I came for a application," Stony said that you had to say an application.

"If you got a word that starts with a, e, i, o, or u then you got to say an instead of a," Stony had said.

Anton Crier's brow knitted and he stalled a moment before asking, "An application for what?"

"A job." There, he'd said it. It was less than a minute and this short white man, just a boy really, had already made him beg.

"Oh," said Anton Crier, nodding like a wise elder. "Uh. How old are you, sir?"

"Ain't that against the law?" Like many other convicts Socrates was a student of the law.

"Huh?"

"Askin' me my age. That's against the law. You cain't discriminate against color or sex or religion or infirmity or against age. That's the law."

"Uh, well, yes, of course it is. I know that. I'm not discriminating against you. It's just that we don't have any openings right now. Why don't you come in the fall when the kids are back at school?"

Anton leaned to the side, intending to leave Socrates standing there.

"Hold on," Socrates said. He held up his hands, loosely as fists, in a nonchalant sort of boxing stance.

Anton looked, and waited.

"I came for an application," Socrates repeated.

"But I told you . . ."

"I know what you said. But first you looked at my clothes and at my bald head. First yo' eyes said that this is some kinda old hobo and what do he want here when it ain't bottle redemption time."

"I did not . . ."

"It don't matter," Socrates said quickly. He knew better than to let a white man in uniform finish a sentence. "You got to give me a application. That's the law too."

"Wait here," young Mr. Crier said. He turned and strode away toward an elevated office that looked down along the line of cash registers.

Socrates watched him go. So did the checkers and bag boys. He was their boss and they knew when he was unhappy. They stole worried glances at Socrates.

Socrates stared back. He wondered if any of those young black women would stand up for him. Would they understand how far he'd come to get there?

He'd traveled more than fourteen miles from his little apartment down in Watts. They didn't have any supermarkets or jobs in his neighborhood. And all the stores along Crenshaw and Washington knew him as a bum who collected bottles and cans for a living.

They wouldn't hire him.

Socrates hadn't held a real job in over thirty-seven years. He'd been unemployed for twenty-five months before the party with Shep, Fogel, and Muriel.

They'd been out carousing. Three young people, blind drunk.

Back at Shep's, Muriel gave Socrates the eye. He danced with her until Shep broke it up. But then Shep fell asleep. When he awoke to find them rolling on the floor the fight broke out in earnest.

Socrates knocked Shep back to the floor and then he finished his business with Muriel even though she was worried about her man. But when she started to scream and she hit Socrates with that chair he hit her back.

It wasn't until the next morning, when he woke up, that he realized that his friends were dead.

Then he'd spent twenty-seven years in prison. Now, eight years free, fifty-eight years old, he was starting life over again.

Not one of those girls, nor Anton Crier, was alive when he started his journey. If they were lucky they wouldn't understand him.

2

There was a large electric clock above the office. The sweep hand reared back and then battered up against each second, counting every one like a drummer beating out time on a slave galley.

Socrates could see the young assistant manager through the window under the clock. He was saying something to an older white woman sitting there. The woman looked down at Socrates and then swiveled in her chair to a file cabinet. She took out a piece of paper and held it while lecturing Anton. He reached for the paper a couple of times but the woman kept it away from him and continued talking. Finally she said something and Crier nodded. He took the paper from her and left the office, coming down the external stairs at a fast clip. Walking past the checkers he managed not to look at Socrates before he was standing there in front of him.

"Here," he said, handing the single-sheet application form to Socrates. Crier never stopped moving. As soon as Socrates had the form between his fingers the younger man was walking away. Socrates touched the passing elbow and asked, "You got a pencil?"

"What?"

"I need a pencil to fill out this form."

"You, you, you can just send it in."

"I didn't come all this way for a piece'a paper, man. I come to apply for a job."

Anton Crier stormed over to one of the checkers, demanded her pencil, then rushed back to Socrates.

"Here," he said.

Socrates answered, "Thank you," but the assistant manager was already on his way back to the elevated office.

HALF AN HOUR LATER Socrates was standing at the foot of the stairs lead-ing up to Anton and his boss. He stood there waiting for one of them to come down. They could see him through the window.

They knew he was there.

So Socrates waited, holding the application in one hand and the borrowed pencil in the other.

After twenty minutes he was wondering if a brick could break the wall of windows at the front of the store.

After thirty minutes he decided that it might take a shotgun blast.

Thirty-nine minutes had gone by when the woman, who had bottled red hair, came down to meet him. Anton Crier shadowed her. Socrates saw the anger in the boy's face.

"Yes? Can I help you?" Halley Grimes asked. She had a jail-house smile — insincere and crooked.

"I wanted to ask a couple of things about my application."

"All the information is right there at the top of the sheet."

"But I had some questions."

"We're very busy, sir." Ms. Grimes broadened her smile to show that she had a heart, even for the aged and confused. "What do you need to know?"

"It asks here if I got a car or a regular ride to work."

"Yes," beamed Ms. Grimes. "What is it exactly that you don't understand?"

"I understand what it says but I just don't get what it means."

The look of confusion came into Halley Grimes's face. Socrates welcomed a real emotion.

He answered her unasked question. "What I mean is that I don't have a car or a ride but can take a bus to work."

The store manager took his application form and fingered the address.

"Where is this street?" she asked.

"Down Watts."

"That's pretty far to go by bus, isn't it? There are stores closer than this one, you know."

"But I could get here." Socrates noticed that his head wanted to move as if to the rhythm of a song. Then he heard it: "Baby Love," by Diana Ross and the Supremes. It was being played softly over the loudspeaker. "I could get here."

"Well." Ms. Grimes seemed to brighten. "We'll send this in to the main of-fice and, if it's clear with them, we'll put it in our files. When there's an opening we'll give you a call."

"A what?"

"A call. We'll call you if you're qualified and if a job opens up."

"Uh, well, we got to figure somethin' else than that out. You see, I don't have no phone."

"Oh, well then." Ms. Grimes held up her hands in a gesture of helplessness. "I don't see that there's anything we can do. The main office demands a phone number. That's how they check on your address. They call."

"How do they know that they got my address just 'cause'a some phone they call? Wouldn't it be better if they wrote me?"

"I'm very busy, sir. I've told you that we need a phone number to process this application." Halley Grimes held out the form toward Socrates. "Without that there really isn't anything I can do."

Socrates kept his big hands down. He didn't want to take the application back—partly because he didn't want to break the pudgy white woman's fingers.

"Do me a favor and send it in," he said.

"I told you . . ."

"Just send it in, okay? Send it in. I'll be back to find out what they said."

"You don't . . ."

"Just send it in." There was violence in this last request.

Halley Grimes pulled the application away from his face and said, "All right. But it won't make any difference."

3

Socrates had to transfer on three buses to get back to his apartment.

And he was especially tired that day. Talking to Crier and Grimes had worn him out.

He boiled potatoes and eggs in a saucepan on his single hot plate and then cut them together in the pot with two knives, adding mustard and sweet pickle relish. After the meal he had two shots of whiskey and one Camel cigarette.

He was asleep by nine o'clock.

His dream blared until dawn.

IT WAS A REALISTIC SORT of dream; no magic, no impossible wish. It was just Socrates in a nine-foot cell with a flickering fluorescent light from the walkway keeping him from sleeping and reading, giving him a headache, hurting his eyes.

"Mr. Bennett," the sleeping Socrates called out from his broad sofa. He shouted so loudly that a mouse in the kitchen jumped up and out of the potato pan pinging his tail against the thin tin as he went.

Socrates heard the sound in his sleep. He turned but then slipped back into the flickering, painful dream.

"What you want?" the guard asked. He was big and black and meaner than anyone Socrates had ever known.

"I cain't read. I cain't sleep. That light been like that for three days now."

"Put the pillow on your head," the big guard said.

"I cain't breathe like that," Socrates answered sensibly.

"Then don't," Mr. Bennett replied.

As the guard walked away, Socrates knew, for the first time really, why they kept him in that jail. He would have killed Bennett if he could have right then; put his fingers around that fat neck and squeezed until the veins swelled and cartilage popped and snapped. He was so mad that he balled his fists in his sleep twenty-five years after the fact.

He was a sleeping man wishing that he could sleep. And he was mad, killing mad. He couldn't rest because of the crackling, buzzing light, and the more it shone the angrier he became. And the angrier he got the more scared he was. Scared that he'd kill Bennett the first chance he got.

The anger built for days in that dream. The sound of grinding teeth could be heard throughout Socrates' two rooms.

Finally, when he couldn't stand it anymore, he took his rubber squeeze ball in his left hand and slipped his right hand through the bars. He passed the ball through to his right hand and gauged its weight in the basket of his fingers. He blinked back at the angry light, felt the weight of his hard rubber ball. The violent jerk started from his belly button, traveled up through his chest and shoulder, and down until his fingers tensed like steel. The ball flew in a straight line that shattered the light, broke it into blackness.

And in the jet night he heard Bennett say, "That's the last light you get from the state of Indiana."

Socrates woke up in the morning knowing that he had cried. He could feel the strain in the muscles of his throat. He got out of bed thinking about Anton Crier and Halley Grimes.

4

"You what?" asked Stony Wile. He'd run into Socrates getting off a bus on Central and offered to buy his friend a beer. They went to Moody's bar on 109th Street.

"I been down there ev'ry day for five days. An ev'ry day I go in there I ask 'em if they got my okay from the head office yet."

"An' what they say about that?"

"Well, the first day that boy, that Anton Crier, just said no. So I left. Next day he told me that I had to leave. But I said that I wanted to talk to his boss. She come down an' tell me that she done already said how I cain't work there if I don't have no phone."

"Yeah," asked Stony Wile. "Then what'd you do?"

"I told 'em that they should call downtown and get some kinda answer on me because I was gonna come back ev'ryday till I get some kinda answer." There was a finality in Socrates' voice that opened Stony's eyes wide.

"You don't wanna do sumpin' dumb now, Socco," he said.

"An' what would that be?"

"They could get you into all kindsa trouble, arrest you for trespassin' if you keep it up."

"Maybe they could. Shit. Cops could come in here an' blow my head off too, but you think I should kiss they ass?"

"But that's different. You got to stand up for yo' pride, yo' manhood. But I don't see it wit' this supermarket thing."

"Well," Socrates said. "On Thursday Ms. Grimes told me that the office had faxed her to say I wasn't qualified for the position. She said that she had called the cops and said that I'd been down there harassin' them. She said that they said that if I ever come over there again that they would come arrest me. Arrest me! Just for tryin' t'get my rights."

"That was the fourth day?" Stony asked to make sure that he was counting right.

"Uh-huh. That was day number four. I asked her could I see that fax paper but she said that she didn't have it, that she threw it out. You ever hear'a anything like that? White woman workin' for a white corporation throwin' out paperwork?"

Stony was once a shipbuilder but now worked on a fishing day boat out of San Pedro. He'd been in trouble before but never in jail. He'd never thought about the thousands of papers he'd signed over his life; never wondered where they went.

"Why wouldn't they throw them away?" Stony asked.

"Because they keep ev'ry scrap'a paper they got just as long as it make they case in court."

Stony nodded. Maybe he understood.

"So I called Bounty's head office," Socrates said. "Over in Torrence."

"You lyin'."

"An' why not? I applied for that job, Stony. I should get my hearin' wit' them."

"What'd they say?"

"That they ain't never heard'a me."

"You lyin'," Stony said again.

"Grimes an' Crier the liars. An' you know I went down there today t'tell'em so. I was up in Anton's face when he told me that Ms. Grimes was out. I told him that they lied and that I had the right to get me a job."

"An' what he say?"

"He was scared. He thought I mighta hit'im. And I mighta too except Ms. Grimes comes on down."

"She was there?"

"Said that she was on a lunch break; said that she was gonna call the cops on me. Shit. I called her a liar right to her face. I said that she was a liar and that

I had a right to be submitted to the main office." Socrates jabbed his finger at Stony as if he were the one holding the job hostage. "I told'er that I'd be back on Monday and that I expected some kinda fair treatment."

"Well that sounds right," Stony said. "It ain't up to her who could apply an' who couldn't. She got to be fair."

"Yeah," Socrates answered. "She said that the cops would be waitin' for me on Monday. Maybe Monday night you could come see me in jail."

5

On Saturday Socrates took his canvas cart full of cans to the Boys Market on Adams. He waited three hours behind Calico, an older black woman who prowled the same streets he did, and two younger black men who worked as a team.

Calico and DJ and Bernard were having a good time waiting. DJ was from Oakland and had come down to L.A. to stay with his grandmother when he was fifteen. She died a year later so he had to live on the streets since then. But DJ didn't complain. He talked about how good life was and how much he was able to collect on the streets.

"Man," DJ said. "I wish they would let me up there in Beverly Hills just one week. Gimme one week with a pickup an' I could live for a year offa the good trash they got up there. They th'ow out stuff that still work up there."

"How the fuck you know, man?" Bernard said. "When you ever been up Beverly Hills?"

"When I was doin' day work. I helped a dude build a cinder-block fence up on Hollandale. I saw what they th'owed out. I picked me up a portable TV right out the trash an' I swear that sucker get ev'ry channel."

"I bet it don't get cable," Bernard said.

"It would if I'da had a cable to hook it up wit'." They talked like that for three hours. Calico cooed and laughed with them, happy to be in the company of young men.

But Socrates was just mad.

Why the hell did he have to wait for hours? Who were they in that supermarket to make full-grown men and women wait like they were children?

At two o'clock he got up and walked away from his canvas wagon.

"Hey," Bernard called. "You want us t'watch yo' basket?"

"You could keep it," Socrates said. "I ain't never gonna use the goddam thing again."

Calico let out a whoop at Socrates' back.

ON SUNDAY Socrates sharpened his pocket knife on a graphite stone. He didn't keep a gun. If the cops caught him with a gun he would spend the rest of his life in jail. But there was no law against a knife blade three inches or less; and three inches was all a man who knew how to use a knife needed.

Socrates sharpened his knife but he didn't know why exactly. Grimes and Crier weren't going to harm him, at least not with violence. And if they called the cops a knife wouldn't be any use anyway. If the cops even thought that he had a knife they could shoot him and make a good claim for self-defense.

But Socrates still practiced whipping out the knife and slashing with the blade sticking out of the back end of his fist.

"Hah!" he yelled.

6

He left the knife on the orange crate by his sofa bed the next morning before leaving for Bounty Supermarket. The RTD bus came right on time and he made his connections quickly, one after the other.

In forty-five minutes he was back on that parking lot. It was a big building, he thought, but not as big as the penitentiary had been.

A smart man would have turned around and tried some other store, Socrates knew that. It didn't take a hero to make a fool out of himself.

It was before nine-thirty and the air still had the hint of a morning chill. The sky was a pearl gray and the parking lot was almost empty.

Socrates counted seven breaths and then walked toward the door with no knife in his hand. He cursed himself softly under his breath because he had no woman at home to tell him that he was a fool.

Nobody met him at the door. There was only one checker on duty while the rest of the workers went up and down the aisles restocking and straightening the shelves.

With nowhere else to go, Socrates went toward the elevated office. He was half the way there when he saw Halley Grimes coming down the stairs. Seeing him she turned and went, ran actually, back up to the office.

Socrates was sure that she meant to call the police. He wanted to run but couldn't. All he could do was take one step after the other; the way he'd done in his cell sometimes, sometimes the way he did at home.

Two men appeared at the high door when Socrates reached the stairs. Salt and pepper, white and black. The older one, a white man, wore a tan wash-and-wear suit with a cheap maroon tie. The Negro had on black jeans, a black jacket, and a white turtleneck shirt. He was very light-skinned but his nose and lips would always give him away.

The men came down to meet him. They were followed by Grimes and Crier.

"Mr. Fortlow?" the white man inquired.

Socrates nodded and looked him in the eye.

"My name is Parker," he continued. "And this is Mr. Weems."

"Uh-huh," Socrates answered.

The two men formed a wall behind which the manager and assistant manager slipped away.

"We work for Bounty," Mr. Weems said. "Would you like to come upstairs for a moment?"

"What for?" Socrates wanted to know.

"We'd like to talk," Parker answered.

THE PLATFORM OFFICE was smaller than it looked from the outside. The two cluttered desks that sat back to back took up most of the space. Three sides were windows that gave a full panorama of the store. The back wall had a big blackboard on it with the chalked-in time schedules of everyone who worked there. Beneath the blackboard was a safe door.

"Have a seat, Mr. Fortlow." Parker gestured toward one of the two chairs. He sat in the other chair while Weems perched on a desk.

"Coffee?" asked Parker.

"What's this all about, man?" Socrates asked.

Smiling, Parker said, "We want to know what your problem is with Ms. Grimes. She called the head office on Friday and told us that she was calling the police because she was afraid of you."

"I don't have no problem with Ms. Grimes or Anton Crier or Bounty Supermarket. I need a job and I wanted to make a application. That's all."

"But she told you that you had to have a phone number in order to complete your file," said Weems.

"So? Just 'cause I don't have no phone then I cain't work? That don't make no sense at all. If I don't work I cain't afford no phone. If I don't have no phone then I cain't work. You might as well just put me in the ground."

"It's not Bounty's problem that you don't have a phone." Parker's face was placid but the threat was in his tone.

"All I want is to make a job application. All I want is to work," Socrates said. Really he wanted to fight. He wanted his knife at close quarters with those private cops. But instead he went on, "I ain't threatened nobody. I ain't said I was gonna do a thing. All I did was to come back ev'ry day an' ask if they had my okay from you guys yet. That's all. On the job application they asked if I had a car or a ride to work — to see if I could get here. Well, I come in ev'ry day for a week at nine-thirty or before. I come in an' asked if I been cleared yet. I didn't do nuthin' wrong. An' if that woman is scared it must be 'cause she knows she ain't been right by me. But I didn't do nuthin'."

There was no immediate answer to Socrates' complaint. The men looked at him but kept silent. There was the hum of machinery coming from somewhere but Socrates couldn't figure out where. He concentrated on keeping his hands on his knees, on keeping them open.

"But how do you expect to get a job when you come in every day and treat the people who will be your bosses like they're doing something wrong?" Weems seemed really to want to know.

"If I didn't come in they woulda th'owed out my application, prob'ly did anyway. I ain't no kid. I'm fifty-eight years old. I'm unemployed an' nowhere near benefits. If I don't find me some way t'get some money I'll starve. So, you see, I had to come. I couldn't let these people say that I cain't even apply. If I did that then I might as well die."

Parker sighed. Weems scratched the top of his head and then rubbed his nose.

"You can't work here," Parker said at last. "If we tried to push you off on Ms. Grimes she'd go crazy. She really thought that you were going to come in here guns blazing."

"So 'cause she thought that I was a killer then I cain't have no job?" Socrates knew the irony of his words but he also knew their truth. He didn't care about a job just then. He was happy to talk, happy to say what he felt. Because he knew that he was telling the truth and that those men believed him.

"What about Rodriguez?" Weems asked of no one in particular.

"Who's that?" Socrates asked.

"He's the manager of one of our stores up on Santa Monica," Weems replied.

"I don't know," Parker said.

"Yeah, sure, Connie Rodriguez." Weems was getting to like the idea. "He's always talking about giving guys a chance. We could give him a chance to back it up with Mr. Fortlow here."

Parker chewed on his lower lip until it reddened. Weems grinned. It seemed to Socrates that some kind of joke was being played on this Connie Rodriguez. Parker hesitated but he liked the idea.

Parker reached down under the desk and came out with a briefcase. From this he brought out a sheet of paper; Socrates' application form.

"There's just one question," Parker said.

7

"What he wanna know?" Stony Wile asked at Iula's grill. They were there with Right Burke, Markham Peal, and Howard Shakur. Iula gave Socrates a party when she heard that he got a job as a general food packager and food delivery person at Bounty Supermarket on Santa Monica Boulevard. She made the food and his friends brought the liquor.

"He wanted to know why I had left one of the boxes blank."

"What box?"

"The one that asks if I'd ever been arrested for or convicted of a felony."

"Damn. What you say?"

"That I musta overlooked it."

"An' then you lied?"

"Damn straight. But he knew I was lyin'. He was a cop before he went to work for Bounty. Both of 'em was. He asked me that if they put through a check on me would it come up bad? An' I told him that he didn't need to put through no checks."

"Mmm!" Stony hummed, shaking his head. "That's always gonna be over your head, man. Always."

Socrates laughed and grabbed his friend by the back of his neck.

He hugged Stony and then held him by the shoulders. "I done had a lot worse hangin' over me, brother. At least I get a paycheck till they find out what I am."

(1997)

Anthony Grooms   (b. 1955)

The oldest of six children, Anthony Grooms was born on January 15, 1955, in Louisa County, Virginia, to Robert Grooms, a mechanic, and Dellaphine Scott, a textile worker. In 1967 Grooms's parents enrolled him in the Freedom of Choice plan to integrate white public schools. After graduating from the College of William and Mary in 1978 with a bachelor's degree in theater and speech, Grooms attended George Mason University, earning a master's of fine arts degree in 1984. He and his wife Pamela Jackson, with whom he has a son, moved in 1988 to Atlanta, Georgia, where Grooms began teaching. He has since taught at numerous institutions of higher education, including the University of Georgia, Emory University, Morehouse College, and the University of Cape Coast in Ghana. Currently, he teaches creative writing at Kennesaw State University, located outside of Atlanta.

Grooms's publications include a collection of poetry, *Ice Poems* (1988); a collection of short stories, *Trouble No More* (1995) — winner of the Lillian Smith Book Award and the Georgia Center for the Book's All Georgia Reads Award; and a novel, *Bombingham* (2001) — also a winner of the Lillian Smith Book Award as well as a finalist for the Hurston-Wright Legacy Award. *Bombingham*, set in 1963 Birmingham, exemplifies Grooms's concern with social justice and the 1960s civil rights movement. His short stories and poems have appeared in numerous literary magazines and journals, including *Callaloo*, *African-American Review*, and *George Washington Review*. Grooms's other literary honors include a Sokolov Scholarship from the Breadloaf Writing Conference, a Lamar lectureship from Wesleyan College, an Arts Administration Fellowship from the National Endowment for the Arts, and a Fulbright Fellowship to lecture at the University College of Southern Stockholm.

"Negro Progress," originally published in *Callaloo* and included in *Trouble No More*, returns to the tense atmosphere he portrayed in *Bombingham*, looking at the 1963 protests from the viewpoints of the everyday people involved. The nonviolent direct action campaign that Grooms references in the story focused on boycotts of local white-owned businesses and marches that involved teenagers and children. In one infamous series of events, local law enforcement officials, under the direction of Public Safety Commissioner Eugene "Bull" Connor, turned fire hoses and police dogs on the marchers.

Negro Progress

The water hunted the boy. It chipped bark from the oaks as he darted behind the trees. It caught him in the back. His lanky legs buckled. Then, as if the fireman who directed the hose were playing a game, the boy's legs were cut from under him, and he was rolled over and over in the mud.

From the distance of half a block, Carlton Wilkes watched the white ropes of water as they played against the black trunks and lime green leaves of the trees. In the sunlight, the streams sparkled, occasionally crisscrossed or made lazy S's like fluttering ribbons.

He had been on his way to his Uncle Booker's building, when he first saw the children. They were wearing school clothes. He remembered that somebody in King's organization had called for a children's crusade, placing teenagers and children as young as six on the front lines of the city's civil rights demonstrations. Even when the first firetruck skidded to a stop across the street from the park and the firemen unwound their hoses and screwed them into the hydrants, he paid little attention. Uncle Booker had quite literally ordered him downtown. "It's only your damn future that's at stake," he had said. Uncle Booker had a way of exaggerating, but when it came to business, his feet were flat on the ground. There was little Negro business that went on in the city that Uncle Booker didn't have a hand in.

Then a child's squeal, the squeal and the whoosh-and-scour of the water, made him look up at the sometimes taut, sometimes lazy ropes the firemen directed. At first, the children taunted the firemen. They danced about, darting under the arcing streams and through the mist of the pressurized water. Then the boy was tripped and rolled with such force that Carlton thought he must have been hurt, and the scene took on urgency. He told himself to move, to run to the boy, but this meant passing the firetrucks. Then he saw the paddy wagons, and the handsome German shepherds. His legs went rubbery.

HIS LEGS SEEMED barely strong enough to push in the clutch, as he drove to Salena's house. He and Salena Parrish had been engaged for six months, but had not set a date for the wedding. She was a nurse at the city hospital, one of the first Negro nurses there. When she opened the door he saw in her expression how harried he looked.

"What happened to you?" she asked, her gray eyes growing wide for a second.

The sight of her made his heart rush. Her light skin blushed in response to his breathlessness. He stumbled across the threshold, stammering. Not until she had taken him by the shoulders, did he manage to speak.

"They . . . they are *hosing* children—shooting them down like . . . like the Boston massacre."

For a moment she looked horrified, then seemed to understand him and relaxed a little. "You mean *spraying* them with water?" She tightened the belt on her robe and turned on the radio. "Just *hosing* them with water?"

There was no news on the radio. She led him to the sofa, spoke soothingly to him, and brought him a drink. It was cheap whiskey, but it calmed him. She took his hand and asked him to tell her what had happened.

"Let me get another drink." He went to the decanter in the dining room. The decanter was made of gaudy cut glass. He poured a finger, swallowed it, and poured another. The trembling stopped; he felt a little more like himself. "Doesn't your old man ever buy good liquor?"

"You know it's only for display."

He talked a moment about what he had seen, but when he got to the part about rescuing the boy, he stopped.

"Then what did you do?" She leaned toward him.

He sipped the whiskey. "I came here."

"What happened to the boy?"

"I don't know."

"Well," she said and sat back on the sofa. "Probably nothing. The radio hasn't said a thing."

The trembling came back. He paced. "I just don't know. I have a sick feeling. I can't explain it. It feels like . . . like my whole insides want to come out." He stopped while she took the curler out of her bangs. "It feels like something bad is going to happen, and if I stay here—I mean if we—stay here we are going to be trapped in it."

"Well, there *is* a civil rights protest."

He took a breath. "Don't be sarcastic."

"I don't mean to be sarcastic. I'm just pointing out to you that something *is* happening. You don't realize it because you don't see it every day. And, well, you have options those people don't have. Money gives you options."

"What is that suppose to mean?"

"Just an observation." Then she added quickly, "Not of you — not so much of you, sweetheart — but of my patients. You feel you may get trapped. But you can afford to go to New York or California. But most of them can't. At least, not in the way I'm talking about."

"What's the difference in New York?" He closed his eyes. "I wish I could really get away from here. From this city. From the whole damn country." He sat on the sofa and took her hand. "I'm serious. Why don't we get married and go overseas. We could go to Amsterdam or Paris. I hear things aren't so bad over there."

"Paris? Oh, sure, *mon cher*. And just what are we going to do in *Paris*? We don't have that kind of money."

"I'll sell Dad's part of the business to Uncle Booker. He buys up everything sooner or later any way."

"He *is* a business man."

Carlton remembered his meeting with his uncle. "And I'm not?"

HE DID NOT GO right away to meet his uncle. Salena decided to go to the hospital and asked him to make lunch for her father. Her father, Mr. Parrish, was a wiry, olive man with patchy gray fuzz on his head. He seemed agitated when he came in from his store and found Carlton in the kitchen warming up string beans and left-over turkey. "Where's Salena, Mr. Wilkes? She done got called in?"

"She went in before they called her."

"Volunteered her time? She know better'n that."

"I believe she felt they would call her anyway with the riot going on downtown."

"Riot?" He went to the washroom just off the kitchen. "I ain't hear tell of no riot. Heard they spraying them children. But spraying ain't a riot."

"No, sir. I guess not." Carlton watched Mr. Parrish's angular hips as he bent over the basin. "Anyway, Salena asked me to warm up some dinner for you." He poured the limp, sweet smelling beans onto the plate with the turkey and candied yams. His stomach growled a little, but he decided not to eat until the old man invited him.

Mr. Parrish put the paper napkin to his collar and began his lunch. "You not in business today?"

"I had an appointment down with Uncle Booker, but . . . the disturbance was in the way."

"That's what I knew. They talk about hurtin' the white man, but they hurtin' the colored, too." Mr. Parrish sawed on his turkey. "Shuttlesworth, and Walker! Call themselves preachers. Preachers ain't got no business in politics, if you ask me. Marchin' in the street ain't never got nobody into heaven." He motioned with the fork to a chair. "Help yourself, Carlton."

"I'm not very hungry."

"Can't work if you don't eat. That's what my daddy always told me. He was a farming man. Worked me sun up 'til midnight. I ain't lying. He was born a slave, you know. Had that slave working mentality. Nothing wrong with a work mentality. Two things I swore when I was a boy. One: I would get ahead anyway I could — but ain't but one way — hard work. After my daddy died, Momma moved us over here to live with her brother who worked at the furnace. That's when I saw how to make it: business. Momma opened the little dry goods store — just a hand full of inventory and I carried it on. My brother, Tom, he went back to farming — still farming — don't own a thing. Ain't got no pension. No nothing."

Carlton wiped sweat from his forehead back into his hair. He was wishing for a drink and the smell of the turkey was making him hungry. "What was the second thing?"

"I'll get to it." Mr. Parrish chewed. "Farming. That's what. Never gone lift another hoe in my life — unless it is to sell it. That's what your average Negro don't understand. He go out break his back whether it's farmin' or minin' or smeltin' — and ain't got a red cent to show for it. You got to be the middle man. The middle man or the owner. It's still hard work, but you got something in the end. Something you can sell if nothing else." He drank water. "Take yourself. You still young. You and Salena both. Well, she doing the best she can for a woman, but nursing — first colored girl or not — that's not what I want for her. She needs to settle in and raise the children and take care of the house. It's nice she got a skill and all to lean back on, in case something happens to you." He winked. "That's one thing that worries me so much about this going on. Interferes with business. White and colored, too."

"Mr. Parrish, did you *see* what was going on downtown?"

"I heard they was spraying children. Children ought to be in school, not the street . . . how do they ever expect to get a job out in the street? I wouldn't hire nay one of them — and what do they expect a white man to say if they have this on their record . . . ?"

"They were not spraying them. They were *hosing* them."

"What's the difference, Carlton?" Mr. Parrish stopped sawing the turkey with his fork. "What's the difference for us? It ain't fixin' to do nothin' but hurt us, one way or the other. Colored people too impatient. They want something and don't know what they gettin'. Now you tell me what sense it make for me to want to go all the way downtown and sit in at a white lunch counter to eat a hamburger, when my friend Harvey Brown got a rib shack not three blocks from here. And in your own business, Carlton, what good it gone be if they let us live up in Mountain Brook? You can't sell no houses in Mountain Brook, and ain't no white ever gone buy a house in Titusville. People talkin' about gettin' their freedom. Freedom ain't worth a dime if you ain't got a dime." He punched the table with his finger. "Every dollar they spend with the white man is a dollar they ain't spent with us." He pushed back from the table and folded his arms. "We got to think this thing through. This marching business liable to drive every colored man in the city out of business."

The two men sat quietly for a moment as if considering this proclamation. Then Carlton shifted, and cleared his throat. "Mr. Parrish, Salena and I have been talking. We figure if things don't get better we might go away."

The old man didn't look up. "Where to? Up North? Colored got the same trouble up North, only difference is they don't know it."

"We were thinking about Europe, maybe Paris."

"Paris, France?" Mr. Parrish looked at Carlton with incredulity. "You don't mean Paris, Kentucky? You mean Paris that in France? What the *hell* you going to do in Paris, France? You speak French? You got any family in France?" He sighed. "Son, white man own Paris just like he own Birmingham. Ain't a place in the world you can go — unlessen it's Red China — that the white man don't own. You can even go back to Africa, and you still got to deal with the white man. So you might as well save yo'self some running and deal with him right here."

UNCLE BOOKER KEPT HIM waiting. From the window in the outer office he could see the park. It showed no evidence of the disturbance. The intercom buzzed.

"Mr. Wilkes," the secretary called to him. "He will see you now." Just before she opened the door for him, she whispered in a matronly way, "Straighten your tie."

Uncle Booker looked at his watch and shook his head.

"I was here on time, Uncle Booker. But there was a riot."

"You let that foolishness stop you?"

"It was more than just a little foolishness." Carlton walked quickly to the window. "Didn't you see it from here?"

"I saw it. But I didn't let it get in the way of what I had to do." Uncle Booker packed and lit his pipe. "Have a seat, son. Believe it or not, I was young once, so I know how it is to get excited about things that don't mean a difference to you one way or the other."

"But . . ."

"I know. I know." Booker waved him silent with a chubby hand. "You're concerned about your rights — about Negro progress — I'm for all that, too. Lord, I'd be a fool not to be. And believe me, sure as the sun comes up every morning, it's coming. Maybe these school children have started something. Maybe not. Maybe we'll be singing their praises or maybe we'll be burying them. Or maybe both." He puffed and swiveled in his chair. "And you got a part in this progress, too."

Carlton's stomach churned. He couldn't see himself marching.

Booker put his pipe in the pipe rest. "This will sound awful hard, but it's the truth. For someone like you, educated up North, and in a white school — and got a little money behind you — the only Negro progress is to make as much money as you can. Now before you say anything stupid, let me remind you that for three generations, even before the end of slavery, the Wilkes family has been in one business or the other. We may not have gotten our rights from the white man, and damn it, I know we didn't get his respect, but we got what we wanted because we had money."

Carlton had heard it before. Uncle Booker recounted the Wilkes businesses, from the small farm and produce store his first free ancestor had, to the white-only barber shops Carlton's grandfather had owned, to the real estate company that Carlton's father had owned, and to Booker's own insurance company. Carlton studied the short, chubby man. It was hard to believe that he was related to him.

"Now, I have a deal for you," Booker continued. "It should make you and your lady very happy — and rich. There is a man, a Northerner — and I may add, a white man, who is proposing to build some stores in various places around the city. Mountain Brook will be the first one. These are what they call *convenience* stores. They'd sell sundries and quick items.

"This man needs a partner — an investor. Someone who knows the area, but yet isn't exactly one of the local okies, if you catch my drift."

After a moment, Carlton spoke. "That would take a lot of money."

"You've got it. You'll need to sell off some of those slum houses your Daddy left you, and it would be tight for a few years. But you're young, and you've got your young lady to fall back on. She's Parrish's only child, and you'll have what he leaves her. But the best part," he puffed the pipe, "the very best part will be if this civil rights thing goes through, then you'll own property in Mountain Brook and black and white alike will already be buying from you."

Uncle Booker leaned back in his swivel chair and laid his intertwined fingers across his stomach. He seemed to have been caught in a daydream. Carlton went to the window, again, and looked out over the park. He remembered how he felt when he had seen the dogs, and turned quickly to Uncle Booker. "I don't know about going into business with a white man. People around here wouldn't like that. It could cause trouble." The mention of "trouble" was strategic. Trouble would be bad for business.

Uncle Booker leaned forward. "Nobody will know who owns what." He leaned back in the chair and frowned. "What's the matter with you, Carlton?"

"It's just that Salena and I had been thinking of leaving Birmingham. You know, going to some place where we could get a good start."

"Like where?"

"Like Paris."

Uncle Booker's face was still for a moment, then he laughed. "How romantic!" He leaned forward and put his thick hands on the desk top. "Son, what do you see when you look out that window at Birmingham? Filthy smokestacks? A shabby little downtown? For certain, it is not Paris. What I see is a town that black people helped to build. I see opportunity on every street corner. Your opportunity. You can't be afraid to claim it."

Carlton looked out of the window again. In the distance he saw the columns of white smoke rising from the steel furnaces in Hueytown. Hueytown was home to the KKK. In another direction, he saw the rooftops of Titusville. Only last week bombs had been tossed into houses in Titusville. Then there was the park just in front of him. He returned to his seat. How could he make Uncle Booker understand. "Everything is changing, here."

"Change can be good."

"It's just that . . . I'm afraid."

Uncle Booker leaned back again. He put the pipe in his mouth. "Of course, there is some risk. If you want to make money, you've got to take risks."

"It's not the business, Uncle Booker. I'm afraid. Afraid of what's happening here —"

"Afraid?" Uncle Booker frowned and rocked forward abruptly. "Afraid? Afraid to make money?"

CARLTON HAD STARTED home after his talk with Uncle Booker, but the sight of the park stopped him. Close up, he could see the scars the water had left on the tree trunks and where it had stripped the leaves from shrubs. Here and there were puddles in the grass. He stood at the place where the boy had fallen. The grass was thin, and the ground had been churned up by running feet. It smelled fresh. Remembering again what he had witnessed, he felt himself begin to shake. He looked at his hand. On the outside he was perfectly still, but on the inside, everything trembled. He knew it was fear; but what did he have to fear?

Uncle Booker was right. He had nothing to lose if he played it smart. Money gave him options. He could invest and become very rich. The boycotts wouldn't hurt him. Or he could go to Europe. He couldn't live like a king in Europe, but he could live well for a very long time.

He looked up from his hands and saw a police car circling the block. In the back, heads against the window, were two dogs.

NO ONE HAD ANSWERED at Salena's, and he had started back to his car when he saw the men gathering on a neighbor's porch. Mr. Shannon, the neighbor, waved. He was carrying a hunting rifle. Several of the half dozen or so men carried guns. The three shots of good bourbon he had had on the way over kept Carlton's stomach still.

Mr. Shannon, a tall, brown man with a wide mouth, beckoned to him. "It's about to come on."

Carlton straightened his tie. "What's that, Mr. Shannon?"

"Walter Cronkite."

Mrs. Shannon opened the window from the inside, and pushed the television to face the men. Walter Cronkite appeared inside the oval screen and spoke about Birmingham. Then pictures of the hosing came up. Carlton saw the lanky silhouettes of the children, dancing about in the white mist. A jet smacked a child and tossed her down.

"God," one of the men said.

The whole news cast was about Birmingham. No one made a sound. Even when the governor made a defiant speech no one said a thing, though Carlton could see Mr. Shannon's forearms tighten.

When the newscast ended, the men looked at each other, their jaws set in anger, and their fists twisted around the barrels of the guns.

"The Klan will be out tonight," one of them said.

"I'd like to see them," another said.

Mr. Shannon relaxed a little. "I don't reckon so. I reckon they're at home watching it like we are. But we'd better be on guard any way."

"Any hooded bastard come sneaking around this neighborhood, I get me a piece of'm," a man said.

"All you do is give Pooler a piece of mortuary business."

"Now, gentleman," Mr. Shannon said, "we got a higher cause than to talk like that." He turned to Carlton. "Mr. Wilkes, won't you join us on watch tonight. Ever since the bombings started, we sit on different porches to see if we can't discourage whoever is doing it."

They looked like an unlikely militia—school teachers, mill workers, and brick masons, fidgeting with their shotguns and hunting rifles. Someone dropped a shell and it rolled and stopped at Carlton's feet. His hand trembled as he picked it up and held it out to its owner. He worried that they would think he was afraid.

"How about it, Mr. Wilkes?" Mr. Shannon asked.

Carlton cleared his throat. "No. Not tonight."

"When?" Mr. Shannon looked directly at him, but spoke softly. "Comes a time when enough's enough, and you got to do what you got to do. I say when the fire department that I pay my taxes to, go and hose little colored girls, then the time's come."

"Amen," someone said.

"Shannon's the next Martin Luther King," another man said and provoked laughter from the group.

Carlton's throat was dry. "I was there this morning, Mr. Shannon. I saw it." The men grunted sympathetically. "What you saw on television, I saw face to face."

"Then you know what I'm talking about." Mr. Shannon held out his gun to

Carlton. "I got another gun in the house. Besides, we'll take turns carrying the guns."

"No. I . . . I wouldn't know how to use a gun."

"Just carry it like you know how," someone chimed in.

Carlton backed down the stairs. "I'm sorry gentlemen, I have an appointment—across town, and I . . ."

"He's G. W. Parrish's son-in-law," one of them said. "He's too worried about business to be free."

"No call for that," Mr. Shannon said. "If the man's got business to do, then he's got business to do. He said he would join us another night."

"May not be another night."

One of the men made a joke. "One Wilkes'll rent you a house; the other one will insure it; Parrish'll sell you your stock; and Pooler will put you under, but nay one of 'em will fight for you." A stiff laugh came from the man who said it, a big, bucked-tooth man Carlton knew as a brick mason. The other men only stared at Carlton, challenging him. He fumbled for an answer, but realized it was no good, and he couldn't stay with them now, even if he had wanted to, but to run would make him a coward, or worse a traitor.

Then a little girl, about five, a fragile wide-eyed child with two erect plaits came to the screen door. "Daddy," she called in a soft, quavering voice, "Daddy, are we going to get bombed tonight?"

Mr. Shannon opened the door, and took his daughter into one arm and wedged the rifle in the crook of the other. "No honey, we ain't gonna get bombed."

CARLTON DROVE AIMLESSLY until after sunset. The police were setting up check points, so he drove back to Titusville and waited around the corner for Salena to get home from her shift. Soon after midnight, he saw her park her car in the driveway, nod to the men on Shannon's porch, and go quickly up the stairs. He caught up to her just before she shut the door.

"You scared me," she said. "God, Carlton, you've been drinking."

"I've been thinking."

"Come in before you wake up the neighborhood. And for God's sake, don't wake up Papa."

Carlton sat on the couch while Salena put away her things. She came back wearing her uniform and no shoes. "Listen. Maybe you should go. Daddy will have a fit if we keep him up on a work night."

A little dizzy from the drinking, Carlton stood. "I just wanted to say . . ." She pulled the pins out of her nurses' hat. In the dim overhead light her features were sullen. "I wish we could listen to music," he said.

"Papa'll . . ."

"I know what he'd do, but—Don't you feel like you're between a rock and a hard place?"

She seemed to think for a moment. "No. What do you mean? I feel very lucky, altogether. Very lucky."

"You want to be more than just lucky. Never mind. I . . ." He put his palm to his head and sighed. "I'm an ass."

She said nothing, but took his elbow and pushed him back to the sofa. "What's on your mind?"

It took him a moment to prevent his voice from cracking. "I want to get away. I'm scared this thing is going to backfire."

She folded her hands around his. "We had a fairly quiet night at the hospital. Mostly white. They were scared too. Scared of the 'race riot.' One old woman said it was Armageddon. But when I saw those pictures of the children on the TV, I was proud. I don't know what will happen to them. I don't think it'll be good, but at least they aren't letting the white people get away with it — I mean, they are at least standing up for something." She took off her hat. Her hair fell down on her neck and she pulled it back and set it with the bobbie pin.

"You weren't scared?" He whispered.

"A little. Who wouldn't be? But you've got to go on with your work."

"What about Paris?"

She sighed. "I guess I could be a nurse in Paris. The question is, what are you going to do?"

He took a flask from his jacket.

"Don't. It's too late. You've got to work tomorrow, don't you?"

Hearing Mr. Parrish on the stairs, Carlton put the flask away.

"Let me see if I can't send him back to bed." Salena went to the foot of the stairs and called to her father, telling him nothing was the matter. The old man complained about his interrupted sleep and kept coming down. Reluctantly, Carlton started toward the door.

"Mr. Wilkes," Mr. Parrish blurted. "What brings you around at this hour?" He was wearing a dingy sleeveless undershirt and trousers. "Something wrong downtown?"

"Everything is fine, Papa."

"Them children up to something?"

Salena tried to turn her father around at the foot of the stairs, but he brushed past her, eclipsed Carlton on the way to the door, and looked out of the sidelight. "Shannon and his crew still sittin' up. Waiting for the Ku Klux Klan!" He faced Carlton. His age showed in the bags and spots under his eyes. "Tell you one thing, the Klan ain't waitin' for them. They in bed gettin' their rest so they can put in a full day. Klan gone strike, he go head and strike and then go home and get a full night. Ain't that right, Mr. Wilkes?" His bare feet scuffed against the scatter rugs as he limped into the dining room. "Mr. Wilkes," he said with a certain sarcasm, "won't you join me in a taste?"

"Oh, Papa!" Salena protested.

Carlton stepped between her and her father, and pulled the flask from his jacket. "I owe you one, Mr. Parrish."

"I suppose you do." Mr. Parrish took a glass from the sideboard and held it for Carlton to fill.

"Papa," Salena said, "Carlton was just leaving."

Motioning to the sofa, Mr. Parrish invited Carlton to sit. "I'm sure he got more gumption than to come into a man's house in the middle of the night, wake him up and then *leave*. Besides, this Paris thing got me so I can't sleep." He sat. "Carlton, I'm a country man and I didn't have the privilege of the education that yo' daddy give you. But I do my share of readin' and I read about these colored fellows that run off to Paris 'cause they can't be free in this country. But you take a look at what they do, and they all singers, and horn players. That's their *work*. I understand that some of them make good money at it, too." He sipped the liquor. "Now you see what I'm gettin' at? I don't hear you or Salena singin' or playing no horn. Lord, the girl's momma couldn't even get her to sing in the church choir. So tell me what you gone do in Paris? You just be livin' off what yo' daddy left you — givin' it all away to another bunch of white men. Now, I know things are supposed to be better overseas, but let me tell you this. No matter how bad it gets, and it done already been a hell of a lot worse than it is now, there is no place like your home." Finishing his drink, he started back up the stairs, then stopped and looked plainly at Carlton and shook his head. "You know, Carlton, Salena my only child."

The old man went up into the darkness, and Carlton turned to Salena. "I could look into getting passports, tomorrow."

Salena threw her head back and sighed. "Carlton . . . I love you, but, really . . . it's a silly idea."

THE SUN WAS ABOVE the rooftops when Mr. Shannon rapped on the window of Carlton's Lincoln. "I just wanted to see if you were all right, Mr. Wilkes."

Carlton's head was cloudy, and his neck ached from having slept on the arm rest. He mumbled a greeting to Mr. Shannon, and felt in his pocket for the keys. "Excuse me, I must have fallen asleep . . ."

"Don't worry about it." Mr. Shannon winked. "I remember when my wife and I were courting — besides, it's good to be young. Why don't you come in and have a cup of coffee and some eggs? Put something solid in your stomach."

Carlton tried to beg off the invitation, but Mr. Shannon insisted and he found himself brushing the wrinkles out of his suit and running his tongue over his stale teeth.

Inside, Mrs. Shannon, her hair in rollers, was scrambling eggs. She was a tall, dark woman with genteel features. Two girls sat at the kitchen table, one the little girl Carlton had seen the day before, and the other an adolescent who seemed much perturbed by his appearance.

"I'll just have coffee."

"Oh no, you won't," said Mrs. Shannon as she scooped grits and soft scrambled eggs onto a plate with sausage patties, toast and jam. The food smelled good and Carlton was hungry, he fidgeted to prevent himself from eating until all were seated and Mr. Shannon had said the grace. The older girl, Gloria, pretended to ignore him. She ate the sausages with her fingers, pinky up. Mrs. Shannon firmly told her to use a fork, and slowly, fastidiously wiping grease from her fingers onto a paper napkin, Gloria conformed. The little girl hardly ate for staring at him. He winked at her, trying to solicit a smile, and asked her name. She turned away, but prodded by her parents she told him, "Bonita."

"That's a pretty name, Spanish isn't it?"

"I believe so," Mrs. Shannon said. "We took it from her grandmother."

Mrs. Shannon asked about the wedding plans. "Salena tells me nothing, you know. Not that it's my business, but a neighbor would like to know."

"We haven't set them yet," Carlton said. "Maybe soon. We've been thinking about going to Europe."

"That would be a nice honeymoon." Mrs. Shannon looked impressed. "I swear, Salena doesn't tell me a thing."

"She hasn't exactly agreed, yet," Carlton confessed.

"It is expensive," Mrs. Shannon said slowly. For a moment it seemed to Carlton that she would give him a sympathetic pat on the hand. "You'd better travel while you are young. Once you have your children you'll be settled for a long time."

"I did get to travel over in the Pacific during the War or 'the Conflict' — whatever they called it. Korea." Mr. Shannon piped in between bites of egg and toast. He stopped chewing and looked at Carlton. "What you think about all this mess that Shuttlesworth and King stirred up, Mr. Wilkes? You think it gonna come to something?" This was not the conversation Carlton wanted. He wanted to ignore Mr. Shannon and to turn back to Bonita with her erect braids and tiny, square, egg-covered teeth.

"We don't need to talk about that at the table," Mrs. Shannon said. And then more softly, "It upsets the children."

"Some children are out there in jail."

Mrs. Shannon scooted back from the table and asked if Carlton wanted a second helping, and barely waiting for him to clear his mouth to reply, she put another spoonful of grits on his plate.

"Some children are in jail," Mr. Shannon repeated. "I can't say that I'm not scared for them, but there comes a time when you got to — "

"Got to do nothing." Mrs. Shannon banged the pot on the stove. "None of mine are going down there to be killed by Bull Connor."

"I'm not scared of Bull Connor," the older girl said.

"You'd better be," her mother replied. She took a breath. "We're going to upset Bonita, so just let it rest."

"It won't rest." Mr. Shannon took his plate to the sink. "Mr. Wilkes, I'm going downtown. I think a lot of us will be marching."

Mrs. Shannon cut a look at him. "You'd better be marching on to work, instead of jail. We don't have any money to get you out."

"Then I'll just stay." He went to the door. "Are you coming, Mr. Wilkes?"

Slowly, Carlton sat back from the table. He nodded toward Mrs. Shannon and stood. He felt a tremble in his knee. Gloria popped up and ran toward her father. "Can I go with you?" she asked.

THE PARK WAS CROWDED with people of all ages. Carlton recognized no one, but Mr. Shannon, a school teacher, greeted many of the people, both adult and children. Policemen and firemen were gathering on three sides of them. Yet there was a quiet festivity, as people greeted friends or sang hymns. Someone was singing: *Gonna lay down my burden, down by the riverside . . .* ; in another place a small group knelt in prayer.

A bull horn crackled, and the crowd began to shift. Carlton's mind tripped over itself as he tried to fathom everything. He couldn't understand the instructions coming from the demonstration leaders. The bullhorn seemed to have been circling the park. He thought it may have been coming from Bull Connor's armored car, yet he couldn't see the car. He looked for Mr. Shannon and saw the top of his curly head several yards away. He tried to follow, but the crowd pressed against him and Mr. Shannon moved even further away. It occurred to him that the people were dressed nicely, in clean dungarees and sun dresses, and that the firemen were preparing to hose them, as they had done to the children the day before.

Behind the firetrucks and paddy wagons he saw Uncle Booker's insurance building. He thought that if he could make it past the trucks, that he might be able to take refuge in the building. What Mr. Parrish had said was evident now. How much business would the storeowners along Fourth Avenue do, if there were rioting in the park. They had mortgages to pay and families to feed.

The demonstrators, singing and chanting, lined up at the park's edge. Carlton was close enough to see the face of one of the firemen. He was a square-jawed young man, covered with freckles. He held the hose against his body with one arm, and gripped the throat of the nozzle with his hand.

Suddenly Bull Connor's armored car rolled down the street between the crowd and the firemen. At the window sat heavy-jowled Bull Connor himself. He wiped his glasses with a white hankie, and spoke into a microphone which was amplified by a speaker on the roof of the car. The demonstrators did not disband, and the car moved on. A line of helmeted policemen and their dogs moved in, cutting off Carlton's retreat to Uncle Booker's building.

The young fireman adjusted the nozzle. It seemed to have been pointed directly at Carlton, but there was some confusion. The fireman was looking back at the pumper and yelling instructions. The men at the pumper had taken out their wrenches and were tampering with the hydrant intakes. The young fireman took aim again and braced himself. Carlton saw him push down the nozzle lever.

There was still an escape route, Carlton thought, if he could get to the back of the crowd and then slip behind the firetrucks. He began to push through the crowd. Things were getting too crazy. Somebody was bound to get hurt. Negro progress was supposed to be good for Negroes; he was a Negro, but this was not good for him. He would go to Europe. He pushed faster through the crowd, not caring whom he shoved or stepped on. If Salena didn't want to go, he would go without her. Someone grabbed his shoulder. He pulled away, and was grabbed again. It was Mr. Shannon. "Hold on a minute, Mr. Wilkes. We are marching on City Hall."

Carlton was still for a moment. Mr. Shannon's hand felt like a vise on his shoulder. Then, he shivered, and Mr. Shannon took away his hand.

"I'm sorry," Mr. Shannon said and looked away. Carlton flushed with embarrassment. Mr. Shannon spoke again, in a steady low voice. "Won't you please walk with me, Mr. Wilkes. If you won't, I'm not sure that I can."

For a while, Carlton could not answer, and the two men stood while the crowd pushed around them. "Mr. Shannon." Carlton's voice quavered. "I'm afraid." The confession was accompanied with a great relief, but relief made him no less afraid. "I'm afraid, too." Mr. Shannon hooked his arm in Carlton's, and slowly the two got in step with the crowd.

"But I feel I don't have much choice about being here. I've got my children to think about, for one thing. You're young, Mr. Wilkes. You don't have children yet, but someday you will. When you have children, then you will know that you have to make a choice to face your fears. I don't know what will happen today. We may be knocked in the head, maybe worse. Just keep thinking about the children. Think about all the children."

"All the children?"

"The children who were arrested."

Carlton tried to imagine the faces of the children. He imagined groups of children, their faces blurred by distance. He saw them as silhouettes, or as flashes of color dashing in and out of the arcs of water. He saw the form of the boy who had been knocked down by the water. But he could not see the children as individuals, as people he knew. Because his father had money, he had been sent away to a boarding school in the North. Except for business, he had had only a little contact with these people, much less with their children. It had been a business errand to the hospital that had brought him and Salena together.

"Salena," he thought out loud. He had no children, but he had a future with Salena. He tried to imagine having children with Salena. How would they look?

Her eyes? His nose? Her mouth and hair? Try as he might he couldn't imagine the child's face.

TWO BY TWO, the demonstrators began to file across the street toward a gap between the police cars and the firetrucks. Secure on Mr. Shannon's arm, Carlton fell into step. They made it to where the park lawn and the pavement met, before the line stopped. The demonstration leaders argued with the policemen. Again, Carlton saw the young, freckled fireman, now dragging the dead weight of his limp hose around and aiming it at the marchers. There was a murmur, and people began to kneel. Kneeling! Carlton thought. Kneeling like lambs to be slaughtered. He tried to pull away.

"Kneel and pray," someone said. "Kneel and pray."

Mr. Shannon held him tightly. "They say pray that the water won't come on, Mr. Wilkes."

Carlton shook his head.

"They are praying that the water won't come on."

They had gone crazy. It was one thing to get hosed when you were on your feet and able to run, but it was suicide to kneel down. Mr. Shannon pulled on him, his knees buckled, and he landed squarely on the edge of the sidewalk.

The water didn't come.

"Oh, God. Oh, God."

People sang and prayed. Carlton dared not move. It was as if the collected will of the crowd had frozen the hydrants. If he could only stay here now. Stay. If he didn't move. If he didn't shiver. If he were as still as ice, then the water wouldn't come on. Time would hold still. He caught his breath. His ears began to ring. But nothing, nothing moved. Except now, a cold molecule of sweat was slowly pushing through a pore at the base of his scalp and swelling into a quavering bead. He must not move! "Oh God, oh God." He imagined the boy, rolled in the streets by the jets of white water, and the dogs — oh God, the dogs. Why was he a Negro, and so scared?

The eyes of the young fireman were round, and the hose had slipped from under his arm. He was backing away from the crowd, looking over his shoulder to his colleagues for support.

Carlton saw the fireman stepping back. It confused him. His concentration slipped and he began to note his surroundings. He was kneeling in a crowd, being held by a man he barely knew, while the firemen backed away and tampered with the hydrants. He had stepped out of his life into something stranger than life. He had a comfortable home which sat on a hill above Titusville. He had a fiancé who was one of the first colored nurses at the white hospital. He had a business to run, and a Lincoln Continental.

Yet he was compelled to stay where he was, on his knees, in front of Bull Connor's firemen, for if he moved, if one hair sprung up from the pomade that held it close to his skull, then the water would come on. The bead of sweat trembled and began to roll in a meandering, ticklish path over his temple and across his cheek. That wasn't his fault! He couldn't help that. He hadn't done anything to cause it to fall.

Now other beads began to roll. He felt each one individually, prickling across his skin. Each one was a cold prod inciting his body to revolt, to shiver, to stand up and run. But if he dared, then it would be the end of him. He would be rolled in the streets, chased and bitten by the dogs. He would be no better than the others.

"Courage, Mr. Wilkes. Courage." Mr. Shannon loosened his grip, and Carlton screamed, and jerked away.

"Kneel, mister," someone said, but Carlton continued stumbling through the kneeling people, stepping on them, picking a route to the rear of the park.

Then there was a whoosh. Carlton turned to see the young fireman brace himself as the hose kicked, and foamed, and shot water. At first the stream scoured the asphalt and sprayed up a milky, prismatic mist; then the fireman gained control of it and directed it at the kneeling demonstrators.

The jets bowled the demonstrators over, and knocked them down as they tried to rise. White arcs came from every direction, and Carlton realized that he was surrounded. He pushed people aside as he ran, instinctively, towards Uncle Booker's building. He made it to the curb just as a column of water came at him. Diving behind a parked car, he escaped the direct force. He edged along the side of the car and peeped around the fender to see in which direction the hose was pointed.

Just inside the park, he saw a young woman in a white dress. She was bent over, and stumbling as she tried to dodge the jets of water. Carlton wiped his eyes to get a better look. His heart skipped a beat. Was it Salena? He wiped his eyes again. The young woman turned in his direction, and he saw without a doubt that it was Salena. Now she had stopped running and was trying to help a heavy-set man out of the mud.

Carlton ducked behind the car again. His head was spinning and the water in his eyes had broken the world into fragments. He had a clear shot to Uncle Booker's building. If he tried to reach Salena the hoses would surely catch him. He tried to convince himself that she would be all right. She was strong, stronger than himself. Maybe she was too strong for him. Maybe he couldn't imagine children with her because they had no future together. She was claiming her future here at the park. His future was in Europe.

He tried to imagine Salena's face. He held it in his mind for a moment, but it seemed the water in his eyes was also in his head. Every time he got the image of her to stand still, it was washed away by rivulets of water. Maybe he didn't love her. If he loved her, then he would be able to see her clearly. He would be able to run to her.

He looked for her again in the crowd and in a moment found her. The white uniform was now gray with mud. She had lost her shoes. She seemed dazed, no longer crouched and running but standing and limping, an easy target. Then he saw a jet of water coming towards her. "Salena!" He stood. The scene kept spinning around him. First Uncle Booker's building, then Salena, then the firetrucks. "Run," he heard someone scream at him. "Run, run, run!" It was himself screaming. He ran. He wasn't sure in which direction. The water punched his ribs and knocked out his breath. It slammed him to the asphalt, shoved his hips against the pavement and beat on his back. He lay and caught his breath as the run-off trickled and fizzed around him. Slowly, he stood, and made a clumsy step toward Salena.

(2006)

Cyrus Cassells   (b. 1957)

orn in 1957 in Dover, Delaware, in a segregated hospital, Cyrus Curtis Cassells III grew up in Southern California, living with his two brothers, his mother, and his father, who was in the military and desegregated the living quarters at West Point in the 1950s. Cassells attended Stanford University, earning a bachelor's degree in 1979. He then traveled widely in Europe, living in Rome, Italy, for six years, before studying at a mystic school in San Francisco.

Cassells's first poetry collection, *The Mud Actor* (1982), was a National Poetry Series selection, and his second volume, *Soul Make a Path through Shouting* (1994), was nominated for a Pulitzer Prize, won the Poetry Society of America's William Carlos Williams Award, was a finalist for the Lenore Marshall Prize for outstanding book of the year, and was named one of the Best Books of 1994 by *Publishers Weekly*. Cassells dedicated the collection's title poem to Elizabeth Eckford — one of the students who integrated Arkansas's Little Rock Central High School in 1957. The volume also memorializes Holocaust victims and survivors and explores the AIDS crisis. Cassells's other collections include *Beautiful Signor* (1997) — winner of the Lambda Literary Award, *More Than Peace and Cypresses* (2004), and *The Crossed-Out Swastika* (forthcoming). Additionally, Cassells's poems have appeared in numerous literary journals and magazines, including *Ploughshares*, the *Kenyon Review*, the *Indiana Review*, *Borderlands*, and the *Crab Orchard Review*. With an international perspective, Cassells frequently addresses violations of human rights under a variety of systems of oppression, including racism and heterosexism. Many of his poems also explore issues of identity, defy stereotypes of African Americans and homosexuality, and advocate breaking down boundaries and binaries, such as that of victim and perpetrator, in order to connect diverse groups of people.

Cassells is the recipient of a Pushcart Prize, a fellowship from the Rockefeller Foundation, and two fellowships from the National Endowment for the Arts. He has worked as a translator, film critic, and actor, in addition to teaching at the College of the Holy Cross, Northeastern University, and Southwest Texas State University. Cassells currently lives in Austin, Texas, and Paris, France.

Soul Make a Path through Shouting

for Elizabeth Eckford

Little Rock, Arkansas, 1957

Thick at the schoolgate are the ones
Rage has twisted
Into minotaurs, harpies
Relentlessly swift;
So you must walk past the pincers,
The swaying horns,
Sister, sister,
Straight through the gusts
Of fear and fury,
Straight through:
Where are you going?

I'm just going to school.

Here we go to meet
The hydra-headed day,
Here we go to meet
The maelstrom —

Can my voice be an angel-on-the-spot,
An amen corner?
Can my voice take you there,
Gallant girl with a notebook,
Up, up from the shadows of gallows trees
To the other shore:
A globe bathed in light,
A chalkboard blooming with equations —

I have never seen the likes of you,
Pioneer in dark glasses:

You won't show the mob your eyes,
But I know your gaze,
Steady-on-the-North-Star, burning—

With their jerry-rigged faith,
Their spear of the American flag,
How could they dare to believe
You're someone sacred?:
Nigger, burr-headed girl,
Where are you going?

I'm just going to school.

(1991)

Honorée Fanonne Jeffers (b. 1967)

Honorée Fanonne Jeffers grew up in Durham, North Carolina, and in Atlanta, Georgia. Her father, Lance Jeffers, was an acclaimed Black Arts movement poet and blues pianist. After graduating from Talladega College, where her mother is a professor, Jeffers earned a master's of fine arts degree from the University of Alabama. She then taught at Knox College in Indiana and at the University of Oklahoma. Her poetry has appeared in numerous periodicals and anthologies, including *Black Issues Book Review, Brilliant Corners: A Journal of Jazz and Literature, Bum Rush the Page: A Def Poetry Jam* (2001), *Callaloo, Dark Matter: A Century of Speculative Fiction from the African Diaspora* (2000), the *Kenyon Review, Ploughshares, Roll Call: A Generational Anthology of Social and Political Black Literature and Art* (2002), and *These Hands I Know: Writing about the African American Family* (2002).

Jeffers has also published three volumes of award-winning poetry: *The Gospel of Barbecue* (2000) — a finalist for the 2001 Paterson Poetry Prize, *Outlandish Blues* (2003), and *Red Clay Suite* (2007), where she explores her family's history. Jeffers was selected by Lucille Clifton as the 1999 winner of the Stan and Tom Wick Prize for Poetry, and in 2002 she won the Julia Peterkin Award for Poetry. Her other awards include those from the Barbara Deming Memorial Fund and the Rona Jaffe Foundation as well as an Alan Collins Poetry Fellowship from the Bread Loaf Writers Conference. Jeffers's poetry employs biblical imagery, the blues, and southern foodways and folkways to explore the enduring legacies of black history, racial and sexual violence, and above all, love of family, heritage, and place. "Confederate Pride Day at Bama" (from *Outlandish Blues*, originally published in *Callaloo*) offers a satiric look at both the enduring symbols of Jim Crow and the naïveté of her white friends. "Giving Thanks for Water" (from *Red Clay Suite*) recovers memories of the 1921 riots in Tulsa, Oklahoma, and considers the possibilities for healing from violent events that happened so long ago.

Confederate Pride Day at Bama

(Tuscaloosa, 1994)

The first time, my liberal white friends try
to prepare me. I might feel ashamed when I hear
rebel yells, see the too familiar flag waving.
You know they're going to sing the song, don't you?

The fraternity boys dressed in gray uniforms,
marching boldly around the yard, then coming home to black
maids, their heads tied up in bright handkerchiefs.

Faces greased to perfection once a year. *Can you believe*
they make those women dress up like mammies?
Southern meals prepared with eye-rolling care.
You should stage a protest. For me or for my mama?

Come day, go day, God sends Sunday and I see those
sisters at the grocery store buying food every week.
We smile and sometimes meet each other's gaze.

Nod.
At the very least, write a letter. Some kinds of anger
need screaming. Some kinds just worry the gut
like a meal of unwashed greens, peas picked

too early from the field. Or a dark woman, her brow
wrapped in red, smiling to herself, then hawking
and spitting her seasoning into a Dixie cooking pot.

(2001)

Giving Thanks for Water

Before moving to Oklahoma,
I read up on the Tulsa riots,
was shocked—I thought they only
did things like that back
home in the Deep South.
I guess I was wrong.

Ugliness is an obsession of mine—
I read the news on 1921
as if that year wasn't gone,
disappeared in smoke, those judges waiting
for the last witnesses, stubborn old folk,
to die and take their goddamned
memories into grace:

Dick and Sarah black shoeshine man
white elevator woman I heard
tell he grabbed her did he grab
her white grabbed her woman Molotov
cocktails dropped black burned
to Sodom's ash man dozens bodies
stacked up hundreds unmarked
graves thousands I heard tell

Skirting this city's edge,
I see a few trees in shy clumps.
I'm driving past Tulsa,
taking a roundabout way home,
with knowledge vindicating—
a bit—my sweet Georgia.
This morning, I took a shower
and gave thanks for water,
for the cleanliness next to God.

If you please Little
Africa burning one girl
hid in a pigpen please she lived
through Black Wall Street
burning if you please

Thank You, Maker,
for swine, filth, and Noah's rain.
Thank you, Lord,
for memory's long-lived,
pointing finger.

(2007)

Chronology of Publication Dates and Historical Events

1865   Post–Civil War Reconstruction begins; Thirteenth Amendment to U.S. Constitution outlaws slavery; the first Ku Klux Klan is formed in Pulaski, Tennessee.

1868   Fourteenth Amendment defines African Americans as citizens, guaranteeing due process and equal protection under the laws.

1870   Fifteenth Amendment extends suffrage to African American males.

1871   The Civil Rights Act or "Ku Klux Klan Act" temporarily puts an end to Klan activities.

1873   *Slaughter-House* cases before the U.S. Supreme Court narrow the Fourteenth Amendment's reach.

1877   Compromise of 1877 marks the end of Reconstruction.

1892   Frances E. W. Harper publishes *Iola Leroy*.
        Tuskegee Institute (now University) records a record number of lynchings at 230; Ida B. Wells begins an antilynching campaign.

1895   Booker T. Washington delivers the "Atlanta Exposition Address" (later published in *Up from Slavery* in 1901).

1896   The U.S. Supreme Court's *Plessy v. Ferguson* ruling institutionalizes racial segregation by allowing for "separate but equal" facilities; the National Association of Colored Women (NACW) is formed.

1899   Paul Laurence Dunbar publishes *Lyrics of the Hearthside*, which includes the poem "Sympathy."

1901   Charles W. Chesnutt publishes *The Marrow of Tradition*, based upon an 1898 race riot in Wilmington, North Carolina.

1903   W. E. B. Du Bois publishes *The Souls of Black Folk*; Dunbar publishes *Lyrics of Love and Laughter*, which contains the first full-length version of his poem "The Haunted Oak."

1906   In September, white mobs riot in Atlanta, Georgia, killing two dozen blacks and wounding many more.

1909   The National Association for the Advancement of Colored People (NAACP) is founded.

1910s   The "Great Migration" of African Americans from the South to northern and western cities begins.

1911   The National Urban League is formed.

1914   Marcus Garvey organizes the University Negro Improvement Association.

1915   The Ku Klux Klan re-forms in Stone Mountain, Georgia.

1917–18 U.S. participation in World War I.

1917   In July, white mobs in East St. Louis, Illinois, kill forty blacks and drive thousands from their homes; later that month, the NAACP stages a Silent Protest Parade in Harlem to protest racial violence.

1919	Mary Burrill's *Aftermath* and Claude McKay's "If We Must Die" appear in *The Liberator* (McKay's poem is later reprinted in his 1922 collection, *Harlem Shadows*).
	During "Red Summer," race riots break out in cities across the nation; the Commission on Interracial Cooperation (CIC) is formed; the U.S. Congress passes the Nineteenth Amendment granting women the right to vote (it is ratified in 1920); Du Bois organizes the Pan-African Congress.
1921	Claude McKay's "America" appears in *The Liberator* (and is later reprinted in his 1922 collection, *Harlem Shadows*).
	White violence in Tulsa, Oklahoma, claims hundreds of lives and wipes out an area known as the "Black Wall Street."
1922	The U.S. House of Representatives passes an antilynching bill sponsored by Missouri's Leonidas Dyer, but the bill fails in the Senate under a threatened filibuster; over the next two decades, subsequent attempts to pass antilynching legislation fail as well.
1923	Angelina Weld Grimké's poem "The Black Finger" appears in *Opportunity*.
	The all-black town of Rosewood, Florida, is destroyed by white mobs.
1925	Alain Locke's anthology, *The New Negro*, including poetry by Grimké, Hughes, and others, provides one herald of a new literary and political consciousness that will come to be known as the "Harlem" or "New Negro" Renaissance.
	A. Phillip Randolph organizes the Brotherhood of Sleeping Car Porters and Maids, an African American labor union.
1926	Langston Hughes publishes his first book of poetry, *The Weary Blues* (where the poem "I, Too" appears).
1927	Grimké's poem "Tenebris" appears in Countee Cullen's anthology *Caroling Dusk: An Anthology of Verse by Negro Poets*; Hughes's "Song for a Dark Girl" appears in the *Crisis* (and is later reprinted in that year's *Fine Clothes to the Jew*).
1929	The Great Depression begins.
1930	The Nation of Islam (NOI) is formed.
1931	In Scottsboro, Alabama, nine African American youths are falsely accused and arrested for raping two white women; the case becomes an international symbol of Jim Crow injustice, generating a widespread response from artists, writers, and activists.
1934	The Southern Tenant Farmers' Union is organized to reform the sharecropping system.
1938	In *Missouri ex rel. Gaines*, the U.S. Supreme Court rules that states must provide equal, if separate, facilities within their boundaries.
1939	The NAACP Legal Defense and Educational Fund is organized, focusing on issues of education, civil rights, and voting rights.
1940	Erskine Caldwell publishes "The End of Christy Tucker" in the *Nation*.
1941–45	U.S. participation in World War II.
1941	A. Phillip Randolph organizes the March on Washington Movement.
1942	The Congress of Racial Equality (CORE) is founded.

1944	In *Smith v. Allwright* the U.S. Supreme Court case outlaws "whites only" voting primaries.
1945	Richard Wright publishes *Black Boy*.
1946	President Harry Truman appoints the Committee on Civil Rights.
1947	Ralph Ellison publishes "The Battle Royal" in *Horizon* magazine (the story later appears as the first chapter of his 1952 novel, *Invisible Man*).
	The Committee on Civil Rights issues a report, *To Secure These Rights*; CORE initiates the Journey of Reconciliation (freedom rides); Jackie Robinson integrates Major League Baseball.
1948	President Truman issues orders to desegregate the military.
1949	Lillian Smith publishes *Killers of the Dream*.
	The U.S. Congress begins investigations, lasting until 1954, of citizens who might have ties to Communism through the House Un-American Activities Committee (HUAC); a number of screenwriters and other individuals are "blacklisted" and prevented from working in the motion picture industry for refusing to provide information.
1951	Hughes publishes *Montage of a Dream Deferred*, which includes the poem "Harlem."
1954	The U.S. Supreme Court rules in *Brown v. Board of Education* that segregation in public schools is inherently unequal and therefore unconstitutional; the first White Citizens' Council is formed shortly afterward in Indianola, Mississippi.
1955	James Baldwin publishes his essay "Notes of a Native Son" in *Harper's* magazine (it appears later that year as the title essay of his first collection).
	In August, Emmett Till is murdered in Money, Mississippi — an all-white jury later finds two local white men not guilty in his death and, afterward, the men confess to killing him; in December, Rosa Parks is arrested for refusing to move from the "white" section of a Montgomery, Alabama, bus, inaugurating a yearlong boycott of local buses and catapulting a local minister, Dr. Martin Luther King Jr., into the national spotlight.
1956	Southern congressmen issue a protest of racial integration known as the "Southern Manifesto."
1957	The Southern Christian Leadership Conference (SCLC) is formed; the U.S. Congress passes the Civil Rights Act of 1957, which bars discrimination in public conveyances and interstate travel; President Dwight D. Eisenhower sends federal troops to Arkansas to protect nine African American teens who are integrating Little Rock's Central High School.
1960	Gwendolyn Brooks publishes *The Bean Eaters*, which contains several movement-related poems, including "The Chicago Defender Sends a Man to Little Rock" and her Emmett Till series.
	In February, students from North Carolina A&T stage a sit-in at a Woolworth's lunch counter in Greensboro, inaugurating similar protests against segregated lunch counters across the South; in April, the Student Nonviolent Coordinating Committee (SNCC) is formed.

1961   Flannery O'Connor publishes "Everything That Rises Must Converge" in
       New World Writing (later reprinted as the title story of a 1964 collection).
       In May, Freedom Rides begin in Washington, D.C.; riders persevere through
       Alabama violence until they are arrested in Jackson, Mississippi.

1962   James Meredith's September enrollment at the University of Mississippi
       provokes riots on campus.

1963   Martin Luther King Jr. writes "Letter from a Birmingham Jail" in April,
       in response to eight Alabama clergymen who condemn the nonviolent
       protests he was jailed for helping to organize; Eudora Welty's story "Where
       Is the Voice Coming From?" — based upon the June murder of Medgar
       Evers in Mississippi — appears in the *New Yorker* a few weeks after his
       death.

       Civil rights protests take place across the South throughout the year; in
       August, 250,000 marchers converge in Washington, D.C., where King
       delivers his "I Have a Dream" speech; in September, a bomb explodes in
       a Birmingham, Alabama, church, killing four girls; President John F.
       Kennedy is assassinated in November.

1964   *Dutchman*, by Amiri Baraka (writing as LeRoi Jones) opens off-Broadway;
       Malcolm X and Alex Haley publish *The Autobiography of Malcolm X*.
       During "Freedom Summer," young adults from across the country converge
       in Mississippi for voter registration drives; three of those civil rights
       workers — James Chaney, Andrew Goodman, and Michael Schwerner —
       are murdered in Neshoba County; in July, Congress passes the Civil Rights
       Act of 1964, which outlaws discrimination based upon race, color, and
       national origin; in December, King is awarded the Nobel Peace Prize.

1965   Dudley Randall's "Ballad of Birmingham," about the 1963 church bombing,
       becomes one of the first publications from Broadside Press; Baraka (writing
       as LeRoi Jones) publishes "A Poem for Black Hearts" in *Negro Digest*, and
       Randall reprints it two years later as a Broadside Press publication.
       In February, Malcolm X is assassinated in New York City; in March, state
       troopers beat back voting rights marchers attempting to cross Selma,
       Alabama's Edmund Pettus Bridge; a second attempt, in March, is success-
       ful; in August, President Lyndon Johnson signs the Voting Rights Act of
       1965, which outlaws discriminatory practices in voting; in August, riots
       erupt in the Watts section of Los Angeles, California.

1966   In June, James Meredith organizes a March Against Fear in Mississippi; after
       he is shot on the second day, SNCC, CORE, and the SCLC continue the march,
       with SNCC leader Stokely Carmichael coining the phrase "Black Power"
       during a Greenwood rally; in October, the Black Panther Party for Self-
       Defense is formed in Oakland, California; the National Organization for
       Women (NOW) is also formed during this year.

1967   Howard Sackler's play, *The Great White Hope*, premieres in Washington, D.C.
       Riots erupt in Newark, New Jersey, and Detroit, Michigan; former NAACP
       counsel Thurgood Marshall is sworn in as the first black U.S. Supreme
       Court Justice; Carl Stokes becomes the first black mayor of a major U.S. city
       (Cleveland, Ohio).

1968	Eldridge Cleaver publishes *Soul on Ice*, with "On Becoming" as its first chapter; Audre Lorde publishes *Coal* (which contains "Rites of Passage") with Norton and *First Cities* (which contains "Suffer the Children") with Poets Press.
	In April, Martin Luther King Jr. is assassinated in Memphis, Tennessee, while participating in a sanitation workers' strike; in June, Ralph Abernathy leads fifty thousand demonstrators to Washington, D.C., for the Poor People's Campaign; in July, the American Indian Movement (AIM) is founded.
1969	Haki Madhubuti (writing as Don L. Lee) publishes the poem "Malcolm spoke / who listened?" in his collection *Don't Cry, Scream*.
	In New York City's Greenwich Village, the "Stonewall Riots" inaugurate the Gay Liberation Movement; "La Raza Unida" is formed to support Mexican American causes and political candidates; massive demonstrations against the Vietnam conflict in Washington, D.C.
1970	Michael S. Harper publishes *Dear John, Dear Coltrane*, which includes the poems, "American History" and "Martin's Blues"; Robert Hayden publishes his collection *Words in the Mourning Time*, which contains his tribute to Malcolm X, "El-Hajj Malik El-Shabazz"; Third World Press publishes Amiri Baraka's poem "It's Nation Time" as the title poem of a collection; Broadside Press publishes Margaret Walker's *Prophets for a New Day* (which includes the movement-related poems reprinted in this anthology and many more); Morrow publishes as one book Nikki Giovanni's two collections *Black Feeling, Black Talk* and *Black Judgement* (containing the poems "Adulthood," "Black Power," and "The Funeral for Martin Luther King, Jr."), which Giovanni had privately and separately printed in 1968.
	Feminist rallies across the nation celebrate the fiftieth anniversary of the Nineteenth Amendment, call for passage of an Equal Rights Amendment, and highlight the need for reproductive freedom.
1971	The Congressional Black Caucus is formed.
1972	Lucille Clifton publishes the collection *Good News about the Earth*, where her poems "apology (to the panthers)," "eldridge," and "malcolm" appear.
	Shirley Chisolm becomes the first African American to seek the Democratic Party's nomination for president.
1973	In *Roe v. Wade*, the U.S. Supreme Court rules that women have the right to an abortion in the first and second trimesters of pregnancy; the last American troops leave Vietnam.
1974	Lucille Clifton publishes the collection *Ordinary Woman*, which includes the poem "jackie robinson."
	Violence erupts over busing in Boston, Massachusetts.
1976	Robert Hayden becomes the first African American to hold the position of poetry consultant to the U.S. Library of Congress (now poet laureate).
1977	June Jordan publishes *Things That I Do in the Dark: Selected Poetry*, which includes her poems "In Memoriam: Martin Luther King, Jr." and "I Celebrate the Sons of Malcolm." On the occasion of activist Fannie Lou Hamer's death this same year, Jordan also publishes a tribute poem, "1977: Poem for Mrs. Fannie Lou Hamer."

Robert Chambliss becomes the first of several men to be tried and convicted for his role in the 1963 Birmingham, Alabama, church bombing that killed four girls.

1978   The U.S. Supreme Court's decision in *Regents of the University of California v. Bakke* begins the process of weakening affirmative action policies.

1982   A public battle against a Warren County, North Carolina, toxic waste dump draws national attention to the issue of environmental racism.

1983   Martin Luther King Jr.'s birthday is made a national holiday.

1986   Wanda Coleman publishes "Emmett Till" in *Callaloo*.

President George H. W. Bush signs the Americans with Disabilities Act.

1987   PBS first airs its six-part civil rights movement documentary, *Eyes on the Prize*.

1989   Virginia's Douglas L. Wilder becomes the first African American elected to any state governorship.

1990   Marilyn Nelson's poetry collection, *The Homeplace*, containing "Tuskegee Airfield," comes out.

1991   Patricia J. Williams publishes *The Alchemy of Race and Rights*, where "The Death of the Profane" appears; Cyrus Cassells's poem "Soul Make a Path through Shouting" appears in *Indiana Review* (later reprinted as title poem of his 1994 collection).

Clarence Thomas replaces Thurgood Marshall on the U.S. Supreme Court after controversial confirmation hearings focus on allegations that he sexually harassed a former employee, Anita Hill; Carol Moseley-Braun becomes the first African American woman elected to the U.S. Senate.

1992   Bebe Moore Campbell publishes *Your Blues Ain't Like Mine*.

Violence erupts in south-central Los Angeles after an all-white jury finds white police officers not guilty of using excessive force in the beating of African American Rodney King.

1993   Novelist Toni Morrison becomes the first African American to win the Nobel Prize for Literature; the Library of Congress names Rita Dove as poet laureate.

1994   David Hernandez's poem "Martin and My Father" is first published in the anthology *Unsettling America*, edited by Maria Mazziotti Gillan and Jennifer Gillan.

The Florida state legislature passes the Rosewood Claims Bill, compensating survivors of the 1923 Rosewood massacre for their losses; Byron De La Beckwith is found guilty in the 1963 murder of Medgar Evers.

1995   In October, the Nation of Islam sponsors a "Million Man March" in Washington, D.C.

1997   Toi Derricotte publishes *The Black Notebooks*; Walter Mosley's "Equal Opportunity" appears in *Buzz* (later reprinted in Mosley's 1998 collection, *Always Outnumbered, Always Outgunned*).

President Bill Clinton begins the "Initiative on Race," a yearlong dialogue in local communities across the country.

1998   Rita Dove publishes "The Enactment" and "Rosa" in the *Georgia Review* (both are reprinted the following year in *On the Bus with Rosa Parks*).

In June, an African American man named James Byrd is chained to the back of a pickup truck and dragged to his death in Jasper, Texas; in October, a gay white man named Matthew Shepard is beaten to death and left hanging on a fence in Laramie, Wyoming; both incidents draw widespread attention to the problem of hate crimes.

2000   Constance Curry, Joan C. Browning, and seven other women publish *Deep in Our Hearts: Nine White Women in the Freedom Movement*, where Curry's "Wild Geese to the Past" appears.

During the close, and later disputed, presidential election between George W. Bush and Al Gore, thousands of African Americans are prevented from voting in Florida because their names have been accidentally purged from voting lists.

2001   Honorée Fanonne Jeffers's poem "Confederate Pride Day at Bama" appears in *Callaloo* (later reprinted in her 2003 collection, *Outlandish Blues*).

On September 11, coordinated airplane attacks bring down the World Trade Centers in New York and damage the Pentagon in Washington, D.C., killing approximately three thousand and renewing national debates on the meaning of "freedom" and "civil liberties."

2005   The U.S. Senate issues a resolution apologizing for its failure to enact anti-lynching legislation during the twentieth century; former Klansman Edgar Ray Killen is found guilty of manslaughter for his role in the 1964 deaths of three civil rights workers (Chaney, Goodman, and Schwerner).

2006   Anthony Grooms's 1995 book *Trouble No More*, in which "Negro Progress" appears, is revised and rereleased.

2007   Jeffers's poem "Giving Thanks for Water" is published in her collection *Red Clay Suite*.

In February, the Virginia legislature issues an apology for slavery, making it the first of several states to do so.

In September, a rally in Jena, Louisiana, draws tens of thousands to protest the prosecution of six black youths known as the "Jena Six" for assaulting white youths who hung nooses in a local tree; before the year's end, between fifty and sixty noose incidents throughout the country will recall this powerful symbol of Jim Crow violence.

2008   While seeking the Democratic Party's presidential nomination, candidate Barack Obama, in a March speech, uses his own racially mixed heritage to address the importance of racial reconciliation.

Selected Bibliography

The following is a selection of reference works, educational resources, and Web sites devoted to civil rights history and literature. The list is not meant to be comprehensive, but to provide students, teachers, and general readers with a starting point to locate further information. Scholarship on the civil rights movement is vast, with its own Library of Congress Subject Heading (and multiple subcategories). Most of the resources listed below, however, also have bibliographies and links to further readings or more specific texts.

Armstrong, Julie Buckner, Susan Hult Edwards, Houston Bryan Roberson, and Rhonda Y. Williams, eds. *Teaching the American Civil Rights Movement: Freedom's Bittersweet Song*. New York: Routledge, 2002.

Birnbaum, Jonathan, and Clarence Taylor, eds. *Civil Rights: A Reader on the Black Struggle since 1787*. New York: New York University Press, 2000.

Bradley, David, and Shelley Fisher Fishkin, eds. *The Encyclopedia of Civil Rights in America*. Armonk, N.Y.: Sharpe Reference, 1998.

Carson, Clayborne, et al. *The Eyes on the Prize Civil Rights Reader*. New York: Penguin, 1991.

Civil Rights Movement Veterans. http://www.crmvet.org.

D'Angelo, Raymond, ed. *The American Civil Rights Movement: Readings and Interpretations*. New York: McGraw-Hill/Dushkin, 2001.

Dierenfield, Bruce J. *The Civil Rights Movement*. New York: Pearson Longman, 2004.

Glisson, Susan M., ed. *The Human Tradition in the Civil Rights Movement*. Lanham, Md.: Rowman and Littlefield, 2006.

Lowery, Charles D., and John F. Marszalek, eds. *The Greenwood Encyclopedia of African-American Civil Rights: From Emancipation to the Twenty-first Century*. 2nd ed. New York: Greenwood Press, 2003.

Luker, Ralph, ed. *Historical Dictionary of the Civil Rights Movement*. Lanham, Md.: Scarecrow Press, 1997.

Martin, Waldo E., Jr., and Patricia Sullivan, eds. *Civil Rights in the United States*. New York: Macmillan Reference, 2000.

Menkart, Deborah, Alana D. Murray, and Jenice L. View, eds. *Putting the Movement Back into Civil Rights Teaching*. Washington, D.C.: Teaching for Change, 2004.

Reporting Civil Rights. 2 vols. New York: Library of America, 2003.

Southern Poverty Law Center. "Teaching Tolerance." http://www.tolerance.org/index.jsp.

Teaching for Change. http://www.teachingforchange.org/.

Whitt, Margaret Early, ed. *Short Stories of the Civil Rights Movement: An Anthology*. Athens: University of Georgia Press, 2006.

William Winter Institute for Racial Reconciliation. http://www.olemiss.edu/winterinstitute/.

Credits

James Baldwin, "Notes of a Native Son." Copyright © 1955, renewed 1983, by James Baldwin. Reprinted by permission of Beacon Press, Boston.

Amiri Baraka, *Dutchman*, "It's Nation Time," and "A Poem for Black Hearts." Copyright © 1979 by Amiri Baraka. Reprinted by permission of SLL/Sterling Lord Literistic, Inc.

Gwendolyn Brooks, "A Bronzeville Mother Loiters in Mississippi. Meanwhile, a Mississippi Mother Burns Bacon" and "The Chicago Defender Sends a Man to Little Rock." Copyright © 1963 by Gwendolyn Brooks Blakely. Reprinted by consent of Brooks Permissions.

Erskine Caldwell, "The End of Christy Tucker," from *The Stories of Erskine Caldwell*. Copyright © 1940 by The Nation Inc. Copyright © renewed 1967 by Erskine Caldwell. Reprinted with permission of McIntosh & Otis, Inc.

Bebe Moore Campbell, chap. 44 from *Your Blues Ain't Like Mine*. Copyright © 1992 by Bebe Moore Campbell. Used by permission of G. P. Putnam's Sons, a division of Penguin Group (USA) Inc.

Cyrus Cassells, "Soul Make a Path through Shouting," from *Soul Make a Path Through Shouting*. Copyright © 1994 by Cyrus Cassells. Reprinted with the permission of Copper Canyon Press, www.coppercanyonpress.org.

Charles W. Chesnutt, selections from *The Marrow of Tradition*, by Charles W. Chesnutt, edited by Eric J. Sundquist. Copyright © 1901 by Charles W. Chesnutt. Introduction © 1993 by Eric J. Sundquist. Used by permission of Penguin, a division of Penguin Group (USA) Inc.

Eldridge Cleaver, selection from "On Becoming," from *Soul on Ice* (New York: McGraw-Hill, 1967). Copyright © 1967 by Eldridge Cleaver. Reproduced with permission of The McGraw-Hill Companies.

Lucille Clifton, "apology (to the panthers)," "eldridge," "jackie robinson," and "malcolm," from *Good Woman: Poems and a Memoir, 1968–1980*. Copyright © 1987 by Lucille Clifton. Reprinted with the permission of BOA Editions, Ltd., www.boaeditions.org.

Wanda Coleman, "Emmett Till," from *African Sleeping Sickness*. Copyright © 1990 by Wanda Coleman. Reprinted by permission of the author.

Constance Curry, selections from "Wild Geese to the Past," from *Deep in Our Hearts: Nine White Women in the Freedom Movement*, by Constance Curry et al. Copyright © 2000 University of Georgia Press. Reprinted by permission of the University of Georgia Press.

Toi Derricotte, selections from "The Club," from *The Black Notebooks: An Interior Journey*. Copyright © 1997 by Toi Derricotte. Used by permission of W. W. Norton & Company, Inc.

Rita Dove, "The Enactment" and "Rosa," from *On the Bus with Rosa Parks*. Copyright © 1999 by Rita Dove. Used by permission of W. W. Norton & Company, Inc.

Paul Laurence Dunbar, "The Haunted Oak" and "Sympathy," from *The Collected Poetry*

Index of Authors and Titles